23rd EG-ICE International Workshop on Intelligent Computing in Engineering (EG-ICE 2016)

Krakow, Poland
29 June - 1 July 2016

ISBN: 978-1-5108-9054-1

Printed from e-media with permission by:

Curran Associates, Inc.
57 Morehouse Lane
Red Hook, NY 12571

Some format issues inherent in the e-media version may also appear in this print version.

Printed by Curran Associates, Inc. (2019)

European Group For Intelligent Computing in Engineering (eg-ice)
c/o Andre Borrmann
Arcisstrasee 21
80333 Munich
Germany

Phone: 498928-925117
Fax: 498928-948789

anything@eg-ice.org

Additional copies of this publication are available from:

Curran Associates, Inc.
57 Morehouse Lane
Red Hook, NY 12571 USA
Phone: 845-758-0400
Fax: 845-758-2634
Email: curran@proceedings.com
Web: www.proceedings.com

TABLE OF CONTENTS

BIMsite – Towards a BIM-based Generation and Evaluation of Realization Variants Comprising Construction Methods, Site Layouts and Schedules

Stefan Krepp[1], Katrin Jahr[1], Sonja Bigontina[2], Maximilian Bügler[1], André Borrmann[1]
[1]Chair of Computational Modeling and Simulation
[2]Institute for Materials Handling, Material Flow, Logistics
Technical University of Munich, Germany
stefan.krepp@tum.de

Abstract. Despite the proliferation of BIM tools in construction process planning, the BIM-based development of a digital representation of the construction phase, including detailed site layout plans, is still in a very early phase. Most planners still use manual methods and rely on experience when it comes to the selection of construction methods and site layout planning. The following paper introduces BIMsite, a recently started research project, focussing on BIM-based site layout planning under the consideration of different construction methods. The project investigates how to generate different variants of construction site layouts based on different construction methods in a semi-automated way; and how to evaluate those variants utilizing construction simulation approaches. The paper provides an overview of the initial research, focussing on first approaches regarding construction site generation, optimization and simulation.

1. Introduction

Until recently, building layouts and construction drawings have been designed and delivered in 2D, leading to problems and delays on the construction site due to insufficient depth of planning. Building Information Modeling (BIM), the digital representation of physical and functional characteristics of a building, has been introduced into the field of civil engineering to improve planning efficiency and planning quality (Eastman et al., 2011; Borrmann et al., 2015). BIM facilitates and accelerates the planning process by the use of semantic construction components and continuous data exchange. However, concerning the selection of construction methods on one hand and planning of construction work and construction schedules on the other hand, most engineers still use manual methods and rely on experience. Up to now, the development of a representation of the construction process in BIM is still in an early phase, giving away the opportunity to optimize the planning process towards time efficiency, robustness, as well as health and safety concerns.

The recently started project BIMsite is focused on the transition from construction planning to construction process. A tool is created to assist engineers during the planning process: different construction variants and materials, as well as the setup of building site facilities are automatically generated, and the construction sequences are simulated. By this means, decisions are supported by extensive evaluation of the costs, robustness and duration of the building process. For example, concrete elements can be constructed using precast concrete components or in-situ concrete, leading to complex influences on costs and duration: Using precast concrete, high-power cranes and longer travel journeys may be necessary; using in-situ concrete, additional storage locations for formwork and reinforcement steel as well as extended curing times have to be taken into account. Up to now, these influences are not considered adequately during the selection of different construction methods and haven't to the best of our knowledge, been part of former research.

BIMsite aims at an early, comprehensive variant analysis with as little user interaction as possible. For the semi-automated generation of a set of site layout plans, a layout generator, which is able to extract as much information from the building information model as possible, will be developed. The project utilizes the Industry Foundation Classes (IFC), an open file format specification used to digitally describe building data. The project comprises three succeeding main steps: "model preparation and simulation", "analysis and evaluation", and "monitoring" (Figure 1).

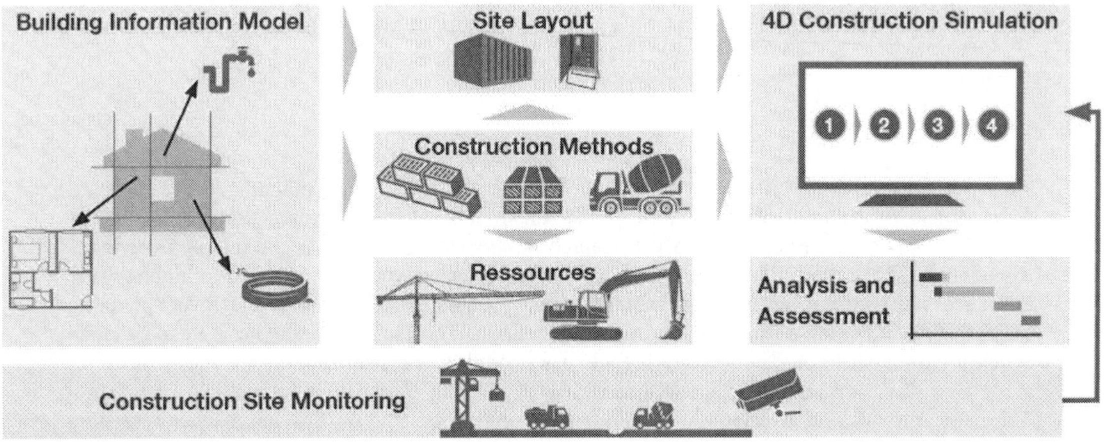

Figure 1:BIMsite – Project Overview

During model preparation and simulation, BIM models are examined for missing and corrupt information; possible ways to integrate required information a-posteriori are identified. The reproduction of construction sequences and building site facilities within a BIM model, as well as commonly used resources are investigated and implemented. Following this, a methodology for a construction sequence simulation is developed. The second step of the project includes the development of systematic evaluation methods to analyze and evaluate the generated building site facility and construction sequence plans. Different design variations are generated and weighed to assist the decision making. During the last step, the developed methods are verified and parameters are calibrated. The construction sequence plans should be robust towards unexpected changes in circumstances Finally, a pilot construction site is being chosen during the planning phase to verify the developed methods and solutions in collaboration with construction companies. One construction site layout plan is selected, and a construction sequence plan is simulated. The construction process is monitored to validate the assumptions. To evaluate the acceptance of the proposed methods, the construction companies are interviewed and suggestions for improvements are requested.

This paper presents a brief overview of selected research topics in the context of BIMsite. In the first part of the paper, it is discussed how building information models will be used within the project context. Furthermore, a brief overview of construction site modeling is given, and process patterns as well as the representation of construction procedures are introduced. The second part of the paper describes boundary conditions of site layouts and discusses different site layout optimization approaches. In the third part of the paper, the simulation of construction sites is discussed and the development of a key performance indicator system is described. Finally, a short summary is given and the further line of research is described.

2. Building Information Models and Construction Site Modeling

Construction site layouts strongly depend on the building itself and the used construction methods. The dimension and position of needed storage areas and corresponding transport ways for instance strongly depend on the geometry of the building and resources such as materials and machinery needed for construction. In conjunction with construction method models, building information models have the potential to serve as a basis for automated site layout planning. The amount of material needed for certain building elements, for example, can be derived from building information models using quantity take-off techniques (Monteiro & Poças Martins, 2013). Therefore, the modeling of computer interpretable construction method models, as well as the question how they can be utilized for automated site layout planning and simulation, form a vital part of the planned research. Furthermore, it will be investigated which kind of information is necessary in building information models to derive the construction methods that can be applied to building sections and elements like walls or slabs automatically or semi-automatically.

Building information models can be defined at different Levels of Development (LOD). The LOD specifies content and reliability of a model. BIMforum (2015) for example specifies six LODs reaching from conceptual information that must be considered approximate on the lowest level, up to more detailed and reliable information on higher levels. Typically, the models of earlier design phases are of lower LODs and therefore do not specify construction details. However, in order to enable an analysis of different construction methods and how they might affect the construction site layout, it will be addressed how models of lower detail and reliability can be used to derive the construction methods that can be applied to building sections and elements like walls or slabs (semi-)automatically. The resulting concept will be integrated into a demonstrator working with IFC-files. Requirements on IFC-files can be specified in a Model View Definition (MVD), which defines a schema that must be satisfied by valid files (buildingSMART International Ltd., 2016). Therefore, a model checker based on a proposed Model View Definition (MVD) will also be part of the resulting prototype. It will be used to validate and check if the building information models provide the information needed for automated site layout planning.

One way of modeling construction methods in a 4D environment (3D + time) is within the scope of pattern based approaches such as proposed by Wu et al. (2010), König et al. (2012) and Benevolenskiy et al. (2012). According to them, a construction pattern is a reusable concept that can be applied or assigned to certain building elements. The pattern defines and models sub-processes and their general set-up like the required workforce, machinery, material and time in order to build the component. For instance, a construction method for in situ concrete columns could be applied to columns in an IFC model by assigning the corresponding pattern. The pattern then determines the needed sub-processes like erecting formwork, installing reinforcement, placing the in-situ concrete, curing the concrete and finally stripping the formwork as well as needed resources. Furthermore, process patterns can be modeled in a hierarchical way which allows the abstraction from single building elements to compositions of elements like rooms, stories or on top-level entire buildings as demonstrated by Wu et al. (2010). Thus adequate process patterns can also be applied to coarse grained building information models of early planning phases. Furthermore, they are a promising approach for the mostly automatic generation of site layout plans and construction schedules based on models not reaching for higher LODs. The assignment of different matching process patterns, defining different construction methods, will allow for an analysis of different construction methods in early planning phases with minimal effort and is therefore an essential component of BIMsite. Consequently, methods of how to extend and combine former pattern based approaches of modeling construction methods will be investigated. Since BIMsite aims to assess site layouts in terms of safety and productivity the formalized construction method models must consequently reflect both aspects.

A characteristic site layout feature, affecting safety as well as productivity, is space. Looking at a snapshot of a large construction site, one will typically notice many construction processes taking place simultaneously. And as each process requires space, spatial conflicts may occur. Either in terms of congestion, like one tower crane operation is blocking another tower crane and thus affecting the overall productivity, or as safety hazard, like construction workers operating directly below suspended crane loads. Akinci et al. (2002) proposed a model that allows the detection of spatial conflicts and their classification regarding type and severity which could serve as a basis of automatic scheduling while avoiding spatial conflicts. Marx et al. (2010) integrated a subset of this model into a discrete event simulation limited to the detection of spatial conflicts between simultaneously operating tower cranes in order to generate optimized schedules. Later they proposed an approach where spatial requirements are implemented alongside process patterns that can be applied to building elements like *IfcWall* components and can be integrated into simulation models as soft constraints in Constraint Based Discrete Event Simulation. However, the rating of severity and the type of spatial conflicts is only implied vaguely (Marx & König, 2013). A more recent approach from Zhang et al. (2015) introduced a more detailed workspace model that integrates into the BIM-IFC world, but focuses mainly on safety. Based on a detailed state-of-the art research and discussion with industry partners, we will combine and refine existing approaches of workspace modeling and will propose a model that can serve as a basis for site-layout planning and site layout simulation. In this regard we will focus on the BIM-based automatic assignment of spatial requirements of construction processes to building elements as well as on general requirements of simulation-based construction site safety and productivity analysis (see section 3).

Both, automated site layout planning and construction simulation depend on models that determine the build order of certain building parts. Most obviously, before the construction process of a slab can be started, the subjacent supporting columns or walls have to be load bearing. The manual scheduling of the corresponding processes is potentially a time consuming task, especially when it comes to large buildings. However, predecessor-successor-relationships can be derived from building information models by applying corresponding rules or templates. In order to do so spatial query languages can be utilized (König et al., 2012). In order to support planners, it will be investigated how query languages like *QL4BIM* (Daum & Borrmann, 2014) and building information models can be used to support the definition of more sophisticated predecessor-successor-relationships.

3. Semi-Automated Generation and Optimization of Site Layouts

For generating the site layouts, external circumstances and boundary conditions are investigated and combined with requirements on facilities to formulate and solve an optimization problem. Different alternative construction methods will lead to site layout variants, which will serve as a basis for site layout simulation and variant evaluation in section 4.

3.1 Boundary Conditions for Site Layout Planning

As an input for the layout problem information about the types of facilities to be placed and the quantity of each facility type and/or the size of each facility is necessary. To generate this information, data about the building geometry, the applied construction methods as well as the time schedule will be extracted from the BIM model.

Tower cranes play a key role in building construction projects. One method of calculating the number of tower cranes is given in Equation (1), in which N_c represents the number of cranes, V the gross volume and C the crane capacity (Schach & Otto 2008, Hofstadler 2007). Reference values for crane capacities depending on the construction method can be found in (Schach & Otto, 2008). M is the time period measured in months, for which the usage of one or more cranes is scheduled. Once the number of cranes is determined, specific tower cranes will be selected using the digital tower crane deployment planner by (Frenz et al., 2014). Their approach is based on providing applicable crane models based on a set of input parameters, such as boom length and lifting capacity for the upper structure. In addition, a 3D-model of the crane with the selected characteristics will be generated automatically using pre-defined construction components.

$$N_c = \frac{V}{C \cdot M} \tag{1}$$

The number of office containers, washrooms and day accommodation strongly depends on the number of site personnel, which can be approximated for building construction projects by Equation (2), in which n represents the number of site personnel and V the gross volume. A stands for the effort necessary for certain tasks, e.g. the masoning of walls, and is measured in hours per unit of quantity (m, m^2 or m^3). T is the total construction time measured in days and t_{AT} are the daily working hours (Berner et al., 2013).

$$n = \frac{V \cdot A}{T \cdot t_{AT}} \tag{2}$$

The necessity and the size of a concrete pump, a concrete mixer and/ or a mortar mixer as well as the size of storage area depend on the construction method. Suggestions for dimensioning are given in (Schach & Otto, 2008). The width of the construction road depends on the engaged construction machines.

In addition to the type, number and size of facilities, restrictions need to be considered for the generation of a layout. These include geometric constraints, e.g. facilities must be placed inside the construction site boundaries and outside of the building space. Other restrictions concern safety aspects, for instance cranes should not lift their loads above office containers, or ground characteristics, e.g. load-bearing capacities must be considered when placing a crane. All constraints will be categorized in either hard constraints (mandatory requirements) or soft constraints (recommendations).

3.2 Generation and Optimization of Site Layout Variants

Commonly, it is up to the planner to decide between different construction methods to realize a construction project. Different construction methods entail different materials, storage spaces, construction equipment and process patterns, leading to overly complex cost and time distribution. To facilitate the process of selecting particular construction methods based on distinct, comparable criteria, different methods are examined.

Depending on the construction methods, the building process can be divided into discrete construction stages according to the construction progress. Each construction stage has different requirements on facilities – some facilities may not be necessary in every construction phase. Therefore, a dynamic site layout model is required. Through varying the site layout plan over the duration of the construction process, optimal layouts can be realized for all construction stages. In the beginning of each construction stage, facilities that are not needed any more are dismantled and may be replaced by other facilities. The number of construction stages and, consequentially, facility alterations, has to be thoroughly pondered: too few construction stages may lead to suboptimal exploitation of the building site, too many construction stages and modifications lead to disorganized and confusing site structures (Kumar & Cheng, 2015).

Correspondingly to the variation of facilities, space requirements and constraints vary over the construction stages. Building site areas are redefined in each stage, leading to a complex layout system. Solely based on the experience of planners, optimal solutions are hardly found. However, taking into account the constraints specified in 3.1, an optimization problem can be formulated to evaluate different layouts. The optimization of the site layout implies the minimization of an objective function with multiple conflicting objectives (Yahya & Saka, 2014). Typical objectives are the reduction of costs and the increase of safety. To measure the costs, which arise on a building site, different parameters are used: A strong indicator of efficiency are the travel distances and frequencies between different facilities to calculate the cost for transportation of materials and workers' travel paths. Setup, dismantling and relocation of facilities on the building site produce additional costs. Khalafallah & El-Rayes (2011) include costs for wildlife control and debris control systems. To minimize the objective function of the optimization problem, various optimization algorithms have been used: Huang & Wong (2015) implement a binary-mixed-integer-linear program, which is solved using a standard branch-and-bound algorithm in a commercial software. Shawki et al. (2010) and Kumar & Cheng (2015) use genetic algorithms for layout creation, starting with random layouts which are crossed and mutated. Several researchers use artificial intelligence to solve the optimization problem. Research includes swarm intelligence based meta heuristic algorithms, implemented by Yahya & Saka (2014) by using an artificial bee colony algorithm and Ning et al. (2010) by using a max-min ant system. Yeh (1995) uses annealed Hopfield neural networks. Another approach, as used by Andayesh & Sadeghpour (2013), uses the theory of minimal total potential energy, moving objects until they reach the equilibrium state. To decide on a suitable and efficient optimization approach, further literature research has to be conducted to analyze advantages and disadvantages of the different approaches.

4. Simulation and Evaluation

As generated variants of site layouts need to be evaluable and comparable, the valuation basis of those variants is central to the research within BIMsite. Therefore, a key performance indicator (KPI) system will be developed with an emphasis on occupational safety and productivity aspects. The calculation of those KPIs will utilize a construction simulation approach that incorporates the model of the formerly defined site layout and thereby induced constraints.

4.1 Simulation

Within the scope of the BIMsite project an approach for construction simulation with an emphasis on site layout evaluation will be developed. A promising and widespread approach is the so called constraint based discrete event simulation (DES) (Beißert et al., 2007). It has been shown, that constraint based DES is applicable to the evaluation of several aspects relevant to site layout evaluation and allows inter alia for simulation models considering available resources such as machinery, available workforce, skills, material and construction processes (König et al., 2012). Furthermore constraint based DES can be used to analyze resource utilization on construction sites in order to identify bottlenecks induced by logistic chains (König et al., 2011). Additionally, the approach of Beißert et al. has been extended by spatial constraints in order to detect and avoid spatial conflicts between tower cranes (Marx et al., 2010) and workspaces in general (Marx & König, 2013). Moreover, discrete event simulation can also be utilized for process schedule optimization (Bügler et al., 2013). Based on the refinement and adaptation of prior research in constraint based event simulation a simulation model will be developed, that explicitly takes the construction site model into account and allows for an extensive construction site simulation. The simulation model will further respect the location where construction processes take place and therefore, in conjunction with building information models and detailed construction process information enable the evaluation of logistic chains and spatial conflicts which will serve as a basis for safety and productivity evaluation.

An advantage of using constraint based DES is that at each event, the simulation engine identifies the processes that can be started by checking the constraints the simulation model has been initially fed with. This reduces the effort regarding input data preparation since no hard coded detailed schedule information needs to be created. Furthermore the approach can be extended by differentiating hard constraints that have to be fulfilled and soft constraints that influence the selection of upcoming processes which allows for the application of more detailed strategies during the simulation process (Beißert et al., 2010). However, the preparation of constraints still remains a potentially time-consuming task, which has been addressed by former research. The utilization of process patterns can reduce the effort needed for data preparation and helps to mitigate repetitive user input (Marx & König, 2011). Since BIMsite aims at the generation and simulation of several site layout variants the development of innovative concepts for automatized generation of simulation input data will also be part of our research. In this context possibilities of how to assign process patterns to building parts based on building information models will be investigated (see section 2).

4.2 Evaluation: Key Performance Indicator (KPI) System

During the simulation a lot of data about the building process is being generated. To evaluate this data, which strongly depends on the applied construction methods and the generated site layout plan, a KPI system will be developed. The emphasis is placed on measuring occupational safety and productivity aspects.

Safety remains a big issue in the construction industry due to high accident and fatality rates (Zhang, Sulankivi, et al., 2015). In the BIMsite project two different aspects of occupational safety will be regarded: Firstly safety related to the applied construction methods and secondly safety related to the positioning of facilities. This involves identifying and quantifying potential risks at different stages of construction considering interactions between the building and workers, the building and facilities, facilities and workers and facilities among themselves.

While safety aspects might influence the reputation of the construction company, keeping a high productivity level is a necessary prerequisite for the financial success of a company. Potential KPIs to measure the productivity are total construction time, utilization rate of construction machines and robustness of the construction schedule. The latter is an indicator for the sensitivity of project objectives to uncertainties such as weather conditions, machine breakdowns or delivery dates and can be measured by the deviation of realized and planned activity start time combined with the deviation of realized and planned order of activities (König, 2011).

5. Conclusion and Outlook

Building Information Modeling is able to facilitate and accelerate the planning process of constructions. However, none of the existing approaches facilitates the analysis of different construction methods and their effects on site layout planning. In this paper, an overview of the recently started BIMsite project is given. Within the project a decision support system for the planning process is developed to analyze construction processes and construction variants with regard to productivity, safety and robustness using a BIM-based approach.

In the paper, necessary properties of the BIM-model are discussed. Furthermore, the concept of process patterns for integrating construction methods as well as approaches for the automatic assignment of spatial requirements are introduced. It is discussed how the information from the BIM-model will be used to generate input parameters and constraints for the mathematical layout optimization problem. Approaches for solving the optimization problem are presented in a brief review. Next, it is examined how generated, optimized site layouts serve as an input for construction simulation. Different simulation approaches as well as key performance indicators for the variant analysis are discussed.

In future research, the presented approaches will be refined and extended. Additionally, methods enabling the validation of the approaches will be developed. These will be used on a pilot construction site, comparing the results from the simulation to parameters from the real process.

6. Acknowledgements

The project BIMsite is funded by the Bavarian Research Foundation (Bayerische Forschungsstiftung). The authors would also like to thank the industrial project partners for their cooperation.

References

Akinci, B., Fischen, M., Levitt, R. & Carlson, R., 2002. Formalization and Automation of Time-Space Conflict Analysis. *Journal of Computing in Civil Engineering*, 16(2), pp.124–134.

Andayesh, M. & Sadeghpour, F., 2013. Dynamic site layout planning through minimization of total potential energy. *Automation in Construction*, 31, pp.92–102.

Beißert, U., König, M. & Bargstädt, H.-J., 2007. Constraint-Based Simulation of Outfitting Processes in Building Engineering. In *Proceedings of CIB-W78 24th International Conference on Information Technology in Construction*. pp. 491–498.

Beißert, U., König, M. & Bargstädt, H.-J., 2010. Soft Constraint-based simulation of execution strategies in building engineering. *Journal of Simulation*, 4(4), pp.222–231.

Benevolenskiy, A., Roos, K., Katranuschkov, P. & Scherer, R.J., 2012. Construction processes configuration using process patterns. *Advanced Engineering Informatics*, 26(4), pp.727–736.

Berner, F., Kochendörfer, B. & Schach, R., 2013. *Grundlagen der Baubetriebslehre 2*, Wiesbaden: Springer Fachmedien Wiesbaden.

BIMForum, 2015. Level of Development Specification. *[Online]*. Available at: http://bimforum.org/lod [Accessed February 28, 2016].

Borrmann, A., König, M., Koch, C. & Beetz, J. eds., 2015. *Building Information Modeling*, Wiesbaden: Springer Fachmedien Wiesbaden.

Bügler, M., Dori, G. & Borrmann, A., 2013. Swap Based Process Schedule Optimization using Discrete-Event Simulation. *Proceedings of the International Conference on Construction Applications of Virtual Reality, London, United Kingdom*.

buildingSMART International Ltd., 2016. Model View Definition Summary. *[Online]*. Available at: http://www.buildingsmart-tech.org/specifications/ifc-view-definition/summary [Accessed February 25, 2016].

Daum, S. & Borrmann, A., 2014. Processing of Topological BIM Queries using Boundary Representation Based Methods. *Advanced Engineering Informatics*, 28(4), pp.272–286.

Eastman, C., Eastman, C., Teicholz, P. & Sacks, R., 2011. BIM handbook: A guide to building information modeling for owners, managers, designers, engineers and contractors.

Frenz, T., Kessler, S. & Günther, W.A., 2014. TEP - der Turmdrehkran-Einsatzplaner Die Anforderungen der Praxis. In *22. Internationale Kranfachtagung 2014 "Krane in Materialflusstechnik und Logistik."* pp. 61–74.

Hofstadler, C., 2007. *Bauablaufplanung und Logistik im Baubetrieb*, Berlin: Springer-Verlag.

Huang, C. & Wong, C.K., 2015. Optimisation of site layout planning for multiple construction stages with safety considerations and requirements. *Automation in Construction*, 53, pp.58–68.

Khalafallah, A. & El-Rayes, K., 2011. Automated multi-objective optimization system for airport site layouts. *Automation in Construction*, 20(4), pp.313–320.

König, M., 2011. Robust construction scheduling using discrete-event simulation. In *Proceedings of the 2011 ASCE International Workshop on Computing in Civil Engineering*. pp. 446–453.

König, M., Habenicht, I. & Spieckermann, S., 2011. On-site logistics simulation in early planning phases. *Proceedings of the International Conference on Construction Applications of Virtual Reality*, pp.728–737.

König, M., Koch, C., Habenicht, I. & Spieckermann, S., 2012. Intelligent BIM-based construction scheduling using discrete event simulation. In *Proceedings of the 2012 Winter Simulation Conference (WSC)*. IEEE, pp. 1–12.

Kumar, S.S. & Cheng, J.C.P., 2015. A BIM-based automated site layout planning framework for congested construction sites. *Automation in Construction*, 59, pp.24–37.

Marx, A., Erlemann, K. & König, M., 2010. Simulation of construction processes considering spatial constraints of crane operations. In *Proceedings of the XIIIth International Conference on Computing in Civil and Building Engineering*.

Marx, A. & König, M., 2013. Modeling and simulating spatial requirements of construction activities. In *Proceedings of the 2013 Winter Simulation Conference (WSC)*.

Marx, A. & König, M., 2011. Preparation of constraints for construction simulation. In *Proceedings of the 2011 ASCE International Workshop on Computing in Civil Engineering*.

Monteiro, A. & Poças Martins, J., 2013. A survey on modeling guidelines for quantity takeoff-oriented BIM-based design. *Automation in Construction*, 35, pp.238–253.

Ning, X., Lam, K.-C. & Lam, M.C.-K., 2010. Dynamic construction site layout planning using max-min ant system. *Automation in Construction*, 19(1), pp.55–65.

Schach, R. & Otto, J., 2008. *Baustelleneinrichtung: Grundlagen - Planung - Praxishinweise - Vorschriften und Regeln*, Springer-Verlag.

Shawki, K.M., Abd EL-Razek, M.E. & Maqboly, S.A., 2010. Optimal Arrangement of Temporary Facilities in Construction Sites. *Journal of Engineering Sciences*, 38(4), pp.949–960.

Wu, I.C., Borrmann, A., Beißert, U., König, M. & Rank, E., 2010. Bridge construction schedule generation with pattern-based construction methods and constraint-based simulation. *Advanced Engineering Informatics*, 24(4), pp.379–388.

Yahya, M. & Saka, M.P., 2014. Construction site layout planning using multi-objective artificial bee colony algorithm with Levy flights. *Automation in Construction*, 38, pp.14–29.

Yeh, I.-C., 1995. Construction-Site Layout Using Annealed Neural Network. *Journal of Computing in Civil*

Engineering, 9(3), pp.201–208.

Zhang, S., Sulankivi, K., Kiviniemi, M., Romo, I., Eastman, C.M. & Teizer, J., 2015. BIM-based fall hazard identification and prevention in construction safety planning. *Safety Science*, 72, pp.31–45.

Zhang, S., Teizer, J., Pradhananga, N. & Eastman, C.M., 2015. Workforce location tracking to model, visualize and analyze workspace requirements in building information models for construction safety planning. *Automation in Construction*, 60, pp.74–86.

Automated building energy performance simulation: a review of approaches and outline of research opportunities

Aurelien Bres[1], Georg Suter[2]

[1]AIT Austrian Institute of Technology, Energy Department

[2]Design Computing Group, Center for Geometry and Computational Design, Vienna University of Technology

Aurelien.Bres.fl@ait.ac.at

Abstract. This paper offers a review of approaches to the automated creation of input data for building energy simulation. Such data may be obtained by translation of available data from architectural and HVAC models. However, a full energy performance model also requires missing data to be completed, either with default values or automated procedures. Following the review, research opportunities for further automation are identified.

1. Introduction

Computational tools that model the variety of processes and interactions relevant to the thermal behavior of buildings have high application potential in building design and operation (Clarke 2001). Despite decades of continuous evolution, building energy performance simulation (BEPS) tools still face challenges when it comes to realizing this potential. Reasons for this are to be found in the simulation model creation workflow, which is considered to be time-consuming and error-prone (Bazjanac 2008). The use of procedures reducing the amount of human intervention for the creation of simulation models, which we will refer to as automation, may address both drawbacks, by reducing the model creation effort and avoiding input errors.

This paper offers a review of approaches that aim to automate the creation of a BEPS model. Organized around the required data, the survey begins with the cases where this data can be translated from existing data, as for geometric data, on which a majority of existing work has focused, before investigating how missing data can be automatically completed. This is followed by a discussion and an outline of research opportunities. Two criteria for the assessment of the reviewed methods are their level of automation and the completeness of the obtained models. In particular, the aim is to create a complete building energy model in the more integrated sense, including the impact of HVAC systems (Barbour et al. 2016, p.1). This paper focuses on data translation and completion, which are relevant in several building energy simulation steps. According to the workflow in figure 1, a simulation user processes information obtained from an architect and an HVAC designer. Part of this existing data can be translated seamlessly into simulation inputs. Section 2 deals with such automated translation, each subsection dealing with a different data domain. In other cases, missing data needs to be completed (Section 3). Default values may be used, notably for constructions and internal loads. More complex procedures might also have to be used, such as for model zoning and for HVAC model creation.

Areas which which are not covered in this review include parametric variations of model attributes, such as building orientation or composition of wall elements, as well as uncertainty analysis and model calibration. The modeling of entire building stocks is not considered, although such a task involves a high degree of automation. Finally, the focus lies on early design phases, for which the potential impact of simulation is assumed to be higher, while time and cost constraints are often incompatible with manual model creation.

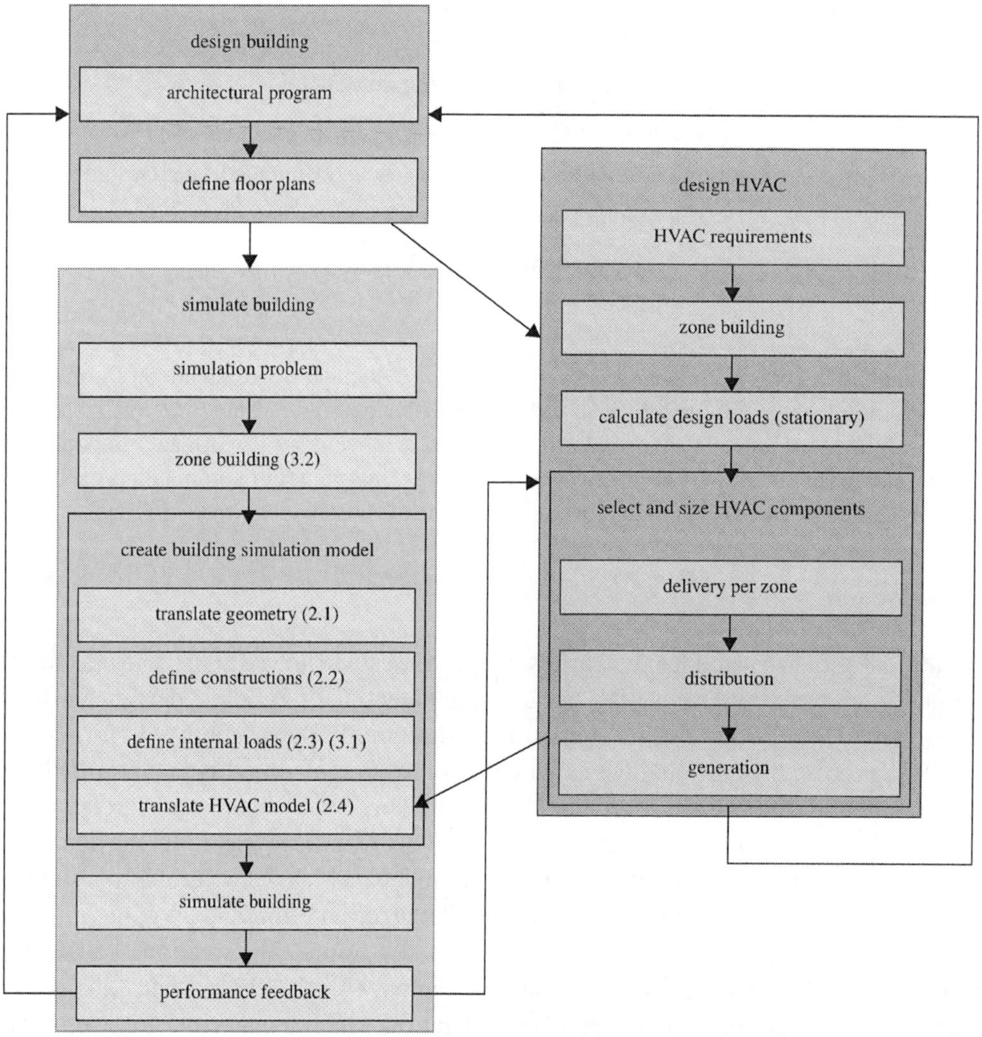

Figure 1: Workflow model for building energy simulation in the design process, with the following roles: architect (red), HVAC designer (blue), simulation user (green)

2. Data translation

2.1 Building geometry

A three-dimensional description of the building geometry is a prerequisite for dynamic thermal simulation. Ideally, this description is derived from a building information model (BIM), a "shared digital representation of physical and functional characteristics of any built object" (ISO 2010), for instance in a format specified by the Industry Foundation Classes (IFC). Characteristic for the thermal view underlying BEPS is the division of buildings into zones, separated from another by space boundaries. Since the flow through a space boundary is to be consistent, there can only be one zone on each of its sides, and it should be assigned a unique construction.

Hence the need to decompose some space boundaries. The methodology for consistent simulation model creation developed at the Lawrence Berkeley National Laboratory (Bazjanac 2008), based on unambiguous rules for data transformation, the use of IFC-based BIM, and model checking, addressed the problem of geometry translation with the definition of different levels of space boundaries (Bazjanac 2010). Fundamental is the partition of first level space boundaries, modeling surfaces in their maximal extent, to obtain second level space boundaries (level 2a in IFC), in blue in figure 2, which come in pairs through which thermal flow is consistent. This partition may also result in sliver surfaces of higher level (level 2b in IFC), through which no heat flows, but which should be present in the model to ensure closed zone volumes.

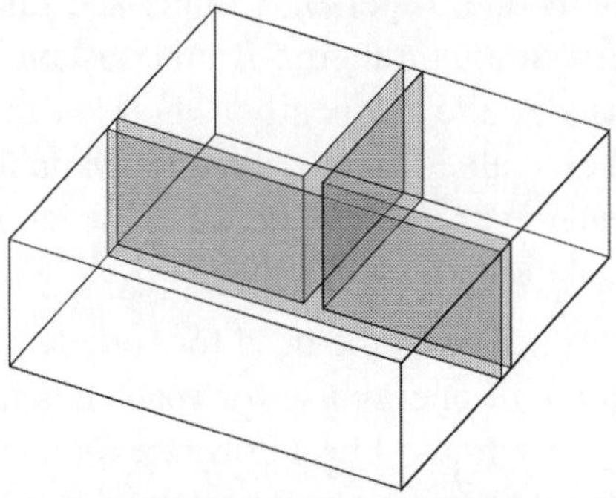

(a) Space boundaries of level 1

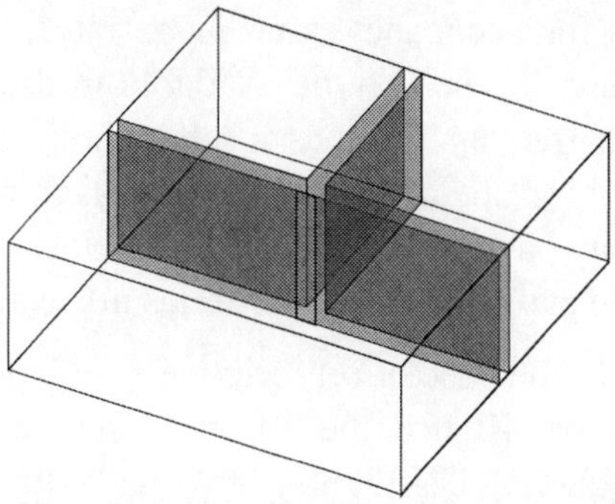

(b) Space boundaries of level 2 (2a IFC) and 3 (2b IFC)

Figure 2: Space boundaries of different levels according to LBNL methodology (Bazjanac 2010) respectively IFC. Level 1 in gray, level two (2a IFC) in blue, level three (2b IFC) in red

Sources other than a BIM may also be considered for geometry translation. Geometry contained in geographical information systems (GIS) may be only two-and-a-half-dimensional (Reinhart & Davila 2016) or necessitate additional semantic mapping, including, for instance, the transformation of overhanging roof surfaces into shading surfaces (Banfi 2013). Traditional CAD drawings without semantic information require additional steps, particularly for the identification and matching of spaces and surfaces (Jones et al. 2013).

2.2 Construction properties

Heat transfer elements, and possibly heat storage elements, are characterized not only by their geometry, but also by thermal and physical properties required for energy performance simulation. Typically, each construction element is composed of a number of layers of homogeneous materials.

Surface properties can be derived from an IFC model (Giannakis 2015, p.79). The boundary type (internal, external, ground) is indicated by the *InternalOrExternalBoundary* attribute of an *IfcRelSpaceBoundary*. However, information about the thermal properties of construction materials, which could be referred to through the *RelatedBuildingElement* attribute, are not exported by current IFC export tools (Giannakis 2015, p.83). BIM authoring tools feature materials that can be retrieved from databases and assigned to building elements (Autodesk 2011, p.1542). Yet presently they are mainly used to define the appearance rather than physical or thermal properties. Databases such as the "Building Component Library" (Fleming et al. 2012) may allow material and construction data to be exchanged.

Modeling of air-tightness presents additional difficulties. Infiltration rates required for simulation differ from potentially available infiltration rates, which are only measured or defined for a given pressure. Thus, direct translation from building data is implausible. Still, a methodology proposed for the modeling of infiltration (Gowri et al. 2009), which implies the calculation and integration of wind-driven pressures on exterior surfaces for the determination of a wind-dependent infiltration coefficient, could potentially be automated.

2.3 Time series

In addition to static data, building performance simulation inputs also include time-dependent values for occupancy, air change rates, or internal gains due to persons, lights and other appliances. These may be available in different time resolutions, ranging from constant values to high-frequency values for the whole simulation period, quite frequently as hourly schedules defined for one or several day types. In most cases, these values are not directly available, and one may have to resort to default values, as for construction properties. However, several cases may be evoked where time series are available for translation:

- In the case of prescriptive simulation, standard values are to be used for some variables. For instance, the European standard for calculation of energy use for space heating and cooling EN 13790 states that "hourly and weekly schedules of heat flow rate for metabolic heat from occupants and dissipated heat from appliances shall be determined on national basis, as a function of building use, (optionally) occupancy class and purpose of the calculation" (ISO 2008, p.45). For this kind of application, the issue is to determine a building's use together with the occupancy classes of spaces defined by the architect in order to retrieve associated schedules. Attention should be paid to the reference quantities used, e.g. net or gross floor areas, which may vary and require conversion.

- In existing buildings, real measured values may be used as inputs. A co-simulation methodology was proposed for the use of dynamic data in BEPS (Giannakis 2015), allowing automatically generated thermal models to be used for model-based control. Since some quantities (e.g. occupant heat output) cannot be directly measured, correlations between sensed quantities and simulation inputs may be required. For instance, building occupancy may be derived from passive infrared motion detectors, carbon dioxide sensors (Lam et al. 2009), doorway counting sensors, or even classroom scheduling data (Davis & Nutter 2010). Occupant heat output would then be obtained by multiplying the estimated number of occupants by an assumed metabolic rate. This also leads to the topic of calibration, for which automated approaches have been proposed (Robertson et al. 2013).

2.4 HVAC data

Data on existing or planned heating, ventilation and air-conditioning (HVAC) systems serving a building may be available and translated for use in energy performance simulation. While all previously considered data may be be obtained from the architect, HVAC data usually stem from a different source. Thus, automated generation of models for integrated building and HVAC energy performance simulation would require multiple exchanges, as illustrated in Figure 1. Several views are also to be distinguished here:

- HVAC system engineers tend to base system design on static calculations, mostly for the full load case (Vandenbulcke et al. 2012). Moreover, pressure distribution plays an important role in their view of HVAC systems.

- For energy performance simulation, the dynamic behavior of systems, and thus part load conditions, are of primary importance. On the other hand, some processes are assumed to be perfect. For instance, the adjustment of pressure resistances to achieve the flow rates required for energy transfer is mostly not explicitly considered.

- Other disciplines are more concerned with the spatial aspects of HVAC systems, including openings and collision avoidance. The corresponding constraints on dimensions and changes in direction influence resistances in distribution systems and noise effects.

Similar to building data, a common format should be able to support these different views. For energy simulation, the modeling of HVAC systems requires diverse data, including construction properties (e.g. of pipe elements) and time series (e.g. set points and operation schedules). The complexity and diversity of HVAC systems and components contribute to making the integration of information relative to HVAC in BIM a challenging issue.

Despite successive extensions of the "HVAC part" of the IFC data model (Bazjanac et al. 2002, Bazjanac & Maile 2004), IFC data do not yet satisfy the requirements for building energy performance simulation (Wimmer et al. 2014, Liu et al. 2013). In order to support BIM based HVAC definitions in Modelica, Wimmer et al. (Wimmer et al. 2014) resort to the SimModel data model, which can store more relevant data for BEPS than current versions of IFC.

3. Automated completion of missing data

3.1 Use of default values

When required data are not available, some assumptions are necessary to complete the building model. Use of default values for unknown variables is common in approaches for automated BEPS (Smith et al. 2011, Ahn et al. 2014, Leal et al. 2014). For instance, standard constructions may be chosen in function of the building age, and internal loads based on room functions. Default values may be taken out of different sources, such as standards, guidelines, or handbooks, with different levels of credibility. Because of uncertainties in data, it would be reasonable to consider value intervals. Uncertainty and sensitivity analysis have indeed been used in conjunction with BEPS, for instance to predict building performance under future conditions (De Wilde & Tian 2010). One study (Ahn et al. 2014) used uncertainty analysis in order to identify the most significant inputs, and determine which inputs require human intervention in the context of semi-automated simulation.

Default values often originate from the aggregation of large amounts of data. In urban building energy modeling, they may be derived from the abstraction of a building stock into a limited number of archetypes (Reinhart & Davila 2016). Mandatory upper limits for U-values or infiltration in recent building codes represent a case of relatively trustworthy default values. Assumptions often come together with simplifications. For instance, assuming a default construction for external walls implies the absence of differentiation between these walls.

It has been argued that a template format encapsulating non-geometrical properties of building zones could allow default values to be well documented and correctly exchanged, contributing to a fast and consistent setup of BEPS models (Cerezo et al. 2014).

3.2 Zoning

Although fundamental for building thermal and HVAC simulation, zoning has received relatively little attention. Most methods for automated BEPS either equate thermal zones to rooms or settle for a mono-zone building model. An appropriate zoning strategy would depend on simulation goals and available information. A recently presented algorithm (Dogan et al. 2015) creates a partition of buildings whose interior space definitions are unknown, based solely on the building outline. Core zones are found by offsetting the floor outline. Perimeter zones with different orientations are derived from the straight skeleton decomposition of the floor-plan polygon. Using simulation for control purposes, one may use coarser zoning for increased speed (Giannakis 2015, p.100). Grouping spaces for this aim may be achieved with the application of clustering algorithms or other mathematical analysis techniques (Georgescu et al. 2012) on the results of a building simulation with fine zoning.

3.3 HVAC system model

State-of-the-art simulation engines make the simultaneous simulation of building structure and HVAC systems possible. However, detailed HVAC simulation requires a high modeling effort. Moreover, its integration in automated procedures for building performance simulation is not well developed, which can be explained by the translation difficulties described in 2.4. State-of-the-art interfaces such as the Simergy GUI for EnergyPlus (Basarkar 2012) or DesignBuilder (DesignBuilder 2015) use automatic data translation from a graphical view familiar to engineers to a simulation model. The HVAC system is manually assembled from different components linked to each other. Pre-defined templates, autosizing features and the possibility to group zones served by the same type of equipment may speed up this process. It is also automatically checked if the restrictions induced by the EnergyPlus simulation engine are respected. For instance, no more than one set of parallel branches should be present on each side of a water loop. A paper (Ahn et al. 2014) distinguishes fully automated and semi-automated building energy simulation. The latter involves human data entry of given uncertain simulation inputs. It highlights the limits of autosizing and default values for HVAC system variables such as chiller performance coefficients or condenser loop set points.

4. Discussion

The present review has revealed that the different types of data necessary for the preparation of a complete BEPS model are unequally automation-ready.

The translation of geometry has been dealt with extensively. Typical for this the IFC-based space boundary decomposition, the implementation of which should rely on the development of three components dealing with the respective domains of geometry, HVAC and internal loads (Bazjanac et al. 2011). While the first component is already in use, the second one is an interoperable HVAC graphical user interface, comparatively less developed, and the third one is not developed yet. Still, difficulties remain for complex building geometries, such as free-form geometries. Many of the difficulties may be ascribed to the quality of the input model, which could be addressed by model checking in authoring tools and training of model creators (Maile et al. 2013). Others have to do with limitations of the simulation tools. Until now, these can only operate with polyhedral geometries. The approximation of curved surfaces with planar elements should consider the trade-off between quality of the approximation and the increase in run-time and potential errors resulting from numerous surfaces.

Existing methods have paid less attention to other aspects influencing building performance. The need to document and exchange building property data is relevant for automated approaches (Cerezo et al. 2014).

The integration of HVAC systems in automated BEPS only began to be tackled recently (Wimmer et al. 2014, Robert et al. 2014). Since current BIM models lack concepts and properties for a detailed modeling of HVAC systems within building performance simulation, the main approach has been to "extend" the IFC format and complete the corresponding models with custom additions.

The reviewed methods show that a high degree of automated model creation through translation is only possible for some domains. For others, only the use of default values may allow full building energy models to be generated automatically. Exemplarily, simulation parameters, describing the simulation itself rather than the simulated building, are bound to be absent from other data sources. This part of the simulation input can only be determined by the simulation user, taking into account the questioning underlying simulation. Eventually, the objective can be summed up as "trying to set as many intelligent defaults as possible to reduce the number of steps required for a successful analysis" (Smith et al. 2011, p.58). The definition of a successful analysis and the appropriate amount of such defaults remains in most cases an open question.

5. Research opportunities

Based on the review, the consideration of HVAC systems represents an important gap in current approaches to automated building energy simulation. Given the difficulty of translating HVAC models for simulation, and their unavailability in earlier design phases, an alternative approach would be the automated creation of a multi-component structure mapped to the building and its zones, based on key HVAC system variables. In the workflow model presented in figure 1, several steps could be automated with an approximated model. The resulting model could probably give more valuable feedback to designers than is achievable with the assumption of ideal loads. Based on a zoned building model, the system creation process would follow the same steps as in HVAC design, beginning with the calculation of design loads, after which delivery, distribution and generation components are successively determined. Autosizing in currently available tools is performed according to similar steps, but, to the authors' knowledge, lacks any explicit representation of the distribution subsystem. As a result, fully automated pump or fan sizing, which would require pressure drop calculations, is not enabled. Automated procedures deriving the configuration of distribution systems from the building model would be desirable (Clarke 2015), but existing examples thereof are not known to the authors. To begin with, they would require a specification of delivery components and their locations. Existing pipe routing algorithms for different plant types (Guirardello & Swaney 2005) may be used.

More generally, the errors introduced by automated procedures should be systematically investigated. Until now, the literature only offers a very limited number of case studies attempting to quantify such errors (Ahn et al. 2014, Dogan et al. 2015). Comparing these errors to those caused by manual data entry, one could investigate the benefits and limits of a fully automated approach, and if needed pinpoint the most important inputs on which human intervention should concentrate.

6. Conclusion

Until now, approaches for automated building energy performance simulation have mostly focused on the translation of geometric data. The consideration of HVAC systems in automated simulation still represents a gap in the state of the art. Models of such systems could be obtained through translation from a BIM model, or approximated by automated procedures based on building data. Moreover, attention should be paid to the question of zoning and the appropriate resolution of automatically generated building models, as well as to quality control at different levels.

References

Ahn, K.-U., Kim, Y.-J., Park, C.-S., Kim, I. & Lee, K. (2014), 'Bim interface for full vs. semi-automated building energy simulation', *Energy and Buildings* **68**, 671–678.

Autodesk (2011), *Revit Architecture 2011 - User's Guide*, Autodesk, Inc.

Banfi, D. (2013), Energiebedarfsanalyse urbaner rume anhand des semantischen modells und austauschformats citygml, Master's thesis, Technische Universitt Mnchen.

Barbour, C., Zogg, R., Cross, E. & Clark, D. (2016), Research and development roadmap for building energy modelingdraftfor review only, Technical report, Prepared by Navigant Consulting, Inc for the U.S. Department of Energy.

Basarkar, M. (2012), 'Mapping hvac systems for simulation in energyplus', *SimBuild 2012* .

Bazjanac, V. (2008), Ifc bim-based methodology for semi-automated building energy performance simulation, *in* 'CIB-W78 25th International Conference on Information Technology in Construction'.

Bazjanac, V. (2010), Space boundary requirements for modeling of building geometry for energy and other performance simulation, *in* 'CIB W78: 27th International Conference'.

Bazjanac, V., Forester, J., Haves, P., Sucic, D. & Xu, P. (2002), Hvac component data modeling using industry foundation classes, *in* '5th International Conference on System Simulation in Buildings'.

Bazjanac, V. & Maile, T. (2004), Ifc hvac interface to energyplus: A case of expanded interoperability for energy simulation, *in* 'SimBuild 2004, Building Sustainability and Performance Through Simulation'.

Bazjanac, V., Maile, T., ODonnell, J., Rose, C. & Mrazovic, N. (2011), Data enviroments and processing in semi-automated simulation with energyplus, *in* 'CIB W078-W102: 28th International Conference. CIB, Sophia Antipolis, France'.

Cerezo, C., Dogan, T. & Reinhart, C. (2014), Towards standarized building properties template files for early design energy model generation, *in* 'Proceedings of the ASHRAE/IBPSA-USA building simulation conference', pp. 25–32.

Clarke, J. (2001), *Energy Simulation in Building Design*, second edition edn, Oxford: Butterworth-Heinemann.

Clarke, J. (2015), 'A vision for building performance simulation: a position paper prepared on behalf of the ibpsa board', *Journal of Building Performance Simulation* **8**(2), 39–43.

Davis, J. A. & Nutter, D. W. (2010), 'Occupancy diversity factors for common university building types', *Energy and buildings* **42**(9), 1543–1551.

De Wilde, P. & Tian, W. (2010), 'Predicting the performance of an office under climate change: A study of metrics, sensitivity and zonal resolution', *Energy and Buildings* **42**(10), 1674–1684.

DesignBuilder (2015), 'Designbuilder software product overview'. [Online; Accessed 14. July 2015].
URL: *http://www.designbuilder.co.uk/content/view/144/223/*

Dogan, T., Reinhart, C. & Michalatos, P. (2015), 'Autozoner: an algorithm for automatic thermal zoning of buildings with unknown interior space definitions', *Journal of Building Performance Simulation* (ahead-of-print), 1–14.

Fleming, K., Long, N. & Swindler, A. (2012), The building component library: An online repository to facilitate building energy model creation, *in* 'Proceedings of the 2012 ACEEE Summer Study on Energy Efficient Buildings', Citeseer.

Georgescu, M., Eisenhower, B. & Mezic, I. (2012), Creating zoning approximations to building energy models using the koopman operator, *in* 'IBPSA-USA SimBuild', pp. 40–47.

Giannakis, G. (2015), Development of Methodologies for Automatic Thermal Model Generation using Building Information Models, PhD thesis, Technical University of Crete.

Gowri, K., Winiarski, D. W. & Jarnagin, R. E. (2009), Infiltration modeling guidelines for commercial building energy analysis, Technical Report PNNL-18898, Pacific Northwest National Laboratory USA.

Guirardello, R. & Swaney, R. E. (2005), 'Optimization of process plant layout with pipe routing', *Computers & chemical engineering* **30**(1), 99–114.

ISO (2008), Energy performance of buildings - calculation of energy use for space heating and cooling, ISO ISO 13790:2008, International Organization for Standardization, Geneva, Switzerland.

ISO (2010), Building information modelling information delivery manual part 1: Methodology and format, ISO 29481-1:2010, International Organization for Standardization, Geneva, Switzerland.

Jones, N. L., McCrone, C. J., Walter, B. J., Pratt, K. B. & Greenberg, D. P. (2013), Automated translation and thermal zoning of digital building models for energy analysis, *in* 'Building Simulation Conference'.

Lam, K. P., Höynck, M., Dong, B., Andrews, B., Chiou, Y.-S., Zhang, R., Benitez, D., Choi, J. et al. (2009), Occupancy detection through an extensive environmental sensor network in an open-plan office building, *in* 'IBPSA Building Simulation 2009', pp. 1452–1459.

Leal, S., Hauer, S., Judex, F. & Gahr, S. (2014), Implementation of an automated building model generation tool, *in* 'Industrial Informatics (INDIN), 2014 12th IEEE International Conference on', IEEE, pp. 457–462.

Liu, X., Akinci, B., Bergés, M. & Garrett, J. H. (2013), 'Extending the information delivery manual approach to identify information requirements for performance analysis of hvac systems', *Advanced Engineering Informatics* **27**(4), 496–505.

Maile, T., O'Donnell, J., Bazjanac, V. & Rose, C. (2013), Bim-geometry modelling guidelines for building energy performance simulation, *in* 'BS2013-13th International Conference of the International Building Performance Simulation Association', pp. 3242–3249.

Reinhart, C. F. & Davila, C. C. (2016), 'Urban building energy modeling–a review of a nascent field', *Building and Environment* **97**, 196–202.

Robert, S., Mazza, D., Hilaire, B., Sette, P. & Vinot, B. (2014), An approach to enhancing the connection between bim models and building energy simulation hvac systems in the loop, *in* 'eWork and eBusiness in Architecture, Engineering and Construction', pp. 149–154.

Robertson, J., Polly, B. & Collis, J. (2013), Evaluation of automated model calibration techniques for residential building energy simulation, Technical Report TP-5500-54084, National Renewable Energy Laboratory.

Smith, L., Bernhardt, K. & Jezyk, M. (2011), Automated energy model creation for conceptual design, *in* 'Proceedings of the 2011 Symposium on Simulation for Architecture and Urban Design', Society for Computer Simulation International, pp. 13–20.

Vandenbulcke, R., Mertens, L. & Janssen, E. (2012), 'A simulation methodology for heat and cold distribution in thermo-hydronic networks', *Building Simulation* **5**(3), 203–217.

Wimmer, R., Maile, T., O'Donnell, J. T. et al. (2014), Data-requirements specification to support bim-based hvac-definitions in modelica, *in* 'BauSIM 2014, Aachen, Germany, September, 2014'.

Impact of occupancy on energy consumption of an educational facility

M.Amore[1], M.Rossoni[1], M.Marengo[1,2] and P.deWilde[3]

1. University of Bergamo, Department of Engineering and Applied Sciences, Dalmine (BG), Italy
2. University of Brighton, School of Computing, Engineering and Mathematics, Brighton, UK
3. Plymouth University, Chair of Building Performance Analysis, Plymouth, UK

pieter.dewilde@plymouth.ac.uk

Abstract. Building energy simulation models are playing an increasing role in the construction industry and estate services and are constantly being improved. However, the accuracy and usability of simulation results is highly dependent on its inputs, many of which remain difficult to determine. Amongst inputs, the definition of occupant behaviour is recognized to be complex, and generally underestimated and neglected. With the trend towards increasingly energy efficient buildings, a proper representation of occupant presence and activities is becoming crucial in the design of buildings, which need to be comfortable, adaptable and resilient towards variable thermal loads. This paper presents a study of the occupancy of a university building in the UK in order to assess discrepancies between assumed and actual occupancy of the facility. Data has been obtained from a range of sources, including the Building Energy Management System, timetabling, and direct observation. The corresponding occupancy patterns have been simulated using DesignBuilder and EnergyPlus. Results indicate a potential energy saving in the order of 10% for set-up control that matches actual building occupancy more closely than current settings.

1. Introduction

Progress in the field of building simulation has made it a tool of choice in the building design and engineering process (Hensen and Lamberts, 2011). Built on a track record of fifty years of research and development, this technology is increasingly important and popular in the construction industry. Increasingly stringent energy efficiency targets, such as those demanded by the European Energy Performance of Buildings Directive (EPBD) are driving further uptake, whereas the increased use of Building Information Models (BIM) is bridging the gap between different tools by providing a common information repository. However, there is still a need to make building simulation more accurate. Significant improvements have already been achieved in terms of fidelity and precision of simulation models, helping the technology to become even more prominent in the design, analysis and maintenance of buildings (Malkawi and Augenbroe, 2004).

Building performance simulation requires a considerable amount of input data. Amongst others this needs to include physical inputs (such as building size, orientation, construction materials, HVAC system size/types, interior and exterior lighting, equipment) and operational inputs varying in time, like occupancy, lighting and HVAC control settings, and plug load profiles. While physical data can be determined with a certain accuracy by using engineering drawings or measurement and observation of the building, other inputs such as control settings and occupancy are more volatile since they can easily vary over time. Understanding these latter factors and how they impact on energy use of a building is crucial to manage the energy efficiency of buildings.

A range of recent research projects shows evidence of discrepancies between the simulation predictions and measured results, discussing what has become known as the 'energy performance gap' (Carbon Trust, 2011; Menezes *et al.*, 2012). An important cause of this gap, especially in buildings for public use, is the fact that the effective future use of the building is unknown at the design stage. Although the energy performance gap needs further research, fundamental causes are likely to be linked with predicting the building occupant behaviour, use and maintenance of the building, rather than problems of design or construction (Korjenic and Bednar, 2012). For a deeper discussion of the gap between simulated and measured results, and the role of issues such as actual weather conditions, modelling errors and uncertainties, see de Wilde (2014).

Due to its complex nature, the influence of occupancy is often under-recognized or misjudged in the design, construction, operation and retrofit of buildings. Especially with regard to public buildings, and specifically to educational ones, the presence of people is extremely variable and difficult to forecast, and requires the use of rather specific quantitative analysis. Occupants interact with the building in both a passive (by contributing a heat load) and active manner (by actively switching equipment and lighting on and off, changing control settings, and opening doors and windows). These interactions all influence the building energy consumption. Unfortunately, predicting the behaviour of people within a building requires long, detailed and precise analysis, so that often the analyst relies on hypothetical or statistics default values for occupation. Since actual occupancy also involves a significant of random behaviour it can be said to be stochastic (Curry *et al.*, 2013). However, efficient energy models require the consideration and combination of all the variables that affect the building. As evidenced by the work of the IEA Annex 66, a deeper understanding of occupancy is a key factor to properly replicate the dynamics that govern energy uses within the building and quantifying its impact is crucial to the design low energy buildings.

2. Aims and Objectives

This paper explores various approaches to capture the occupancy within a university building and compares and contrasts this with the use of typical default assumptions in a commercial software tool. The key factor in this work is occupant presence; occupant actions are not taken into account at this stage. The work aims at exploring the amount of energy that may be saved by using control settings in terms of switching on/off the HVAC system that are more closely aligned to real facility usage.

3. Methodology

3.1. Case study building

The case study building analysed for this work is selected on the basis of the variety of uses and its role within the University Campus, since it is used for many activities, including non-academic. A great number of variables affect the presence of people, such as special events, number and time of lessons, available time of people, ways to cross the building and allocation of the rooms. All these parameters confirm the difficulty to predict the number of people in a common space for an educational facility. This is the Roland Levinsky Building, a striking building on the campus of the University of Plymouth in the UK. Built between 2003 and 2007, it currently houses the Faculty of Art and Humanities. One of the aspects that contributes to increasing the buildings value within the campus and the whole city is the fact that it is a multi-purpose building, having been realized both for university and public use. In addition to classrooms, laboratories and offices, it contains two large lecture theatres, the Jill Craigie Cinema, three performance rehearsal studios, digital media suites and a public art gallery housing Plymouth's Peninsula of Art, which displays works by students and both internal and invited artists. Thank to this variety of spaces and functions, the building facilitates the interaction of different subjects, and stands out as one of the main cultural meeting points in Plymouth. It has generated significant urban development in the adjacent areas. The building has a gross floor area of 12,660 m^2 distributed over 10 levels. The east side is characterized by a high tower visible from all over the town. The central part of the building, that connects the tower to the west, which consists of two floors, is three storeys high and is characterized by an aesthetic impactful central atrium that internally connects the two areas. In addition to the unique geometry that characterizes the building, an important role is played by the materials used. The base of the building is made of slate walls, alternating with the lightness of the glass walls extending to the upper floors. The most memorable feature of the building is probably the "wrap", a shell made from copper sheets that envelops the building along the west and the east elevation and covers the roof surfaces. While outside shapes, materials and colours are interwoven to create a complex and innovative solution, the interior of the building recalls an industrial context, with extensive use of exposed concrete and, again, impressive windows that bring together the different activities within it. The interior spaces are flexible and designed so that they can be varied and adapted according to the different activities carried out within the building.

Figure 1: South facade of the Roland Levinsky Building

3.2. Data collection

A sample of ten rooms was selected for an in-depth study of building occupancy. These rooms were chosen in such a way as to represent a range in functionality and frequency of use, allowing the scaling up of findings in such a way as to estimate indicatively the occupancy of all the rooms of the building, by associating each room to one reference room that has been studied in depth. The following rooms were selected: classroom, studio space, offices with various types of occupants, special event space, a restaurant, and a large classical lecture theatre.

The analysis period covered the fall semester (October-December 2015). As university buildings are also used for additional activities, significant efforts were invested in defining the occupancy scenarios both on weekday and weekends, and in properly considering academic activities and special events days. Some particular vacation days are subject of the analysis as well. This was then scaled up to cover the whole facility. A longitudinal study over three months allowed getting some understanding of discrepancies in student attendance over term.

Three sources of information on building occupancy were studied in order to understand the differences between the timetabling forecasts and the actual use of every room:

University timetable. The university timetable provides online access to the timetable for all individual rooms in the building. This has been taken as reference for the predicted occupancy values. The occupancy has been assumed to make use of all available seats within every room. The timetable includes information on the timing of regular lectures as well as workshops and special events.

Building energy management system. The building energy management system (BEMS) manages the whole HVAC system of the building. It sets temperatures and times of activation and shutdown for each space and allows determination of energy consumption and reporting of the effective internal temperatures at any instant. Therefore, on the basis of these data, it is possible to obtain an additional source of predicted occupancy, namely that which is programmed into the building services.

Manual collection. Data was collected by direct observation of the occupancy of the selected representative rooms within the building, across the fall semester. This data collection involved an hourly observation of the number of people present in these rooms, and was undertaken from 8 AM until 8 PM.

3.3. Dynamic energy simulations

The final stage consists of thermal simulation of the building subject to different occupancy patterns, which allows studying their impact. To this end, two simulation models are used: a DesignBuilder model, created specifically for the purpose of this work, as well as a legacy EnergyPlus model used in earlier research. The use of two models allows cross-comparison and reduces the risk of model bias in the final comparisons.

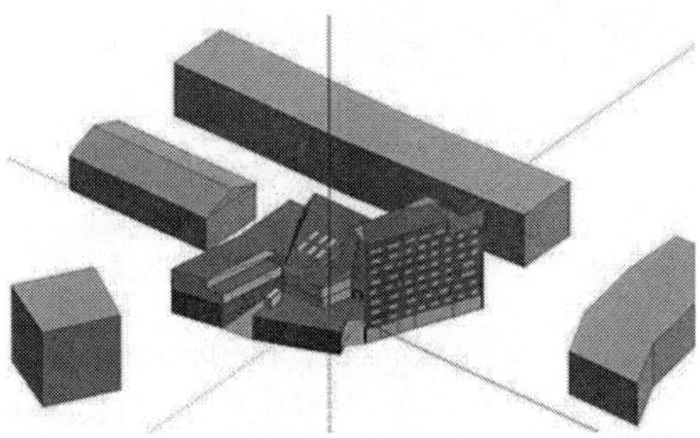

Figure 2: Model of the RLB and its surrounding in Design Builder

Figure 3: Model of the RLB in EnergyPlus (OpenStudio)

Both models are as faithful as possible to reality in terms of weather file, geometry, materials and constructions. Using the same features for both models allows avoiding influences of these parameters on the final results addressing them only to the occupancy. However, as shown in Figure 2, the DesignBuilder model also contains the surrounding buildings that may have an impact on the studied building. Since their contribution on the results is minimal, because of their north orientation and distance from the Roland Levinsky buiding, they are not created into the existing Open Studio model. Heating and cooling systems were modelled for the specific rooms studied, while the remaining services were represented by a mechanical ventilation system, controlled according to BEMS settings. Electric equipment (i.e. computer, printers and projectors) within the facility was manually counted and specific values of heat emission were investigated by means of literature. Similarly, approximate values were established for interior lighting. In modelling the occupancy, heat emissions were assumed for adult males at 120W for seated person (i.e. for offices and teaching rooms), 200W for a slowly walking person (i.e. circulation zones and toilets) and 230W for a medium working/eating person (i.e. laboratories, restaurant and rooms used for special events).

In the simulations, three main scenarios were created in order to analyse how occupancy affects energy consumption in different situations. Such schemes were simulated using both the DesignBuilder and EnergyPlus model, by changing schedules for each of them

Default: a base case was defined in the first stage of the simulation strategy to consider the gap between the two models and reality. In DesignBuilder, all the values of occupancy are automatically associated to their own functions as a default; into EnergyPlus standard values are manually chosen. In this first case, the HVAC system is set according to the BEMS.

Predicted: subsequently, the density of people was determined as the maximum number of possible people within a room, provided by the timetable in terms of number of seats, divided by its area. As in the previous case, the HVAC system was modelled according to BEMS settings. These last ones, represent a further prediction of the presence of people within a room.

Real: finally, in the last and most significant case, the manual investigation is considered. The occupant density (persons/m^2) was determined considering the peak of the average hourly number of people, considered separately for every room and for weekdays, weekends and special events. The effective occupancy is represented by a percentage number of the aforementioned density. Firstly, the case in which the HVAC system is set according to BEMS is considered. After that, some different assumptions are made with respect to the real occupancy, as shown in Table 1.

4. Results and discussion

This section first analyses the results of the manual data collection of number of people. Further it focuses on the gap between reality and the two energy simulations. Finally, it provides some values in terms of consumptions by varying the HVAC system as a function of the occupancy. Figure 4 and 5 describe the average trend of people of the Career and Employability room, which is a public office and the BEMS settings, whose curve indicates the operating time interval of the HVAC system. Figure 4 shows a regular usage with two peaks, a slight one at 2pm and another at 11am, where the number of visitors is double than the number of working people. Conversely, during the considered special weekend day, which is an Open Day, shown in Figure 5, it is possible to notice a non-regular attendance starting at 9 am, namely the beginning of the event, followed by a gradual decrease. The same graph shows a peak of 63 people, which corresponds to a great contribution of visitors to internal gains. In both cases it is interesting to observe that the schedule time of the BEMS is coherent with the real occupancy.

In the same way, an academic research office has been studied because of the necessity to understand the differences between different kind of offices, namely public and administrative/research ones. According to the results, the BEMS data for operation hours are coherent with the real occupancy times. Moreover, for this room, the average trend shows a decrease of occupancy corresponding to lunch breaks.

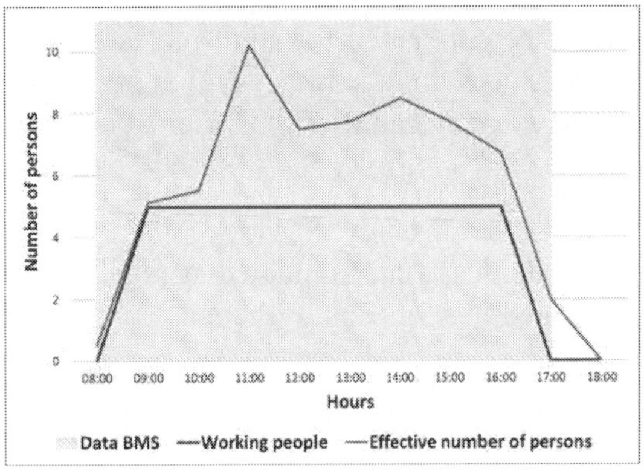

Figure 4: Career and Employability – Average of weekdays

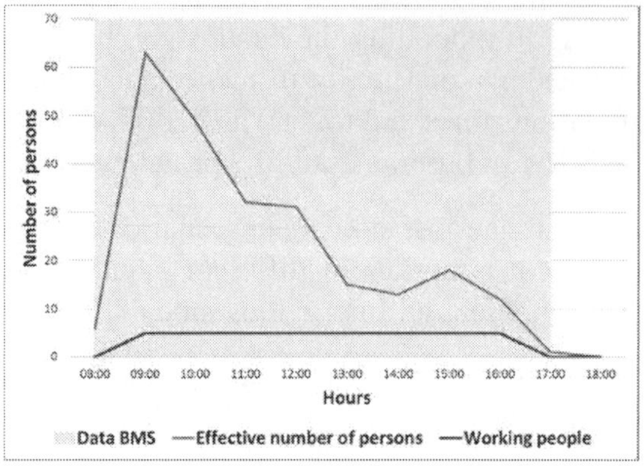

Figure 5: Career and Employability – Saturday 10th October (Open Day)

One of the two lecture theatres within the building is studied. This is used in accordance to their particular function, but is also used for public events, in addition to the normal classes. Figure 6 shows a changeable situation in accordance to lessons change. At the end of the day, the room is often used by small groups of people for recreational activities. It can be noticed that the prediction of people expected in the room is overestimated for the whole day. In the same graph, the variation of the predicted average number of people, namely those from the timetable, is due to not forecasted activities in some hours of some weekdays. Considering the average trend, it is possible to observe that the BEMS data are coherent with the predicted occupancy but not with the real observed data. However, considering a specific day, as shown in Figure 7, there is no correspondence between BEMS data and predicted number of people. It is possible to notice a big discrepancy between the number of people really present and both the timetable prediction and BEMS data. Thus a regular rearrangement of BEMS settings would be able to save energy.

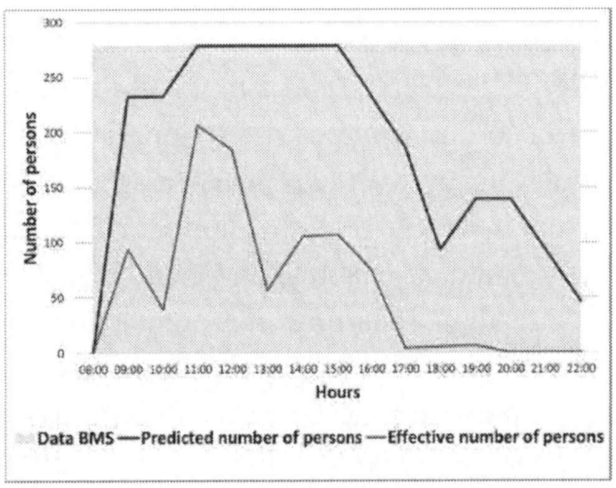

Figure 6: Lecture Theatre 1 – Average of weekdays

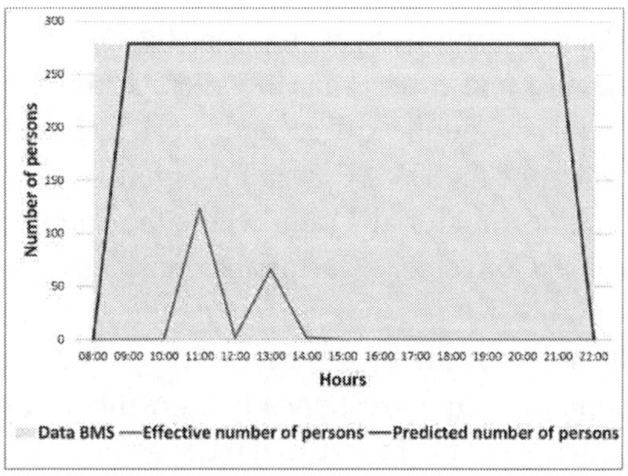

Figure 7: Lecture Theatre 1 – Wednesday 21st October

In Figure 8 it can be noticed that the trend of people within a common teaching room changes over time; this is especially true for Wednesdays. Furthermore, there is a marked decrease of the number of people in the middle of the semester, while at the beginning and the final days of the term, they fill the room; this may be due to increased interest in academic information such as grouping for coursework at the start, and exams at the end. Figure 9 shows that occupancy predictions from the timetable are reasonable, and the effective number of hours in which the room is occupied is almost always less than the predicted.

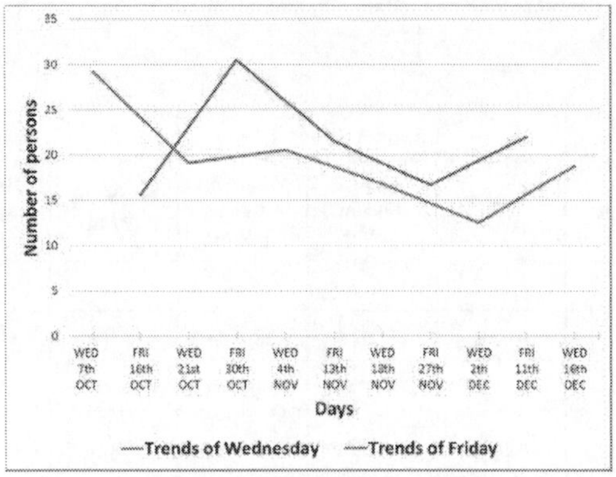

Figure 8: Teaching room 209 – Trend of real presence of people

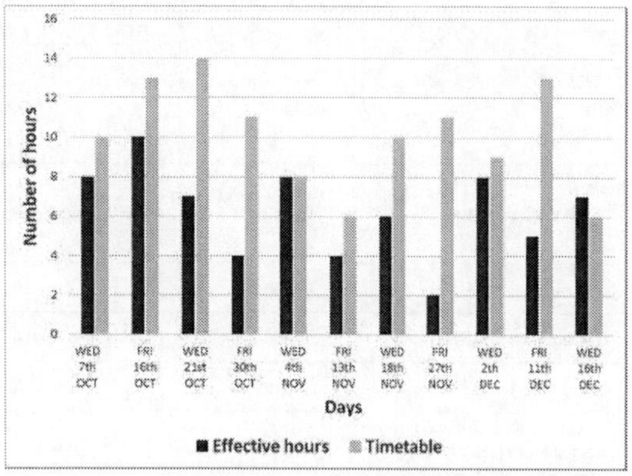

Figure 9: Teaching room 209 – Number of hours with occupied room

Figures 10 and 11 show the trend of a particular room, which is mainly used for workshops and practical independent activities, rather than lessons. It is possible to notice how the occupancy increases in the third week of each chosen month. This seems to indicate that the room is more occupied in days close to academic deadlines, which are normally set in the last week of each month. Accordingly, during the first week of the month, only few students are in the room. By looking at the hours really occupied and the predicted ones from the timetable, the gap between reality and prediction based on university events can be appreciated.

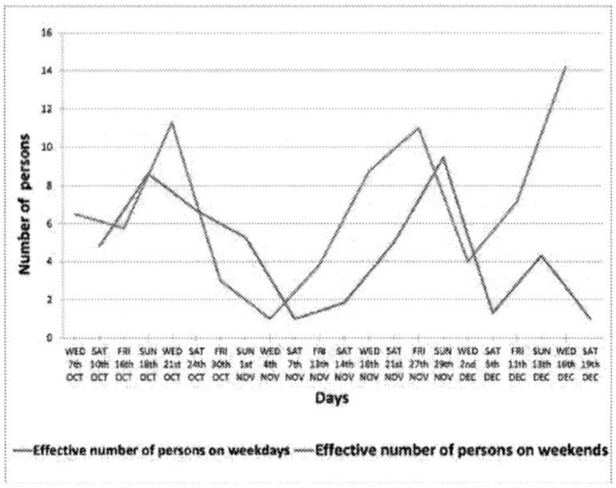

Figure 10: 3D Design studio 211 – Trend of real people

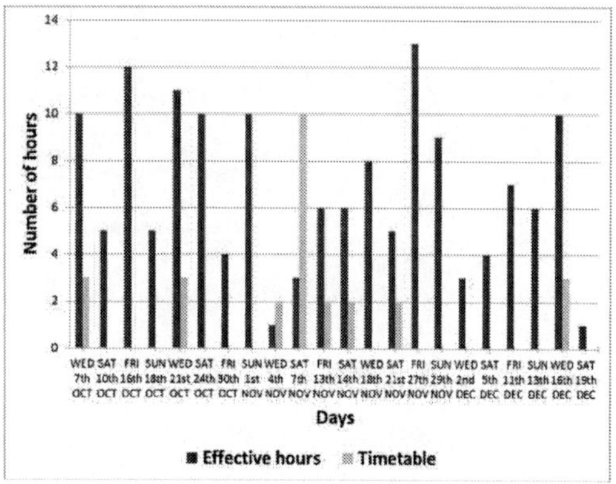

Figure 11: 3D Design studio 211 – Number of hours with occupied rooms

Table 2: Simulations results and evaluation of different solutions of occupancy

					Design Builder			EnergyPlus		
	Occupancy	HVAC system	Lights	Electric Equipment	Electricity [kWh]	HVAC system [kWh]	Total End Uses [kWh]	Electricity [kWh]	HVAC system [kWh]	Total End Uses [kWh]
1	Default	According to BEMS	Default	Default	1,271,607.00	317,662.00	1,589,269.00	917,312.00	308,040.00	1,225,352.00
2	Predicted	According to BEMS	Default	Default	0.00%	+11.43%	+2.29%	0.00%	+5.71%	+1.44%
3	Real	According to BEMS	Default	Default	0.00%	-4.44%	-0.89%	0.00%	-3.43%	-0.54%
4	Real	According to BEMS and when at least one person occupies the rooms	Default	Default	0.00%	+31.58%	+6.31%	0.00%	+24.33%	+6.12%
5	Real	When at least one person occupies the rooms	Default	Default	0.00%	+6.32%	+1.26%	0.00%	+5.98%	+1.5%
6	Real	When at least one person occupies the rooms - without weekends	Default	Default	0.00%	-2.64%	-0.53%	0.00%	+2.04%	+0.51%
7	Real	When at least 5% of the people avarage peak occupies the rooms	Default	Default	0.00%	-2.79%	-0.56%	0.00%	-3.05%	-0.77%
8	Real	When at least 5% of the avarage peak of people occupies the rooms - without weekends	Default	Default	0.00%	-9.32%	-1.86%	0.00%	-8.34%	-2.1%
9	Real	When at least one person occupies the rooms	When at least one person occupies the rooms	Default	-0.87%	-8.22%	-2.34%	-2.18%	-4.25%	-2.7%
10	Real	When at least one person occupies the rooms	When at least one person occupies the rooms	When at least one person occupies the rooms	-9.91%	-7.82%	-9.49%	-13.14%	-3.76%	-10.78%

Table 2 shows how occupancy affects energy consumption in different situations through the results of the energy simulations. It allows the understanding of the incidence on electricity, HVAC consumption and total end uses of the variation of different parameters, namely occupancy, set up of HVAC system, lighting and electric equipment. The impact of the occupancy is more evident in Design Builder, while in Energy Plus a more significant contribution in terms of energy consumption is associated to interior lighting and equipment. The high value of electricity consumption, which exceeds the HVAC one, is due to the considerable number of electric devices, necessary for this kind of educational facility. The first row shows the situation in which just default conditions are considered and the HVAC system works in accordance to BEMS data, in order to compare the gap between the two models without the influence of further assumptions made subsequently. The results show that the model created by means of Design Builder is characterized by higher values of consumptions than the EnergyPlus one. In particular, the raising rate is 27.86% as regards electricity, 3.12% in terms of HVAC consumption and 29.70% for total end uses.

In the two following rows the incidence of occupancy is analysed by considering the predicted number of people according to timetable and the real one measured by means of manual collection. In the first case, the high affluence of people increases the HVAC consumption because the additional energy required for the cooling system exceeds the saved heating energy. Conversely, in the second case, corresponding to the reality, a lower number of people decreases the HVAC consumptions due to a significantly lower usage of the cooling system.

As can be observed in the fourth row, the maximum consumption is reasonably obtainable by considering the HVAC system working in accordance with the BEMS and when at least one person occupied the room, namely the maximum usage of the system.

In the subsequent rows the HVAC system working according to the real use of each room; in fact, initially it works when at least one person fills the room, and then when 5% of the average peak of people does it. This percentage is associated to specific time slots, such as the hours before and after classes, offices opening time, cleaning hours, etc, where the rooms are not used for their main purposes. In addition, cases without considering weekends are considered, as happens in the reality. As can be seen, the fifth row is characterized by an increase of consumptions with respect to the basic model. Conversely, the following two rows show a decrease with respect to the default conditions but it increases with respect to the real case. Finally, the seventh case is the only one of these last four mentioned cases that reduces the consumptions.

Regarding the aforementioned considerations, is also possible to notice that electricity consumptions do not vary because lighting and electric equipment have not been changed.

The last two rows consider that HVAC system and lighting and then electric equipment turn on when at least one person occupies the room, thus, it is possible to obtain the best prediction due to a saving of HVAC consumption and electricity as well. In the last case, the higher impact of electric equipment on electricity consumption than lighting is shown.

5. Conclusions

This paper has compared various ways of exploring the effect of occupancy in a university building on the energy performance. The work highlights the discrepancies between the default occupancy values typically used in building simulation tools, occupancy according to timetabling, occupancy assumptions in the BEMS, and observation done. Deep observation of a representative selection of rooms was scaled up by associating occupancy patterns to rooms with similar functions and features; findings allow a more accurate simulation of the whole building. However, the result of the collection of data has underlined limits in the estimation of the exact presence of occupants within common spaces, such as circulation zones and dining room. Two models were used, one created in DesignBuilder and the other in EnergyPlus. Despite the fact that Design Builder is based on EnergyPlus, it is more immediate and user-friendly. Conversely, EnergyPlus is more systematic and requires more efforts to fill every schedule; however, it allows obtaining a wider number of outputs enabling to check initial hypothesis. The main differences between the results obtained with the two software is due to the different ways in which data are insert. While in DesignBuilder some values are automatically associated when assigning a specific function, such as specific lighting devices, in EnergyPlus each parameter is necessary manually added; thus, some of them could be not taken into account. The analysis of different cases made possible to consider all the possible advantages and disadvantages obtainable by varying the HVAC system operation time according to the real occupancy. In particular, the best solution is the one in which the HVAC system works when at least 5% of the average peak of people occupy the room because, since, even if it corresponds to only a slight decrease in terms of consumptions, it guarantees the required indoor conditions for all the rooms during the main activities (both on weekdays and weekends). Results indicate a saving potential in the order of 10% for control regimes that match real building occupancy more closely than current settings.

References

Carbon Trust. (2011). *Closing the gap: Lessons learned on realising the potential of low carbon building design*. London: Carbon Trust.

Hensen, J.L.M. and R. Lamberts, eds. 2011. *Building performance simulation for design and operation*. Abingdon: Spon Press

IEA-EBC Annex 66, http://www.annex66.org

Korjenic, A., Bednar, T., 2012. Validation and evaluation of total energy use in office building: A case study. Automation in construction, 23, 64-70

Malkawi, A. and Augenbroe, G., 2004. Advanced building simulation. Taylor and Francis

Menezes, C., Cripps, A., Bouchlaghem, D. and Buswell, R., 2012. Predicted vs. actual energy performance of non-domestic buildings: Using post-occupancy evaluation data to reduce the performance gap. *Applied Energy*, 97, 355-364

de Wilde, P., 2014. The gap between predicted and measured energy performance of buildings: a framework for investigation. *Automation in Construction*, 41, 40-49

de Wilde, P. and W.Tian, 2012. Management of thermal performance risks in buildings subject to climate change. Building and Environment, 55, 167-177.

Curry, E., O'Donnell, J., Corry, E., Hasan, S., Keane, M. and O'Riain, S. (2013). Linking building data in the cloud: Integrating cross-domain building data using linked data. Advanced Engineering Informatics, 27, 206-219.

Personal/Team, Engineering Knowledge Modeling in Context of Product Development Stage

Jerzy Pokojski
Warsaw University of Technology, Poland
jerzy.pokojski@simr.pw.edu.pl

Abstract. The paper deals with the actual state-of-the-art of the personal/team systems for engineering knowledge storage. On the basis of the state-of-the-art a general, descriptive model of an engineering personal assistant system is created. The model is associated with different product development stages.

1. Introduction

In the paper the actual state-of-the-art of the personal/team systems for engineering knowledge storage is shown. The presented characteristics of the systems concentrate on the applied knowledge representations, the implemented functionalities and scenarios, the system interoperability and the software/hardware solutions which were used.

On the basis of the characteristics a general, descriptive model of an engineering personal assistant system is created. The model is associated with different product development stages and considers new areas of a personal assistant application and its new functionalities development.

The whole complex approach is presented in the context of automotive components design.

2. State-of-the-art

It is well-known that a designer is the master of any design activity as he has the suitable knowledge and is able to apply this knowledge when solving design tasks (Pahl 2007, Pokojski 2004, Ullman 2002).

The designer's knowledge (Chandrasegaran 2013, Pokojski 2004, Ullman 2002) may be gained through educational processes or acquired from other external knowledge sources but it can also be the outcome of engineering tasks performed in the past. Moreover, the knowledge may result from an actually solved engineering problem. In this case it can be applied immediately.

It is possible to make a designer's knowledge available for other designers (Moran 1996, Regli 2000) directly by communication or indirectly with the help of other means, for instance computer representations. Likewise, computer representations can be exploited as a form of personal notes which can relatively easily be shared with other people.

Designers' knowledge is stored in different computer representations. Unfortunately, it is impossible to express all issues connected with certain engineering topics this way (Pokojski 2004) therefore only the main knowledge sources are reflected; this means sources of which the designer knows each topic widely. Because only when the designer knows the multi-aspect and multi-context of the knowledge he is able to operate with it. Very often this knowledge results from the reflection on situations in the past and is remembered by its creator. In many cases though, this knowledge development undergoes an evolutional progress.

The articulation of comprehensive knowledge, usually requires big effort from the designer. Consequently, this process often results in a compromise between completeness and pragmatism (Pokojski 2010a, 2011a).

A designer's personal knowledge is acquired by him, created by him, remembered by him, edited by him and developed by him (Pokojski 2004). Any attempt of its formal modeling with the help of computer representations is very difficult; mostly it has an insufficient and incomplete form. When validating his personal knowledge, the designer makes a selection and gives it certain formal representations. While doing so he can estimate his trust in particular knowledge elements. He can check whether an element is risky or confidential or valuable and recommendable. In many situations these evaluations are made permanently for actual and obvious reasons or according to expected problems and limitations.

Personal/team knowledge can be expressed and exposed by designers and later stored in suitable computer representations. There are computer tools for the storage of engineering knowledge and for its effective management. These tools have a history of more than 20 years. Their development can be divided into three stages (phases).

In the first stage we notice many diverse attempts of applying computer tools for knowledge storage and re-using (Clarkson 2000, Court 1997, 1998ab, Fenves 1998, Hildre 1999, Hong 1996, Lowe 1999, O'Leary 1998, Regli 2000, Turkiyyah 1996). They vary in the way of a general functioning model, knowledge representation, intents connected with the system development, applied tools and solutions as well as the areas of applications. The great conceptual diversity of the applied solutions and the fact that most of the proposals are prototypes, are the most important features of that stage. Industrial applications were very rare at that time.

The inspirations for the developed solutions were in most situations concrete areas of application with their specific circumstances, limitations and requirements. Classics taken from artificial intelligence had strong influence on the applied solutions. The influence of achievements from different design theories (proposed by different authors) was relatively little. Most of the proposed solutions may be described as routine detail design. The growing scale of applications which had to be considered pressed developers to apply more system-oriented solutions. Usually, the aspect of personal knowledge was not especially regarded in those papers. Although many solutions could work at any stage of the design process, they were mostly applied for detailed design tasks.

During the second stage of the development (beginning in about 2000) a significant improvement of the tools ensued (Bracewell 2009, Ding 2009, Fruchter 2009, Hicks 2002, Hisarcikliar 2009, Keraron 2009, Kim 2007, Kitamura 2004, Sim 2003, Lenne 2009, McMahon 2004, Pokojski 2006, 2007ab, Sevilmis 2007, Wallace 2006). Specialized tools for certain processes with well prepared representations and actions were developed. It became evident that the tools gained the spearheading role in real life design offices with considerable computer resources (Pokojski 2004, Wallace 2006).

Tools acompanying designers and allowing for solidifying important issues of the realised processes were built as well.

Along with that, solutions appeared which could reflect about the respective project. They mostly had the form of "best practice solutions" (McMahon 2004). At the same time, designers noticed the lack of dedicated, personalized tools for searching available knowledge resources (Sevilmis 2007). Sometimes computer tools appeared which were surprisingly efficient, clear and not complicated (Bracewell 2009). Generally, very good solutions resulting from a limited scale of projects could be noticed.

During the third phase, which began about 10 years ago, a very intensive, unexpected development of tools for knowledge storage and management took place (Chen 2010, 2012, Chen Y-J 2012, Chungoora 2013, Dongmina 2012, Hahm 2014, Khattak 2013, Monticolo 2015, Nomaguchi 2013, Ouertani 2011, Song 2013, Wang 2012, Xu 2010, 2011ab, Xiaofang 2013, Zhen 2012). Elements of that way of thinking gradually were implemented to the concepts of engineering knowledge modeling. In certain cases highly developed applications came about. After a while that thinking concentrated less on the specificity of engineering applications but rather on their universal issues. However, there are not many papers which deal with engineering design reality and the application of those advanced tools.

On the whole the literary output of this domain is relatively high but it does not have significant influence on real, industrial reality. Analysing computer applications which are used by people responsible for product development, it becomes obvious that text files, spreadsheets and e-mails still play the main role, where e-mails are used as a personal repository of knowledge and information.

Looking at the above survey of literature, we try to group the key features of the applied approaches. Especially the works of the first phase (Pokojski 2004, Regli 2000) favour the following features in their descriptions: general model, knowledge representation, intent of the project, applied tools, exemplary problems, domain of application, literature, etc. (Pokojski 2010b) use similar classifications as a basis for their comparison: functionalities, metaphors, knowledge representations, scenarios, areas of application, applied computer tools, etc.

The third phase brought about very advanced tools in knowledge engineering.

A slightly different conceptualization of the above categorisation is presented in (Gorman 2010, Volkel 2010). It refers to more general aspects of the human personal knowledge modeling.

3. Descriptive model

On the basis of the survey from chapter 2 it is possible to establish a descriptive model of software which can assist a designer:

a) description on the basis of the first phase

A designer's personal knowledge is very useful as it can significantly accelerate design processes and improve their quality. The main goal of this software is to capture different traces of operations made by designers and to back them up immediately with the help of computer representations. During this process the new knowledge can be selected and validated and at the same time be integrated with the knowledge which has already been stored. Furthermore, inferencing modules may be added. The resulting content usually carries the author's thumbprint. This class of tools often looks like a personal notepad, where each publication needs the author's agreement.

b) description on the basis of the second phase:

The second phase takes up concepts and solutions from the first phase. But additionally it develops concepts and solutions which pay attention to the actual state of real life knowledge sources – for instance large design repositories in industries. This means tools were built to search particular design knowledge in text reports or documentations which were made with the help of CAD/CAE systems. There was also an improvement of tools which could make annotations integrated with engineering documentation parallel to the design process. Along with that it became popular to create design recommendations which somehow reflected on earlier performed activities. Graphic interfaces and integration tools got upgraded as well.

c) description on the basis of the third phase:

The third phase elaborated and refined the elements from the previous phases. Numerous advanced knowledge models were built and many tools for storing and searching knowledge were designed. But often those solutions were not deeply enough embedded in the specificity of engineering knowledge modeling.

4. Descriptive model and real-life applications

4.1 Real-life applications

In real life practice we meet various applications of tools supporting processes of knowledge acquisition, storage and management. Mostly these tools have a limited area of application. However, they fulfil their limited functionalities quite well.

Their development concepts mainly aim at cost-cutting and a rather short time perspective. Such an attitude usually results in a large plurality of forms, functionalities and informatic solutions. Only rarely, an advanced software with a high complexity level, universality and versatility is developed.

This problem will be illustrated with the help of a few examples of different problems and processes.

Example 1 (Linkiewicz 2007, Pokojski 2008)

The following example deals with the analysis of design knowledge owned and used by designers. Two students were observed while carrying out projects. These projects were realised one after the other with a 10 months' interuption. Both projects were about the designing/re-designing of automotive bodies. The first project was performed by 9 persons, the second by 2 (these two persons also participated in the first project).

The development of engineering design knowledge of both paticipants with different engineering activities was analysed. A progressive evolution of those activities together with certain knowledge development during the two projects (treated as a whole) could be observed. (Sim 2003) presents some activities with their knowledge sources context and typologies taken from design theories. (Pokojski 2008) describes how engineering knowledge evolved, what states and contexts became obvious.

The accomplished study showed what kind of knowledge could be stored and what functionalities were regarded useful. As an outcome a specification of the personal assistant system for storing engineering knowledge development was obtained which concentrated on geometric modeling.

Example 2 (Pokojski 2007a)

This example deals with product fault detection in manufacturing with a machine shaft as an examination object. The concept of the approach is developed on the basis of (Aoyama 2006). In the paper it is assumed that different engineers, i.e. designers, people who prepare the manufacturing process, predict product faults or carry out experiments use personal assistant systems. Hence in case of faults for example, the content of all personal assistants of the engineers participating in the whole development process can be traced back and analysed. The given example shows a prototype version of a personal assistant software.

Example 3 (Pokojski 2013)

Environments for building KBE (Knowledge Based Engineering) applications offer many different methods and tools - starting from those belonging to CAD/CAE systems to such solutions developed by programming and integrated with CAD/CAE systems (Pokojski 2010a, 2011ab, 2012).

Generally, the building of real life industrial KBE applications has to regard many very detailed conditions. Often the competences needed for developing this class of software exceed the possibilities of a single person.

The author of this paper and his team frequently realize projects of KBE applications development (most of them are done by students). The majority is accomplished in cooperation with industrial partners or on the basis of external partners' specifications. Each team member specializes in certain computer modeling aspects of engineering knowledge.

The competences of individual team members differ concerning the tools and the type of modeled products. The team members specialize in certain solutions and observe their progress. Sometimes the team memeber – the developer also participates actively in the solutions' development. Usually, developers have their own repositories of KBE solutions in the form of descriptions of concepts and examples of their applications. The development of the KBE tools is kept in the personal resources of the team members.

However, watching and analyzing personal resources of team members while building a new KBE application is common practice.

To make these activities more efficient, a special environment in data base form for storing and sharing KBE solutions was developed. The following elements *Projects, Solutions, links, Persons, Software, Applications, etc.* were modeled in that system.

4.2 Descriptive model and its functions/elements/features

The presented examples illustrate attempts of individual, partial computer tools applications for the storing of engineering personal/team knowledge and its re-using. The attempts vary in the area of their application, functionalities and used knowledge representations. Therefore it is very difficult to unify the applied software.

Research in design theory and psychology proves that the individual way and style of work of certain designers may differ significantly (Dorner 1999). These aspects surely influence the content of the personal assistant systems and eventually the personal assistant functionalities.

The software supporting engineering activities is usually classified according to its main functionalities. This classification can be done with the use of the personal assistant. According to Pahl and Beitz, a special version of a personal assistant for different stages of design processes (Pahl 2007) may be developed (clarification, conceptual, embodiment, detail) or according to Ullman (Ullman 2002) types of design problems may be defined (selection, configuration, original, parametric, re-design).

When working with real life problems we should remember that rarely one person takes on only one role and works with one project only. Usually, the various projects and roles have a dynamic structure. These aspects are shown with the example of a personal/team knowledge creation/using/sharing/transfer in the processes of KBE (Knowledge Based Engineering) applications' development (the author of the paper knows the reality of the domain). Selected tasks and processes are presented in a 2-dimensional space time/project. All tasks were performed by one team during a period of about 10 years. The persons cooperating with each other used different knowledge resources and filled several roles in different periods of time. In figure 1 the dependencies between realized projects and performed knowledge transfers in single projects or between projects are depicted. Capital letters mark the developers of the different tasks. Thus it is possible to analyze who was doing what in different projects and when.

The analysis of the various activities and roles of certain developers reveals that each participant took on different roles. As a consequence the type and range of the performed operation changed in each case. This observation suggests building a personal assistant in multi-profiled form, for instance with profiles for: clarification, concept development, detail solution design.

Working with the personal assistant system it should be possible to use all these tools, according to the actual operations and their contexts.

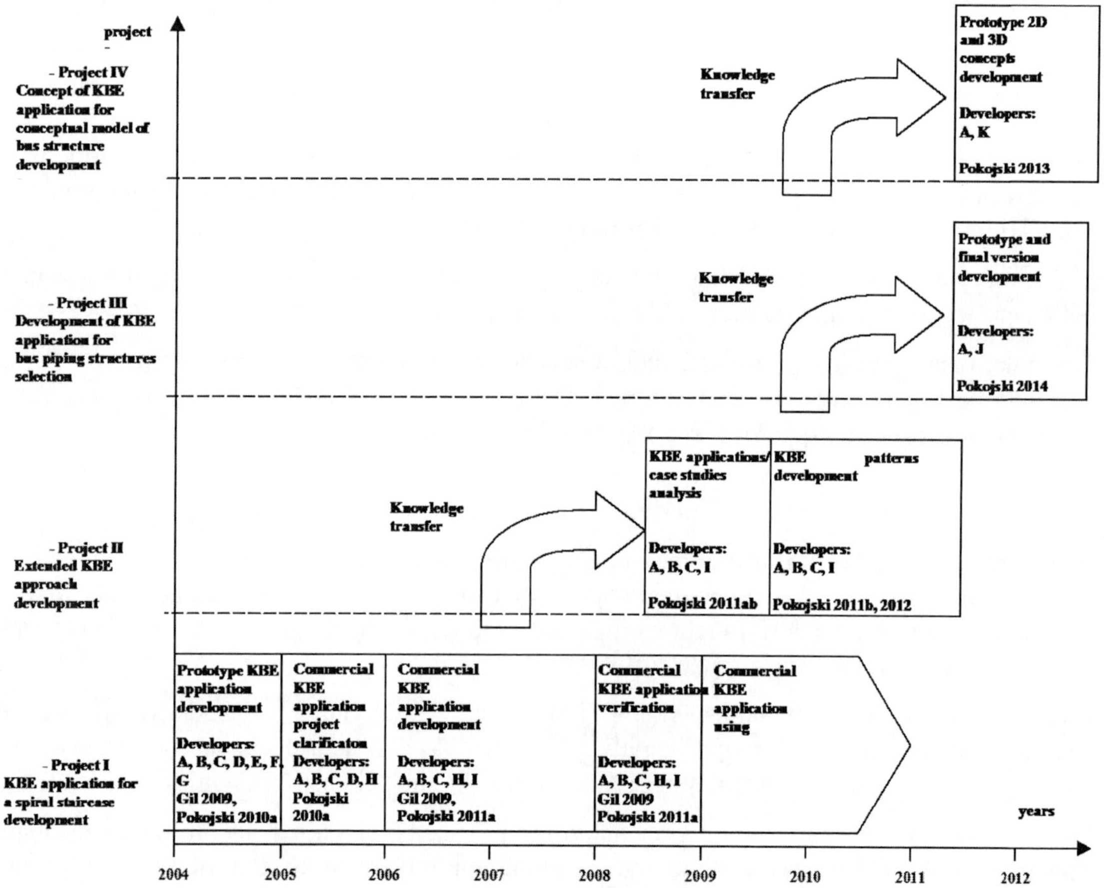

Figure: 1. Diagram time /project.

The prototype development of project I (figure 1), which was done without a personal assistant application but with standard computer and paper tools, involved penetrating many knowledge sources as well as domain terminology, suitable terms and definitions learning. All those findings were stored with appropriate classic representations. At the same time attempts were made to use the acquired knowledge actively in the form of partial models which were at once tested and verified. Different versions of the models or their process iterations were developed as well.

As soon as some degree of sophistication with the partial models' development was achieved, complex models could be created. For that purpose it was very useful to keep the direct mapping of the earlier stages of the whole process.

Project I
Prototype KBE application development

Knowledge operations' characteristic

Stage 1
Delivery of text documents, drawings, sketches by industrial partner.
Stage 2
Initial, prototype software structure development; MS Excel used as transparent integration tool; other program modules integrated with MS Excel. Design process computer simulations performed under supervision of representatives of industrial partner and developers. Clarification process.
Stage 3
Problem decomposition on: a) core components of design process (developers C, D), b) processes directly resulting from core components of design process (developers: E, F), c) proceses resulting indirectly from core components (developer G). Design process computer simulations performed under supervision of representatives of industrial partner and developers. Clarification process.
Stage 4
Integration of each process with CAD system. Design process computer simulations performed under supervision of representatives of industrial partner and developers. Clarification process.

- **Each developer organizes his private knowledge repository.**
- **Stages 1-4 performed iteratively.**

Project I
Commercial KBE application project clarificaton

Knowledge operations' characteristic

Stage 1
Developer H selects knowledge elements (concerning product development) suitable for object oriented modeling. First attempts of building partial object oriented models.
Stage 2
Attempts of engineering knowledge modeling (for partial problems) in form of procedural, declarative and object-oriented representations. Product process and model clarification.
Stage 3
Design product and process model for whole design process development – first iteration.

- **Each developer organizes his private knowledge repository.**
- **Stages 1-3 performed on iterative way.**

Figure: 2. Characteristic of selected knowledge operations in project I.

Processes of clarification, concept developments and others may overlap each other. Every single one of them has its specificity, its most suitable representations and functionalities.

As developers using personal assistant software often work successively or parallel in different projects, it would be very helpful if the suitable knowledge elements could be linked, associated and shared.

Many of the activities described can be developed in different existing environments, for instance MS Visual Studio, UML tools, etc. But they should be integrated with a personal assistant system of the respective developer.

It would be very useful to achieve automatically performed operations which show the stored design records together with their background knowledge sources in a suitable, well synchronized context.

Functionalities which allow an after-project reflection and are integrated with their knowledge resources would be very helpful as well.

Additionally, the opportunity to model different resources according to their access or filtration would be desirable.

The above concepts as well as numerous concepts in literature indicate that it is possible to develop many ad hoc, short-life, personal assistant solutions. But thinking of long-term applications it would be much better to develop a system of standards which is deeply integrated with the existing engineering software. The possibility to profile standard engineering designers, their knowledge and their knowledge development could significantly help with that.

The problem of structuring presented above might be directly integrated with Pahl- Beitz's proposals (or other design methodological concepts) and treated as a reference solution.

Decision making while performing design activities is a permanent process. Designers build concepts of their design processes, precise certain steps and connect activities with them. Later the processes are carried out. Results achieved earlier certainly influence subsequent decisions. Improvements can be made but occasionally an iterative approach may appear.

During these processes engineering knowledge is applied and sometimes also methods supporting decision making are employed. Knowledge used by a single designer, who is the owner of his/her personal assistant software system, may be derived from the resources of a personal assistant belonging to another designer. This external knowledge can be treated as someone's recommendations as well as a personal way of inferencing and used nearly automatically. But it may also be analysed on the attempt to understand somebody's way of seeing a certain problem. In this case - "understanding somebody's way of seeing a certain problem" would mean a first step to transdisciplinarity– the approaching and overlapping of separate disciplines.

The developed personal assistant structures can be categorized from different perspectives:

- sets of available functionalities,
- graphic metaphors used,
- models of knowledge representation,
- possible scenarios of use,
- domain and field of application,
- set of available personal assistants belonging to different people,
- integrated computer tools.

A developed personal assistant software should be reconfigurable with the possibility of user-oriented profiles modelling.

The integration of all available components is one of the main issues of a personal assistant development. Obviously, different solutions are possible. But it is difficult to integrate everything with everything. General solutions are rather expensive and not efficient (Pokojski 2004 – blackboard architecture).

Therefore it is more practical to build tools with which different components can be linked. This means to operate on a micro level of the system. Gradually the whole system will be complete. This is a usual way of developing multi-disciplinary systems which are based on multi-components integration (Stjepandic 2015).

Small and medium enterprises require different integration possibilities than large corporations. With smaller firms the applied solutions are mostly more flexible and complex, but also more risky. Bigger companies, however, tend to apply rather standard and durable technologies.

5. Conclusions

Summing up, it is possible to make a descriptive model of the personal/team assistant system, which might be a vision of the next step concerning the personal assistant. The model bases on the literature survey and the author's considerations. The descriptive model of the new concept consists of three groups of components:

The first group bases on the first stage of development (from the chapter 2)

where the personal/team assistant systems store engineering knowledge. The stored knowledge can be used by the owners of the personal assistant but can also be shared with other people. The engineering knowledge is stored in various computer representations and is strictly connected with the design process stages according to the Pahl-Beitz approach (clarification, conceptual, embodiment, detail).

The second group bases on the second stage of development (from the chapter 2)

The components from group 1 are extended to standardized possibilities of functioning in distributed environments so that they can correspond with actually applied solutions in this kind of processing. Strongly developed solutions based on achievements of graphic interfaces together with standard and new metaphors and archetypes are applied. Classic methods and tools for data mining, case-based reasoning applications are used and different knowledge based approaches and decision making techniques are implemented. The special representations are developed for the storage of engineering knowledge for MDO (Multi-Disciplinary Optimization) processes.

The third group bases on the third stage of development (from the chapter 2)

The components from the groups 1 and 2 are extended to new, advanced functionalities: ontologies change management, reflection processes modeling, traceability modeling, new knowledge representations modeling and management, multidisciplinarity analysis, personalized searching, etc.

Most of the components enumerated above already exist. But they only exist as isolated or limited solutions, or as solutions "with different form". The main problem is to integrate all available solutions in one functioning and effective system.

6. References

Aoyama, K., Koga, T., (2006). Supporting system for design and production with sharing and access of product failure, Leading the Web Concurrnet Engineering, pp. 25-31.

Bracewell, R., Wallace, K., Moss, M., Knott, D., (2009). Capturing design rationale, Computer-Adied Design 41, pp. 173-186.

Chandrasegaran, S. K., Ramani, K., Sriram, R. D., Horváth, I., Bernard, A., Harik, **R. F.**, Gao, W., (2013). The evolution, challenges, and future of knowledge representation in product design systems. Computer-Aided Design **45**, pp. 204–228.

Chen, Y., (2010). Knowledge integration and sharing for collaborative molding product design and process development. Computers in Industry 61, pp. 659-675.

Chen, Y. , Liu, Z., Xie, Y., (2012). A knowledge-based framework for creative conceptual design of multi-disciplinary systems. Computer-Aided Design 44, pp. 146-153.

Chen, Yuh-Jen, Chen, Yuh-Min, Wub, M., (2012). An empirical knowledge management framework for professional virtual community in knowledge-intensive service industries, Expert Systems with Applications **39** , pp. 13135–13147.

Chungoora, N., et al., (2013). A model-driven ontology approach for manufacturing system interoperability and knowledge sharing, Computers in Industry 64, pp. 392-401.

Clarkson, P.J. , Hamilton, J.R. , (2000). "Signposting", A Parameter- driven Task-based Model of the Design Process. Research in Engineering Design 12, 18-38.

Court, A.W. , (1997). The Relationship Between Information and Personal Knowledge in New Product Development, International Journal of Information Management vol. **17,** No. 2, pp. 123-138.

Court, A. W. , (1998a). Issues for integrating knowledge in new product development: reflections from an empirical study. Knowledge-Based Systems **11** , pp. 391-398.

Court, A.W. , Ullman, D.G. , Culley SJ, (1998b) A Comparison Between the Provision of Information to Engineering Designers in the UK and the USA. International Journal of Information Management Vol. **18** No. 6, pp. 409-425.

Ding, L., Davies, D. McMahon, Ch. A., (2009). The integration of lightweight representation and annotation for collaborative design representation, Res. Eng. Design 19, pp. 223-228.

Dongmina, Z., Dachaoa, H., Yuchunb, X. Hong, Z., (2012). A framework for design knowledge management and reuse for Product-Service Systems in construction machinery industry, Computers in Industry 63, pp. 328–337.

Dorner, D., (1999). Approaching design thinking research, Design Studies **20**, pp. 407-415.

Fenves, S., (1998). Towards Personalized Structural Engineering Tools. In: Lecture Notes in Artificial Intelligence, V Workshop Application of Artifical Intelligence in Structural Engineering, Ian Smith (Ed.); Springer-Verlag, Ascona, Switzerland, pp. 86-91.

Fruchter, R., Damian, P., (2009). Effective visualization of design versions: visual storytelling for design reuse, Res. Eng. Design 19, pp. 193-204.

Gil, M., Pokojski, J., Skotnicki, S., Szustakiewicz, K., (2009). Object Oriented Modeling for the Computer Aided Design Application for a Spiral Staircase. Conference: AIMETH 2009, Recent Developments in Artificial Intelligence, pp. 113-120.

Gorman, G.E., Pauleen, D.J., (2010). The Nature and Value of Personal Knowledge Management. In Pauleen, D. & Gorman, G. (eds.) Personal Knowledge Management: Individual, Organizational and Social Perspectives. Gower:London.

Hahm, G. J. , Yi, M. Y., Lee, J. H., Suh, H. W., (2014). A personalized query expansion approach for engineering document retrieval, Advanced Engineering Informatics **28**, pp. 344-359.

Hicks, B.J., Culley, S.J. , Allen, R.D., Mullineux, G., (2002). A framework for the requirements of capturing, storing and reusing information and knowledge in engineering design. International Journal of Information Management 22, pp. 263-280.

Hildre, H.P., (1999). CAE from first day designing complex machines. In: Proceedings of International Conference on Engineering Design ICED99; Munich, Germany, pp. 715-720.

Hisarcikliar, O., Boujut, J-F., (2009) An annotation model to reduce ambiguity on design communication, Res. Eng. Design 20, pp. 171-184.

Hong, J., Toye, G., Leifer, L.J., (1996). Engineering design notebook for sharing and reuse. Computers in Industry, vol 29, pp. 27-35.

Keraron, Y., Bernard, A., Bachimont, B., (2009). Annotations to improve the using updating of digital technical publications, Res. Eng. Design **20**, pp. 157-170.

Khattak, A.M., et al., (2013). Change management in evolving web ontologies. Knowledge-Based Systems 37, pp. 1-18.

Kim, H.L., Choi, J. H., Kim, H.G., Hwang, S.H. , (2007). A Personal Knowledge Management System on Social Software Agent Technologies, KES-AMSTA 2007, LNAI 4496, pp. 785–794.

Kitamura, Y., Mizoguchi, R., (2004). Deployment of an ontological framework of functional design knowledge, Advanced Engineering Informatics 18, pp. 115-127.

Lenne, D., Thouvenin, I., Aubury, S., (2009). Supporting design with 3D annotations in a collaborative virtual environment, Res. Eng. Design 20, pp. 148-155.

Linkiewicz, G., Marowski, W., Pokojski, J. (eds.), (2007). Computer Aided Design in Distributed Environment", WNT. (in Polish)

Lowe, A., McMahon, C., Shah, T. , Culley, S., (1999). An analysis of the content of technical information used by engineering designers. In: Proceedings of the 1999 ASME Design Engineering Technical Conferences, CD.

McMahon, C.A. , Liu, Y., Crossland, R., Brown, D., Leal, D., Devlukia, J., (2004). A best practice advice system to support automotive engineering analysis processes, Engineering with Computers 19, pp. 271-283.

Monticolo, D., Badin, J., Gomes, S., Bonjour, E., Chamoret, D., (2015). A meta-model for knowledge configuration management to support collaborative engineering, Computers in Industry 66, pp. 11–20.

Moran, T.P., Carroll, J.M. , (1996). Design rationale: concepts, techniques, and use. Lawrence Erlbaum Associates, Publishers, Mahwah New Jersey, USA.

Nomaguchi, Y. , Fujita, K., (2013). Knowledge representation framework for interactive capture and management of reflection process in product concepts development, Advanced Engineering Informatics 27, pp. 537-554.

O'Leary, D. , (1998). Using AI in Knowledge Management: Knowledge Bases and Ontologies. IEEE Intelligent Systems May/June, pp. 34-39

Ouertani, M.Z. , Bad'na, S., Gzara, L., Morel, G., (2011). Traceability and management of dispersed product knowledge during design and manufacturing, Computer-Aided Design **43**, pp. 546–562.

Pahl G, Beitz W, and al., (2007). Engineering Design: A Systematic Approach, Springer-Verlag.

Pokojski, J., (2004). IPA (Intelligent Personal Assistant) – Concepts and Applications in Engineering, Springer-Verlag, London.

Pokojski, J., (2006). Knowledge Based Engineering and Intelligent Personal Assistant Context in Distributed Design, in: Intelligent Computing in Engineering and Architecture, LNAI 4200, Springer-Verlag, pp. 519-528.

Pokojski, J., Cichocki, P., (2007a). Personal Knowledge Structuring – Issues Concepts and Application in Engineering, ProSTEP iViP Science Days Proceedings, Bremen, pp. 32-40.

Pokojski, J., Cichocki, P., (2007b). Intelligent Personal Assistant Concept in Context of Fault Analysis, Computer Assisted Mechanics and Engineering Sciences 14 No 4, pp. 591-600.

Pokojski, J., Gil, M., Szustakiewicz, K., (2010a). Engineering Knowledge Modeling in Design. In: New World Situation: New Directions in Concurrent Engineering: Proceedings of the 17th ISPE International Conference on Concurrent Engineering (Advanced Concurrent Engineering), Editors: Jerzy Pokojski, Shuichi Fukuda, Józef Salwiński, Springer-Verlag, pp. 257-266.

Pokojski, J., Gil, M., Szustakiewicz, K., (2011a). Extended KBE in Mechanical Engineering- discussion of concepts, In: Improving Complex Systems Today: Proceedings of the 18th ISPE International Conference on Concurrent Engineering (Advanced Concurrent Engineering), Springer-Verlag, by Daniel D. Frey, Shuichi Fukuda and Georg Rock (2011), pp, 267-274.

Pokojski, J., Gil, M., Szustakiewicz, K., (2011b). Extended KBE in Mechanical Engineering- discussion of solutions, In: Improving Complex Systems Today: Proceedings of the 18th ISPE International Conference on Concurrent Engineering (Advanced Concurrent Engineering), Springer-Verlag, by Daniel D. Frey, Shuichi Fukuda and Georg Rock (2011), pp. 275-284.

Pokojski, J., Niedziółka, K., (2013). Extended KBE model of bus. Unpublished report, Institute of Machine Design Fundamentals, Warsaw University of Technology, 2013.

Pokojski, J., Niemczewski, T., Matysiak, P., (2008). Study of Design Knowledge Development of Two Students' Projects, In "Design Methods for Industrial Practice", edited by R. Rohatyński, P. Poślednik, Oficyna Wydawnicza Uniwersytetu Zielonogórskiego, pp. 325-332.

Pokojski, J., Szustakiewicz, K., (2012). Extended KBE – Scenario of an Application Development. In J. Stjepandic, G. Rock, C. Bil, Concurrent Engineering Approaches for Sustainable Product Development in a Multi_Disciplinary Environment. Proceedings of the 19th International Conference on Concurrent Engineering, Springer (2012), pp. 291-302.

Pokojski, J., Pruszyński, J., Oleksiński, K., (2010b). Concepts of applications supporting process of design knowledge storage. Institute of Vehicles Scientific Papers **4** (80), pp. 71-82.

Pokojski, J., Szustakiewicz, K., Jusis, J., (2013). Collaborative engineering knowledge modeling for KBE applications development. Mechanik nr 7 (2013), pp. 701-710. (in Polish)

Pokojski, J., Woźnicki, Ł., (2014). KBE application development for selection-type design process. Mechanik **7** (2014), pp. 607-614. (in Polish)

Regli, W.C., Hu, X., Atwood, M., Sun, W., (2000). A Survey of Design Rationale Systems: Approaches, Representation, Capture and Retrieval. Engineering with Computers 16, pp. 209-235.

Sevilmis, N., Stork, A., (2007). A Semantic –based Approach for Concurrent Engineering , ProSTEP iViP Science Days 2007, Proceedings, Bremen (2007), pp. 136-145.

Sim, S. Kok, Duffy, A.H.B., (2003). Towards an ontology of generic engineering design activities. Res. Eng. Design 14, pp. 200-223.

Song, F., Zacharewicz, G., Chen, D., (2013). An ontology-driven framework towards building enterprise semantic information layer, Advanced Engineering Informatics 27, pp. 38-50.

Stjepandic, J. ,Wognum, N., Verhagen, W.J.C., (2015). Concurrent Engineering in the 21st Century: Foundations, Developments and Challenges, Springer.

Turkiyyah, G.M. , Fenves, S.J. , (1996). Knowledge-Based Assistance for Finite-Element Modeling; IEEE Experts June , pp. 23-48.

Ullman, D.G., (2002). The Mechanical Design Process, McGraw-Hill (Third Edition).

Völkel, M. , (2010). Personal Knowledge Models with Semantic Technologies. Herstellung und Verlag: Books on Demand GmbH, Norderstedt.

Wallace, K., (2006). How engineering designers retrieve information. Design Methods for Practice, ed. R. Rohatyński, Zielona Góra , pp. 171-180.

Wang, H., et al., (2012). The retrieval of structured design rationale for re-use of design knowledge with and integrated representation, Advanced Engineering Informatics 26, pp. 251-266

Xu, J., et al., (2011a). Fostering continuous innovation in design with an integrated knowledge management approach, Computers in Industry 62, pp. 423-436.

Xu, Y., Bernard, A., (2010). Measurement of enterprise knowledge by state characterization, Expert Systems, The Journal of Knowledge Engineerin vol. 27 no 5, pp. 374-387.

Xu, Y., Bernard, A., (2011b). Quantifying the value of knowledge within the context of product development. Knowledge-Based Systems 24 (2011), 166-175.

Xiaofang, Y. Z. , Li, J., Buis, J. J. , (2013). A semantic representation model for design rationale of products, Advanced Engineering Informatics 27, pp. 13-26.

Zhen, L., Song, H. T. , He, J.T., (2012). Recommender systems for personal knowledge management in collaborative environments, Expert Systems with Applications 39, pp. 12536–12542.

Shape control for self-stress following deployment of a tensegrity footbridge

Ann C. Sychterz, Ian F.C. Smith

Applied Computing and Mechanics Laboratory (IMAC), School of Architecture, Civil and Environmental Engineering (ENAC), Swiss Federal Institute of Technology (EPFL), CH-1015 Lausanne, Switzerland

ann.sychterz@epfl.ch

Abstract. Shape control is a combination of control commands with measurements to achieve a desired form. Tensegrity structures are pin-jointed assemblies of struts and cables, held together in a stable state of stress. Applying shape control to a near-full-scale deployable tensegrity structure presents a unique opportunity to study and control the effects of large shape changes on a closely coupled multi-element system. Simulated cable-length changes provide an initial activation plan to reach an effective sequence for self-stress. Controlling internal forces is more sensitive than controlling movements through cable-length changes; internal forces are thus a better objective for small adjustments to the structure. Due to modeling simplifications and eccentricities in joints, cable-length changes that have been determined only through simulation may not be effective. This paper compares two algorithms for implementing self-stress according to two goals. The first goal is to create sufficient stabilizing axial forces in elements. The second goal is to improve the position of nodes so that they are as close as possible to the design configuration. Applying these algorithms to full-scale structures such as tension-cable structures, tents, and domes, can change shape and stiffness properties in service.

1. Introduction

Most deployable structures today are one-degree of freedom structures such as draw bridges, retractable roofs, and spacecraft appendages (Pellegrino 1995). Tensegrity structures easily change shape in multiple directions due to the closely-coupled nature of the strut and cable systems. These structures require self-stress; otherwise the structure is unstable due to mechanisms (Schenk et al. 2007). Actuation of elements allows the structure to move and adapt. During a movement such as deployment, folding, and shape correction, elements may be in positions that are not prescribed by the design. At the end of deployment, nodal positions need to be restored as close as possible to the design configuration to ensure that behaviour is as intended. Model improvement and control algorithms for movement are the two topics studied in this paper.

Tensegrity structures are light-weight and deformable structures, useful in applications such as slabs (Csölleová 2012), shells (Skelton and Oliveira 2009), and towers (Schlaich 2003). These structures are composed of bars in compression surrounded by a network of cables in tension to maintain stability (Motro 2011; Snelson 2012; Pellegrino and Calladine 1986).

Form-finding is an analysis method that determines deformed shape (Pagitz and Mirats Tur 2009; Tibert and Pellegrino 2003). A drawback of many form-finding methods is the inability to prescribe cable stress given a required shape when behavior is non-linear. Force density is a linear analysis method for form-finding using force-length ratios to determine the equilibrium state of the network (Schek 1974). The tangent stiffness matrix for a structure under self-stress was developed for tensegrity structures (Guest 2006). Dynamic relaxation (DR) (Barnes 1988) is a vector-based pseudo-dynamic static analysis. The advantage of DR is the ability to calculate the equilibrium and form of a non-linear system without matrix inversion. While other form-finding methods require multiple steps, dynamic relaxation involves a direct calculation of the form with the member stresses. While dynamic relaxation has been used for control through stochastic search (Domer and Smith 2005), a multi-criteria algorithm has not yet been proposed to control the geometry of a deployable structure to improve performance.

Research into in the deployment of tensegrity structures has involved aspects such as friction effects, construction limitations and deployment methods. Friction effects at joints were included in a minimum-time method that optimized structural control of a tensegrity structure (Aldrich and Skelton 2003). As the scale and degree of movement in a tensegrity structure increased, difficulties associated with construction of the joints connecting struts and cables also increased (Rieffel et al. 2009). In order to control the structure, either struts (Amendola et al. 2014; Averseng and Dubé 2012) or cables (Sultan 2014) were actuated for shape control. A further improvement on the fluidity of control was the use of actuated continuous cables (Bel Hadj Ali et al. 2011). This reduced the number of actuators required for effective control as proposed by Moored and Bart-Smith (2009). For the movement of a space structure, control loops for coarse and fine adjustments were developed to optimize computation time and accuracy (Rhodes et al. 2012). However, the use of preference (soft) constraints to manage solutions provided by control algorithms has not yet been explored.

Soft constraints are limits that can be relaxed should the deviation from that limit show overall improvement to performance of the system (Tanrikulu et al. 1997). Hard constraints are those that cannot be relaxed. For example, a safe load for experimental testing is a soft constraint that can be exceeded whereas the ultimate failure load is a hard constraint that cannot be exceeded. A combination of hard and soft constraints has been used for multi-modulus blind frequency analysis (Akande et al. 2016; Abrar et al. 2005). Smith and Boulanger (1994) explored the use of soft constraints in decision making processes for design. Hierarchical selection for multi-objective shape control of an adaptable tensegrity structure applied objectives sequentially to reduce the solution set until one solution remained (Adam and Smith 2008). The concept of multiple-limit criteria with levels of importance has not been applied to control algorithms for deployable structures.

Recent work involved a study of active control for mid-span connection of a near-full scale "hollow-rope" tensegrity footbridge. This topology was proposed by Motro et al. (2006) and a laboratory structure was built by Rhode-Barbarigos et al. (2010). Experimental testing established that deployment with continuous cables was feasible (Veuve et al. 2015). In the first stage, it was observed that deployment completed with large variations in end-node coordinates. In a second stage, control feedback has made corrections possible to join the connector nodes and ensure successful locking of the two halves (Veuve et al. 2016).

This paper describes a novel multi-criteria strategy to introduce self-stress after deployment. Following an overview of the analysis methods, a multi-criteria strategy is proposed to control shape and axial forces in elements. Two algorithms are evaluated by simulating pre-stress in the tensegrity structure after deployment. A discussion of results related to nodal position and element forces compares the usefulness of soft and hard constraints. Stress control in deployable structures offers another optimization criterion for shape control and movement.

2. Analytical study

2.1. Overview

Simulations of cable actuation sequences for self-stressing of the deployed tensegrity structure have been carried out. Control command sequences combines a stochastic-search method, Probabilistic Global Search Lausanne (PGSL)(Raphael and Smith 2003), and dynamic relaxation (DR), a vector-based pseudo-dynamic static analysis. These commands are governed by the minimization of a cost function based on maximum element forces and minimal nodal distances between design and deployment.

Table 1 outlines control phases and goals of the tensegrity footbridge. Deployment requires greatest shape change of all the phases. Self-stress is an important phase once the two halves of the structure are connected since this determines behaviour in service. Self-stress sets the structure in an optimal configuration with respect to geometric and internal forces. In the last phase, service, the goals are to ensure that internal forces are within elastic limits and that structural deflections are acceptable. This paper focuses on control algorithms for the second phase, self-stress.

Table 1: Control phases and goals of the tensegrity footbridge

Phase	Goal
Deployment	Unfold from both supports and connect bridge halves at mid-span
Self-stress	Bring structure to design specifications (position and internal forces)
Service	Modify structure in order to reduce effects of unexpected damage and loading (wind, seismic, temperature)

2.2. Test structure

Figure 1 shows a 1/4-scale "hollow-rope" tensegrity footbridge after mid-span connection and after an initial self-stress (Bel Hadj Ali et al. 2010; Motro et al. 2006). The structure is 4 m long and each bridge half weighs 100 kg. Each pentagonal ring module has fifteen springs, twenty non-continuous cables, thirty struts, and five continuous active cables. Struts are 1.35 m long, 28 mm in diameter, and 1.5 m thick S355 steel tubes. Cables are stainless steel 3 mm in diameter and braided. Steel springs are less stiff at the supports (2.0 kN/m) than in the rest of the structure (2.9 kN/m).

The deployment and connection of two halves are ensured by active cables (five for each side). Deployment is aided by energy stored in springs. Dynamic relaxation was employed for form-finding and static analysis. Five continuous cables run along the length of each half and slide through channels at joints that are frictionless connections (Bel Hadj Ali et al. 2011).

A program developed in LabView was used to control cable length changes. PGSL and DR were included in the program to evaluate stresses and position from cable length changes. Without the presence of self-stress, a tensegrity structure would not be stable under service loading. Two properties that describe tensegrity structures are the number of self-stress states and the number of infinitesimal mechanisms (Pellegrino and Calladine 1986). The near-full-scale tensegrity structure has no infinitesimal mechanisms and six independent states of self-stress.

The shape of the structure after mid-span connection is more irregular and not aligned between the two supports. In Figure 1 a) more of the structure is above the reference line whereas in 1) b), the structure is centered. The tensegrity bridge halves are potentially more similar to the design configuration after self-stress than before. Irregular configurations risks unexpected joint angles and undesirable internal forces.

The goals during self-stress are to remove slack in cables and to align the structure. Alignment has been verified using an optical tracking system with eight infrared cameras, four on each bridge support. Cable tension has been measured using a handheld spring-actuated cable tension-measuring device. The self-stress phase improves the tensegrity structure node positions to obtain a well-aligned, uniform shape that is close to the design configuration.

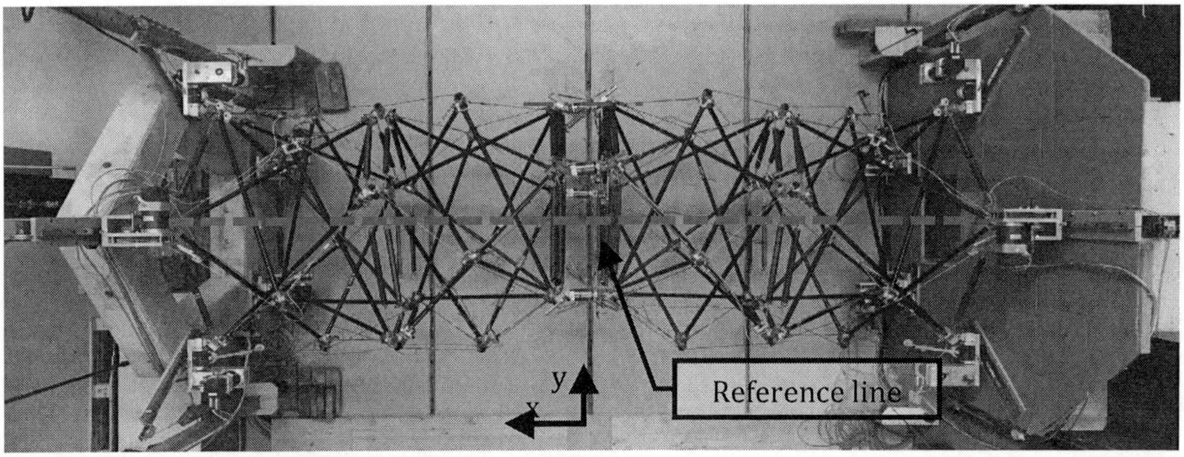

a) View from above after mid-span connection

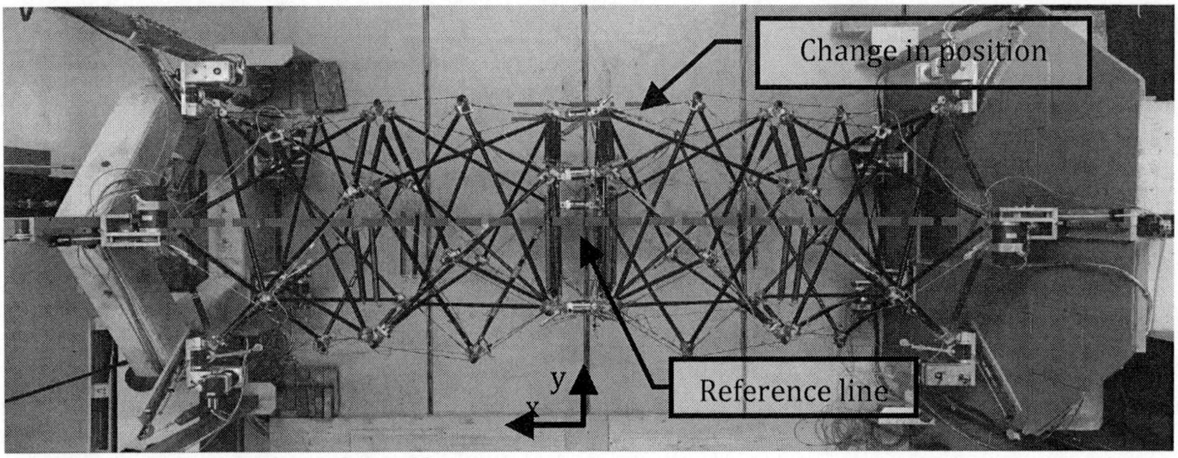

b) View from above after self-stress

Figure 1: View from above of laboratory tensegrity structure a) post mid-span connection and b) after an initial self-stress is imposed. In b), the structure is centered about the reference line.

2.3. Algorithms for self-stress

In addition to attaining desired stabilizing element forces, control during self-stress also involves achieving nodal positions that are close to the design configuration. The PGSL search algorithm was implemented to find control commands for mid-span connection of the two bridge halves. Although many algorithms are possible such as those proposed by Papalambros and Wilde (1989), algorithms based on two types of constraint were investigated.

The cost function to be minimized includes a term that represents the distance between the end nodes on each bridge half. Figure 2 is a flow chart of the algorithm for self-stress. Two versions of this algorithm built on previous work (Veuve and Smith 2015) are evaluated. The goal of the algorithms for the structure to be in the design configuration with cables having their prescribed self-stress values.

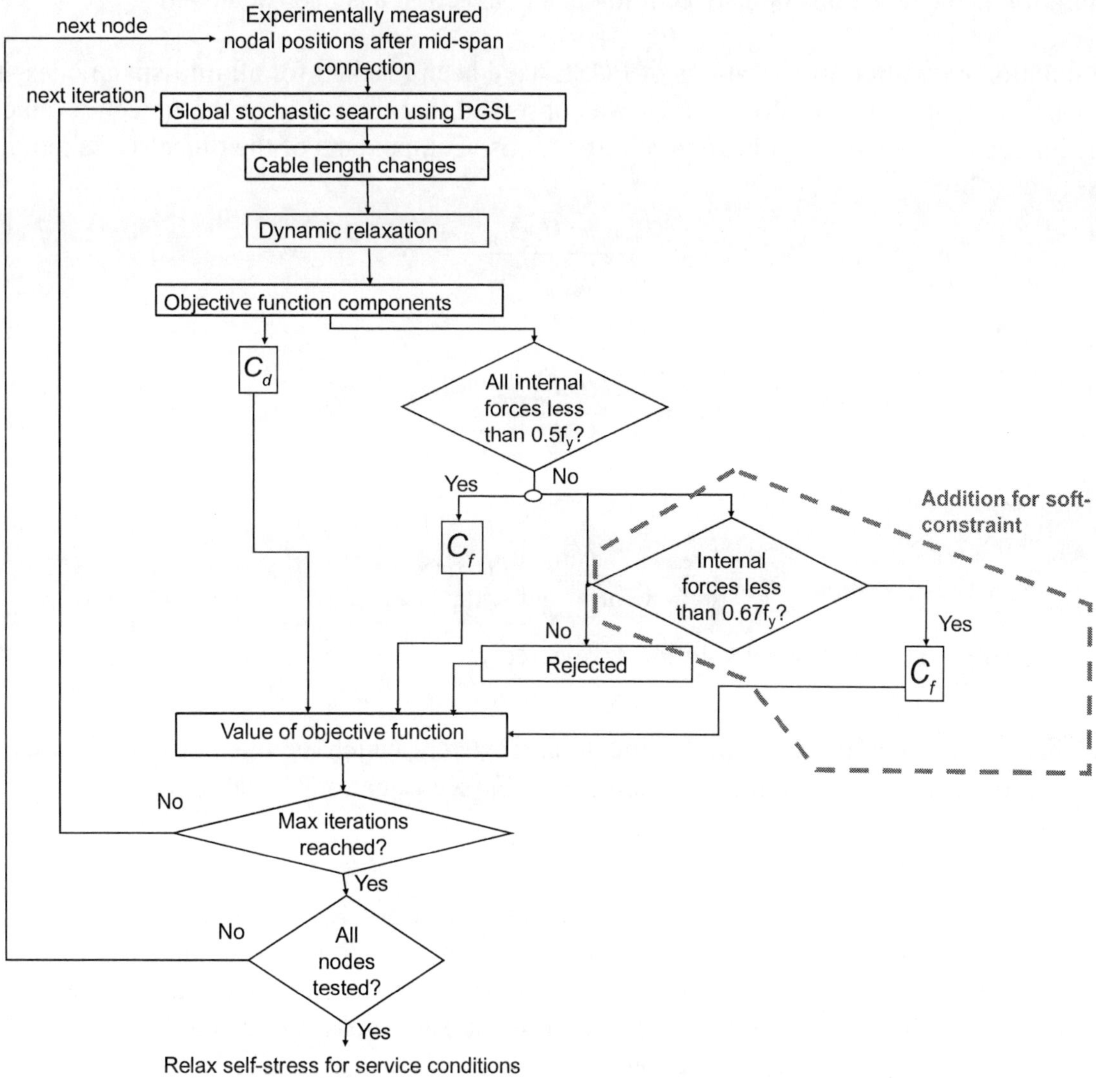

Figure 2: Evaluation of the multi-criteria objective function within PGSL. Cable-length changes govern the objective function value.

Both algorithms compute an objective function value from the normalized nodal position distances and the normalized element internal forces. This configuration is evaluated based on the two criteria of the objective function; current distance away from design configuration, (difference between $d_{current}$ [mm] and d_{design} [mm]), and internal force limits. A hard-constraint algorithm, called the initial algorithm, rejects the element internal force, $f_{current}$ [kN], if the axial forces are greater than half of the material yield value, $0.5f_y$ [kN]. This value is conventionally taken for the purposes of experimental work. A soft-constraint algorithm adds a condition where a penalty factor, P, of value 1.25 if the element internal force is greater than $0.5f_y$ and less than $0.67f_y$, is applied to the surcharge of the objective function in PGSL.

The flowchart consists of two nested loops, the outer loop executes the algorithm to each mid-span node and the inner loop executes the iterations of stochastic search. The starting configuration is the nodal positions once mid-span connection has been achieved.

The simulation ends after 400 iterations of PGSL have been reached for all mid-span nodes. This number is fixed a-priori to be 400 since it was observed that the value of the objective function did not change the overall result beyond 300 iterations. Components of the objective function are expressed as follows:

$$C_d = \frac{d_{design} - d_{current}}{d_{design}} \qquad [1]$$

If $f_{current} < 0.5f_y$, then [2]

$$C_f = \frac{0.5f_y - f_{current}}{0.5f_y}$$

If $0.5f_y < f_{current} < 0.67f_y$, then [3]

$$C_f = \left(\frac{f_{current} - 0.5f_y}{0.5f_y}\right) \bullet P + 1$$

If $f_{current} > 0.67f_y$, then the control solution is rejected [4]

The objective function is taken to be the total cost, C, which is the cost of the distance component, C_d, added to the axial force component, C_f (see Equations [2] and [3]).

$$C = C_d + C_f \qquad [5]$$

The goal of both algorithms is to find a state of self-stress for the structure to be in the configuration closest to the design specifications. Element axial forces must be relaxed to prepare for the service phase. Although nodal positions of the structure while in service may not be exactly as designed, the structure benefits from the self-stress phase that corrects for mis-aligned elements after mid-span connection.

3. Results

In order to study the effects of self-stress-control commands, element internal forces after mid-span connection and after applying the initial self-stress algorithm are compared in Figure 3. Results from a soft-constraint algorithm are presented in Figure 4. The vertical axis is the axial force [kN] in elements where tension is positive. Element numbers are shown on the horizontal axis.

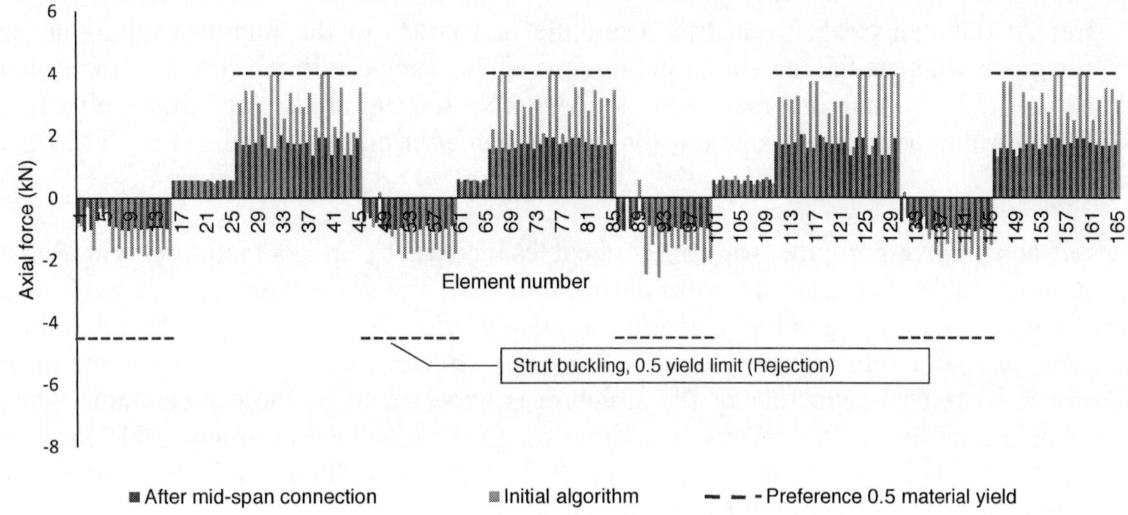

Figure 3: Comparison of an example of element internal forces after mid-span connection and after the initial self-stress algorithm

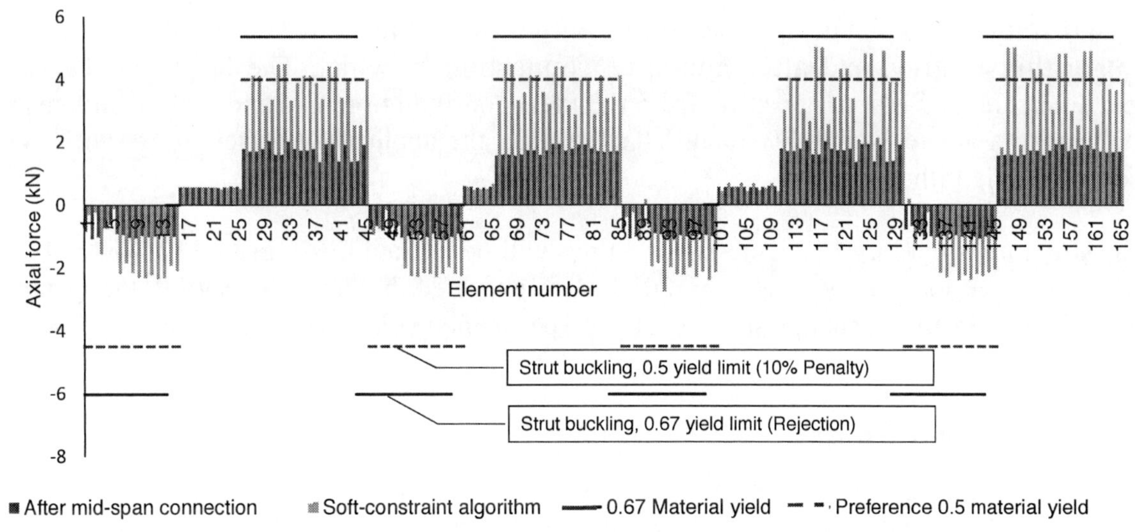

Figure 4: Comparison of an example of element internal forces after mid-span connection and after a self-stress soft-constraint algorithm

Dark grey vertical bars indicate element internal forces after mid-span connection. Light grey vertical bars denote results of the self-stress search function. Struts can sustain an axial force of 9 kN in compression whereas cables are able to resist 8 kN in tension. Limits are shown with a horizontal dash line are set to be half of the material yield limit as described earlier. Since the tensile limit of struts is 31 kN, it is not shown. Application of the self-stress algorithm increases the magnitude of axial forces in elements.

The objective is to maximize internal forces to the limits depicted by the horizontal grey dashed bars while improving the shape. Cables are more affected by the self-stress algorithm than struts.

Using the initial algorithm, axial force in discontinuous cables increases with the application of the self-stress. Continuous cables that run from the end nodes to the middle support nodes increase in tension whereas the remaining continuous cables decrease in tension. The minimum cable force is 1.33 kN and the maximum is 3.98 kN. Execution of the initial self-stress successfully algorithm has higher cable tension values than after mid-span connection. The final value for C is 57.5.

With the soft-constraint algorithm, axial forces in cables increase by up to a factor of eight. Some of the continuous cables exceeded the soft constraint of $0.5f_y$ in the solution selected by PGSL. The cable tension values are more uniform throughout the structure than with the initial algorithm and just after mid-span connection. Since the structure has been designed for ideal near-uniform axial forces, behaviour of the structure is expected to be more predictable when element forces are uniform. This results in a value for C of 50.6. The minimum cable force is 2.53 kN and the maximum is 5.02 kN. The soft-constraint self-stress algorithm is thus better than the initial algorithm for attaining uniform pre-stress.

For each structural node, Figure 5 shows the distance [mm] to the design position after mid-span connection, after applying the initial algorithm, and after applying the soft constraint algorithm. The nodal distance from the design due to the soft-constraint algorithm are in black, to the initial algorithm in grey, and after mid-span connection in white. The length of the bar indicates the distance of a nodal position from the ideal configuration. Distances after mid-span connection have a greater variability than distances after the application of self-stress with the initial self-stress algorithm.

When the structure is put in service, pre-stress values will be relaxed to a range of 12.5% to 20% of the yield stress (Rhode-Barbarigos et al. 2010). It is expected that upon relaxation, the results obtained in Figure 5 will not change significantly. Experimental confirmation of this behaviour is underway.

4. Conclusions and future work

The multi-criteria soft-constraint algorithm for self-stress described in this paper successfully lowers the variability of axial forces in cables and improves the tensegrity structure position such that nodal positions are close to the design configuration. The algorithm using only a hard constraint is less successful in achieving these goals.

This work contributes to the development of algorithms that are necessary to ensure effective deployment, connection, self-stressing and serviceability requirements for a closely coupled structure that has many degrees of freedom. Future work includes studies on calculating penalty values and the relative importance of force and position criteria. In the future, this strategy will provide a basis for enhanced active structural control for situations such as dynamic loading.

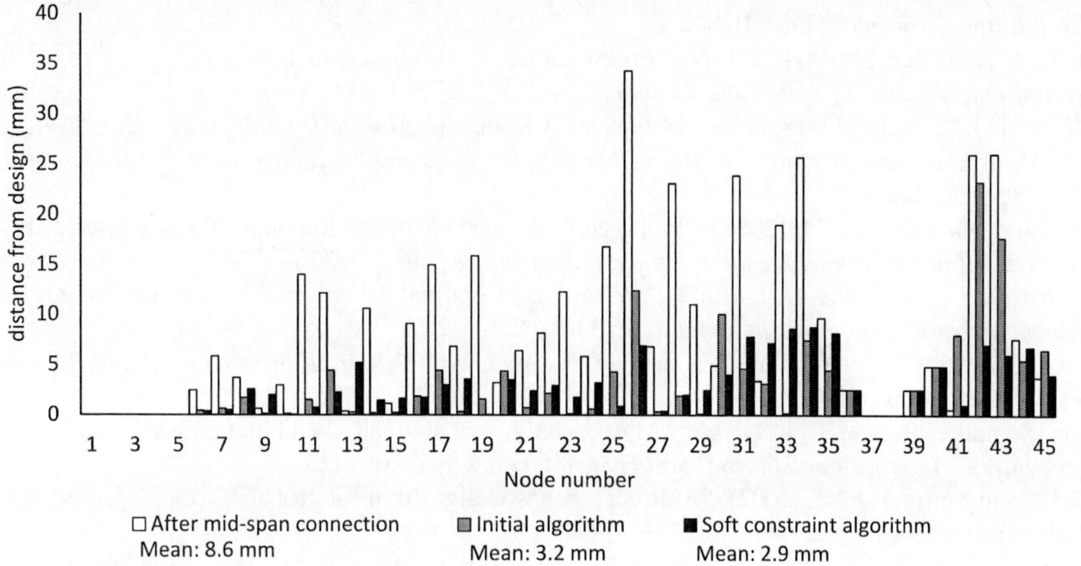

Figure 5: Comparison of nodal-position distances [mm] after mid-span connection, after application of the initial self-stress algorithm, and after application of self-stress soft constraint algorithm of the deployable tensegrity structure.

5. References

Abrar, S., Zerguine, A., and Deriche, M. (2005). "Soft constraint satisfaction multimodulus blind equalization algorithms." *IEEE Signal Processing Letters*, 12(9), 637–640.

Adam, B., and Smith, I. F. C. (2008). "Active tensegrity: A control framework for an adaptive civil-engineering structure." *Computers & Structures*, 86(23-24), 2215–2223.

Akande, K., Iqbal, N., Zerguine, A., and Chambers, J. (2016). "Normalised frequency-domain soft constraint satisfaction multimodulus blind algorithm." *Electronics Letters*, 52(3), 239–241.

Aldrich, J. B., and Skelton, R. E. (2003). "Control/structure optimization approach for minimum-time reconfiguration of tensegrity systems." *Smart Structures and Materials*, (R. C. Smith, ed.), 5049(Modeling, Signal Processing, and Control), 448–459.

Amendola, a., Carpentieri, G., de Oliveira, M., Skelton, R. E., and Fraternali, F. (2014). "Experimental investigation of the softening–stiffening response of tensegrity prisms under compressive loading." *Composite Structures*, 117(November), 234–243.

Averseng, J., and Dubé, J. F. (2012). "Design, Analysis and Self Stress Setting of a Lightweight Deployable Tensegrity Modular Structure." *Procedia Engineering*, 40(July), 14–19.

Barnes, M. R. (1988). "Form-finding and analysis of prestressed nets and membranes." *Computers and Structures*, 30(3), 685–695.

Bel Hadj Ali, N., Rhode-Barbarigos, L., Pascual Albi, A. a., and Smith, I. F. C. (2010). "Design optimization and dynamic analysis of a tensegrity-based footbridge." *Engineering Structures*, 32(11), 3650–3659.

Bel Hadj Ali, N., Rhode-Barbarigos, L., and Smith, I. F. C. (2011). "Analysis of clustered tensegrity

structures using a modified dynamic relaxation algorithm." *International Journal of Solids and Structures*, 48(5), 637–647.
Csölleová, Z. (2012). "The Analyses of Triangular Tensegrity Prisms' Pairs." *Procedia Engineering*, 40(2), 74–78.
Domer, B., and Smith, I. F. C. (2005). "An Active Structure that Learns." *Journal of Computing in Civil Engineering*, 19(1), 16–24.
Guest, S. (2006). "The stiffness of prestressed frameworks: A unifying approach." *International Journal of Solids and Structures*, 43(3-4), 842–854.
Moored, K. W., and Bart-Smith, H. (2009). "Investigation of clustered actuation in tensegrity structures." *International Journal of Solids and Structures*, 46(17), 3272–3281.
Motro, R. (2011). "Structural morphology of tensegrity systems." *Meccanica*, 46(1), 27–40.
Motro, R., Maurin, B., and Silvestri, C. (2006). "Tensegrity rings and the hollow rope." *IASS Symposium*, IASS, Beijing, China.
Pagitz, M., and Mirats Tur, J. M. (2009). "Finite element based form-finding algorithm for tensegrity structures." *International Journal of Solids and Structures*, 46(17), 3235–3240.
Papalambros, P. Y., and Wilde, D. J. (1989). "Principles of optimal design-modeling and computation." *Mathematics and Computers in Simulation*, 31(3), 286.
Pellegrino, S. (1995). "Large retractable appendages in spacecraft." *Journal of Spacecraft and Rockets*, AIAA, 32(6), 1006–1014.
Pellegrino, S., and Calladine, C. R. (1986). "Matrix analysis of statically and kinematically indeterminate frameworks." *International Journal Solids Structures*, 22(4), 409–428.
Raphael, B., and Smith, I. F. C. (2003). "A direct stochastic algorithm for global search." *Applied Mathematics and Computation*, 146, 729–758.
Rhode-Barbarigos, L., Bel Hadj Ali, N., Motro, R., and Smith, I. F. C. (2010). "Designing tensegrity modules for pedestrian bridges." *Engineering Structures*, 32(4), 1158–1167.
Rhodes, J., Dobke, B., Booth, J., and et.al. (2012). "Space-quality data from balloon-borne telescopes: The High Altitude Lensing Observatory (HALO)." *Astroparticle Physics*, 38(1), 31–40.
Rieffel, J., Valero-Cuevas, F., and Lipson, H. (2009). "Automated discovery and optimization of large irregular tensegrity structures." *Computers & Structures*, 87(5-6), 368–379.
Schek, H.-J. (1974). "The force density method for form finding and computation of general networks." *Computer Methods in Applied Mechanics and Engineering*, 3(1), 115–134.
Schenk, M., Guest, S. D., and Herder, J. L. (2007). "Zero stiffness tensegrity structures." *International Journal of Solids and Structures*, 44(20), 6569–6583.
Schlaich, M. (2003). "Der Messeturm in Rostock - ein Tensegrityrekord." *Stahlbau*, 72(10), 697–701.
Skelton, R. E., and Oliveira, M. C. De. (2009). *Tensegrity Systems*. Springer Dordrecht Hiedelberg London New York, New York.
Smith, I. F. C., and Boulanger, S. (1994). "Knowledge representation for preliminary stages of engineering tasks." *Knowledge-Based Systems*, 7(3), 161–168.
Snelson, K. (2012). "The art of tensegrity." *International Journal of Space Structures*, 27(2-3), 71–80.
Sultan, C. (2014). "Tensegrity deployment using infinitesimal mechanisms." *International Journal of Solids and Structures*, 51(21-22), 3653–3668.
Tanrikulu, O., Constantinides, A. G., and Chambers, J. A. (1997). "New normalized constant modulus algorithms with relaxation." *IEEE Signal Processing Letters*, 4(9), 256–258.
Tibert, A. G., and Pellegrino, S. (2003). "Review of Form-Finding Methods for Tensegrity Structures." *International Journal of Space Structures*, 18(4), 209–223.
Veuve, N., Dalil Safaei, S., and Smith, I. F. C. (2016). "Active control for mid-span connection of a deployable tensegrity footbridge." *Engineering Structures*, 112(1), 245–255.
Veuve, N., Safaei, S. D., and Smith, I. F. C. (2015). "Deployment of a Tensegrity Footbridge." *Journal of Structural Engineering*, 141(2006), 1–8.
Veuve, N., and Smith, I. F. C. (2015). "Mid-span connection of a deployable tensegrity footbridge." *22nd EG-ICE workshop 2015*, Eindhoven.

Cooperative Design Methods for Energy Active Façade Elements Based on BIMserver and Multi-Agent Services using JADE

Wagner A, Rüppel U
TU Darmstadt, Germany
wagner@iib.tu-darmstadt.de

Abstract. The renewable energies expansion is increasing worldwide. To satisfy the demand, large surface areas converting wind and solar power are needed. Accessible areas on building envelopes provide potential. However, various problems complicate the application of active façade elements. They need to be planned and integrated as early as possible, implying assumptions to be made. Also, cooperation among different stakeholders is necessary and needs to be organised. Small alterations of the building design can have huge impacts on an elements' efficiency.

This work presents a methodology to solve these problems. Presented is an innovative software-architecture approach using a BIMserver storing building models and a Multi-Agent-System (MAS) establishing intelligence on a collaboration platform. The developed methodology allows an easy and early integration of energy active façade elements into planning and construction processes, and is transferrable to other problems in civil-engineering. This paper discusses the platform's structure with its focus on the MAS.

Introduction

The Renewable Energy Sources Act (EEG) introduced in 2000 by the German Federal Parliament has laid the foundation for the expansion of renewable energies in Germany (*EEG*, 2014). In order to successfully transition towards renewable energy generation, large surface areas are needed to convert wind and solar power (Henning and Palzer, 2015). To prevent substantial encroachments to nature, accessible areas on roofs and façades of buildings provide an enormous potential. However, an economic and reliable integration of energy active façade elements (EAFE) into the planning, construction, and operation processes is missing. Also, information regarding the requirements on the EAFE when the building model component holding it is deleted or altered in any other way inducing a change in the component's identifier.

With our research we are developing an integration of photovoltaic and solar thermal systems into the planning process of building façades (solconpro, 2016). For this purpose, a collaboration platform is being developed. This paper presents the concept of the corresponding Multi-Agent-System (MAS) used to establish an Object-oriented Versioning History (OVH) and communication between different software applications, the underlying server, and the user. To achieve the OVH, functionalities of the BIMserver are used that compare different versions and filter the changes made in the model. This comparison is limited to the Globally Unique Identifier (GUID) of the elements; a semantic relation between previous and current elements cannot be detected. At that point, the MAS analyses the recorded changes to deduce the semantic relation. As an example, the life cycle of a building element and its depiction by software-agents will be shown in this paper.

After this brief introduction, methods applied in this research and related work will be presented in chapter 2. Next, chapter 3 will discuss the concept of the developed collaboration platform in general. Afterwards, a closer look on the structure of the MAS will be given in chapter 4, and finally, chapter 5 completes this work with an outlook and conclusion.

Related Work

Energy Active Façade Elements (EAFE)

EAFE convert utilisable energy forms of the environment into usable forms like electricity or heat. Façades using those elements do not only behave as the building envelope, but rather have various additional functions. Therefore they are being called multifunctional façades. This work concentrates on such façades, particularly on active solar façades.

Building elements related to active solar façades convert solar energy into usable energy forms. Those elements can either be added on top of a non-active building envelope or integrated directly into the façade components. The two element types considered in our research are integrated directly into the façade components: Building Integrated Photovoltaic (BIPV) elements, which produce electricity and are sensitive to clouding and shading of other components or buildings, and Building Integrated Solar Thermal (BIST) elements. The latter cover aspects of Heating, Ventilation and Air Conditioning (HVAC) and by that are more complex to integrate into the building process chain, even though they are more resistant towards clouding or staining.

Multi-Agent-System (MAS)

A MAS consists of multiple agents within an environment. These agents can be human as well as software-agents, a combination of both is possible. Software-agents are defined to be software entities performing tasks caused by requests or information gained from other entities (Shehory and Sturm, 2014). To be able to run, software-agents need an environment usually set on a platform. The platform itself can host multiple container on which the software-agents live. To avoid a confusion of these platforms with our developed collaboration platform, they will be called 'agent-platform'.

The software-agents have various properties, many of which are not bound to be present in them. Next, the properties relevant for this work will be mentioned and briefly illuminated (Shehory, 2014).

Software-Agent Properties

The most relevant properties for agents working in a multi-agent environment are autonomy and sociality. Autonomy enables agents to pursue goals that are not explicitly instructed in its program and to perform unsupervised actions. Sociality allows agents to collaborate with other agents and thereby is a premise for agents in a MAS.

Another possible property is intelligence. Since it is already hard to define intelligence if it is non artificial, a few examples of possible results of intelligence in agents are stated. First, it could mean that the agent is able to learn or reason. Also, planning and making educated decisions can arise from it. Another interesting consequence could be the agent behaving rationally and goal-orientated, which is advantageous for autonomous agents.

Additionally, mobility can be an agent's property. Though its meaning seems unambiguous, it can imply two different features. On one hand, it can describe an agent's ability to move between different agent-platforms and even computers. On the other hand it might stand for the agent-platform the agent is living on itself is moving. By doing so, e.g. when a smartphone with a MAS is physically moving, the physical environment, like location or brightness, can change. If sensors register this and send the information to a mobile agent, it would be able to react to those changes without having to reset its goals or beliefs.

Finally, the ability of an agent to communicate with other agents is essential for agents living in a MAS. To ensure an agent's autonomy, it cannot have public methods, since a program using it would have to reference to that specific agent (Theiß, 2005). Thereby, another way to communicate has to be established. The communication can be direct or indirect by a third-party translator. The exchanged messages have to be of a common language, which means they need to use the same syntax, format and semantics. This implies that a common vocabulary needs to be defined and stored. Ontologies are convenient methods to store such vocabularies.

Agent Communication Language (ACL)

As mentioned above, a common language needs to be employed in a MAS to guarantee a complication-free communication between agents. For this purpose, the Foundation for Intelligent Physical Agents (FIPA) developed the ACL. It determines a structure for the premise message header including a message protocol. The header contains among other information a so called 'Performative' defining what is demanded of the receiving agent regarding the submitted information's processing.

Also, it defines features to save the previous messages, if the sent message is a reply to a series of previous communication acts. The language's ontology clarifies the composition of the messages in relation to its Performative and can be modified and extended by the user (FIPA, 2002).

Construction Process Phases

Since this research pursues the goal of developing a software-platform independent solution, an international approach to describe the planning and construction process is desirable. With the same intention the 5DInitiative was founded by leading European construction companies. The initiative aims to set an international standard for processes management in the field of the construction industry.

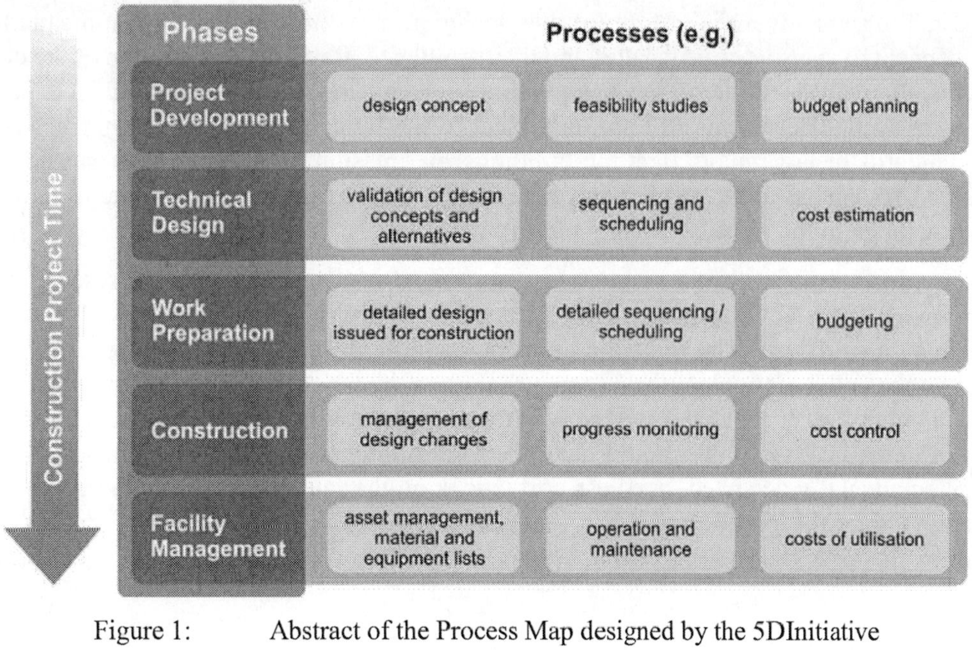

Figure 1: Abstract of the Process Map designed by the 5DInitiative

As a part of their research they determined a process map that is regardless of national process definitions or scales of fees like the German HOAI or the British RIBA plan of work. Figure 1 shows an abstract of the designed map (Ed. Züblin AG, 2012). The collaboration platform designed within this research project is based on this process map.

Further Publications

This work is part of a research project and only depicts a part of the already acquired knowledge. (Leifgen et al., in press) shows the concept of the project and the architecture of the collaboration platform which is the foundation of the developed software solution.

Furthermore, an overview of the MAS as well as a suggestion of an extension of the Industry Foundation Classes (IFC) for representing BIPV/BIST and other active building elements are given by (Franz et al., in press).

Concept

In this chapter we present the concept of our collaboration platform with a special focus on the architecture of the applied MAS. First, the requirements and constraints to the system will be discussed. After that, a brief overview of the platform and its parts will be given.

Requirements to the System

During the building process various stakeholders are involved. Thus, diverse software packages are used, which are not necessarily hosted in the same environment. Also, every project participant has his own operating system he is working on, so an overall system needs to be distributed. Another important aspect that has to be considered for the concept of our platform is the usage of different data formats used by the project participants for the exchange of data. The data exchange over the course of all building phases, from planning until recycling, has to be managed and unified.

Since the field of regenerative energies is funded and its usage promoted by governments (*EEG*, 2014), its progress advances in form of new techniques and methods. This can mean changes in the concept of energy active façades and their appliance. Besides the evolution of the physical elements, the software solution regarding their efficiency and dimensioning can be expected to develop as well. The changes do not only meet to the industry but to the authorities as well. New standards or laws may affect the buildings' permission progress or their subsidies. Our developed system has to be modular and expandable to assure possible amendments in this field can be included in the already existing platform.

A quality attribute of software solutions is user friendliness. Referred to our research project the following issue can be defined: Our platform will check the building model for geometric and semantic collisions. The semantic collisions will be detected with the help of a rule base placed on the collaboration platform (e.g. a change in the façade causing shadows cast on solar active elements). If the planner receives warning messages and improvement suggestions he does not deem necessary, he should have the opportunity to declare rules himself. This will prevent accidentally accepted, needless corrections on the model and facilitate the work flow. To achieve this, the platform needs to act autonomously, without constant confirmation or control by the user.

Platform Architecture

The design of our collaboration platform with focus on the MAS can be seen in Figure 2. For its development we considered the constraints determined above. One of those were distributed systems of the project participants. To cover this aspect, we decided a server every player can access to be the base of our platform. This means that every participating computer application has to be extended by a plugin that connects to the collaboration platform for communication and stream of information. The extensibility of programmes constitutes another constraint; programmes without an Application Program Interface (API) cannot directly be regarded in our advance. Though, it is possible to connect an agent indirect to such programmes by setting them to listen on changes in the files themselves the user is working on.

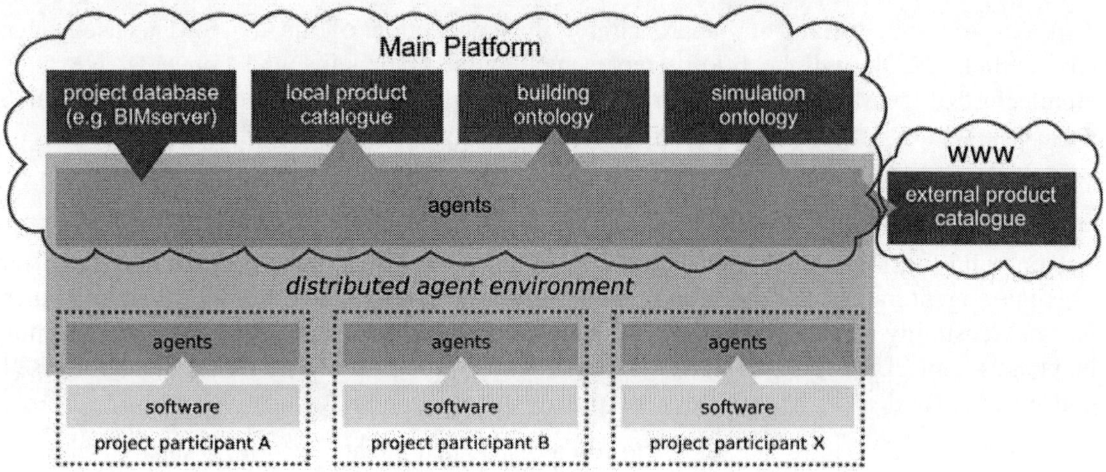

Figure 2: Overview of the Developed Collaboration System

To secure the data exchange and handling, a project database is set on the platform. We decided to use BIMserver for this purpose since it comes with valuable features and is open source (BIMserver, 2016). It allows users to check in and out complete building models or just parts of it. When a new model is uploaded to the BIMserver, the models can be controlled for geometric and semantic collisions as well as the change of individual building components can be detected. This is important for further analysis regarding the effects of applied changes.

Next to the BIMserver, ontologies store specified information relating to building components and simulations. Also, a central product catalogue is located on the main platform in case information about active components are needed. The platform is able to connect to online catalogues as well, since manufacturers provide digital information about their products and it is conceivable that a central, national online catalogue (as already developed in the UK) may be extended to product data of energy active façade elements (RIBA, 2016).

Finally, a MAS is set up on the main platform to perform processes that can be automated and help users with their decision making. The exact structure of the MAS will be shown in the following chapter. For further information about the platform set up see (Leifgen et al., in press).

Object-oriented Versioning History (OVH)

To ensure no information is lost during updates of the building model, the versioning provided by the BIMserver does not suffice. This is due to its limitation to the IFC GUID. If an element is replaced by another element (e.g. a window being replaced by a BIPV), the GUID of those elements will not be identical. A further investigation regarding their relation needs to take place. The MAS should be able to detect connections between varied elements of consecutive BIM versions.

An OVH is of importance within the integration of EAFE since requirements and specifications to the applied system are already made and suggested at early planning stages. The information is usually stored in textual form as an attribute of the not yet active building element. As soon as the element is switched for a more detailed or the originally planned active element, these attributes will be lost, unless a relationship between those elements is established.

Conception of the Multi Agent System

This chapter will explain our approach for the conception of the MAS. The used agent environment JADE will be briefly represented with its benefits and concepts. Next, the architecture of the MAS will be illustrated and expounded. After the introduction of the MAS, a use case will be defined and the MAS applied to it.

JADE

After careful consideration we decided to use JADE as our agent framework. JADE is an object-orientated agent framework based on Java. Its advantages relating to our research among others is its extensibility. It can be extended to support web services and rule based programming languages (e.g. CLIPS), to run on a .NET environment, to apply Belief Desire Intention (BDI) concepts, and to deal with workflows and processes (Sturm and Shehory, 2014).

It provides an architecture that allows to run a distributed agent platform. Instead of different platforms, the computers host containers that are located on the same platform; this is only possible, if the computers are connected via network and the firewall allows it. As consequences, permissions for deploying and killing agents are universal and communication is easier and more resource-efficient. Besides, the framework is consistent with the FIPA standards and regulation.

Thereby, the communication between the agents is realised with ACL. If the agents are living in the same container, messages do not have to be wrapped and Java objects can be exchanged. Furthermore, agents can exchange ontology objects while communicating as long as both parties use the same ontology. This is very helpful in respect of building components and their classification by the IFC (Caire, 2002). To establish communication between an application and agents, the application needs to own the controller of the agent's platform. The controller then can be used for an Object to Agent (O2A) communication, allowing them to share serialisable Java objects.

Another feature is the Directory Facilitator (DF). It is also known as the 'yellow pages service' and administers registrations of other agents with their names, used ontologies and languages, as well as service description. One agent can register multiple service description and it is possible to search for all agents using a specific service. This allows agent groups to be formed and addressed directly.

Architecture of the Multi Agent System

The MAS' architecture and its ways of communication are shown in Figure 3. The central part of the system including its logic is hosted on our main platform. Every used application of participating planners starts a minor container connecting to the major one. This forms a distributed MAS with the ability of communication or migration of agents between different platforms. As stated earlier it also involves the constraint of programmes to possess an API if a direct connection to the main container is necessary.

The so called 'client-agents' placed on the application's containers (e.g. container A, B, and C in Figure 3) have two assignments: listening on input from the project participant in form of changes made on the building model or directly submitted commands/information and communication resp. migration to other containers. With the task of migrating to other containers, client-agents need to be mobile. These agents are not meant to make any decisions but to observe and share their knowledge or gain information by communication with other platforms (e.g. importing IFC-based product data models). The communication with proprietary software is handled with the O2A communication. This requires the software to start the agents' container, so it owns the so called 'container controller'. With the controller, information can be exchanged between the agents and the software's related extension.

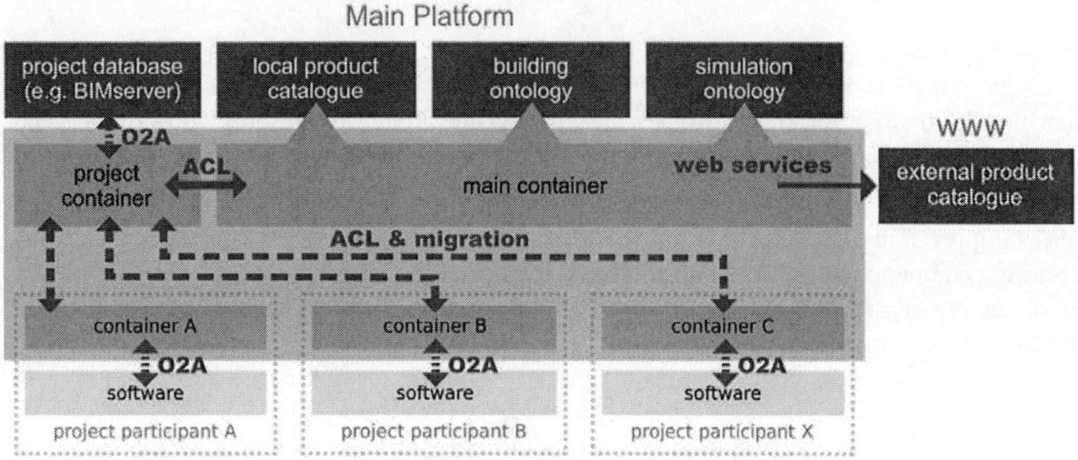

Figure 3: Architecture of the Multi Agent Platform and Ways of Communication

On our collaboration platform, the environment of the MAS on which the agents are operating is set. This induces the main container to be placed on it. To avoid redundancies, we also decided to store the systems logic in this container, meaning agents qualified to read information from data bases like the local product catalogue and ontologies. Additionally, agents that can use web services are living on that container.

The majority of the agents are so called 'element-agents'. Each element-agent represents one building component, is deployed when its component is first instantiated, and holds needed information for identifying the element. This includes the element's IFC GUID, the unique IDs configured by proprietary applications in which it is used as well as the name of the IFC entity it is assigned to.

A hierarchy within the element-agents makes sure that no information will be lost during the building's phases. The relationships between various agents are administered by the DF in the form of service description. The lowest element-agent of the hierarchy represents a specific building element (e.g. window) while the highest represent the abstract idea of the building part (e.g. façade). Any element-agent can have children, depending on the Level of Detail (LoD) used in the model; until it has a child, it will be handled as a representative of a defined component. Only after its children are started, the element-agent gets the state of being abstract. If a lower LoD is asked of the building model (e.g. if the construction planner does not need to know the concreting sections), the abstract parent agents can be used instead of the detailed child agents.

Since the attributes of element-agents are set from information filed in the BIMserver, the agents should be able to communicate with it. As with other software application, this necessitates the BIMserver extension to own the container controller. A BIM-agent living on this container is in permanent contact to the BIMserver and listens for requests made or information shared by it. If a new building element is created within the IFC stored in the BIMserver, the agent starts a new element-agent on the main container. Also, element-agents can communicate with the BIMserver in order to gather information.

Element-agents are placed on the main container since (Cortese et al., 2002) show the performance of inter-agent communication within the JADE framework decreases when the agents are living on the same host but different containers. Since it is more likely for the element-agents to communicate with agents connecting to web-services, ontologies, product databases, and simulations, they are placed on the main container instead of the one started by the BIMserver.

To ensure a clear communication between the agents, ontologies are used. Two separate ontologies are to be distinguished: the building ontology containing the structure of the IFC and their translation to proprietary software classes and the simulation ontology describing needed data for specific simulations depending on the state of the planning process. The agents can, regarding to the subject of their communication, switch between those ontologies.

For examples of application see (Franz et al., in press) who give a brief overview of our MAS' working. They applied our MAS to facilitate the decision making process on where to install energy active façade elements by first checking the applicability based on the selected surfaces and then integrating the selected modules autonomously.

Use Case

For better understanding, the MAS is displayed on a façade in the course of the planning process until the building is put into operation (see Figure 4). In the first picture, the façade is vague and without detail. It only describes the envelope and form of the building. As a simplification of the use case, we assume the building has the form of a cuboid. The façade will be expressed as four surfaces in IFC, which means that four element-agents (A, B, C, and D) are started. Those agents know that they are parts of the building's façade including their cardinal direction. The elements, however, already have attributes describing the functionality and requirements to the façade.

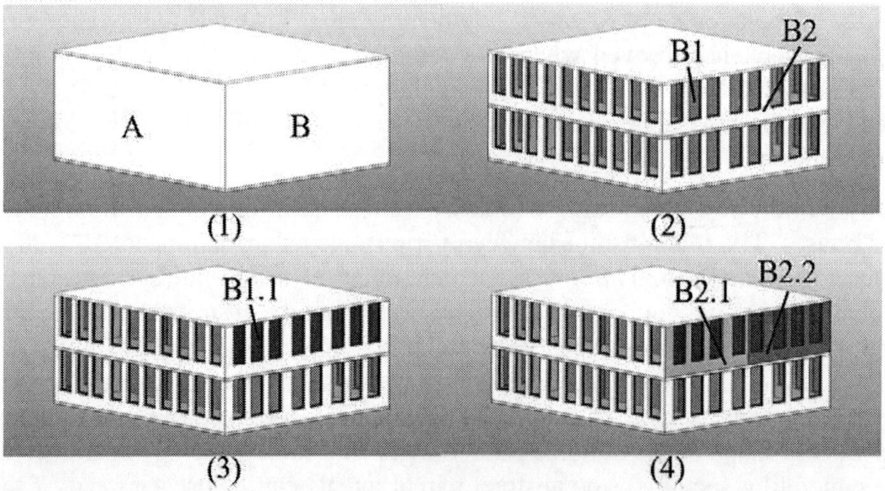

Figure 4: Changes Made on a Building Façade during its Planning Process

Next, we focus on the façade on the front of the building (B). The architect determines the façade to be facing concrete with large windows and sets their dimensions (2). For every window element and concrete wall, an element-agent is started. Each newly started agent (B1 and B2) will search for other agents with the same or related types of building elements. The relation between e.g. façade and window is stored within an ontology. The agents will send messages to semantically matching agents including their location and dimension. If one of the contacted agents lies within these boundaries and does not exactly fit to them, as B does, a reply is sent informing B1 and B2 of the connection between those agents. B1 and B2 will each, after receiving the reply, register their parent B as a service to the DF while B itself deregisters its service since its described component does not exist in the current model anymore.

In the next frame, the architect decides to replace the upper-storey windows of B with BIPV elements. The following actions of the MAS are exemplarily shown on the agents B1 and B1.1. The original agent B1 notices after getting the message of B1.1's dimensions that they are set on the same spot and have the same size. This suggests B1 that it was substituted by B1.1. To prevent redundancies, B1 will send B1.1 a message asking for its attributes and requesting B1.1 to kill itself. The original agent overwrites its former attributes, but keeps its GUID as one of the predecessor elements. After sharing its attributes, B1.1 kills itself.

Another trouble spot occurs when the execution planning is prepared. In the example shown in Figure 4 (4), the execution planner splits the upper-storey wall into two concreting sections. To present them in the model, he splits the wall B2 in two separate walls B2.1 and B2.2. These changes are adopted in the IFC model; other planners would – without the assist of the MAS – have lost information about former process steps the original wall passed. This problem appears only to one of the new walls, though, because the other one (B 2.1) still has the same GUID as B2 since only one wall is newly created. Consequently, one new agent (B2.2) is started. This agent behaves as B1 and B2 did in relation to B; B2, however, does not deregister as its corresponding component is still part of the IFC model. It clones itself and changes its attribute 'relevant revision ID' to the last ones. The clone B2.1 then registers B2 as its parent, too.

Conclusion and Outlook

This work presents the concept of a MAS which is the centre of a collaboration platform designed to facilitate the holistic integration of energy active façade elements. The MAS performs as an OVH in order to prevent information-loss due to varying GUIDs of replaced, altered or split elements. As a result, it allows planners to look up changes made on the model from the very beginning of the planning process independent from radical changes of the model. It also simplifies the handling of different scopes (LoDs) of the model, as information of parent elements can be exchanged, if the concerned planner does not need the detailed version of it.

The presented paper focuses only on the general approach to realise a MAS for generating an Object-oriented Versioning History with the example of energy active façade elements. However, the concept could also be adapted to other problematic civil engineering tasks such as fire safety.

After the architecture of the MAS is implemented, the processes of the integration of energy active façades will be analysed and gained knowledge has to be translated to be machine processible. These rules and processes then need to be integrated into the agents' behaviour and intelligence. Finally, a use case needs to be defined to verify the developed system and its rules.

To enhance the OVH, an email server could be added to the collaboration platform. The agents then could collect information from the email exchange regarding the development of their corresponding building elements. Also, additive information could be linked to the elements, since the first general functional descriptions or wishes expressed by the building owner usually are phrased before the first building model is created.

Acknowledgments

This work is part of the research project *Holistic Integration of Energy Active Facade Components in Building Processes* founded by the German Federal Ministry for Economic Affairs and Energy (BMWi).

References

BIMserver [WWW Document], 2016. . Open Source BIMserver Heart Your BIM. URL http://www.bimserver.org/ (accessed 3.15.16).

Caire, G., 2002. JADE Tutorial Application-Defined Content Languages and Ontologies.

Cortese, E., Quarta, F., Vitaglione, G., Lab, T.I., Direzionale, C., Message, J., System, T., 2002. Scalability and Performance of JADE Message Transport System.

Ed. Züblin AG, 2012. 5D Initiative [WWW Document]. 5D Initiat. URL http://www.5d-initiative.eu/home.php (accessed 2.26.16).

EEG 2014 Gesetz für den Ausbau erneuerbarer Energien, 2014. , EEG 2014.

FIPA, 2002. FIPA ACL Message Structure Specification (Standard No. SC00061G). FIPA, Geneva, Switzerland.

Franz, S., Rüppel, U., Kuhn, T.E., Teizer, J., in press (2016). A Multi-Agent-Based Platform for the Early Integration of Photovoltaic Systems in Building Façades. Presented at the ICCBE 07-2016.

Henning, H.-M., Palzer, A., 2015. Was kostet die Energiewende? - Wege zur Transformation des deutschen Energiesystems bis 2050. Frauenhofer ISE, Freiburg.

Leifgen, C., Kuhn, T.E., Rüppel, U., Teizer, J., in press (2016). BIM-based Collaboration Platform for the Holistic Integration of Energetically Active Façade Components. Presented at the ICCBE 07-2016.

RIBA, 2016. National BIM Library [WWW Document]. Natl. BIM Libr. - Free--Use BIM Objects. URL http://www.nationalbimlibrary.com/ (accessed 3.15.16).

Shehory, O., 2014. Agent-oriented software engineering : reflections on architectures, methodologies, languages, and frameworks. Springer, Berlin [u.a.].

Shehory, O., Sturm, A., 2014. Chapter 1, A Brief Introduction to Agents, in: Agent-Oriented Software Engineering : Reflections on Architectures, Methodologies, Languages, and Frameworks. Springer, Berlin [u.a.].

SOLCONPRO, (2016). solconpro - solar constuction process, http://www.solconpro.de/, accessed February 2016

Sturm, A., Shehory, O., 2014. Chapter 14: The Evolution of MAS Tools, in: Agent-Oriented Software Engineering : Reflections on Architectures, Methodologies, Languages, and Frameworks. Springer Berlin Heidelberg, Oxford, UK.

Theiß, M., 2005. Agentenbasierter Modellverbund am Beispiel des baulichen Brandschutzes in der Gebäudeplanung, Berichte des Instituts für Numerische Methoden und Informatik im Bauwesen. Shaker Verlag, Aachen.

Hypergraphs and Extremal Optimization in 3D Integrated Circuit Design Automation

Katarzyna Grzesiak-Kopeć, Piotr Oramus, Maciej Ogorzałek
Department of Information Technologies, Jagiellonian University in Krakow, Poland
katarzyna.grzesiak-kopec@uj.edu.pl

Abstract. The circuit design task poses an extremely difficult intellectual challenge. The solution has to meet a number of specific requirements and satisfy a variety of constraints. Efficient search of huge and discontinuous spaces requires new non-deterministic and heuristic algorithms. The goal of the research is to minimize the total wire-length of interconnects between sub-circuits. The paper presents a knowledge intensive 3D ICs layout hypergraph representation together with the elaborated neighbourhood optimization heuristics. The results of the Extremal Optimization (EO) implementation applied to the MCNC set of benchmark circuits are reported.

1. Introduction

The spatial arrangement of components which complies with the given requirements and satisfies the set of various constraints is one of the fundamental engineering design tasks. Among the others, it applies to floorplanning of integrated circuits design, building model generation or building reconstruction. It is important not only for scientific research and everyday practical problems, such as urban planning, crisis management or analysis of alternative energy sources, but also for entertainment or virtual reality modeling, as well. It often takes several years of work by a team of specialists to generate an artificial complex and developed 3D environment, like a city. Efficient search of huge and discontinuous spaces which consist of components, objectives and restrictions requires new non-deterministic and heuristic solutions. The automatic generation of three-dimensional (3D) spatial configurations is especially important in the field of architectural design (Müller et al. 2006) and integrated circuits floorplanning (Nain and Chrzanowska-Jeske 2011).

The circuit design task poses an extremely difficult intellectual challenge. The solution has to meet topological, wiring, heating or manufacturability requirements. Floorplanning is the essential and most critical phase in electronic design. It provides early feedback which evaluates architectural decisions, estimates chip areas, and estimates delay and congestion caused by wiring. Even though it has been solved in two-dimensional (2D) spaces, the third dimension cannot be easily adopted to the elaborated algorithmic approaches. The computational complexity and the solution space of the task in 3D is much greater than the one in 2D (Li et al. 2006) and stochastic methods are needed to obtain a globally near-optimal solution.

In (Grzesiak-Kopeć et al. 2014a) a novel approach to 3D ICs layout design has been presented. The proposed method is generic and separates the semantic layer of the specific design task from the presentation layer and the optimization methodology. The design knowledge is provided in the form of predicates that are fed into the generation and optimization procedures. The designer defines a simple shape grammar. The shape grammar supervised by the intelligent derivation controller generates feasible candidate design solutions. The overall search time may be drastically reduced by the application of the emergence phenomenon. The total wire-length of the achieved result may be further optimized with the use of a knowledge intensive 3D ICs layout hypergraph representation

(Grzesiak-Kopeć et al. 2015a) together with the elaborated neighborhood optimization heuristics (Grzesiak-Kopeć et al. 2015b).

The current goal of the research is to minimize the total wire-length of interconnects between sub-circuits. The results of the Extremal Optimization (EO) implementation applied to the MCNC set of benchmark circuits are reported (MCNC 2015).

2. Design Representation

There are many commercial electronic design automation (EDA) tools for 2D ICs layout design. Floorplans may be classified into two categories: slicing floorplans and the non-slicing ones. A slicing floorplan is obtained by recursively cutting the floorplan horizontally or vertically (Nain and Chrzanowska-Jeske 2011). In this case, the solution space is restricted which implies a simpler data structures representation and a faster runtime. However, a non-slicing structure is more general and suitable for most of the real design examples. Hence, various non-slicing floorplan representations has been proposed, namely sequence pair (SP) (Murata et al. 1996), bounded sliceline grid (BSG) (Nakatake et al. 1998), O-tree (Guo et al. 1999), B*-tree (Chang et al. 2000), corner block list (CBL) (Hong et al. 2000), and transitive closure graph (TCG) (Lin and Chang 2001).

Due to the present 3D ICs technology limitations such as a fixed height of the inter-layer or a predefined number of device layers, two classes of 3D floorplans representations are considered: : the true-3D and the quasi-3D ones. Commonly, the true-3D representations are the extensions of the existing 2D ones by introducing the third dimension, like a sequence triple (Yamazaki et al. 2000), a 3D TCG (Bazargan et al. 1999) or a 3D slicing tree (Cheng et al. 2005). Still, since the z-axis generates too much redundancy, the quasi-3D representations (also called 2½D) using arrays of 2D representations for different device layers are in use, e.g. BSG (Deng and Maly 2001) or TCG (Cong et al. 2004).

2.1 Hypergraphs

Graphs are data structures that are particularly suitable for presenting relational structures. Nevertheless, the classical graphs are limited only to binary relations, which may not be sufficient to represent real life problems. This restriction has been removed by hypergraphs that introduce hyperedges to connect not only two but any number of vertices. They have been successfully employed to solve practical problems from many different domains, like architectural design, linear algebra, data mining or information retrieval. They have also been used for ICs layout design (Karypis et al. 1997), especially in respect of the wire-length connection minimization. The connectivity of an electronic circuit is described by a netlist that can be easily map into a hypergraph (Fig. 1). Still, the previously described hypergraph representations and partitioning algorithms split the netlist into tiers using only a single dimension just like in 2D. They assign vertices of a hypergraph to k disjoint nonempty partitions to minimize the sum of weights of hyper-edges that are cut between partitions, and to balance the total vertex weight in each partition. Hence, the k-way partitioning often fails to find a near optimal solution.

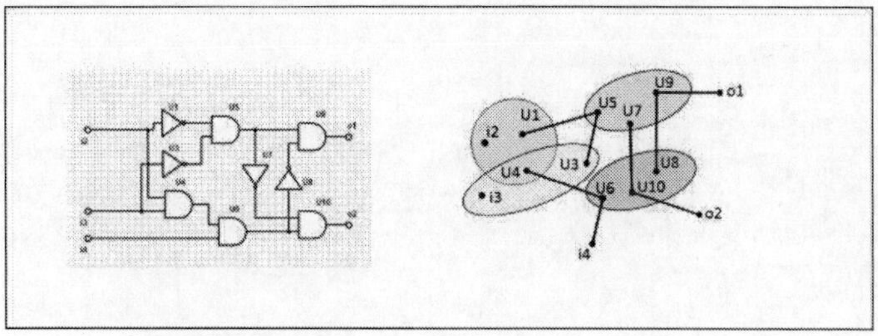

Figure 1: Example: simple logic circuit and the corresponding hypergraph.

2.2 Hierarchical Layout Hypergraphs

The more advance technology becomes, the bigger number of modules has to be placed. To cope with the scalability problem, hierarchical approach should be applied. The hierarchical layout hypergraphs defined in (Grabska et al. 2006) to represent floor-layouts in architectural design are adopted. After (Grabska et al. 2006), a two-step *hierarchical layout hypergraph* (HHG) is introduced. At first, the *layout hypergraph* (HG) is defined and then a *child nesting function* that realizes the hierarchy relation is added.

For $n \in N$, let $[n]$ represent the finite set $\{1,2,\ldots,n\}$, with $[0]=\varnothing$. A function $w:[n]\rightarrow A$ is called a *string* over a set A, where $w=a_1a_2\ldots a_n$ and $w(i)=a_i$ for $i\in[n]$. Let Σ_V, Σ_E be non-empty alphabets of node and hyperedge labels respectively, where $\Sigma_E=\Sigma_C\cup\Sigma_R$ and $\Sigma_C\cap\Sigma_R=\varnothing$. A *layout hypergraph* over $\Sigma=\Sigma_V\cup\Sigma_E$ is a system HG=(V, E, att, lab, ext) where:

1. V is a finite set of vertices,
2. $E=E_C\cup E_R$ is a finite set of hyperedges, where E_C represents object components, E_R represents relations, and $E_C\cap E_R=\varnothing$,
3. $att=(att_S, att_T)$, where $att_S:E\rightarrow V^*$ and $att_T:E\rightarrow V^*$ are attachment functions that assign to hyperedges sequences of source and target nodes respectively, in such a way that $\forall e\in E_C$, $att_S(e)=att_T(e)$,
4. $lb=(lb_V,lb_{EC},lb_{ER})$, where $lb_V:V\rightarrow\Sigma_V$, $lb_{EC}:E_C\rightarrow\Sigma_C$, $lb_{ER}:E_R\rightarrow\Sigma_R$ are labeling functions,
5. $ext:[n]\rightarrow V$ is a mapping specifying a sequence of hypergraph external nodes.

The *external nodes* mapping is added to enable the embedding mechanism of a hyperedge replacement grammar that may be very useful in further research.

The example simple circuit, introduced in Fig. 1, together with the corresponding layout hypergraph is presented in Fig. 2. The hyperedges representing the circuit components are depicted in the form of rectangles and labeled by the corresponding components names (i2, i3, i4, U1, U3, U4,…, U10, o1, o2). The hyperedges reflecting the wire relation are outlined as ellipses. There are 12 wire hyperedges and four of them connect three components while the others are binary connections. Nodes specify pin points for potential connections and are drawn as black dots. Each hyperedge has attached a sequence of source and target nodes and is called non-directed when two sequences are identical.

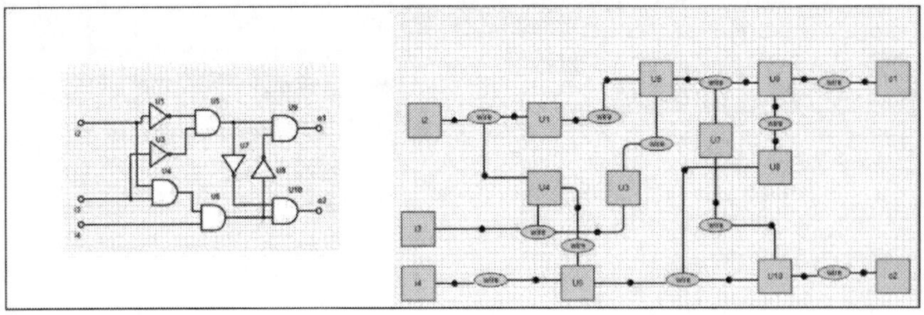

Figure 2: Example: simple logic circuit and the corresponding layout hypergraph.

Now let us add a *child nesting function* $ch:E_C \rightarrow P(A)$, where $A=V \cup E$ is called a set of hypergraph atoms. A *hierarchical layout hypergraph* over $\Sigma=\Sigma_V \cup \Sigma_E$ is a system HHG=(HG, ch) where HG is a layout hypergraph and the following conditions are satisfied:

1. one atom cannot be nested in two different hyperedges: $\forall a \in A \forall e_1, e_2 \in E_C \; a \in ch(e_1) \wedge a \in ch(e_2) \Rightarrow e_1=e_2$,
2. hyperedge cannot be its own child: $\forall e \in E_C \; e \notin ch^+(e)$, where $ch^+(e)$ denotes all descendants of a given hyperedge e,
3. source and target nodes are nested together with their hyperedge: $\forall e_1 \in E \; \exists e_2 \in E_C \; e_1 \in ch(e_2)$: $\forall v_1$ of $att_S(e) \wedge \forall v_2$ of $att_T(e)$ $v_1 \in ch(e_2) \wedge v_2 \in ch(e_2)$.

The hierarchy can be presented at different levels of details. Depending on the currently considering design aspects the hypergraph may be either collapsed or expanded. For example, a single hyperedge may represent the whole components placed in a specific layer.

3. 3D Layout Hypergraph Partitioning

A k-way partitioning of a (hyper)graph is an assignment of vertices to k disjoint and nonempty sets. Usually, it minimizes the sum of hyperedge weights that span multiple partitions and tries to balance the total vertex weight in each partition. Such a constraint k-way partitioning problem is NP-complete for both hypergraphs and graphs (Lengauer 1990).

The most popular and widely used state-of-the-art (hyper)graph partitioners apply Fiduccia-Mattheyses algorithm (Fiduccia and Mattheyses 1982) which is not only computationally effective (a linear time heuristics) but easily adjustable to different objective functions as well. The approach scheme can be divided into three steps, that is coarsening, initial partitioning and uncoarsening. In the time of the coarsening phase, the (hyper)graph is successively contracted until it is small enough to be feasibly partitioned in the initial partitioning phase. The overall quality of the partition is highly dependent on the selected coarsening strategy. The more similar structural properties the smaller graphs exhibit, the better quality of the overall partition is achieved. During the uncoarsening phase the contraction is reversed. The initial partition is projected to the more detailed and expanded graph and a local search algorithm is applied to improve the quality of the partition.

Nevertheless, the state-of-the-art approach scheme completely neglect the third dimension in the 3D space. The 3D partitioning procedures of the netlists into layers are identical in both

2D and 3D spaces. In consequence, they often fail to obtain an acceptable quasi-optimal solution.

3.1 Topological partitioning

Instead of the k-way partitioning of the netlist hypergraph, the 3D topological partitioning of the layout hypergraph has been proposed (Grzesiak-Kopeć et al. 2015b). The main goal is to optimally group interconnected 3D neighborhoods rather than produce the minimal and balanced cut of the graph. Taking into account the grid like structure of a chip, the von Neumann neighborhood definition was chosen. It outlines a diamond-shaped set of cells surrounding a given cell on a 3D grid. To measure the distance between two cells in the IC grid the taxicab metric (the Manhattan distance) is used. It calculates the absolute difference of the Cartesian coordinates of considered cells.The building block hypothesis was adopted that the optimal global solution is the sum of the optimal local neighborhoods.

Considering the layout hypergraph structure, where two different kinds of hyperedges are defined, two different procedures may be applied to generate the initial solution. On the one hand, the chip component hyperedges and their degree (the number of connections) may be first considered. In this case, all the components are sorted in descending order according to the number of connections. At each step, the component with the highest number of connections, that is not placed in the layout, is randomly located in a chip. Then, all of its neighbors (connected components) are located in the nearest possible neighborhood according to the von Neumann neighborhood. On the other hand, the chip wiring hyperedges and their degree (the number of components in one network) may be first considered. In this approach, the biggest networks are placed in a chip before the others. Such an initial solution can be further optimized with a use of some optimization technique.

3.2 Extremal Optimization Implementation

Inspired by self-organized critical (SOC) models and co-evolution the Extremal Optimization (EO) is a generic coevolution approach for hard optimization problems (Boettcher 2000). Unlike the others evolutionary computations that manipulate on the whole population of possible solutions, EO evolves only a single solution $S=\{x_1,x_2,\ldots,x_m\}$by successively eliminating its unsatisfactory features. Every feature has assigned a fitness value. The sum of all this fitness values is the fitness of the solution S. Step by step the feature (x_i) with the worst fitness is eliminated by generating a random solution S' where (x_i) must change. In order to avoid dead ends that may appear in some implementations, a τ control parameter is introduced (the *τ-extremal optimization*). All the features are sorted in ascending order by their fitness values. The new solution S' is generated by swapping two features drawn from a probability distribution:

$$P(k)\propto k^{-\tau},\quad 1\le k\le m \tag{5}$$

In the self-organized critical state, nearly all features are much better than random ones and preserve good values for a long period of time, unless they neighbors are low-adopted.

The solution improves its quality for some time to crash it suddenly (avalanche) just like described by punctuated equilibrium. These avalanches move the search process to different parts of the search space and enable to escape the local optima. This emergent behavior is a result of the negative component selection which is the fundamental principle of the approach. In this manner, the EO is a robust hill climbing technique with embedded diversity mechanism that resembles multiple starting points search. In other words, there is a potential for large hill-climbing fluctuations at any stage of the optimization process (Boettcher 2000).

To implement topological partitioning heuristics the τ-EO was applied. The task is to distribute integrated circuit components in a 3D space to minimize the total wire-length. The search space is defined by a grid cube with predefined maximal volume $X \times Y \times Z$. Each cell in the grid, $(x, y, z) \in X \times Y \times Z$, is either occupied by a component or empty. Every component designate one feature of the solution. The optimal local arrangement of a component is the minimal range neighborhood containing all of its neighbors. Thus, a component fitness value is evaluated as follows:

$$fitness_c = \frac{optimal\_fitness_c}{\sum_{c'} D\left(c_{(x,y,z)}, c'_{(x,y,z)}\right)} \quad (6)$$

where c' is a component connected to c and $c_{(x,y,z)}$ denotes the current grid cell occupied by the component c. Such a definition assures that $fitness_c \in (0,1\rangle$, so the optimal fitness of the solution S is equal to the number of components.

The τ-EO algorithm proceeds in the following way:

```
Create initial solution S and set Sbest=S
Until !STOP repeat:
    (1)for each c evaluate fitnessc
    (2)rank all components according to the fitness value
    (3)draw k1, k2 from P(k) for given τ
    (4)flip a coin and replace component k1 with k2 or put k1 in some free cell in
       a grid
    (5)put k2 in k1 before change
    (6)create S' accordingly and update Sbest if necessary
    (7)S=S'
Return Sbest
```

4. Experimental Results

The MCNC block packing instances is the most common set of benchmark circuits for floorplanning and placement problems (MCNC 2015). They are given in a YAL file format. This benchmark contains five block packing instances. The details of these instances important for our research are given in Table 1. For the three smallest MCNC instances, namely *apte*, *xerox* and *hp*, the optimal wirelength in 2D has been calculated (Funke et al. 2016). The authors also stated that currently, computing wirelength optimal packings for the two largest instances (33 and 49 components) is far beyond the realms of possibility. The optimal wirelengths results together with the results reported in (Funke et al. 2016) for *ami33* and *ami49* are given in Table 2.

The extremal optimization procedure was successfully evaluated in (Grzesiak-Kopeć et al. 2015c). This time, not only the approach itself is examined but also different initial solution generation procedures and their influence on the final result. The YAL files are parsed into hierarchical layout hypergraphs and series of τ-extremal optimization experiments for different $\tau \in \{1.8, 1.9, \ldots, 3.0\}$ were carried out. The τ value equal to 2.7 was selected and results for 1 000 000 runs for each packaging instance are reported in Table 3. The columns denote: (YAL datafile) the instance file name, (grid size) the chip grid size, (optimal fitness) the optimal value for the fitness function, (result fitness/component) and (result fitness/wire) are the obtained fitness values where the initial solution considered either the component hyperedges and its degree or the chip wiring hyperedges and its degree, respectively, (avg optimum) the average optimal solution defined by the size of the average neighbors number (see Table 1), (result optimum) the optimum neighborhood arrangement result.

Table 1: Characteristics of the MCNC benchmark instances.

YAL datafile	Blocks	Nets	Neighbors no		
			Min	max	Avg
apte.yal	9	97	8	8	8
xerox.yal	10	203	9	9	9
hp.yal	11	83	5	10	7
ami33.yal	33	123	32	32	32
ami49.yal	49	408	2	35	18

Table 2: Optimal wirelengths for apte, xerox, and hp for the original die size (after Funke et al. 2012). Wirelegth for ami33 and ami49 after (Funke et al. 2016). Areas are given in μm^2.

YAL datafile	original size	Wirelength *optimal
apte.yal	10 500 × 10 500	513 061*
xerox.yal	5 831 × 6 412	370 993*
hp.yal	4 928 × 4 200	153 328*
ami33.yal	2 058 × 1 463	58 627
ami49.yal	7 672 × 7 840	640 509

The average optimal solution is received by a calculation from the formula (3). For *ami49* where the average neighbors number is 18, the average distance from a component to its neighbors is the sum of 6 neighbors at distance of 1 and 12 at distance of 2 which is 30.

Table 3: The τ-EO results for the MCNC benchmark.

YAL datafile	grid size	optimal fitness	result fitness		avg optimum	result optimum
			component	Wire		
apte.yal	2×2×3	9	5,8307	5,9865	10·9=90	136
xerox.yal	2×2×3	10	6,8295	6,8295	12·10=120	178
hp.yal	2×2×3	11	7,7867	7,8075	6·11=66	140
ami33.yal	3×3×4	33	22,8793	22,8885	66·33=2178	3184
ami49.yal	4×4×4	49	27,3801	27,0710	30·49=1470	2698

As demonstrated by the numerical data, the initial component layout basically does not matter for the final result, which was expected for a fine defined extremal optimization task. Graphing the solution quality over the algorithm iterations (time) shows the highest dynamics diversity in the case of *ami49* circuit. It is more sparse than other instances which makes it more appropriate for the proposed method. The results are presented both as the optimal fitness function value and as the total sum of neighbors distances as well. The second value (result optimum in Table 3) is the one that describes the probable total wire-length given in the number of intercellular grid connections. Such an approach goes far beyond current technological capabilities. However, what is not possible today may be possible tomorrow and the range of this numbers comparing to the actually viable solutions given in Table 2, even taking into account the units conversion, is encouraging.

Generated layout examples for each MCNC instance are presented in Fig. 5 and Fig.6. The chip grid size is no smaller than the number of components that is why there are some empty cells present. The cell sizes are adjusted to the component dimensions.

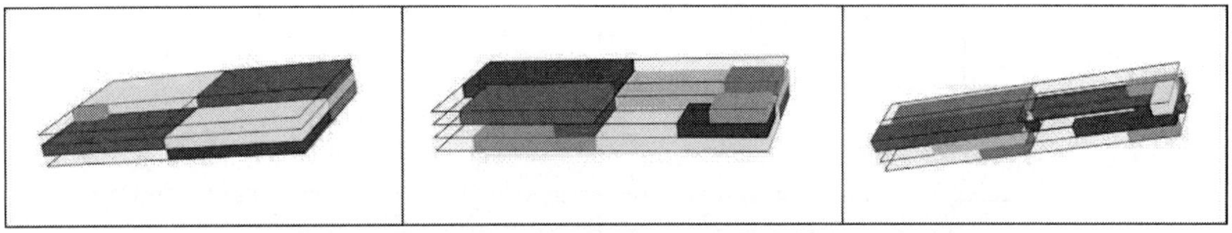

Figure 5: The solution for *apte*, *xerox* and *hp.*

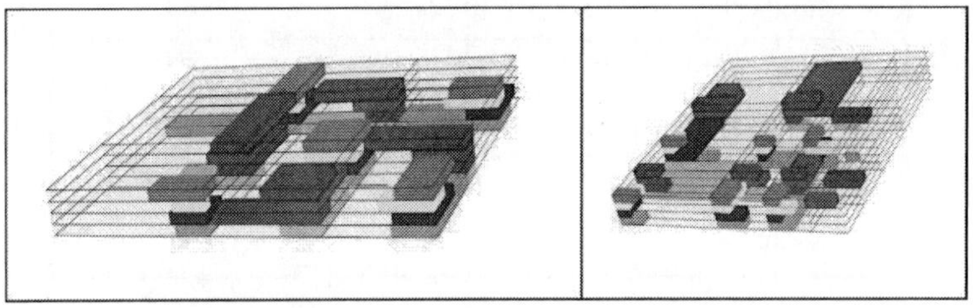

Figure 5: The solution for *ami33* and *ami49.*

5. Conclusions

This paper presents a new approach to the total wire-length minimization in the 3D ICs design. It combines a layout hypergraph representation that perfectly reflects possible relations among chip components and the original optimal neighborhood heuristics. Instead of the minimal and balanced cut of the hypergraph, the optimal grouping of interconnected 3D neighborhoods was applied and implemented with the use of the τ-extremal optimization algorithm. The proposed approach was successfully evaluated using the MCNC set of benchmark circuits.

Acknowledgements

Research supported by FNP under the Program "Master": "New computational approaches for solving next generation microelectronic design problems".

References

Karypis, G., Aggarwal, R, Kumar, V., Shekhar, S. (1997). Hypergraph Partitioning: Application in VLSI domain, In Proceedings of 34th Annual Conference on. Design Automation, DAC 1997, pp. 526–529.

Grabska, E., Grzesiak-Kopeć, K., Lembas, J., Łachwa, A., Ślusarczyk, G. (2006). Hypergraphs in Diagrammatic Design, in K. Wojciechowski et al. (eds.), Computational Imaging and Vision 32, Springer, pp. 111-117.

Li, Z., Hong, X., Zhou, Q., Cai, Y., Bian, J., Yang, H.H., Pitchumani, V., Cheng, Ch.-K. (2006) Hierarchical 3-D Floorplanning Algorithm for Wirelength Optimization, in Circuits and Systems I: Regular Papers, IEEE Transactions on , vol. 53(12), pp. 2637-2646.

Grzesiak-Kopeć, K., Ogorzałek, M. (2014a) Computer-Aided 3D ICs Layout Design, Computer-Aided Design and Applications, 2014, vol. 11(3), pp. 318–325.

Grzesiak-Kopeć, K., Ogorzałek, M. (2015a) 3D ICs layout hypergraph representation, Computer-Aided Design and Applications, vol. 12 (4) , pp. 425–430.

Grzesiak-Kopeć, K., Ogorzałek, M. (2015b) Extremal Optimization Approach to 3D Design of Integrated Circuits Layouts, The 7th International Conference on Advanced Computational Intelligence (ICACI), pp. 411-414.

Grzesiak-Kopeć, K., Oramus, P., Ogorzałek, M. (2015c) Using shape grammars and extremal optimization in 3D IC layout design, Microelectronic Engineering, vol. 148, pp. 80-84.

MCNC (2015) The MCNC set of benchmark circuits: http://lyle.smu.edu/~manikas/Benchmarks/

MCNC_Benchmark_Netlists.html, Retrieved on June 9, 2015.

Lengauer, T. (1990) Combinatorial algorithms for integrated circuit layout. John Wiley & Sons, Inc., 1990.

Fiduccia, C. M., Mattheyses, R. M. (1982) A Linear-time Heuristic for Improving Network Partitions, DAC, pp. 175-181.

Boettcher, S. (2000) Extremal optimization: heuristics via coevolutionary avalanches, Computing in Science & Engineering, vol. 2 (6), pp. 75–82.

Funke, J. and Hougardy, S. and Schneider, J. (2016) An Exact Algorithm for Wirelength Optimal Placements in VLSI Design, Integration, the VLSI Journal, vol. 52, pp. 355-366.

Nain, R.-K.; Chrzanowska-Jeske, M. (2011) Fast placement-aware 3-D floorplanning using vertical constraints on sequence pairs, IEEE Transactions on Very Large Scale Integration (VLSI) Systems, 19(9), pp. 1667–1680.

Müller, P., Wonka, P., Haegler, S. et al. (2006) Procedural modeling of buildings, ACM Trans. Graph. 25(3), pp. 614–623.

Cong, J., Wei, J., Zhang, Y. (2004) A thermal-driven floorplanning algorithm for 3D ICs, in Proc. ICCAD, Nov. pp. 306–313.

Nakatake, S., Fujiyoshi, K., Murata, H. et al. (1998) Module packing based on the BSG-structure and IC layout applications, Computer-Aided Design of Integrated Circuits and Systems, IEEE Transactions, 17(6), pp. 519-530.

Guo, P., Cheng, Ch., Yoshimura, T. (1999) An O-tree representation of non-slicing floorplan and its applications, Design Automation Conference, pp. 268-273.

Chang, Y., Chang, Y., Wu, G. et al. (2000) B*-trees: a new representation for non-slicing floorplans, Design Automation Conference, pp. 458-463.

Hong, X., Huang, G., Cai, Y. et al. (2000) Corner block list: an effective and efficient topological representation of non-slicing floorplan, Computer Aided Design, ICCAD-2000, pp. 8-12.

Lin, J., Chang, Y. (2001) TCG: a transitive closure graph-based representation for non-slicing floorplans, Design Automation Conference, pp. 764-769.

Yamazaki, H., Sakanushi, K., Shigetoshi. N. et al. (2000) The 3D-Packing by Meta Data Structure and Packing Heuristics(Special Section on Discrete Mathematics and Its Applications), IEICE Trans. Fundamentals, 83(4), pp. 639-645.

Bazargan, K., Kastner, R., Sarrafzadeh, M. (1999) 3-D floorplanning: simulated annealing and greedy placement methods for reconfigurable computing systems, Rapid System Prototyping, pp. 38-43.

Cheng, L., Deng, L., Wong, M. (2005) Floorplanning for 3-D VLSI design, Design Automation Conference, 2005. Proceedings of the ASP-DAC, pp. 405-411.

Deng, Y., Maly, W. (2001) Interconnect characteristics of 2.5-D system integration scheme. In Proceedings of the 2001 international symposium on Physical design (ISPD '01). ACM, New York, NY, USA, pp. 171-175.

How To Predict Behavior At Risk – Educational Game Story Analysis

Iwona Grabska-Gradzińska
Faculty of Physics, Astronomy and Applied Computer Science,
Jagiellonian University, Kraków, Poland
iwona.grabska@uj.edu.pl

This paper discusses the prospects of using layered graphs for eye-tracking video game analyzing especially serious game, where player attention affects learning activity. It is shown how the user strategy can be described by graph structure. Eye tracking system is used for examination of user's attention and interest and perception related to understanding and recall. Comparing user decisions with eye-tracking data give us possibilities to make correlations between user's perception of object shown during the gameplay and his decisions. Visual elements of game scene impact on user's decision and can support or disturb learning process. Two types of games were analysed for this paper: adventure game and serious game based on occupational safety and health.

1. Introduction

The challenge of the narrative game design process, especially game with educational aim, is to show real word dependencies both in easy, attractive and educationally effective way. The means that knowledge base (e.g. rules how to escape building in fire) have to be transformed into authentic and adequate scenarios and have to push player to act. It is extremely important to examine which elements of gameplay environment are the base of user decisions: object of scene, components of HUD (heads-up display, i.e. display several pieces of information including the main character's health, items, and an indication of game progression as a part of user interface), dialogs with Non-Player Characters (NPCs) or player general knowledge. The holistic model based on the gameplay graph that represents the current state of the game and eye-tracking data system associated with every state help to compare users' strategies and to recognize visual factors impacting on decision. [1,2]

In game design eye-tracking systems are used both in character control [14] and analysis, both top-down or bottom-up approaches. [15] Eye tracking systems are often used during the examination of user's attention and interest and perception related to understanding and recall. [10] Especially in serious game research it is used for checking which elements of the game grasp players' attention and how it influences the learning activity. [13] One connected to the gameplay graph gives possibility to analyze information of user perception of game environment in the moment and just before, making the decisions in the gameplay. [11]

1.1 Apparatus and Participants

Two types of games were chosen to take into consideration: one is adventure game based on classic Polish folktale with no education aim. It is academic teaching project with no commercial use. Second is a serious game based on occupational safety and health (OSH) rules. Player has to find the way out of the burning building. This game is used in Jagiellonian University as a part of OSH training for students and stuff since 2008.

Data was collected during the sessions of gameplay (students of the Jagiellonian University and the author). The used equipment was The Eye Tribe tracker (specification at https://theeyetribe.com/)

2. Aim

The questions were: which element of scene was taken into consideration a while before decision? (for example: emergency exit pictograms, fire extinguisher, doors, windows), which HUD components impacted on the decision: (equipment list, scene description)? How long does it take to change location (what influenced that?), how long was the whole game, how many breaks (too long brake may suggest seeking for answer in external sources). Answers were associated with user strategies.

The first game Shoemaker and Dragon (further called SD) gives the user three different ways to achieve the essential aim. There were no clear instructions about possible moves, only the introduction to the narrative, which is based on the old polish about a young shoemaker and a dragon. The player takes the role of the young Shoemaker and his quest is to defend the land against a Dragon. After doing it, he may marry the Princess and get right to rule the land as a consequence. Thus we can track graph productions that reflect players' decisions and compare them.

There are four sources of knowledge used during the gameplay: text summary of the scene in the top left part of the screen, player's equipment tray in the right corner, image shown characters in the scene and potential source of information: knowledge of this folktale got at school or while reading children's books.

For every player it was possible to retrace his moves and decisions and compare to his eye's gaze. Due to graph system we can check not only checkpoints during the game (what is provided in many other gameplay analysis) but also sequences of activity categorised as generic productions. The variety of solving the problem give us different interesting strategy graphs.

Fig 1. Screenshot from the game SD.

While playing the second game John in Distress (further called JD) user has only one strategy of behaviour, he has to run out of the burning building and its strategy is clearly said in the introduction to the game. The challenge is to do it as quick as it is possible and not be killed by the fire in the meantime. The decision to be made is where to go, right or left and take or not elements of equipment e.g. fire extinguisher, and answer questions about safety rules.

In general, the right decision brings us closer to the final goal, and wrong decision terminate the game as our death in fire. The strategy graph is very simple, but we got additional information e.g. time spent to make the right decision and the eye movement before making it, so researches can check elements influenced the decision.

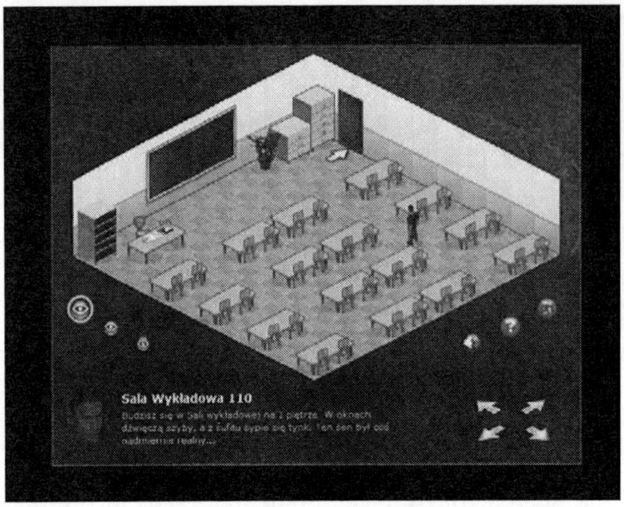

Fig 2. Screenshot from the game JD.

3. Formal Definitions

Graphs used for gameplay modeling were formally defined in our previous paper [3], which in turn was inspired by [7]. Let us recall those definitions.

Let L be an alphabet of labels for nodes and edges. Let A be a nonempty, finite set of attributes. For every $a \in A$, let D_a be a fixed, nonempty set of its admissible values, called the domain of a. If f is a function, then let f^+ be its transitive closure.

Definition 1. A *hierarchical graph* is a system

$$G = (V, E, s, t, ch, lab, atr),$$

where:

- V and E are finite disjoint sets of *nodes* and *edges*, respectively,
- $s : E \rightarrow V$ *and* $t : E \rightarrow V$ are *edge source* and *edge target functions*,
- $ch : V \cup E \rightarrow 2^{V \cup E}$ is a *child nesting function* such that $\forall x \in V \cup E : x \notin ch^+(x)$,
- $lab : V \cup E \rightarrow L$ is a *labeling function*, and
- $atr : V \cup E \rightarrow 2^A$ is an *attributing function*.

Child nesting function enables to define hierarchical graphs.

Let par: $V \cup E \rightarrow V \cup E \cup \{\perp\}$ be a function such that $\forall x, y \in V \cup E : par(x) = y \Leftrightarrow x \in ch(y)$. This inverse of the children function is known as a *parent function*.

Def. 1 determines types of attributes for nodes and edges. A graph instance needs values of attributes and is defined as follows:

Definition 2. By a *graph instance* we mean:

$$I = (V, E, s, t, ch, lab, atr, val),$$

where:

- $(V, E, s, t, ch, lab, atr)$ is a hierarchical graph,
- $val : (V \cup E) \times A \rightarrow D$, with $D = \cup_{a \in A} D_a$, is a partial function such that for all $x \in V \cup E$ and for all $a \in A$ if $a \in atr(x)$ then $val(x, a) \in D_a$.

Let us assume that L (the set of labels) consists of three disjoint subsets Σ_V, Σ_D, and Σ_U, which are used to label nodes, directed edges and undirected edges. Furthermore, let $Y = \{Y_1, Y_2, \ldots Y_n\}$ be a partition of Σ_V.

Definition 3. Graph G or instance I is *layered* if and only if:

$$\forall x \in V : lab(x) \in Y_i \Rightarrow lab(V \cap ch^+(x)) \in Y_i$$

(i.e., a node and all its descendant nodes have labels from the same layer).

Gameplay graphs have four layers, thus:

$$Y = \{PLOT, CHAR, LOC, ITEM\}.$$

Morphisms are mappings between graphs. They preserve graph structure (two nodes connected by an edge in the source graph must be mapped to target graph nodes which also have an edge between them), labels, attributes, and parent-child relations.

Definition 4. A *graph morphism* from G into H is defined as a function

$$f : V_G \cup E_G \rightarrow V_H \cup E_H$$

such that:

- $f(V_G) \subset V_H, f(E_G) \subset E_H$,
- $\forall e \in E_G : f(s_G(e)) = s_H(f(e)) \wedge f(t_G(e)) = t_H(f(e))$,
- $\forall x, y \in V_G \cup E_G : x \in ch_G(y) \Rightarrow f(x) \in ch_H(f(y))$ and $par_G(x) = par_G(y) \Rightarrow par_H(f(x)) = par_H(f(y))$,
- $\forall x \in V_G \cup E_G : lab_G(x) = lab_H(f(x))$,
- $\forall x \in V_G \cup E_G : atr_G(x) \subset atr_H(f(x))$.

In this paper, morphisms are used in two places: to establish correspondence between common parts of the left- and right-hand sides of the production, and to fix a match between the left-hand side and a fragment of the gameplay instance graph.

Formally, in the second case it is not a morphism, because morphisms map graphs into other graphs. Let us call it "a match", and define as a function from a graph into a graph instance such that it has the same properties as morphisms.

Definition 5. G is a subgraph of H if and only if:

- $f(V_G) \subset V_H, f(E_G) \subset E_H$,
- $s_G, t_G, ch_G, lab_G, atr_G$, are defined as restrictions of $s_G, t_G, ch_G, lab_G, atr_G$, respectively.

I is a *subinstance* of J if and only if:

- $f(V_I) \subset V_J, f(E_I) \subset E_J$,
- $s_I, t_I, ch_I, lab_I, atr_I, val_I$ are defined as restrictions of s_J, t_J, ch_J, lab_J, atr_J, val_J, respectively.

Definition 6. A *graph production* is defined as a triple:

$$p = (r : L \rightarrow R, \pi, F)$$

where:

- L and R are graphs and r is an injective partial graph morphism,
- π is an application condition, i.e. a function which takes as its arguments the instance being transformed and the match, and returns a Boolean value,
- F is a family of attribute valuators, i.e. functions which take the same arguments as π and return values for attributes in newly created nodes and edges,
- $\forall x \in V_R \cup E_R,\ a \in atr_R(x) : \exists!\, f_{x.a} \in F$ *with* D_a as its range.

Nodes and edges mapped by r are known as "the context", and are preserved when the production is applied. This definition is based on the definition of single-pushout productions [8], with π and F added. Another way of extending the SPO formalism hinges on generalizing the notion of label matching, so that the left-hand side can, e.g., have a node labeled as „any label from the plot layer".

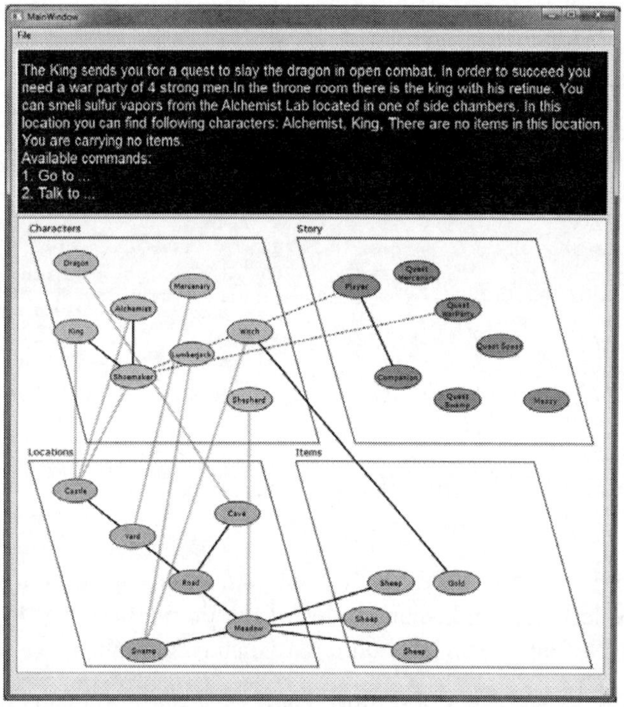

Figure 3: Screenshot of the game with the debugging graph.

Definition 7. A *generic production* is a production in which L and R are defined over $\Sigma_V \cup Y$ as their set of node labels.

That is, a node can have either an ordinary label (Σ_V is the set of node labels used in the gameplay graph), or it can be labeled with a name of a layer (Y is the set of gameplay graph layers). This special Y-labels can be only assigned to nodes from L, and to those nodes from R corresponding to them.

Generic productions cannot be applied directly. They are merely a notational shortcut, able to represent a whole family of ordinary productions in a compact way. To expand a generic production, find one of Y-labeled nodes; let us assume that we found $x \in L$ which has Y_i as its label. Y_i is a set of ordinary node labels. Generate a set of derived productions by assigning consecutive elements from Y_i as labels for x (and for $r(x)$, if it is defined). Repeat the whole procedure until there are no more nodes with Y-labels.

The resulting set of productions contains ordinary productions, which can be applied to graph instances.

The process of applying a production to a graph instance I begins with searching I for a fragment which matches the left-hand side, i.e. for an injective match $m : L \rightarrow I$. After the match is found, the application condition π is evaluated. If π returns false, then the production cannot be applied at this place and the whole process must restart at an alternative match. Fail if no more matches can be found.

If π is true, then the construction of the resulting instance J can begin. Start by assuming $J = I$. In the first step remove from J nodes and edges belonging to $m(L - r^{-1}(R))$, i.e., those nodes and edges from the left-hand side which are not part of the context. Delete recursively any children, if they had them. Delete any dangling edges that may be left after node removal.

In the second step add to J a copy of $R - m(L)$. Reroute edges which were attached to context nodes to their corresponding nodes in J, i.e., if an edge was attached to $r(x)$ for some $x \in L$, then reroute it to $m(x)$.

In the third step define $m' : R \rightarrow J$. Let $m'(x) = m(r^{-1}(x))$ for $x \in m(L)$, $m'(x) = x$ for $x \in R - m(L)$. Then go over F and calculate new attribute values. Let $val_J(m'(x), a) = f_{x,a}(I, m)$ for all $x \in V_R \cup E_R$, $a \in atr_R(x)$. It can be noticed that this not only assigns values to newly created nodes and edges, but can also update values in the context.

4. Game Story Structure Analysis

Participant task was to complete the game and he had several different paths to do so. The story provokes various user strategies. Thus we can track graph productions that reflect players' decisions and compare them. All users' decisions were included in User Strategy Graph. Every game session was recorded and eye movement information was collected. Heat maps and gaze plots for every scene were created and statistics for eye movement were prepared.

Problem: In which decision moment user is confused and not sure what to do

The first question about decision made by user is to find the situations in the game, where user is not sure what to do and find out what influence his final decision.

Researcher can analyse production used by user during the gameplay to find schemas suggesting uncertenity. First indicator was the time of gameplay compared to average (7,25 s for JD and 4,32 for SD). Into consideration was taken 7 longest gameplays od each game. The next step was to use generic productions category to distinguish the story important productions and the trivial ones. There were calculated indicators:

- Obscurity: the ratio of all productions where the player character was involved (story-important and trivial) to unique story-important ones. High obscurity suggests that the player just wandered aimlessly.
- Ramification: the ratio of total unique story-important productions performed to the actual shortest path to victory. High ramification means that the player followed longer

storylines or multiple storylines simultaneously and this suggests that he could not easily foresee the story or felt intrigued by other possibilities.

- Replayability: the ratio of all story-important productions the game offered to unique story-important productions performed. High replayability suggests the game could be played again in a different way.

Then there was taken into consideration the longest time periods between two story-important productions and eye-tracking gaze path was analyzed.

The conclusion gives us the schema of uncertainty in SD: players quickly collect all items which can be taken from ground and keep by user, but then walk around all locations and try to talk to all NPCs (perhaps seeking for additional items in every available location). Some players give up in this moment, some spend lot of time to seek the hint. Gameplay speed up again when player found himself in the cave in front of dragon with only the dead sheep and the sulfur. Players guessed that they can use this equipment to poison the dragon, but, what is interesting, nobody give one look to the equipment tray, which turned out completely useless.

Figure 4: Typical process of looking for solution of difficult situation in the game. No single look on the equipment tray on the right.

An unexpected result of our research was finding a fault in the story by our students. Some of them fed a sheep to the dragon again and again and let him grow into power. The sheep was designed to be fed to the dragon, but according to the original story it should have been stuffed with sulfur before. Designers knew the story and didn't try to feed the dragon with a raw sheep.

In the JD game there was no moment of uncertainty while choosing the way out of the building. The delay between story-important productions was connected with the longitude of corridors (in this game time of changing location depend of the longitude, in JD the time of movement was fixed). The problem for players were to make the right decision: about fire extinguisher usage, way of opening doors and windows. Wrong decisions were death sentences and the game ended with defeat. That's why story-important and trivial productions interlaced regularly with no long periods of just trivial ones.

This result of absolute certainty where to go insinuate doubts of researchers and made us pose the next question:

Problem: Perception of emergency signs in decision-making process

The question was: if fire exit signs influenced user decision where to go while running out of the building? In real situations they are the main indicator of emergency way in unknown building. There were such signs visualized in the gameplay. If they were omitted by player, there is next question: what gives the user advise where to go?

Figure 5: Emergency exit sign used in the game

Scenes with fire exit signs visible on the wall was taken into consideration. The big facilitation was the fact, that it is the platform game, that means among others, that we see the stage from the same point of view above all the time.

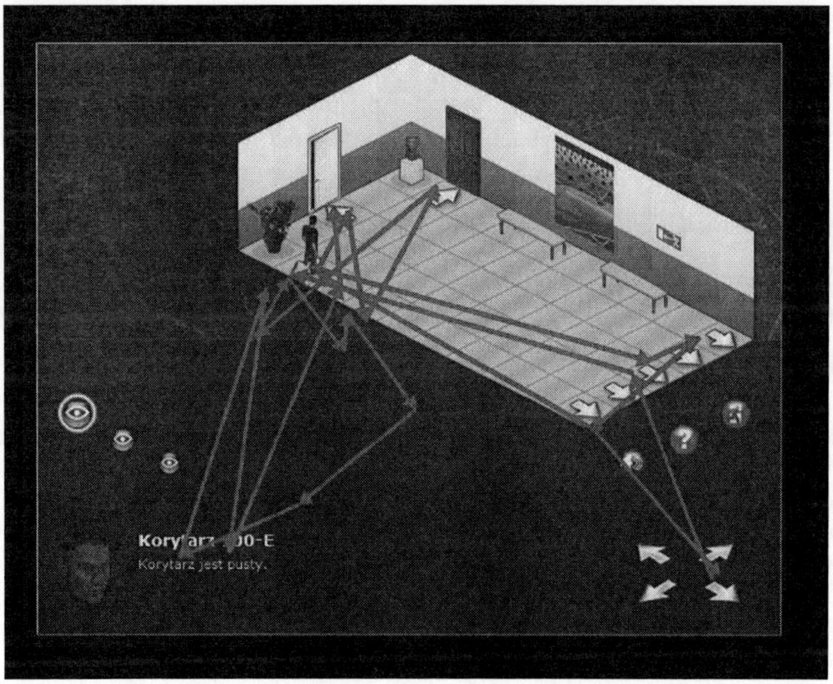

Figure 5: Typical process of seeking the way out

The results were unexpected and worrying. This educational game does not teach users to pay attention for emergency signs during the evacuation from the fire, because there are very attention-grabbing yellow arrows showing possible movement on the stage (elements of

HUD, not the scenery) and they were the only noticed tips where to go. Players in 90% cases chose the one of the top-left yellow arrow. No one gave a single look to emergency signs.

5. Implementation

The graph model is currently developed in the Games Technology Department of Jagiellonian University. A game engine was built in C++ using Qt5. Communication with the eye-tracking system (The Eye Tribe tracker, 60 Hz, with latency <20 ms) was established with open API that relies on the standard TCP/IP protocol using open-source runtime environment Node.js and Java application.

6. Conclusions

There are benefits of using graphs for representing knowledge – representing gameplay models and their modifications in mathematical terms of graph grammars will give us an opportunity to formally reason about their properties, and automatize analysis of gamers decision under given conditions. Thanks to generic productions researcher can categorize all users actions into groups of different importance and find schemas and interlaces of decisions of different categories. In typical gameplay analysis without graph support we can only use milestones between long sequences of player movements. There is a problem with implementation of the strategy graph in big entertainment games with a lot of characters and side quests, but in simple decision games possibility to find activity and decision schema and take it into consideration on different levels of detail (levels of subgraphs or nodes and productions and generic productions) is very useful.

Comparing user decisions with eye-tracking data give us possibilities to make correlations between user's perception of object shown during the gameplay and his decisions. Visual elements of game scene impact on user's decision. Sometimes the wrong decisions in level design make wining the game (which means – make learning the right reactions in case of emergency) significantly harder.

References

1. C.Aldrich, Simulations and Seriuos Games, 2002.
2. J.Juul, "What computer games can and can't do", 2000.
3. I.Grabska-Gradzińska, B.Porębski, W.Palacz, E.Grabska, "Towards a graph-based model of computer games", AITC 2012, pp. 34-39, ACEEE, 2012.
4. J.Dormans and S.Bakkes, "Generating Missions and Spaces for Adaptable Play Experiences", IEEE Trans. on Computational Intelligence and AI in Games, 2011.
5. A.Paszyńska, E.Grabska, M.Paszyński, "A Graph Grammar Model of the hp Adaptive Three Dimensional Finite Element Method". Fundamenta Informaticae, vol. 114 no. 2, 2012.
6. I.Grabska-Gradzińska, B.Porębski, W.Palacz, E.Grabska, "Graph-Based Data Structures of Computer Games", Procedings of CGAT 2013.
7. W.Palacz, "Algebraic hierarchical graph transformation", JCSS, 2004.
8. G.Rozenberg (ed.), Handbook of Graph Grammars and Computing by Graph Transformation, World Scientific, 1997.
9. R.D.Coyne, M.A.Rosenman, A.D.Radford, M.Balachandran, J.S.Gero: Knowledge-based Design System, Sydney, 1990.

10. NHM Zain, FHA Razak, A Jaafar, MF Zulkipli, Eye tracking in educational games environment: evaluating user interface design through eye tracking patterns, Visual Informatics: Sustaining Research and Innovations, 64-73
11. C. Conati, N. Jaques, M. Muir, Understanding Attention to Adaptive Hints in Educational Games: An Eye-Tracking Study, Artif Intell Educ (2013) 23:136–161
12. Duchowski A. Eye Tracking Methodology: Theory and Practice, Springer-Verlag New York, Inc. Secaucus, NJ, USA ©2003
13. K. Kiili, H. Ketamo, M. D. Kickmeier-Rust, Eye Tracking in Game-based Learning Research and Game Design, International Journal of Serious Games, Volume 1, Issue 2, April 2014
14. V. Sundstedt, Gazing at Games: An Introduction to Eye Tracking Control, Morgan & Claypool, 2012.
15. S. Alkan, K. Cagiltay, Studying computer game learning experience through eye tracking. British Journal of Educational Technology 2007, 38(3), 538-542.

Knowledge based Bridge Engineering - Artificial Intelligence meets Building Information Modeling

Dominic Singer, Maximilian Bügler, André Borrmann
Chair of Computational Modeling and Simulation
Leonhard Obermeyer Center, Technische Universität München, Germany
dominic.singer@tum.de

Abstract. In the research project "KBE4Infra", knowledge-based engineering (KBE) techniques for capture, storage and reuse of engineering knowledge in bridge engineering are investigated. A rich data source of bridge engineering knowledge, are Bridge Management Systems (BMS). The work present addresses the question, whether it is possible to gain knowledge by the use of data in bridge management systems and how this knowledge can be used beneficially in conceptual bridge design phases. To achieve this, we propose the use of a Bayesian network. Thus, we introduce and review well known network learning and inference algorithms for Bayesian networks. Then, promising methods are matched to the needs of the proposed approach. Finally, a proof of concept will show the practicality of the chosen approach.

1. Introduction

In the research project "KBE4Infra", knowledge-based engineering (KBE) techniques for capture, storage and reuse of engineering knowledge in bridge engineering are investigated (Singer et al. 2015). In the course of this project, generation and comparison of various design alternatives in early design phases are mainly taken into account. KBE aims at the *"the use of advanced software techniques to capture and re-use product and process knowledge in an integrated way"* (Stokes 2001). Compared to previous approaches, the present system is strongly based on building information modeling. Furthermore, visual programming is used for the geometric semantic modeling of the bridge. This enables the possibility of real-time modelling, evaluation, and optimization of bridge structures. While setting up a knowledge base and an inference engine, formalizing engineering knowledge in computer interpretable rules is the most important and difficult step.
In recent years, Artificial Intelligence (AI) techniques have been intensively researched in civil engineering (Lu et al. 2012; Schneider et al. 2015). In the course of these studies, the use of expert systems, rule-based systems, knowledge-based engineering, case-based reasoning, neural networks, machine learning, and their underlying technologies like first order logic, fuzzy logic, forward and backward chaining, semantic networks, genetic programming were investigated to enhance typical civil engineering tasks. In bridge engineering, the application of AI methods was considered for various tasks throughout bridge lifecycle phases, like in conceptual design, analysis, construction, operation, and maintenance. To the present day, these systems have hardly reached a broader use in practice for several reasons (Reich 1995): The research was often focused on narrow and specialized engineering subtasks, not on larger and more integrated problems. In addition, a building product model was not yet established and therefore not used. However, a product model, acting as a communication base, is indispensable to gain reliable design solutions, since in bridge engineering design tasks interact closely and influence each other.

Currently, a fundamental change in the Architecture, Engineering and Construction (AEC) industry by the introduction of the Building Information Modeling (BIM) technology (Eastman et al. 2011) takes place. BIM aims to represent the complete building facility in a digital product model (Eastman 1999), which is used throughout the whole life-cycle. Furthermore, parametric modeling is more and more incorporated for the design of infrastructure facilities (Boeykens 2012). Apart from that, the Industry Foundation Classes (IFC), a non-proprietary data-format for the exchange of product models, has already reached a convenient level. This data format has the potential to increase the integration of existing analysis tools in the design workflow of bridges dramatically in the near future. Figure 1 shows a building information model of reinforced concrete road bridge in a low to mid level of detail.

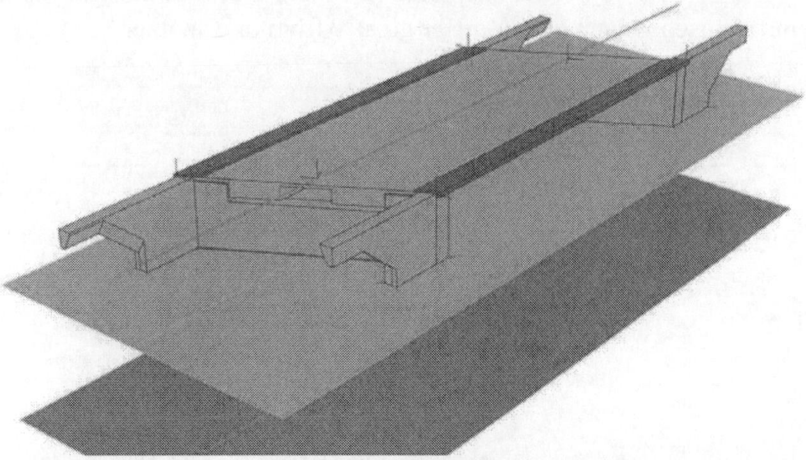

Figure 1: Building information model of a bridge

As part of knowledge modeling, knowledge representation and inference, suitable existing AI methods have to be chosen. In this paper, we propose to use a Bayesian network to achieve these tasks. Therefore, we introduce and review well known network learning and inference algorithms for Bayesian networks. Then, promising methods are matched to the needs of the proposed KBE approach for bridge engineering. Finally, a proof of concept will show the practicality of the chosen approach.

2. Problem definition

Preliminary design focuses on the exploration of various design options leading to an optimal or near-optimal design solution with regard to technical, ecological, creative, and economic aspects of the planned structure. The generated design solution serves as a basis for determining the construction costs, preparing the tendering, elaborating the detailed design, and finally executing the construction work itself. The design of bridge structures is a highly iterative process, which is heavily dependent on external conditions, such as the location and the intended function of the structure.

As part of the bridge design, a bridge structure is described by the essential design elements like superstructure, substructure, foundation, abutment, bearing, bridge equipment, materials and construction methods. For each component a very large number of corresponding regulations and guidelines specifying the design and function exists. The design for each bridge is mainly dependent on the boundary conditions like alignment and traffic type or the existing terrain and soil conditions found in-situ. Beyond the engineering knowledge in codes and guidelines, knowledge is implicitly represented by existing bridges. It is desirable to get useful hints towards possible design solutions for the present circumstances. We aim to use this data to gain knowledge for new design problems and narrow the design space.

A rich data source to achieve this, are Bridge Management Systems (BMS). BMSs are software systems to manage large infrastructure assets. They are usually operated by the road authorities of each country. A BMS consists of a database where all information belonging to a bridge structure is documented. The database typically holds general information like the name of the bridge structure, the location, as well as construction data, the condition of bridge parts, pictures, and drawings. For our work, data like bridge type, bridge length, number of piers and superstructure type are important information stored in the database. In Germany the bridge management system "SIB Bauwerke" depicted in Figure 2 is well known; All over the world several systems are used, which do not differ greatly from one another.

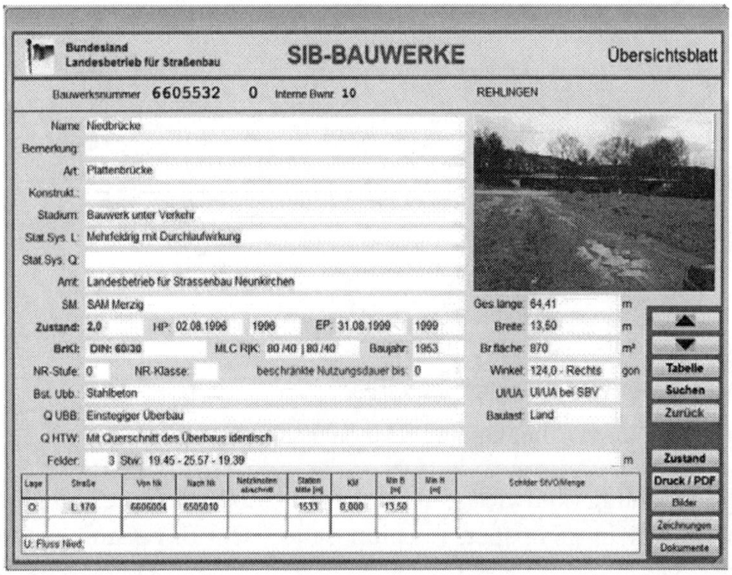

Figure 2: General view in the bridge management system SIB-Bauwerke (WPM - Ingenieure 2015)

This paper addresses the question, whether it is possible to gain knowledge by the use of data in bridge management systems and how this knowledge can be used in conceptual bridge design phases. With the help of the present approach we want to support bridge engineers throughout their planning tasks, for example a feasibility analysis, by answering questions like the following ones: (i) Which construction type, materials, superstructure types are usually used to build a bridge crossing a river with a width of 10m? (ii) Which superstructure height needs to be reckoned for a certain span width and superstructure type? (iii) Which design options cannot be used for the conditions in-situ? The information delivered by the system and further settings given by the bridge engineer are then used to generate BIM models for each variant of the bridge. With the help of these models further simulation and analysis processes could be performed.

3. Methods

3.1 Bayesian network

In artificial intelligence various methods for knowledge representation exist. To represent knowledge in an uncertain domain and to perform probabilistic reasoning Bayesian networks are well known. They are based on Bayes' theorem, which describes the conditional probability $P(A|B)$ of an event A for a given event B. It is defined as:

$$P(A|B) = \frac{P(B|A)P(A)}{P(B)}$$

A Bayesian network is defined by a directed acyclic graph (DAG), where each node N represents a discrete or continuous random variable $X = \{X_1, \ldots, X_n\}$ and the edges E represent conditional dependencies among variables. A directed link from node X to node Y says that X is a parent of Y. An arrow between two variables is usually interpreted as a direct influence of X (cause) on Y (effect). If no connection between two nodes exists, they are conditionally independent of each other. This is very intuitive and makes it easy for domain experts to formalize dependencies in the domain. Once the topology of the graph is defined, each node of the graph is associated with a conditional probability distribution $P = (Xi \mid parents(Xi))$, which determines the impact of the parents of one node. The probabilities are denoted in conditional probability tables (CPT). The joint probability for a set of variable values $x = \{x_1, \ldots, x_n\}$ can be calculated by multiplication of each probability distribution:

$$P(X_1 = x_1 \wedge \ldots \wedge X_n = x_n) = P(x_1, \ldots, x_n) = \prod_{i=1}^{n} P(x_i|parents(x_i))$$

To set up the Bayesian network, two main tasks occur. First, one needs to learn the network structure, second is to calculate the A-priori conditional probability distributions for each node. In order to perform these steps, a sufficient amount of training data sets is needed. In the following sections, algorithms are introduced that allow to automatically generate the topology of the graph and the conditional probability distributions. After setting up the Bayesian network, it is possible to perform probabilistic reasoning tasks. For the present application this means that we take existing data sets from BMS to learn the network structure and to calculate the probability distribution tables and then perform probabilistic reasoning for a new bridge design problem.

3.2 Structure learning

Beside the possibility to define the graph structure by the help of a domain expert, it is also feasible to define the graph structure of a Bayesian network by learning from training sets in an automated manner. Therefore, algorithms like the CI-based search algorithm (De Campos 2006) or the K2 algorithm (Cooper et al. 1992) exist. The Tree Augmented Naive Bayes (TAN) method was introduced by (Friedman et al. 1997). This algorithm creates a Bayesian network structure the following way.

1. Compute the mutual information function $I(X_i, X_j)$

   for each pair of variables where $i \neq j$

   $$I(X,Y) = \sum_{x,y} P(x,y) \log \frac{P(x,y)}{P(x)P(y)}.$$

2. Generate a undirected graph where the edges are weighted by $I(X_i, X_j)$.
3. Find a maximum weighted spanning tree, applying Kruskal's algorithm.
4. Set a root variable and set the direction of all edges to be outward from it.

3.3 Inference in Bayesian networks

After setting up the Bayesian network, we would like to reason on this network. First, we need to differentiate between exact inference methods and approximate inference methods for Bayesian networks. Part of exact inference are the variable elimination algorithm and clustering algorithms. Common known algorithms for approximate inference in Bayesian networks are direct sampling methods, rejection sampling and likelihood weighting.

Also well-known are the Markov chain Monte Carlo (MCMC) algorithms. Unlike the before mentioned algorithms, samples are not generated randomly from scratch. Here, based on the current sample, the next sample is generated by performing small random changes. A particular form of a MCMC is called Gibbs sampling (Neal 1993) which is well suited for inference in Bayesian networks.

Gibbs sampling in Bayesian networks works as follows:

1. Start with an arbitrary state. Fix the evidence variables.
2. Initialize all other variables.
3. Repeat n times:
    a. Randomly choose a non-evidence variable X
    b. Resample this variable X from P (X | all other variables)
    c. Count current state
4. Normalize.

Usually a pre-sampling or burn-in is performed to begin the Gibbs sampling from a more realistic starting state.

4. Proof of concept

In the following is to be demonstrated that the use of a Bayesian networks permits the determination (at least with a certain probability) of bridge design parameters on the basis of given boundary conditions. Up to now, it has not been possible to get access to real data from a bridge management system. However, in order to proof our approach, we generated random test data sets by the help of a knowledge-based system. We assume, that the generated output data is compliant to the current codes and guidelines. We focused on reinforced concrete road bridges. We choose the following variables to generate our test sets, also depicted in Figure 3: terrain depth, bridge length, cross section, horizontal curvature, bridge crossing angle, bridge type, number of piers, material type, superstructure type and superstructure height. In Table 1 the chosen minimum and maximum values as well as the discretization for each variable is shown. Furthermore, the use as an input or output design parameter is indicated.

The minimal necessary amount of data sets is mainly dependent on the number of connections in the network structure. In order to count a sufficient number of samples for all possible combinations and each variable, an either high number of training data or a very heterogenic set is necessary. In order to get meaningful results, we generated 10,000 training data sets. SIB Bauwerke contains about 8,000 data sets for bridges in the state Bavaria along motorways. The number would be much higher if all states in Germany and the other road types would be taken into account. For those data sets, the proposed approach could be used the same way. Comparable BMS systems in other countries typically hold a similar number of data sets.

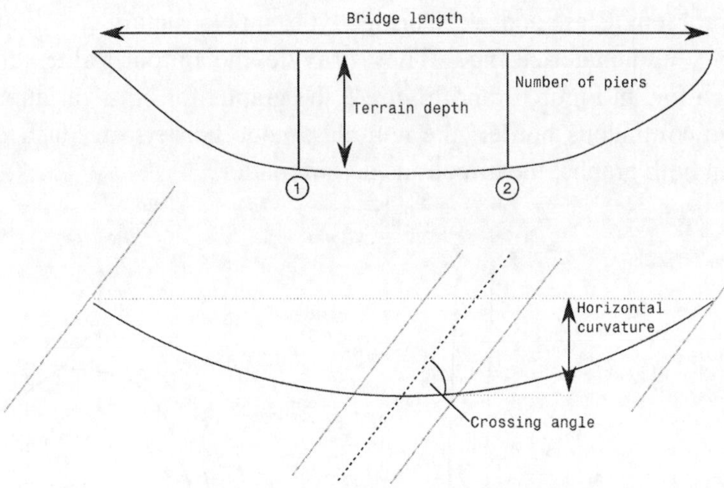

Figure 3: Chosen bridge parameters

Table 1: Discretization of variables

Variables	Type	Min value	Max value	Discretization	Used as
Bridge length	Continuous	0	100	25	Input
Crossing angle	Continuous	0	60	5	
Cross section	Discrete	{RQ 7.5, RQ 9.5, RQ 10.5, RQ 15.5}			
Horizontal curvature	Continuous	0	13	1	
Terrain depth	Continuous	-50	0	10	
Bridge type	Discrete	{frame bridge, continuous girder bridge, arc bridge}			Output
Material type	Discrete	{reinforced concrete, pre-stressed concrete}			
Number of piers	Continuous	0	6	1	
Superstructure height	Continuous	0.5	5	0.5	
Superstructure type	Discrete	{plate, T-beam, girder box}			

We considered two variants for the generation of the Bayesian network. First is the generation by the help of the Tree Augmented Naive Bayesian Network Algorithm (TAN). Therefore, the algorithm was extended to work with multiple class nodes (Van Der Gaag et al. 2006). The spanning tree is generated as usual, excluding all class nodes. Instead of then connecting all class nodes to all nodes in the spanning tree, which would create a very strongly connected network, only the edges to the class nodes with high mutual information are connected. Strongly connected networks cause large probability tables which require larger amounts of data to be populated. Edges are added in order of mutual information values until the desired connectivity is reached. This can be a maximum information spanning tree. Otherwise a threshold can be set on the minimal MI to create an edge. Furthermore, the interconnections among the class nodes have been set by an expert a-priori, in order to reflect the order in which the design choices are commonly made.

The second considered variant was the completely manual creation of the Bayesian network by a knowledge engineer. Both the necessary nodes as well as the edges in between are solely defined by a domain expert. In both cases the same class and non-class variables were chosen. Non-class nodes are bridge length, terrain depth, cross section, crossing angle, and horizontal curvature. The non-class nodes are used as input values and describe the boundary conditions of a certain design problem. Class nodes are bridge type, superstructure type, number of piers, superstructure height, and materiel type. They provide the output values for the design parameters we search for. In Figure 4 and Figure 5 the graphs for both variants are depicted. Class variables have continuous border; the non-class node borders are dashed. Continuous styled edges occur in both graphs; the directions do not matter.

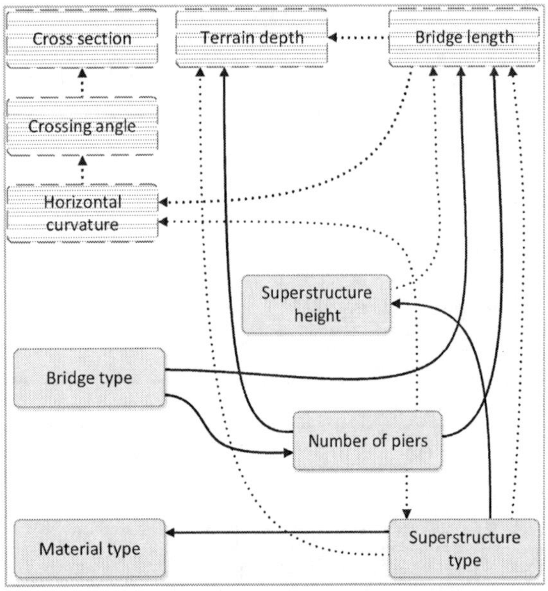

Figure 4: Variant 1 - TAN generated graph

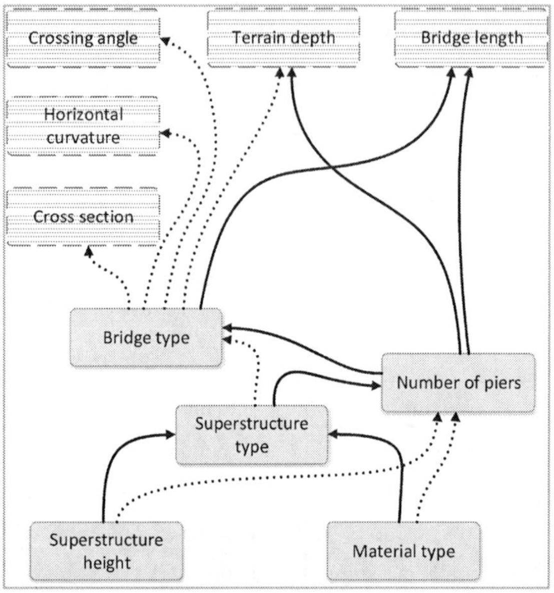

Figure 5: Variant 2 - Manually created graph

As you can see in the diagrams above, the input variables terrain depth und bridge length are the most important variables and the main conditions for the output variables in both variants, which reflects the reality as expected. The input variables horizontal curvature, crossing angle und cross section have minor influence on the output variables in both networks. Since we work with generated test data to learn the network structure in variant 1, the way of their generation could have main impact on the appearance of the network. It is possible that some conditions are implicitly effected by the generation algorithm. The manually created graph fits better to the design procedure bridge engineers usually perform than the automatically generated one (bridge length → bridge type → number of piers → superstructure type → superstructure height → material type).

In order to sample results from the network, all non-class nodes are assigned with the respective input values, and all class nodes are then sampled using the Markov Chain Monte Carlo (MCMC) algorithm, counting the occurrences of all combinations of values for all class nodes. Therefore, a likelihood for each possible class parameter combination can be calculated. Combination that never occur are discarded and the remaining combinations are ranked accordingly (Zheng et al. 2011). In Table 2 the conditional probability table for the class node superstructure type is exemplarily shown for variant 1. Given the number of piers equal to 2, a probability distribution of 37%, 33%, and 30% for the given superstructure types can be derived. This means that in the training data set an almost equal number of bridges with two piers for each superstructure exists. For variables with more than one condition the table gets more complicated. For bridges with more than four piers only bridges with a plate superstructure occur.

Table 2: Conditional probability table for superstructure type for variant 1

Number of piers	Plate	T-beam	Girder box
0	31%	37%	32%
1	41%	13%	46%
2	37%	33%	30%
3	60%	30%	10%
4	95%	5%	0%
5	100%	0%	0%

In order to test the generated Bayesian network, we set up two test scenarios. The scenario No. 1 describes the use case of an ordinary road (RQ 10.5) crossing a valley or river with a bridge length of 100m and a maximum height of 37m. Scenario No. 2 specifies a design problem for a bridge with a length of 57m and a maximum height of 15m for a motorway (RQ 15.5). To simplify the test, the variables crossing angle and horizontal curvature are set to 0 for both scenarios.

This experiments showed that the analysed input parameters returned a small set of feasible design variants with strong preferences that can be determined by those with distinctively high numbers of occurrences. The network generating small sets of possible designs implies that the number of possibilities is reduced successfully. If the information in the network would be sparse, all possible design combinations would be generated with uniform probability in the worst case. Since the truth is far from that, the results are meaningful. Exemplarily, the best four sample results for two different design scenarios and the two different graph generation variants are shown in Table 3 to 6. The two design scenarios differ in the values assigned to the non-class nodes which are denoted in the table description.

Table 3: Design scenario No. 1 – variant No. 1: Best sample results for evidence variables bridge length=100, horizontal curvature=0, terrain depth=-37, crossing angle=0, cross section = RQ10.5

Bridge type	Superstructure Type	Material Type	Superstructure Height	Number of piers	Probability
frame	plate	pre-stressed	1.0	4.0	32,95%
frame	plate	pre-stressed	1.0	6.0	11,97%
frame	plate	reinforced	1.0	4.0	10,22%
arc	plate	pre-stressed	1.0	4.0	7,37%

Table 4: Design scenario No. 1 – variant No. 2: Best sample results for evidence variables bridge length=100, horizontal curvature=0, terrain depth=-37, crossing angle=0, cross section = RQ10.5

Bridge type	Superstructure Type	Material Type	Superstructure Height	Number of piers	Probability
frame	T-beam	pre-stressed	1.0	3.0	10,83%
frame	T-beam	pre-stressed	1.0	2.0	8,60%
frame	girder box	pre-stressed	2.0	2.0	8,32%
frame	plate	reinforced	1.0	3.0	6,03%

Table 5: Design scenario No. 2 – variant No. 1: Best sample results for evidence variables bridge length=59, horizontal curvature=0, terrain depth=-15, crossing angle=0, cross section = RQ15.5

Bridge type	Superstructure Type	Material Type	Superstructure Height	Number of piers	Probability
continous girder	girder box	pre-stressed	1.0	0.0	61,78%
continous girder	T-beam	pre-stressed	1.0	0.0	12,62%
continous girder	plate	pre-stressed	1.0	0.0	9,05%
continous girder	girder box	pre-stressed	2.0	0.0	5,78%

Table 6: Design scenario No. 2 – variant No. 2: Best sample results for evidence variables bridge length=59, horizontal curvature=0, terrain depth=-15, crossing angle=0, cross section = RQ15.5

Bridge type	Superstructure Type	Material Type	Superstructure Height	Number of piers	Probability
continous girder	girder box	pre-stressed	1.0	0.0	23,29%
frame bridge	T-beam	pre-stressed	1.0	2.0	7,68%
frame bridge	girder box	pre-stressed	2.0	2.0	7,51%
frame bridge	T-beam	pre-stressed	1.0	3.0	5,55%

The outcome for the chosen test scenarios looks promising and showed that the approach works in principle. However, we expected more suitable advices. For example, in scenario No. 1 variant No. 1 only superstructure types of type plate are listed Alternatives with less piers and therefore other superstructure types are not mentioned. In Table 5 continuous girder bridges are combined with a number of piers equal to 0 for all entries and several superstructure types, which makes no sense from a bridge engineering perspective. The chosen discretization step of 1m for the variable superstructure height is too big. To achieve more feasible advices, more design variables and a finer discretization of those must be taken into account. Furthermore, a Bayesian network based on real-life data and not on randomly generated test data will provide much more realistic outcomes. Generally, the calculated probabilities for variant 1 are higher than for variant No. 2. This is because the generated network fits better to the generated training data sets than the manually created one. However, the manually created is the one which supports the bridge design process in a more intuitive way.

5. Conclusion and Outlook

In artificial intelligence Bayesian networks are well established for probabilistic reasoning in big data sources. We presented an approach to use Bayesian networks for purposes in preliminary bridge design phases, namely to gain knowledge implicitly stored in bridge management systems. It needs to be mentioned that the existing knowledge used in early bridge design phases cannot be captured in explicit if-then rules since it is highly uncertain. Thus, the use of a Bayesian networks perfectly fits this need.

It could be shown that, in principle, our approach is suitable to support the bridge design engineer by providing proper design solutions. To achieve more feasible advices, more design variables and a finer discretization of those must be taken into account. The hypothetical case is limited on early design stages. In order to include further life-cycle aspects (e.g. operation and maintenance) into the decision making process, information like the operation cost of the bridge structure must be included. BMSs usually provide this type of information. We then can think about answering questions like, which construction type works well under which boundary conditions concerning the maintenance costs?

In future work, we will apply the shown concept to real world data from bridge management systems. Additionally, we want to develop methods to extend the Bayesian network with explicit knowledge to achieve a hybrid knowledge representation for bridge engineering. Furthermore, we will think of machine learning techniques to fill knowledge gaps in the knowledge base. Moreover, other artificial intelligence methods like artificial neural networks could be assessed for their applicability.

References

Boeykens, Stefan (2012): Bridging building information modeling and parametric design. In: *eWork and eBusiness in Architecture, Engineering and Construction: ECPPM 2012*, S. 453.

Cooper, Gregory F.; Herskovits, Edward (1992): A Bayesian method for the induction of probabilistic networks from data. In: *Machine learning* 9 (4), S. 309–347.

De Campos, Luis M (2006): A scoring function for learning Bayesian networks based on mutual information and conditional independence tests. In: *The Journal of Machine Learning Research* 7, S. 2149–2187.

Eastman, Charles M. (1999): Building product models. Computer environments supporting design and construction. Boca Raton, Fla.: CRC press.

Eastman, Charles M.; Teicholz, Paul; Sacks, Rafael; Liston, Kathleen (2011): BIM handbook. A guide to building information modeling for owners, managers, designers, engineers and contractors. 2nd ed. Hoboken, NJ: Wiley.

Friedman, Nir; Geiger, Dan; Goldszmidt, Moises (1997): Bayesian network classifiers. In: *Machine learning* 29 (2-3), S. 131–163.

Lu, Pengzhen; Chen, Shengyong; Zheng, Yujun (2012): Artificial Intelligence in Civil Engineering. In: *Mathematical Problems in Engineering* 2012 (6), S. 1–22. DOI: 10.1155/2012/145974.

Neal, Radford M. (1993): Probabilistic inference using Markov chain Monte Carlo methods.

Reich, Yoram (1995): Artificial Intelligence in Bridge Engineering: Towards Matching Practical Needs with Technology.

Schneider, Ronald; Fischer, Johannes; Bügler, Maximilian; Nowak, Marcel; Thöns, Sebastian; Borrmann, André; Straub, Daniel (2015): Assessing and updating the reliability of concrete bridges subjected to spatial deterioration - principles and software implementation. In: *Structural Concrete* 16 (3), S. 356–365. DOI: 10.1002/suco.201500014.

Singer, D.; Borrmann, A. (2015): A Novel Knowledge-Based Engineering Approach for Infrastructure Design. In: The Fourth International Conference on Soft Computing Technology in Civil, Structural and Environmental Engineering. Prague, Czech Republic.

Stokes, M. (2001): Managing engineering knowledge. MOKA: methodology for knowledge based engineering applications. London: Professional Engineering Pub.

Van Der Gaag, Linda C; De Waal, Peter R (2006): Multi-dimensional Bayesian Network Classifiers. In: Probabilistic graphical models. Citeseer, S. 107–114.

WPM - Ingenieure (2015): Übersichtsblatt SIB Bauwerke. Online verfügbar unter http://www.wpm-ingenieure.de/images/produkte/sib_bauwerke/uebersichtsblatt.jpg, zuletzt geprüft am 08.02.2015.

Zheng, Fei; Webb, Geoffrey I. (2011): Tree augmented naive Bayes. In: Encyclopedia of Machine Learning: Springer, S. 990–991.

A Graph Transformation Based Method for the Semi-Automatic Generation of Parametric Models of Shield Tunnels

S. Vilgertshofer, A. Borrmann
Chair of Computational Modeling and Simulation, Leonhard Obermeyer Center
Technical University of Munich, Germany
simon.vilgertshofer@tum.de

Abstract. During the design of large infrastructural projects like inner-city subway tracks, it proves necessary to consider differing model scales, ranging from kilometers to centimeters. This problem can be addressed by using multi-scale product models comprising multiple levels of detail (LoD). Ensuring consistency across the different LoDs can be achieved by applying parametric modeling techniques while creating the model. However, the correct application of constraints and dependencies has shown to be too complex to be handled manually. To address this issue, this papers presents an automated detailing mechanism, which is based on the use of graphs and graph transformations. We show how procedural parametric models based on two-dimensional sketches can be represented by graphs and how refinement steps can be realized through the rule-based transformation of such a graph.

1. Introduction

The ongoing digitalization of planning processes in the building sector has led to increasing demands on the complexity of the underlying digital models. One requirement on such a digital model is its capability to represents substantially diverging scales and levels of details. In particular, this is the case in the planning of large infrastructure facilities ranging over several kilometers (tunnels or roads). To efficiently assist planners, the corresponding models need to support the efficient modeling and management of geometric objects on both, large and small scales.

One approach to representing spatially extended facilities with an adaptive semantic and geometric resolution is the use of multiple levels of detail (LoDs). This approach is well established in the domain of Geographic Information Systems (GIS). Previous research extends the LoD concept used in the GIS domain towards consistent multi-scale representations of building information models, particularly used for the modeling of shield tunnels. One conclusion of this research is that the manual creation of these consistency preserving models is very complex, time consuming and error-prone and should be supported by automation mechanisms (Borrmann et al., 2014b).

This paper presents one possible approach to realize these automation mechanisms. It describes a detailing automation approach, which is based on the use of graphs and graph transformations. It further shows how procedural parametric three-dimensional geometric models based on two-dimensional sketches can be represented by graphs and how refinement steps can be realized through the rule-based transformation of these graphs.

The prospected benefit of this approach for end users is the reduction of the effort to manually create the consistency preserving models. Doing so, it allows them to focus on the conceptual and engineering aspects of the design process instead of time-consuming and repetitive modeling operations.

This paper is structured as follows: In Section 2 related works and the theoretical background of the research are outlined. Section 3 discusses the general approach of using graphs to represent a parametric 3D model. Section 4 focuses on the development of a specific graph rewriting system as a case study and describes the prototypical software tool that is used to interpret the graph-based representation and creates the actual 3D model. The paper concludes with a summary and a discussion of future work.

2. Related Work and Theoretical Background

2.1 Multi-Scale Modeling of Shield Tunnels

The idea of modeling and visualizing buildings and infrastructure facilities in different LoDs has been well established in the GIS domain for several years. The general concept is to provide different geometric representations of a semantic object. Which of these representations is actually used to display the object depends on the particular context, for example with respect to the user's requirements. An important example is CityGML, an XML-based data model for the representation of mainly static 3D city models (Kolbe 2009). CityGML defines five LoDs where representations in coarser LoDs are generated from finer ones by abstraction. In contrast, the design process of construction projects starts with a very general representation that gets gradually refined and more and more detailed as planning evolves (Borrmann et al. 2014). Additionally, the concept of CityGML does not include any automated consistency preservation mechanisms to ensure that changes in one LoD are propagated to the other LoDs due to the independent storage of an object's geometry in each LoD.

To fulfill the needs of consistency-preservation and multi-LoD representation, a multi-scale product model for shield tunnels has been developed by Borrmann and Jubierre (2013), which is based on a single scale model introduced by Yabuki et al. (2013). This multi-scale model uses procedural geometry description and parametric modeling techniques to provide mechanisms for automatic consistency preservation across the different LoDs. A 3D representation of the five LoDs of the tunnel model is depicted in Figure 1.

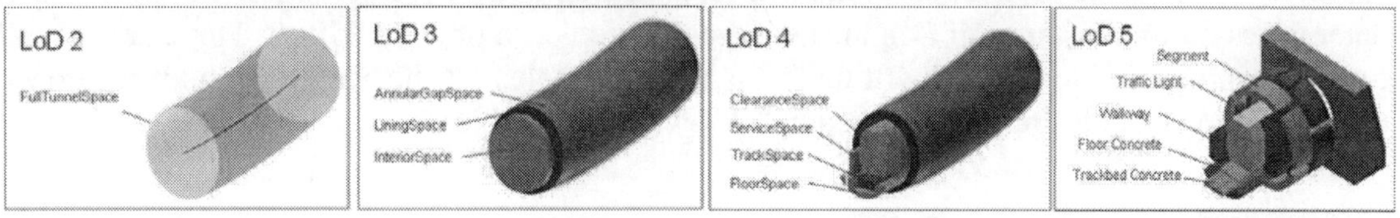

Figure 1: A 3D representation of the LoDs of the multi-scale shield tunnel product model (Borrmann and Jubierre, 2013). The first LoD, which only represents the alignment, is not depicted.

2.2 Parametric and Procedural Modeling

The concept of parametric modeling was developed in the 1990s (Shah and Mäntylä 1995) and is by now well established and used in many commercial and open source CAD applications e.g. Autodesk Inventor, Siemens NX and FreeCAD. While mainly applied in mechanical engineering, the concept has also been used to create flexible models of infrastructure facilities (Ji et al., 2013).

Parametric geometric 2D models (sketches) are composed of geometric objects and parametrical constraints. A system of constraints and objects is defined during the creation of a sketch in a parametric CAD application and forms a constraint problem, which can be solved by an implemented geometric constraint solver (GCS) (Fudos and Hoffmann, 1997; Owen, 1991). The set of parametric constraints that is implemented by all major constraint solvers is defined as the *standard geometric constraint language* by (Schultz et al., 2015). It comprises the dimensional constraints for distances and angles as well as the following geometric constraints: *coincident, collinear, tangential, horizontal, vertical, parallel, perpendicular* and *fixed*.

The core concept of procedural modeling is to store not only the final outcome of a modeling process, but instead the sequence of single sketching and modeling operations. Models created this way are called procedural models or construction history models. They use the concept of parametric modeling to create flexible 2D sketches. These sketches form the basis for the procedural operations that generate 3D geometry by extrusions, sweeps, lofts or Boolean operations (Borrmann et al., 2012; Mun et al., 2003).

The presented approach uses parametrical constraints as listed above in combination with the procedural modeling of geometry to define dependencies between geometric objects belonging to different LoDs as described in (Borrmann et al., 2014a). Thus, the consistency of the model across multiple LoDs can be ensured.

2.3 Graph Rewriting

The proposed concept for automating the detailing process is based on graph theory and graph rewriting methodology (Rozenberg 1997). Graphs and graph rewriting mechanisms are employed to enable the representation and the modification of the procedural parametric models. An application of graph rewriting to semi-automatically create and alter parametric sketches has been presented in Vilgertshofer and Borrmann (2015).

Graph rewriting operations are used to create a new graph out of an existing graph by altering, deleting or replacing parts (subgraphs) of the existing graph. The changes are formalized through graph rewrite rules written as $L \rightarrow R$. A graph rewrite rule is defined by a pattern graph L and a replacement graph R. When a rule is applied to a graph (called the host graph), this graph is searched to find a subgraph that matches the graph pattern defined by L. If the matching succeeds L is replaced with R under the consideration of a preservation morphism that determines how an instance of L in the host graph is replaced or altered by R. There are several different approaches to graph rewriting. Two main examples are the Single-Pushout Approach (SPO) and the Double-Pushout Approach (DPO) (Heckel, 2006).

3. Conceptual Approach

To represent and detail a procedural parametric model, three major challenges are discussed after the general design of the graph representing a model is addressed. First, the so called *graph metamodel* is introduced. The metamodel defines a library of the node and edge types that the graph may consist of as well as possible attributes they may have. Secondly, to create and alter a graph based on this metamodel the requirements on graph rewrite rules are evaluated. These rules formally describe detailing steps that an end user can apply instead of manually executing the underlying procedural or parametric modeling operations. Last, we discuss the process of developing the graph metamodel and rewrite rules. These must meet requirements concerning the representation to be unambiguous and translatable into an actual geometric 3D model by interpreting the graph-based representation.

3.1 Definition of the Graph Metamodel

To create and detail a multi-scale geometric model by using graph rewrite operations, it is necessary to determine the composition of the graph which is used to represent this model. This is achieved by the definition of the graph metamodel. The metamodel defines the types of graph entities (nodes and edges) that may be used by a graph rewriting system to assemble a graph that represents a specific model. Besides the mere types of graph entities, the metamodel furthermore defines their attributes as well as conditions that determine which nodes and edges may be incident or which node types can be adjacent.

Formally, we define the graph representing a procedural geometry model as a directed multigraph with loops $G = \{V, E\}$. V is the set of vertices that represent either procedural modeling operations in the context of the procedural graph or geometric objects in the sketch graph. E on the other hand is a set of edges that connect these vertices. The edges are used to represent the general relations between the procedural operations or specific parametric constraints between geometric objects in a sketch graph. Thus, we define V_P and E_P as vertices and edges conceptually belonging to the procedural graph G_P. Further V_S and E_S are defined as the vertices and edges conceptually belonging to the sketch graph: The complete graph representing a model is described as $G = \{V_P + V_S, E_P + E_S\}$. The metamodel describes the sets of possible objects that V and E may contain.

The graph metamodel that was successfully used to generate models up to LoD 3 and parts of a LoD 4 model of a shield tunnel is described in Section 4.

3.2 Design of the Graph used for Model Representation

In a preliminary concept (Vilgertshofer and Borrmann, 2015) two individual types of graphs were considered necessary to represent two-dimensional sketches (*sketch graph*) and the procedural operations (*procedural graph*). While the conceptual separation of these graphs, which is caused by the different nature of the relations in parametric sketches and procedural operations, persists, the sketch graph needs to be integrated into the procedural graph. This is due to the fact that sketches are the basis for procedural operations used to create 3D objects by extrusion or sweeping. For this reason, the evaluation of a procedural operation will always need a reference to the sketch that this operation is based on.

To handle this interlinkage of the two graphs, three different possibilities supported by the used graph rewriting tool GrGen.NET (Jakumeit et al., 2010) were considered. In the case of an *Integration by reference*, a graph entity representing a sketch would only store a reference to an independent graph which represents the actual sketch (described by its geometry and constraints). The second possibility is an *Integration by using subgraphs*, where a sketch graph is stored inside a graph entity representing a sketch, without connecting it to the procedural graph. Last, an *Integration by combination of the graphs* was considered. In this case each graph that represents a sketch is an actual subgraph of the procedural graph and thereby a part of it.

While each of these solutions is generally possible, the third option proved to be the most advantageous. This is caused by the requirements on the necessary relations between the two graphs. The first two possibilities induce a conceptual separation of the sketch graphs from the procedural graph. This increases the complexity of rewrite rules that need to transform a sketch graph as well as the procedural graph, but does not yield any benefits.

When using the third option on the other hand, relationships between sketch graphs can be modeled much more straight-forward. The combination of the graphs is realized by connecting all nodes belonging to a sketch graph with the respective sketch node of the procedural graph, thereby turning it into a subgraph of the procedural graph. The application of this concept is shown in Figure 2 exemplarily for a graph representing a LoD 2 tunnel model. Here the edges *$9* and *$A* are used to assign the nodes *ProjectedPoint* and *Circle* to the *Sketch* node and thereby create an integrated graph. The edge *$8:project* is introduced for defining the location of the *ProjectedPoint* to be derived from the alignment. This information would otherwise have to be kept as an attribute of the *ProjectedPoint* node.

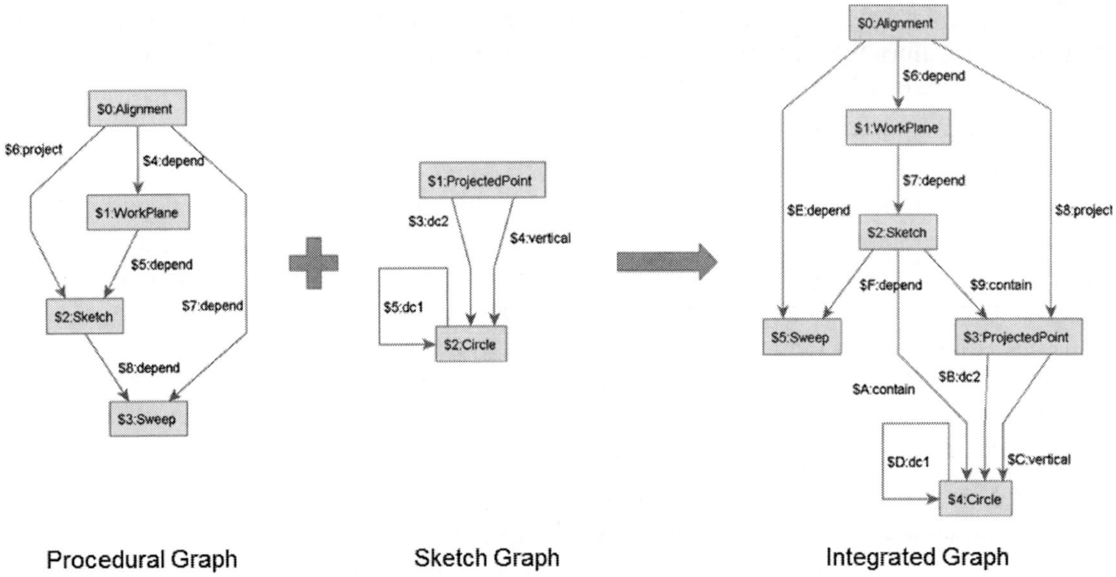

Figure 2: Integration of sketch and procedural graph.

The integration of the graphs is not defined as an actual graph transformation. In fact, it is the conceptual basis for the definition of all graph rewrite rules, as they should only create and transform an integrated graph.

Although only the integrated graph is used for the representation of a complete model, the terms sketch graph and procedural graph will continue to be used in order to indicate which part of the graph is referred to in a particular context.

3.3 Formalizing Modeling Operations as Graph Rewrite Rules

Graph rewrite rules are used to create different instances of the graph that represents the product model based on the graph entities available from the metamodel. The more abstract task of a rewrite rule is to combine a set of modeling operations (procedural or sketch related) that would otherwise have to be carried out manually. Thus, to formally define a rule, it needs to be determined which model parts are to be used or altered (e.g. the creation of a sketch requires a work plane that the sketch is drawn upon). Thereby, the pattern part of the rule is constructed out of the nodes and edges that represent the respective model entities. Next, the designated result of the represented modeling operation needs to be formalized in the rewrite part of the rule by adding, altering or removing new or existing nodes and edges. Additionally, we need to ensure that the application of any rule on the graph-based representation of a model will lead to another valid representation. This means that the representation is interpretable and can be used to successfully create an evaluated model.

The execution of the rules is to be initiated by the end user. To this end, he can choose among a set of predefined rules that are integrated in the graph rewrite system. Currently the definition of rewrite rules by the user is not intended. This is caused by the fact that the creation of a rule requires deep insight in parametric and procedural modeling as well as in the process of graph rewriting and should remain hidden from the end user. He should rather be only concerned with the execution of those rules that lead to the model geometry he requires - which is naturally limited by the set of the predefined rewrite rules.

3.4 Requirements on the Graph to Allow Successful Interpretation

The main requirement on any graph describing a certain model is its validity, insofar as that the interpretation of the graph must be possible (i.e. without conflicts and inconsistencies) and result in a usable procedural geometry model. Therefore, the graph must always represent the result of a modeling process which could also have been performed manually. Procedural modeling applications support this manual process by preventing user actions that would destroy the procedural or parametric structure of the model. For example, they do not to allow the deletion of a sketch while keeping a dependent extrusion. As this is not a-priori assured by automated graph generation, special care has to be taken regarding the consistency of the graph.

In the context of the procedural graph this means, that every node representing a procedural operation has to have all necessary preceding operations (or input parameters) present in the graph in form of the respective nodes connected by proper edges. For example, a sketch node *S* always needs a work plane *WP* node connected by an incoming *depend* edge *d*: *d=(WP, S)*.

Additionally, a subgraph representing the 2D geometry of a sketch must always describe a fully constrained sketch. Otherwise the interpretation of the graph would not lead to an unambiguous solution. The aspects of sketch graphs in this regard are discussed in detail in Vilgertshofer and Borrmann (2015). There, the structure of sketch graphs is defined and the development of and requirements on rewrite rules, which always produce an interpretable graph are shown. The main tools for achieving an unambiguous representation shown there are the definition of ports (definition of the part of a geometric element that a constraint applies to) and the use of temporary coordinates to support the GCS.

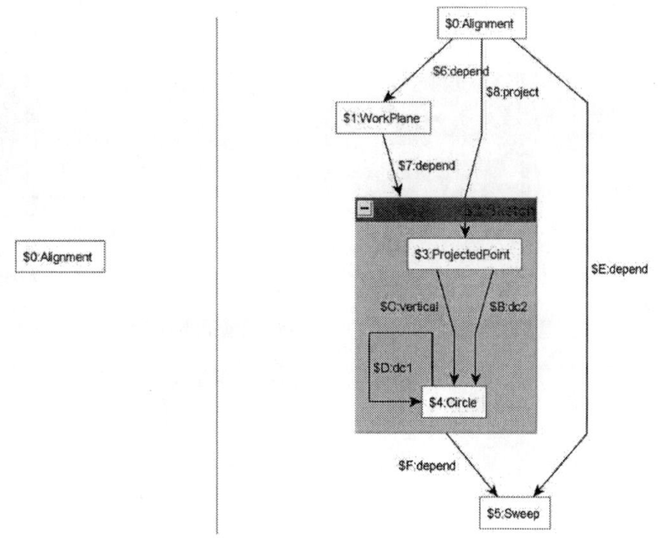

Figure 3: Pattern (left) and replacement (right) part of a rewrite rule that details a model from LoD 1 to LoD 2.

4. Prototypical Implementation

The developed concept of using graph transformation to automatically create consistent multi-scale product models has been implemented as a case study. For the definition of a graph rewrite system consisting of a metamodel and appropriate graph rewrite rules, the graph rewrite generator GrGen.NET has been used while the generation of the evaluated sketch is performed with the commercial parametric CAD application Autodesk Inventor.

4.1 A Graph Rewrite System for the Creation of a Shield Tunnel

GRGEN.NET (Graph Rewrite GENerator) is an open source software development tool that provides programming languages optimized for graph structured data. More concretely, it provides the possibility to create a graph metamodel and respective graph rewrite rules implementing (as default) an SPO-based approach (Blomer et al., 2014).

As a proof-of-concept we implemented a graph rewrite system with GRGEN.NET. It allows us to create the graph based representation of the shield tunnel model stepwise up to LoD 4 without any manual modeling operations. We defined rather comprehensive rewrite rules for this first evaluation of the approach as our primary focus was to proof that a graph created by these rules could actually be used for the creation of an evaluated model.

An overview of our graph metamodel is given in Table 1. It shows the different types of the nodes and edges that we use as well as whether they conceptually belong to a sketch graph or to the procedural graph. In Figure 3 an exemplary rewrite rule consisting of the pattern and the replacement graph is depicted. A graph representing a LoD 3 model is shown in Figures 4.

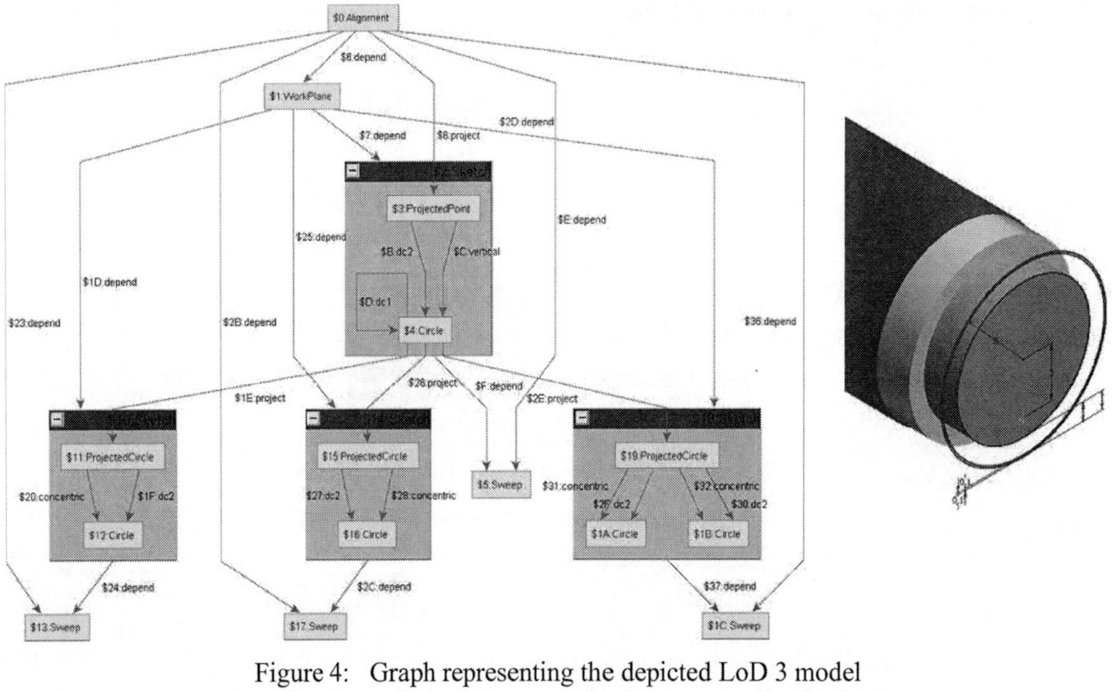

Figure 4: Graph representing the depicted LoD 3 model
(the sketch graphs have been grouped to improve readability)

Table 1: The Metamodel of the Developed Graph Rewriting System

	sketch graph	**procedural graph**
nodes	V_S: – point / projected point – line / projected line – circle / projected circle – arc / projected arc *projected geometric elements are used to create relationships between different sketches*	V_P: – alignment – sketch – work plane – sweep
edges	E_S: dimensional constraints: – dimension of one element (dc1) *(e.g. radius, length)* – dimension between two elements (dc2) *(e.g. distance, offset)* geometric constraints: – concentric – equal – horizontal – vertical – parallel – perpendicular – collinear – coincident	E_P: – contain *relates geometric elements to a certain sketch node* – depend *defines procedural dependencies* – project *defines the source geometry of a projected element*

4.2 Application of Rewrite Rules and Generation of the Evaluated Model

While a graph is used for the representation and alteration or detailing of the model, it is not particularly useful for engineering purposes. Therefore, an actual three-dimensional model, the *evaluated model,* needs to be generated from the graph-based representation for display and further use in a parametrical modeling system. A software tool to enable this generation has been prototypically developed. It combines the functionalities to create and transform the graph with the predefined metamodel and rewrite rules as well as the evaluation of the graph-based representation. Thereby, it generates the geometry and thus the evaluated model in the commercial parametrical modeling system Autodesk Inventor. A short overview of the functionality follows.

The developed program uses the API of the graph rewrite tool GrGen.Net to access the metamodel and rewrite rules predefined in the syntax of this tool. While the user triggers the execution of a rule the actual rewrite operation is performed by GrGen.Net. After the consecutive execution of any number of desired rules the current state of the graph is used to create the evaluated model. Therefore, the nodes and edges are interpreted and their equivalent objects are sequentially created by calling the respective methods of the API of Autodesk Inventor. During this process, the connections and relationships defined by the graph are used to determine the correct order of the construction operations and the necessary dependencies of the objects to be created within Inventor.

5. Conclusion

This paper presents a concept for the graph-based representation of product models and their automatic detailing by performing graph transformation operations based on formal rules defined in a graph rewriting system. It focuses on product models of shield-tunnels as the automated creation of multi-scale versions of such models is the overall purpose of this research.

The main contribution is the description of the development of a graph rewriting system that enables the generation of graphs representing those product models. We give an overview of the main requirements on the graph in terms of its ability to be evaluated in order to create the actual 3D procedural model in a parametric CAD application. We further described how we improved our approach by combining the graphs representing 2D sketches and the procedural operations by integrating them. Using only one graph to represent the complete procedural geometry of the product model allows a much better handling of the graph and makes the definition of rewrite rules and the interpretation of the graph much easier. To prove the feasibility of our approach, the graph rewriting system has been implemented in the graph rewriting tool GRGEN.NET. Additionally, a software prototype was developed that enables to automatically create an evaluated model in the parametric modeling system Autodesk Inventor.

Further research is focusing on creating a larger set of rewrite rules, which enables end users to create more diversified models. Additionally, we will further extend the graph to realize the affiliation of the created objects to a certain LoD.

Acknowledgements

We gratefully acknowledge the support of the German Research Foundation (DFG) for funding the project under grant FOR 1546.

References

Blomer, J., Geiß, R., Jakumeit, E., 2014. The GrGen.NET User Manual.

Borrmann, A., Flurl, M., Ramos, J., Mundani, R., Rank, E., 2014a. Synchronous collaborative tunnel design based on consistency-preserving multi-scale models. Advanced Engineering Informatics 28, 499–517.

Borrmann, A., Ji, Y., Jubierre, J.R., Flurl, M., 2012. Procedural Modeling: A new approach to multi-scale design in infrastructure projects. In: Proc. of the EG-ICE Workshop on Intelligent Computing in Civil Engineering. Herrsching, Germany.

Borrmann, A., Jubierre, J.R., 2013. A multi-scale tunnel product model providing coherent geometry and semantics. In: Proc. of the 2013 ASCE International Workshop on Computing in Civil Engineering. Los Angeles, pp. 291–298.

Borrmann, A., Kolbe, T.H., Donaubauer, A., Steuer, H., Jubierre, J.R., Flurl, M., 2014b. Multi-Scale Geometric-Semantic Modeling of Shield Tunnels for GIS and BIM Applications. Computer-Aided Civil and Infrastructure Engineering 30, 263–281.

Fudos, I., Hoffmann, C.M., 1997. A Graph-constructive Approach to Solving Systems of Geometric Constraints. ACM Transactions on Graphics 16, 179–216.

Heckel, R., 2006. Graph Transformation in a Nutshell. Electronic Notes in Theoretical Computer Science 148, 187–198.

Jakumeit, E., Buchwald, S., Kroll, M., 2010. GrGen.NET. International Journal on Software Tools for Technology Transfer.

Ji, Y., Borrmann, A., Beetz, J., Obergrießer, M., 2013. Exchange of Parametric Bridge Models Using a Neutral Data Format. Journal of Computing in Civil Engineering 27, 593–606.

Kolbe, T.H., 2009. Representing and Exchanging 3D City Models with CityGML. In: Lee, J., Zlatanova, S. (Eds.), Proceedings of the 3rd International Workshop on 3D Geo-Information, Seoul, Korea, Lecture Notes in Geoinformation and Cartography. Springer Berlin Heidelberg.

Mun, D., Han, S., Kim, J., Oh, Y., 2003. A set of standard modeling commands for the history-based parametric approach. Computer-Aided Design 35, 1171–1179.

Owen, J.C., 1991. Algebraic solution for geometry from dimensional constraints. In: Proceedings of the First ACM

Symposium on Solid Modeling Foundations and CAD/CAM Applications. ACM, pp. 397–407.

Rozenberg, G., 1997. Handbook of Graph Grammars aand Computing by Graph Transformation. World Scientific.

Schultz, C., Bhatt, M., Borrmann, A., 2015. Bridging qualitative spatial constraints and feature-based parametric modelling: Expressing visibility and movement constraints. Advanced Engineering Informatics.

Shah, J.J., Mäntylä, M., 1995. Parametric and feature-based CAD/CAM: Concepts, Techniques and Applications. ohn Wiley & Sons, New York.

Vilgertshofer, S., Borrmann, A., 2015. Automatic Detailing of Parametric Sketches by Graph Transformation. In: Proc. of the 32nd ISARC 2015. Oulu, Finnland.

Yabuki, N., Aruga, T., Furuya, H., 2013. Development and application of a product model for shield tunnels. In: Proceedings of the 30th ISARC. Montréal.

Geometric correct objects and systems with a predictable and traceable behavior

Jakob Kirchner*, Wolfgang Huhnt*, Thomas Gust**, Konrad Polthier**
* Technische Universität Berlin, Germany ** Freie Universität Berlin, Germany
jakob.kirchner@tu-berlin.de

Abstract. The introduction of Building Information Modeling (BIM) requires models enriched with information and modeled constraints that describe the design intent. As subsequent modifications are part of a normal planning process, the models have to react with an appropriate behavior and guarantee to preserve all defined constraints. Current BIM software systems do not support the modeler in working with constraints sufficiently. Applying subsequent modifications result in unpredictable states or not traceable fails. As a first step, requirements to a geometric model and its behavior have to be defined. A concept for a geometric model including constraints is presented. It is shown how the requirements can be met in the modeling of geometric objects. An example based on an implemented prototype is included. Finally the work is summarized and future steps are discussed.

1. Introduction

The application of BIM (Building Information Modeling) requires CAE (computer-aided engineering) software systems which support a modifiable 3D-Model of a building. The paradigm of parametric modeling includes parameters to control geometric relations and constraints that specify valid geometric relations which have to be preserved. As an example, the thickness of a wall can be fixed to a constant value by a constraint. Borrmann and Berkhahn (2015, p. 34) state parametric modeling '...is a very important trend in civil engineering...' and results in '... flexible models ... which can be adapted fast and efficient to changing boundary conditions'. Adaptions of a model also known as subsequent modifications require software systems strongly supporting the modeler in initializing changes. That means a modification and its results have to be traceable, predictable, thus comprehensible. Traceable means, that the software offers sufficient information of correlations of the calculated changes. Dependencies and conflicts have to be presented appropriately. Specifying parts of the modeler's intent by constraints is an intuitive way and constraints in geometric objects and between geometric objects enrich the model. However, Lee et al. (2006) explain: 'Even with a clear guide map, parametric modeling can still be a very complex and time-consuming activity'.

Parametric modeling is state of the art, but Bettig and Hoffmann (2011) clarify "Over the last decade, the fundamental representations underlying parametric control of geometry in CAD systems has changed little.' and '... it has also been recognized that the one-way dependencies inherent in parametric operations severely limit the flexibility of parametric CAD for designers and cause it to map poorly to recognized systematic design processes.' That's why new approaches have to be developed.

At present time, existing tools support constraints exclusively in their proprietary data format. Exchanging models between different proprietary software systems using open standards, such as IFC (Industry Foundation Classes), do not support geometric constraints yet. The transferable geometry is a static geometry and has lost most information of the design process. A constraint model is needed to close this gap in the exchange of building models.

This paper represents the beginning of research for a comprehensible and traceable building model behavior in the case of subsequent modifications. An overview of geometric constraints and relating research is given. There follows a summary of our previous investigations in constraint-based modelling features of existing BIM software. The main part consists of a presentation of requirements to an object model that can handle subsequent modifications and is traceable and comprehensible to the modeler. The basic concept is explained and the detailed modeling to meet the requirements for a valid model and the used algorithm in case of modifications is shown. The paper finishes with an example of the implemented prototype and conclusion. Limitations set to our current approach are explained in the concept part. Our pilot implementation can only handle 2 dimensional objects. We make use of an orthogonal Cartesian grid coordinate system and limit modifications to vertical or horizontal 1 unit movements.

2. Geometric constraints

Modeling of geometry by geometric constraints is an intuitive possibility to specify requirements to a building, but a predictable behavior in the case of subsequent modifications is necessary. Geometric dependencies in objects and between objects can be explicitly defined by constraints including parameters. Parametrization with constraints is an intuitive way to specify dependencies in a model, because its semantics can be translated from the architect's or engineer's intention. As an example for a constraint in an object, the distance of wall faces describes the statement: 'the wall has to have a thickness of 30 cm". Geometric modelling with constraints limits modifications of objects and thus reduces the degree of freedom of the entire system. Sarfraz (2013, p. 199) classifies a constraint system:

- *Over-constrained*: More constraints exist than are necessary to fix the objects in their current position.
- *Well-constrained*: Exactly as many constraints exist to fix the objects in their current position.
- *Under-constrained*: Less constraints exist than are necessary to fix the objects in their current position. There are flexible parts and more than one valid system state.

A system of constraints can have only one valid state, if it's over- or well-constrained, and many possible valid states if it's under constrained. Applying a modification in geometry like moving an object requires the computation of a new valid state. As it's a so-called CSP (Constraint Satisfaction Problem) the solving process is not trivial.

3. Related work

Using constraints to design a building model has been investigated in the past, and results have been published in literature. Two different research areas can be distinguished.

The first one deals with the question of how constraints can be created appropriately from artificial or natural languages. Donath and Böhme (2007) present a constraint-based design approach. Constraints are specified as a description of requirements for a building model. A solution that fits these requirements is automatically obtained, if it exists. Difficulties still exist in describing the design intent in a scripting or programming language. Niemeijer et al. (2014) investigated on using an 'automated interpretation of natural language input' to create design constraint for a building model. They asked architectural students for formulations of requirements for specific design problems. The computed constraint specifications consisted of inequations and equations.

The second research area is, how subsequent modifications can be applied and constraints can preserve the original design intent. That means all modifications have to be traceable and comprehensible for the modeler. Vries et al. (2000) use constraints for creating architectural building models which '... respond to designer's actions in a user-intuitive way'. The responding action is defined as behavior. The model consists of geometric objects specified as axis aligned bounding boxes. A system of constraints is introduced. The constraints specify valid values for the size of a bounding box and positioning of two bounding boxes to each other. Constraints are defined by equations or inequations. The work describes a solver and a strategy for finding an acceptable solution if no solution is found. It also includes a strategy if more than one solution is found by choosing a solution which is as near as possible to the original state.

In literature, the term 'Dynamic Geometry' is introduced for increasing the plausibility of constraint solving for the user (Kortenkamp, 1999). The idea of Dynamic Geometry is to solve under-constrained models following a strategy of choosing a plausible solution. It is primarily used in software for teaching mechanical relationships. As an example it tries to avoid 'jumping elements" (Kortenkamp, 1999, p. 28) by giving weight to continuity as a modification is applied.

4. Analysis of an existing BIM tool

The analysis of possibilities of constraint modeling in Autodesk Revit 2015 as an example of current CAE software was part of research of our group (Köhler 2015). Different building models including constraints were created and subsequent modifications were applied. The results of smaller (more than 5 explicitly defined constraints) and larger (up to 308 explicitly defined constraints) models show a lack of feasibility in the use of constraint modeling. The intention of defining a minimal distance as constraints is not possible. Constraints were used which fix the distance to a certain value, e.g. the statement: 'the wall has to have a thickness of at least 30 cm' had to be modeled as a fixed distance. In larger models subsequent modifications resulted in error messages which did not support the user in a detailed analysis thus were not comprehensible. Another problem is the difficulty to predict the impact of a modification. For example a simple model consisting of two walls and a fixed angle between them results in 'jumping' elements and unpredictable new positions if you try to rotate one of the walls. The assumption is that an arbitrary solution is computed by the implemented constraint solver.

5. Requirements for handling subsequent modifications

As a result of our investigations in current CAE software as given in the previous section, we specified a set of requirements for an object model that can handle subsequent modifications. We regard the following requirements of usability as essential:

- *Valid geometry*: A valid geometry has to be preserved in every phase of modeling. That requires valid space partitioning including closed surfaces.
- *Consistent model*: All kinds of parametric relations have to be defined and treated equally. The constraint system consists of constraints defining the relation between

objects and constraints defining an object itself. A comprehensible behavior requires equally defined and treated constraints for these different kinds of constraints.

- *Traceable modifications*: Any modification has to be propagate with continuity. It consists of a transparent path of changes in the model including the affected elements in case of failure or success.
- *Predictable result*: A modification has to result in a unique solution and a modification in geometry has to be propagated only as far as necessary.
- *Local changes*: The impact of modifications has to be as small as possible to get an efficient calculation process and an understandable behavior.

6. Concept

The concept consists of three parts: the geometry model, the constraint model and a strategy to propagate changes in case of a subsequent modification. Meeting the requirements of usability as good as possible can only be achieved by an appropriate interaction between these parts.

The developed geometry model is based on a Boundary Representation (brep) in 2-dimensional space. An object is described by its closed boundary. Every boundary segment is bounded by two points and defined by a straight line connecting these points. All points are included in a point set *P*. The identity of two points does not depend on their geometry, it's determined by the point's object reference. That means a boundary segments geometry is controlled by its two defining points.

The constraint model consists of a constraint set *C*. Every constraint of this set is defined by two points of the geometry model, an interval and a normalized direction vector. The direction vector defines the direction of the connecting vector from the first point to the other. A constraint is valid as long as the distance of the two related points lies in the bounds of the interval and is defined in the direction of the vector. A constraint graph consists of every point of *P* representing a node and every constraint of *C* representing a connecting edge. Every constraint includes the information how in case of a violation a point has to be moved to make the constraint valid again.

The strategy of propagation is to spread changes by violated constraints themselves. As a modification moves a point, all constraints of that point have to be validated. In case of a violation a constraint has to be made valid again without changing the triggering point. If a constraint is made valid again by moving the other point all other constraints of that point have to be validated and the change spreads. The propagation graph *W* consists of every moved point of *P* representing a node and every temporarily violated constraint of *C*.

According to Lee et al. (2006) we define behavior as a response of an object '...to internal or external stimuli...'. We introduce the following classification of behavior:

- *Object behavior* is the response which is necessary to make constraints in the interior of an object valid again. It is defined by the subgraph of the propagation graph which includes only points of the object's boundary.
- *Local behavior* is the result defined by the subgraph of the propagation graph including a point with violated constraints to adjacent points.
- *System behavior* is the response defined by an entire propagation graph.

The current state of development includes the following limitations:

- Geometry is defined in regular 2-dimensional Cartesian grid coordinate system. That means boundary segments have to be vertically or horizontally aligned. It is needed because of a simplification of the calculation of neighboring objects.
- Each modifications is limited to moving a point exactly by 1 unit.

These limitations result in constraints which are explained in the next section.

7. Object modelling

Because we introduced constraints as relations between points, modeling geometric objects representing building components has to meet requirements of being constructible. We expect building components to have a correct geometry, which means the used bounding representation has to be correct. We define an object to be correct if its boundary has no gaps (watertightness), is oriented anti-clockwise and no boundary segments touch each other except at the endpoints (self-intersecting and no material content). These requirements can be met by defining a minimal set of constraints. These constraints have to guarantee an intended object behavior to preserve these properties.

In a 2-dimensional coordinate system objects are watertight if their boundary segments contains no gaps. In our model 0-distance-constraints in every direction between a pair of two overlapping points of the boundary are added. That means every pair of points with the same geometric location on the boundary has to be at the same place.

For convex objects preventing self-intersection and touching of opposite boundaries can be guaranteed by specifying constraints on the two endpoints of every boundary segment. The type of constraint is called larger-0-constraints with an interval of $]0, \infty]$. That means the length of a line segment has to be larger than 0. Because the used constraints are directed it also prevents negative lengths, thus it also prevents a partial reversal of the direction of the closed polygonal chain. For non-convex objects it is necessary to define additional 0-distance-constraints between points of boundary segment laying on opposite sides.

As an additional requirement in a regular Cartesian grid coordinate system, we have to keep every line segment axis parallel. Therefore between the two endpoints of every boundary segment there has to be defined a 0-distance-constraint in normal direction.

A

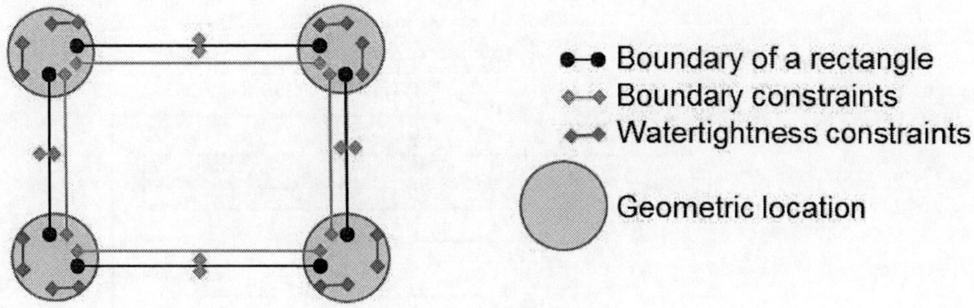

rectangular object in a regular Cartesian grid can be constrained as shown in Figure 1.

Figure 1: The modeled boundary geometry and used constraints for a rectangular object

Additional constraints can be specified for an object as long as they do not violate the described constraints.

Constraints between objects can be specified by constraining one point of an object to another point of another object. A correct building model has to prevent overlapping of building components. As soon as two boundary segments with opposite directed normal vectors get in touch with each other, an additional constraint is created. This constraint guarantees the larger-0-constraints between a point of one and a point of the other boundary. The direction of the constraint has to be the normal direction of one boundary segment. It is removed as soon as both of the boundaries lose their touch.

8. Algorithm

The system state before a modification is introduced is always valid. That means all constraints are not violated. A user-introduced modification is applied as an operation. An operation includes information about the point which is moved, the new coordinates of the point and triggering operations. The idea is to propagate an applied modification as near as possible but as far as necessary. Therefore intermediate states are generated as violated constraints get fixed. These states include temporarily violated constraints, which will be fixed in following steps. As long as constraints are not yet fixed, the algorithm will not terminate. The resulting state includes only non-violated constraints. The process of the algorithm is shown in Figure 2.

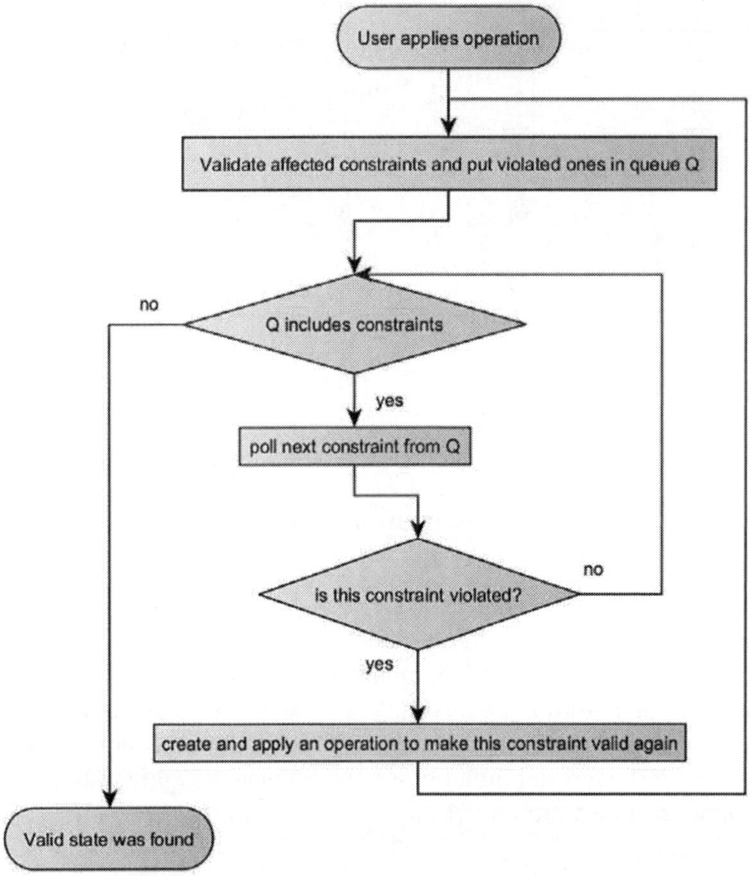

Figure 2: Flowchart of the algorithm for the propagation of a modification.

As we used a regular Cartesian grid the directions are independent. The algorithm always terminates because the created and applied operations do always have an impact in one direction and they move points exactly 1 unit. That's why cycles in the propagation graph always have a valid solution. This solution is the movement of all affected points in the same direction. That also means there is always a global solution consisting of the movement of all points in one direction.

9. Implemented example

The prototype was used to model different examples of a 2-dimensional plan view of a simple building. The description of the modeled geometry and constraints is: 4 walls enclosing a room with two columns Col1 (deep blue) and Col2 (green) and a half-dividing wall W1 (red) in one horizontal line. All walls have a fixed thickness. All horizontal walls have a fixed length except W1. The length of W1 has to be larger than 0. The vertical walls have a length of larger than 0. W1 is fixed on the right hand to the bounding wall. All enclosing walls are aligned flush on the outside. The columns have also a fixed thickness. The state at the beginning is shown in Figure 3.A. The number of constraints per object is 16 as explained in section 'object modeling'. 10 constraints exist between objects.

Modifying W1 by dragging a point of the left boundary 1 unit to the left extends W1. The new state is shown in Figure 3.B. Because the Col2 and W1 get in touch additional constraints are created to guarantee the avoidance of overlapping parts between them. Continuing the extension of W1 moves Col2 because of the just created constraints. In Figure 3.C Col2 and Col1 get in touch and additional constraints are created to avoid overlapping between them. Moving Col1 1 unit to the left results in a new state shown in Figure 3.D. Because Col1 and Col2 have lost their touch, additional constraints are removed.

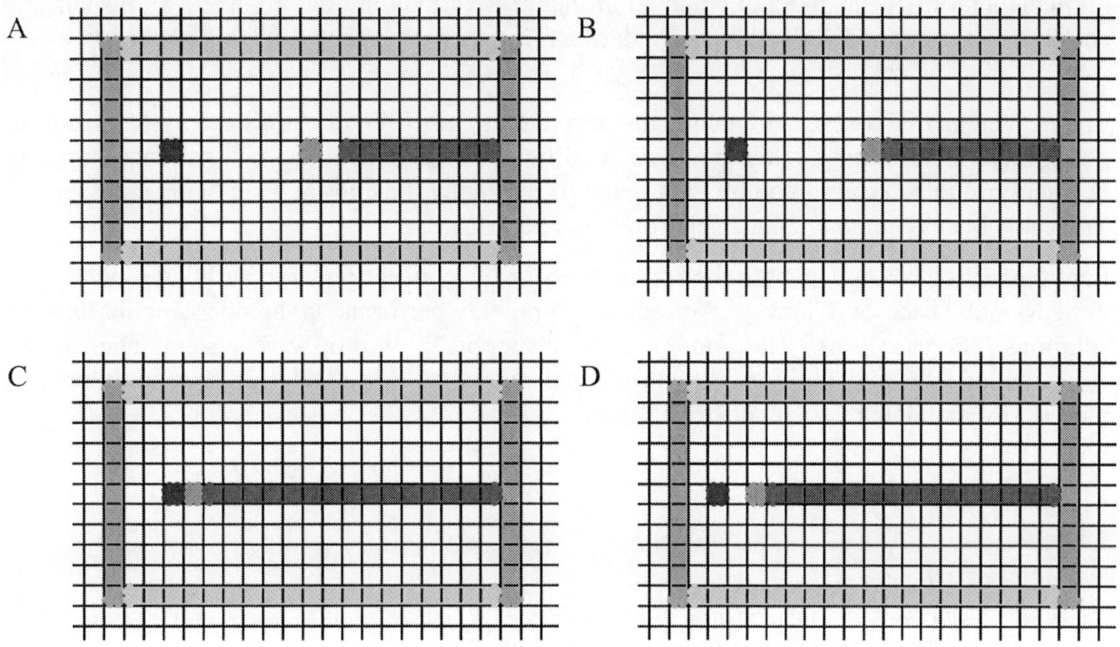

Figure 3: 4 different states of the example as a result to modifications of wall W1 (red) in the order A→B→C and column Col1 (blue) in the order C →D.

Additional modifications of the example show that it's possible to create a high number of possible states by dragging points on the boundary of Col1, Col2 and W1 without changing the geometry of the surrounding walls.

The examples modeled and tested in an implemented prototype showed the fulfillment of the requirements for subsequent modifications given in section 5. The validity of geometry has been preserved by using well-defined constraints on the boundary. The model is completely consistent and the chosen algorithm treats all kind of constraint equally. The modifications are traceable, because it is possible display every process step of the propagation. A predictable result is calculated by making the operations as small as possible and by defining them only in one direction. That leads to only one possible solution. Additionally the algorithm only propagates local changes. That limits the impact of modifications to the smallest necessary propagation.

10. Conclusion and future work

In this paper we presented first results of research for a comprehensible and traceable building model behavior in the case of subsequent modifications. The analysis of a current BIM software demonstrated the necessity for that kind of behavior. The requirements for handling subsequent modifications in a geometric model are defined. These requirements are intended to support the user in modeling correct geometry and comprehensible system behavior.

A concept for a model that meets the requirements was presented and it was shown how to use constraints in the model to preserve correct geometry. Interval constraints are used to transfer more of the modeler's intent into the model and allow a higher flexibility to modifications. Furthermore an algorithm to handle modifications and to create behavior was explained. Finally an example was given which was created with a prototypic implementation. So far the implementation includes various limitations like a Cartesian grid coordinate system and orthogonal boundaries. The results presented in this paper are a first step.

The next steps of our research include the introduction of different coordinate systems and the possibility of specifying other types of modification, for example the rotation of objects. Furthermore the concentration on the impact of removing the current limitations is important. Traceable behavior and a unique solution could be affected.

Future research has to deal with the applicability of the concept on large building models in 3-dimensional space and how the presented approach performs in comparison to existing solutions. The user has to get a more extensive support by the software system. The support could include the possibility of structuring the model by a hierarchy or analyzing existing models, for example by their constraint graph.

References

Bettig, B., M. Hoffmann, C. (2011). Geometric Constraint Solving in Parametric Computer-Aided Design. J. Comput. Inf. Sci. Eng 11, 021001–021001. doi:10.1115/1.3593408

Borrmann, A., Berkhahn, V. (2015). Grundlagen der geometrischen Modellierung. In: Borrmann, A., König, M., Koch, C., Beetz, J. (Eds.). Building Information Modeling. Springer Fachmedien Wiesbaden, Wiesbaden, pp. 25–41.

Donath, D., Böhme, L.F.G. (2007). Constraint-Based Design in Participatory Housing Planning. International Journal of Architectural Computing vol. 6 - no. 1, pp. 97-117 6. doi:10.1260/147807708784640081

Kortenkamp, D.-M.U. (1999). Foundations of dynamic geometry (dissertation). Swiss Federal Institute of Technology Zurich.

Köhler, T. (2015). Auswirkungen nachträglicher geometrischer Änderungen auf und in Gebäudemodellen (bachelor thesis). TU Berlin, Berlin.

Lee, G., Sacks, R., Eastman, C.M. (2006). Specifying parametric building object behavior (BOB) for a building information modeling system. Automation in Construction, Knowledge Enabled Information System Applications in Construction 15, 758–776. doi:10.1016/j.autcon.2005.09.009

Niemeijer, R.A., de Vries, B., Beetz, J. (2014). Freedom through constraints: User-oriented architectural design. Advanced Engineering Informatics 28, 28–36. doi:10.1016/j.aei.2013.11.003

Sarfraz, M. (2013). Geometric Modeling: Techniques, Applications, Systems and Tools. Springer Science & Business Media.

de Vries, B., Jessurun, A.J., Kelleners, R.H. (2000). Using 3D geometric constraints in architectural design support systems. Presented at the WSCG2000.

A Next Generation Platform for Building Energy Modeling Based on Smart Metering Data, Point Cloud Scans, GIS and Building Typology

Robert Irmler, Christian Eller, Uwe Rüppel
Technische Universität Darmstadt, Germany
irmler@iib.tu-darmstadt.de

Abstract. About 28 % of German total final energy consumption is caused solely by the residential sector. In order to reduce this amount, energy simulations can give insights into how retrofits and modifications can influence a buildings energy performance. Due to the complexity of such simulations and their underlying models this is a task which is usually performed by experts. To make residential energy simulations accessible to a wider audience this paper proposes a concept for developing a holistic building simulation model based on a minimum of user inputs. The concept bases on the combination of different information sources like geodetic data sets, building and material typologies and indoor point cloud scans. In addition, smart metering data is used to adjust archetypal assumptions. This paper gives an overview of the different parts of the proposed framework and discusses first results.

1. Introduction

The responsible and efficient use of our planet's resources is one of the main challenges of our time for politics, industry and consumers. More than 20 % of the worldwide final energy consumption is caused by the building sector (EIA, 2013). Due to more energy-dependent living standards this amount is even higher within most OECD countries. In Germany, the residential building sector accounts for about 28 % of total final energy consumption. As part of their energy efficiency strategy the German government set the goal to reduce the primary energy consumption of the building sector by 80 % by 2050.

Residential buildings make up more than 60 % (~ 19 million buildings) of the German building stock. The current refurbishment rate is at roughly 1 %. To achieve the aforementioned goal by 2050, this rate needs to be doubled (German Energy Concept, 2010). Unfortunately, house owners and investors often show hesitation and concerns when it comes to investment decisions regarding retrofitting measures. Common reasons for that are that they are not fully aware of all energy saving potentials and the complexity of the topic repels them or leads to poor decisions. Therefore, recent studies demand alongside greater financial incentives an increase in transparency and validity of appropriate information tools (Prognos, 2015). In this context, suitable methods for modeling the energy consumption of residential buildings are important in order to simulate and optimize retrofitting measures. To encourage as many owners as possible to carry out refurbishment measures, information tools should be easily accessible and should not require expert knowledge regarding building energy simulations.

The energy performance of a building is determined by many different factors such as geometry, weather conditions, occupant behavior, electrical equipment and insulation quality. As these parameters vary greatly among the residential sector, the development of a reliable energy simulation model can be challenging. There are different approaches for modeling a buildings energy consumption which can be roughly divided into engineering methods and data-mining, i.e. statistical, methods. If historical measuring data is present, machine learning algorithms like artificial neural networks or support vector machines can be used to develop an abstract model of a buildings energy consumption via training and optimization processes.

Recent reviews on the application of these techniques are given by Zhao and Magoulès (2012) and Ahmad et al. (2014). However, such supervised learning models crucially rely on the presence of historical consumption information. Therefore, it can be difficult to simulate the change of building characteristics, i.e. the impact of retrofitting measures. On the other hand, engineering methods model the energy consumption of a building based on physical principles, e.g. heat balance and transfer algorithms. Those models are often used by common software solutions like eQuest, EnergyPlus, Autodesk Green Building Studio or TRNSYS. Unfortunately, the development of such models usually requires much more detailed input information. From a house owner's perspective such comprehensive information can be difficult to obtain. Moreover, the correct setup of an engineering model requires expert knowledge and a deep understanding of the utilized software. Therefore, efforts have been made to develop simulation models that require less input information. These approaches usually utilize some sort of typology or archetype library to supplement missing model parameters (Kalogirou et al., 1997; Parekh, 2005; Rhodes et al., 2015). In addition, there are also suggestions for the use of geographic information models as a basis for urban-scale energy simulations (Nouvel et al., 2013). While it has been shown that such models can yield acceptable results in some cases, unverified archetypal defaults as well as over-simplification often lead to major discrepancies in energy estimations.

For that reason, this paper proposes a new concept for developing holistic energy simulation models for German residential buildings based on a minimum of user inputs. In accordance with existing research in the field, our concept bases on building typology libraries and geographic datasets to obtain envelope geometry and define archetypal building characteristics. We then further propose the integration of two additional information sources. We will use indoor point cloud scans from next generation mobile devices for modeling the interior geometry and smart metering data in order to adjust the archetypal defaults for building characteristics. The aim of this approach is to develop an easy-to-use platform that provides house owners with guidance for retrofitting measures based on detailed energy simulations. The platform shall serve as an initial information tool and should not require expert knowledge or any complex user inputs. We therefore aim at automating the model development as far as possible by fusing the aforementioned information sources.

This paper consists of five sections including the introduction. Section 2 presents a brief overview of models and methods dealing with building energy simulation based on reduced user input and the inclusion of different information sources. The modules of the proposed framework are discussed in Section 3. Section 4 provides a short discussion of first simulation results of generated building archetypes. Finally, Section 5 summarizes conclusions and discusses topics for further research.

2. Literature Review

There are a number of models and methods that focus on assessing a buildings energy performance based on simplified input data. Kalogirou et al. (1997) trained an artificial neural network to predict the required heating load of buildings based on spaces. The authors chose 5 input parameters to cover information on window area, external wall area, partition area, floor area and design room temperature of a space. They further used three additional inputs for type codes which represented different thermal qualities of windows, walls, and roof / ceiling. The classification of construction elements by type codes can be understood as a rudimentary definition of construction archetypes. The network was trained with 225 known cases and showed a maximum error of 10 % on test datasets. The results demonstrate that the use of archetypal information can yield acceptable results for energy predictions. However, the presented method would not be suitable for simulating the impact of retrofitting measures. This is partially due to the fact that the used classification only comprise a small sample of construction configurations. To enable the network to simulate the full spectrum of possible construction settings, a more detailed classification and a larger training dataset would be required. Moreover, the simulation of new technologies, for example new strategies to include renewable energies, would be virtually impossible as there would not be any training data available.

Considering the variety of possible retrofitting measures, energy simulations based on bottom-up engineering models seem to be the most appropriate method as they provide great flexibility in model configuration. As mentioned before, these models require extensive information about all sorts of building characteristics. The type of data required depends on the specific simulation engine used. Models usually require information on: location, climate conditions, geometry, materials and thermal parameters of envelope components, HVAC systems, appliance schedules and occupancy levels. To simplify the user depended input a common approach is the use of an archetype library. Archetype libraries are meant for providing appropriate defaults about geometry and thermal characteristics of a building. These characteristics usually include typical dimensions, make and composition of envelope components as well as predominant HVAC systems. An archetype library is typically based on a detailed survey of the building stock and provides some sort of classification referring to construction period, building type and region. Parekh (2005) describes the development of an archetype library for the Canadian residential housing stock. By examining and correlating different surveys and statistical findings, various representative archetypes were modeled with respect to the following three major components: geometric, thermal and operational configurations. The geometric configuration distinguished various housing forms, different plan layouts as well as foundation and roof types. The required geometric inputs were: footprint dimension, house form, number of levels, shape of the house and the roof and foundation type. The thermal configuration was based on survey data and included characteristics of the envelope components, heating and hot water equipment and parameters regarding airtightness and ventilation. Subsequently, based on the location of the house and the year of construction (or latest retrofitting), all thermal characteristics of a specific archetype could be generated. The operational parameters were intended to reflect the occupants' behavior and utilization of appliances. A dataset of highly monitored houses was used to reason typical operating profiles. Those profiles included assumptions for base loads associated with lighting and other energy consuming appliances, levels of occupancy, thermostat settings and average hot water use. The author makes the conclusion that archetype information simplifies the data input and can serve as a basis for quick energy analysis. On the downside, it is also pointed out that unverified archetypal defaults can lead to unacceptable discrepancies in energy estimations, especially for houses that had been subject to retrofitting. To avoid such discrepancies, the author suggests that envelope characteristics as well as space and heating inputs should be confirmed and the number of default values should be limited.

It becomes clear that the sole reliance on archetypal information cannot appropriately account for the individual characteristics of a single building. Therefore, this approach is not considered sufficient for the task of simulating refurbishment measures as part of a reliable information tool for house owners and investors. To reduce the amount of default data, a reasonable approach can be the use of data provided by geographic information systems. Depending on the data model these information systems can provide footprint dimensions or even the whole envelope geometry of a building. Nouvel et al. (2013) propose an integrated process for urban-scale heating demand calculation based on 3D CityGML models. They state that due to its spatial-semantic model, CityGML can serve as an excellent database for automated heating demand diagnostics. Because CityGML models can present in different levels of detail, the accuracy of simulation results may vary. Results of two case studies showed mean deviations between simulated and real heating consumption of less than 10 % when detailed information about thermal building attributes were available. If the 3D model did not include such data, local building typology libraries were used for estimation based on construction / refurbishment years. In such cases the heating demand calculations for a district resulted in an error of around 20 %.

There are also several software solutions and web interfaces with varying capabilities which allow for a simplified generation of building energy simulation models. One example is BEopt™ (Building Energy Optimization) which is developed by the National Renewable Energy Laboratory of the U. S. Department of Energy. The desktop application provides capabilities to model single or multiple residential buildings based on a simple geometry generator. Parameters regarding envelope characteristics, appliances, occupancy levels etc. are given by default and are adjustable within a predefined range. BEopt can be used to analyze existing buildings as well as new constructions with respect to cost-optimal design and energy efficiency measures. Rhodes et al. (2015) performed a case study utilizing BEopt to predict residential energy usage of 54 homes in Austin (Texas) and compared their results to the actual meter reads. To assess the accuracy of the simulation program they investigated four different scenarios of input data. The best result, an aggregated error of 2.4 %, was obtained when using measured weather data, energy audits and survey data to adjust some of the default building characteristics and to account for user behavior. They state that model results for an individual house may vary significantly (up to 30 %), especially for homes with particularly low consumption.

We can summarize that the use of building archetypes can yield acceptable results on urban-scale energy simulations and is a useful tool for quick energy analysis. Geographic information systems can provide geometry data and in some cases even additional semantic information to support model development. However, on a single-building scale archetypal defaults often lead to major inconsistencies when the assumptions differ significantly from the individual building properties. The main pitfalls that can compromise a simulation model are unverified envelope geometry or thermal characteristics and an assumed user behavior. As a verification of construction attributes can only be achieved by field surveys - which would contradict the idea of simplification - another way of verifying the model assumptions is needed. Under the prospect of increasing dissemination of smart metering devices, high frequent monitoring data is considered an applicable source for adjusting default assumptions. Furthermore, next generation mobile devices offer an easy-to-use way to perform point cloud scans. If such information can be utilized, it can support model generation with more precise information on the interior geometry, i.e. thermal zones.

3. Conceptual Framework for Model Generation

Following the thought of simplifying the input process our aim is to develop an integrated web application that makes residential energy modeling accessible to a wider audience. The web application shall provide users with the ability to easily develop a building model and to perform specific queries and modifications on it. Figure 1 shows the component model of the proposed framework.

The framework consists of three major components: the geometry module, the generator module and the calibration module. Each will be described in the following subsections. The central part is the generator module which performs the task of assembling the simulation model based on user inputs and different data sources. We chose EnergyPlus as target platform for energy simulation because it is a powerful, open-source and widely acknowledged simulation engine (see Maile et al., 2007). To automate the model generation as far as possible we further use the open-source middleware OpenStudio® which includes a powerful API that provides object-oriented access to the building model.

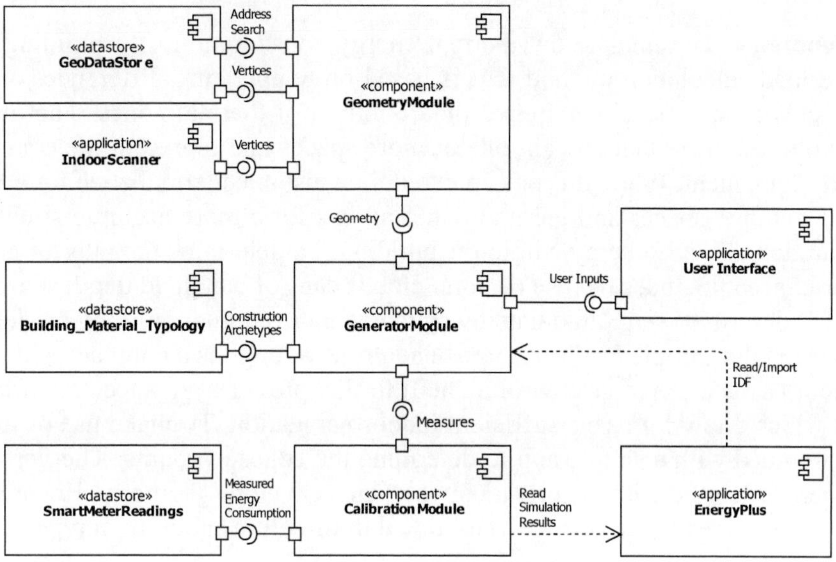

Figure 1: UML Component Model for EnergyPlus Model Generation

3.1 Geometry Module

The geometry module serves the purpose of providing envelope and interior geometry information for the generator module.

Envelope Geometry. Since 2014 the complete German building stock is modelled in CityGML. The OGC Standard CityGML is an open geospatial model for the representation, storage and exchange of 3D city and landscape models (Gröger et al., 2012). CityGML describes 3D objects with respect to their geometry, topology, semantics and appearance. The standard defines five different levels of detail (LoD). The simplest representation is LoD0 which is the plain building footprint, LoD1 models a building as a simple rectangular block, LOD2 adds the roof form and other outer installations, LoD3 adds openings, and LoD4 finally includes interior installations. The German building stock is currently mostly modeled in LoD1. The countrywide transition to LoD2 is scheduled and some regions have already finished it.

Within the proposed concept the envelope geometry of a building is determined based on its address. Because German federal CityGML models do not provide a georeferenced address it is not possible to directly search for a specific building. However, each federal CityGML model can be identified by a globally unique ID which is linked to the federal land register (ALKIS). Therefore, we first perform an address search on the land register to determine the ID of the building and then obtain the respective CityGML model. Depending on the level of detail the CityGML models then provide different kinds of geometric information. In case of a LoD2 model, footprint dimensions as well as wall and roof surfaces can be obtained. If the building is only modeled in LoD1 we can obtain the footprint dimensions and some information about the building height. It should be noted that the LoD1 building height is often not reliable and usually has an accuracy of only 5 meters. Therefore, our concept mainly focuses on LoD2 models. As an intermediate solution for LoD1 models we can generate the wall and roof surfaces depending on user inputs for roof type and number of stories. Because the federal CityGML models are based on airborne laser scanning they do not provide information about structures below the surface, i.e. basements. Information about the existence of a basement has to be either given by the user or is determined by the specifications of the utilized building typology.

Interior Geometry. To simulate the thermal energy consumption of a building EnergyPlus uses a space load calculation method that is based on temperature differences and boundary conditions between spaces. This requires the definition of thermal zones. Thermal zones are isothermal volumes of air that contain one or more spaces and represent the connection point to the HVAC equipment. While it is possible to define just one thermal zone for a building, the definition of multiple spaces and thermal zones allows for a more accurate simulation of the actual distribution of loads/energy within the building. To determine the interior geometry of a building our concept includes the use of point cloud scans of handheld depth sensors. Franz & Rüppel (2015) describe a semi-automated way to generate a digital building model from depth sensor data using the Google Project Tango. The Project Tango is a compact tablet device that is able to record a 3D mesh of its environment. It further provides advanced feature recognition capabilities which allow for a self-sufficient indoor navigation. To make use of this scan data the user is provided with a simple app to determine the edges of rooms. The vertices of these edges can then be merged with the previously obtained envelope geometry. Regarding the later assignment of schedules and appliances, additional information about room types can be added.

3.2 Generator Module

The generator module fuses the geometry data provided by the geometry module with additional user inputs and archetypal building characteristics. The result of this process is an Input Definition File (IDF) which is the main input file for EnergyPlus. Given the wall and roof surfaces as well as the interior space partitioning, the generator module has to add information about: openings (windows and doors), construction materials of building elements, the HVAC system, the hot/cold water loops, appliances and schedules.

Construction & Materials. The construction and material parameters are derived from a building and material typology with respect to the user inputs for construction period and type of the building.

The building and material typology used in this framework is based on the combination of two specific typologies. The first one is the IWU-typology which is developed by the Institute of Living and Environment (IWU) in Darmstadt. The latest update was published in February 2015 in connection with the EU projects Tabula and Episcope (Loga et al., 2015). The typology now covers 12 major construction periods, 4 basic building size types as well as a number of special cases. This classification results in a total number of 50 different building archetypes. For each archetype the typology offers statistical information on various building characteristics like typical floor area, roof type, window-to-wall ratios and thermal properties of building elements. Because the IWU-typology does not contain information about specific materials we further include a typology developed by the German Center for Environmentally Conscious Construction (ZUB, 2009). The ZUB-typology consists of detailed information about typical materials and constructions with respect to the construction period and region of a building. About 60 % of the German residential building stock consist of single family houses, townhouses or duplex houses. Because we expect multi-family buildings to require special solutions to account for different parties and therefore different consumption patterns, we currently limit our investigations on single family houses and townhouses. Table 1 shows the structure of the building type matrix of the IWU-typology referring to single family houses (SFH) and townhouses (TH).

Table 1: Part of the Building Type Matrix of the IWU-Typology (Loga et al., 2015)

Construction Period		A	B	C		L
		until 1859	1860 - 1918	1919 - 1948		2016 - ...
Building Size Types	SFH	SFH_A 	SFH_B 	SFH_C 	...	SFH_L 
	TH	-	TH_B 	TH_C 		TH_L 

The OpenStudio API allows for the definition of construction sets. These objects encapsulate specific construction definitions of building elements for easy reuse. By adapting the building type matrix shown in Table 1, construction sets for each building type were defined. Such a construction set consists of construction definitions for the following types of building elements: exterior wall, interior wall, ground contact wall, slab, roof, floor, ceiling, window and door. During model generation construction sets provide the ability to easily assign or change the characteristics of all building elements depending on the desired building type. The construction sets are stored in a relational database along with the respective material definitions and other typology parameters.

Openings. Because the available CityGML models do not provide information about windows and doors, these building elements have to be generated according to the window-to-wall ratios of the IWU-typology. The typology provides statistical window-to-wall ratios for north, east, south and west walls. Depending on the orientation of the building, which is given provided by its CityGML model, openings are defined and evenly placed on each exterior wall surface.

HVAC System & Water Supply. Depending on the user inputs regarding the type of heat and hot water supply, e.g. gas or electric, standard heating systems as well as the hot/cold water loops are defined.

Electrical Appliances, Schedules & Occupancy Levels. The power consumption of the building is modeled by standard load profiles for summer, winter and intermediate seasons provided by an energy contractor. These load profiles are scaled according to available smart meter readings. In the same fashion we define default occupancy levels based on a detailed time-use survey (Destatis, 2015) and the user input *NumberOfPeople*.

3.3 Calibration Module

The building simulation model developed by the generator module still includes various archetypal assumptions especially regarding window sizes, construction definitions and thermal properties. To achieve a more realistic model of the investigated building the calibration module has to adjust these assumptions where it is necessary.

OpenStudio allows for the definition of so-called 'measures' to change properties of a building model. In OpenStudio a measure is a set of programmatic instructions that makes changes to a building model. OpenStudio offers a library of about 300 predefined measures but it is also possible to write individual measures. These measures may also take arguments which influence their impact on the model. For example, it is possible to write a measure that takes a certain R-Value and then adds insulation to all exterior wall elements until the R-Value is reached. By using measures, the calibration module can easily adjust building parameters. Table 2 gives an overview the different measures that are developed to adjust essential building characteristics.

Table 2: Measures and parameters to adjust building properties

Measure	**Parameters**	**Description**
M_EWALL	R_EWALL	Assign an exterior wall construction that matches the R-value (R_EWALL).
M_GWALL	R_GWALL	Assign a ground wall construction that matches the R-value (R_GWALL).
M_ROOF	R_ROOF	Assign a roof construction that matches the R-value (R_ROOF).
M_SLAB	R_SLAB	Assign a slab construction that matches the R-value (R_SLAB).
M_WIN	R_WIN, A_WIN	Assign a window construction that matches the R-value (R_WIN). Change the window area evenly across all surfaces to match the given area (A_WIN).
M_TEMP	T_SPACES	Change all thermostats to control a given operative temperature.

Finding the right mix of measure parameters represents an optimization problem. The concept for calibration therefore includes a genetic algorithm (GA) to determine the optimal set of arguments. As any other GA, this algorithm is based on the evolution of a population of individuals. Each individual represents a set of measure parameters and therefore a solution to the optimization problem. GAs use fitness functions to evaluate the fitness of each individual, i.e. the quality of each particular solution to the given problem. To determine how well a certain individual serves the purpose of calibrating the model we calculate the coefficient of variation (CV) between the measured thermal energy consumption and the simulated consumption for the same period. The optimization problem can be summarized as:

$$\text{P: } minimize\ CV(f(X), m)$$

where m are the metered consumption values, $f(X)$ are the simulated consumption values and $X = \{R_{EWALL}, R_{GWALL}, R_{ROOF}, R_{SLAB}, R_{Win}, A_{WIN}, T_{SPACES}\}$ denotes the set of measure parameters, i.e. the genome of an individual.

Figure 2 gives a schematic overview of the proposed calibration algorithm. The initial population is based on a random distribution with respect to the parameters of the initial archetypal model. The fitness evaluation for each individual consists of 3 steps: 1. Making a copy of the initial archetype and applying the measures; 2. Simulation of the thermal energy consumption for a given period; 3. Computing the CV with respect to the metered consumption of the same period. If the CV value satisfies a certain threshold the algorithm terminates. Otherwise the fittest individuals are selected and a new population is created by applying genetic operators.

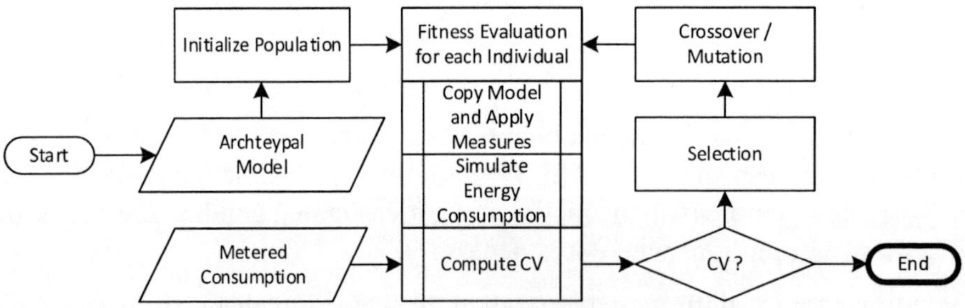

Figure 2: Concept for model calibration algorithm

4. Results and Discussion

As a first step towards implementing the proposed framework we focused on the development of the generator module. To test the feasibility of automated model generation we generated a number of SFH archetypes for different construction periods. A generic floor layout was used and scaled according to the characteristic floor areas given by the IWU-typology. The HVAC system was set to a gas heating system.

Figure 3 shows the simulated end use consumption per year and square meter for each archetype. The simulation was performed with a typical weather data file for the German region of Frankfurt. The results are compared to the average consumption of different classes of German residential buildings with respect to their construction period (BMWi, 2014). The tests show that the simulation results for archteypes refering to earlier construction periods are in accordance with the statistical average. On the other hand, for archetypes refering to more recent construction periods, the energy consumption is highly underestimated. In such cases the simulated energy consumption differs up to 60 % from the statistical average. The reason for that could not be definitely determined yet, but it also demonstrates that the sole reliance on archetypal information is not always reliable.

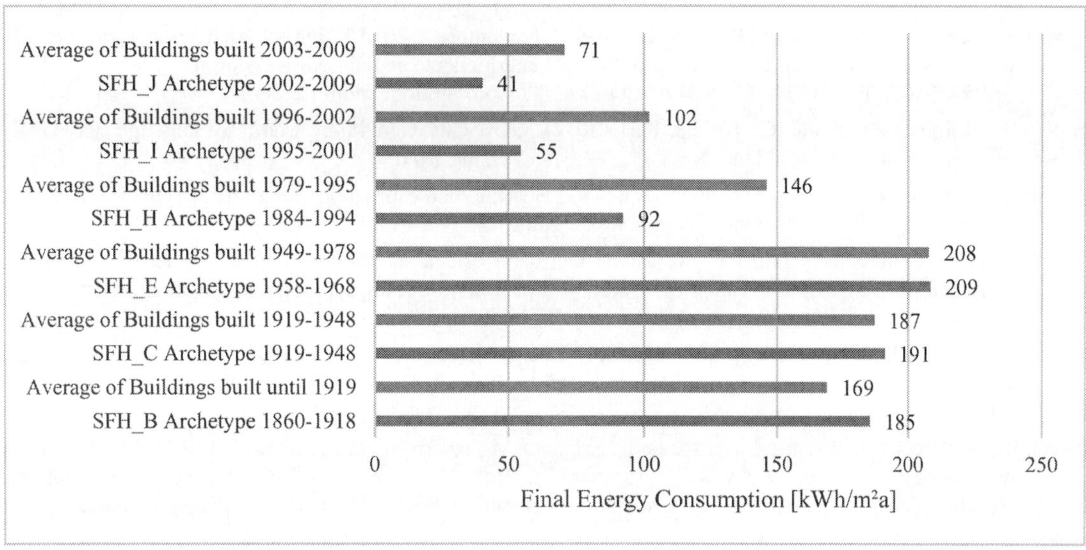

Figure 3: The simulated final energy consumption of archetypes compared to the average final energy consumption of German residential buildings for different construction periods

5. Conclusions

This paper presented a conceptual framework for generating a holistic building model for residential energy simulations by fusing different information sources. The different steps of assembling a simulation model as well as a method to calibrate archetypal assumptions were described. As a first step we implemented the typology-based generation of building archetypes. The feasibility of this approach was demonstrated but simulation results for archetypal models also showed varying accuracy compared to statistical data. Other parts of the framework are still conceptual and their feasibility remains to be proven. Therefore, the next steps of development will focus on the inclusion of the proposed geometry data sources and the implementation of the calibration algorithm. We further believe that the inclusion of handheld depth sensor devices like the Project Tango has great potential because these devices do not only provide point cloud data but also image information. In this context, feature recognition algorithms may provide the ability to automatically detect building elements, e.g. windows and doors. This would eliminate another group of default assumptions and may therefore lead to a more realistic model.

References

Ahmad, A.S.; Hassan, M.Y.; Abdullah, M.P.; Rahman, H.A.; Hussin, F.; Abdullah, H. & Saidur, R. (2014). A review on applications of ANN and SVM for building electrical energy consumption forecasting. In: Renewable and Sustainable Energy Reviews, 33, 2014, Pages 102-109.

BMWi - Federal Ministry of Economy and Energy (2014). Refurbishment Requirements of the Building Stock (German language). Web. 4th January 2016. https://www.bmwi.de/BMWi/Redaktion/PDF/E/sanierungsbedarf-im-gebaeudebestand,property=pdf,bereich=bmwi2012,sprache=de,rwb=true.pdf

Destatis - Federal Office of Statistics (2015). Time-use survey 2012/2013 (German language). Available at: https://www.destatis.de/DE/Publikationen/Thematisch/EinkommenKonsumLebensbedingungen/Zeitbudgeterhebung/Zeitverwendung5639102139004.pdf?__blob=publicationFile

Franz, S. & Rüppel, U. (2015). Supporting forensic fire cause analysis with next generation mobile devices by assembling a BIM based on multiple integrated sensor data. In: 22nd EG-ICE International Workshop, 13.-15. Juli 2015, Eindhoven, Netherland.

German Energy Concept (2010). Web. 19th November 2015. https://www.bundesregierung.de/ContentArchiv/DE/Archiv17/_Anlagen/2012/02/energiekonzept-final.pdf;jsessionid=E685AEA0F50FA91874AE7171E0F70DA7.s3t2?__blob=publicationFile&v=5

Gröger, G., Kolbe, T.H., Nagel, C., Häfele, K.H (2012). OGC City Geography Markup Language (CityGML) Encoding Standard. OGC Doc. No. OGC 12-019, Version 2.0.0.

Kalogirou, S.A.; Neocleous, C.C.; Schizas, C.N. (1997) Heating load estimation using artificial neural networks. In: Proc. of CLIMA 2000 Conf., Brussels (Belgium) 1997.

Loga, T.; Stein, B.; Diefenbach, N.; Born, R. (2015). German Residential Building Typology (German language). Darmstadt, 2015, Available at: http://www.building-typology.eu/downloads/public/docs/brochure/DE_TABULA_TypologyBrochure_IWU.pdf

Maile, T.; Fischer, M.; Bazjanac, V. (2007). Building Energy Performance Simulation Tools - a Life-Cycle and Interoperable Perspective. CIFE Working Paper #WP107, Stanford: Stanford University, December 2007.

Nouvel, R.; Schulte, C.; Eicker, U.; Pietruschka, D. & Coors, V. (2013). CiytGML-based 3D city model for energy diagnostics and urban energy policy support. In: Proceedings of the 13th Conference of International Building Performance Simulation Association, Chambéry, France, August 2013, Pages 218-225.

Parekh A. (2005). Development of archetypes of building characteristics libraries for simplified energy use evaluation of houses. In: IBPSA, Ninth International Conference, Montreal, Canada, August 2005, Pages 921–928.

Prognos (2015). Background Paper on Energy Efficiency Strategy Building (German language). Web. 4. April 2016. https://www.bmwi.de/BMWi/Redaktion/PDF/E/energieeffizienzstrategie-hintergrundinformation-gebauude,property=pdf,bereich=bmwi2012,sprache =de,rwb=true.pdf

Rhodes, J.D.; Gorman, W.H.; Upshaw, C.R.; Webber, M.E. (2015). Using BEopt (EnergyPlus) with energy audits and surveys to predict actual residential energy usage. In: Energy and Buildings, Volume 86, January 2015, Pages 808-816.

Swan, L.G. & Ugursal, V.I. (2009). Modeling of end-use energy consumption in the residential sector: A review of modeling techniques. In: Renewable and Sustainable Energy Reviews, Volume 13, Issue 8, October 2009, Pages 1819-1835.

U.S. Energy Information Administration (EIA) (2013). International Energy Outlook 2013. Web. 19th November 2015. http://www.eia.gov/forecasts/ieo/pdf/0484(2013).pdf

Zhao, H. & Magoulès, F. (2012). A review on the prediction of building energy consumption. In: Renewable and Sustainable Energy Reviews, 16, 2012, Pages 3586-3592.

ZUB (2009). Catalog of typical regional materials in existing buildings with respect to the building age and derivation of typical constructions of building components (German language). Available at: http://www.zub-systems.de/files/downloads/Deutschlandkarte-2009-10.pdf

Incorporating knowledge on construction methods into automated progress monitoring techniques

Braun A., Tuttas S., Stilla U., Borrmann A.
Technical University of Munich, Germany
Leonhard Obermeyer Center
alex.braun@tum.de

Abstract. The research conducted in this publication focuses on automated progress monitoring. The recording of the as-built state of a construction site is achieved by photogrammetric methods (e.g. UAVs) and compared to an as-planned (4D) BIM model. Comparison results of those two parts show that especially parts which were "under construction" are difficult to detect. The authors provide a method that uses the additional information on the construction methods provided by the respective construction elements including e.g. formwork or material colors. In conclusion, the overall detection rate of built elements and those that are currently under construction can be improved and therefore optimize the whole monitoring process.

1. Introduction

In construction, process supervision and monitoring is still a mostly analog and manual task. To prove that all work has been rendered as defined per contract, all performed tasks have to be monitored and documented. The demand for a complete and detailed monitoring technique rises for large construction sites where the complete construction area becomes too large to monitor by hand and the number of subcontractors rises. Main contractors that control their subcontractors' work, need to keep an overview of the current construction state. Regulatory issues add up on the requirement to keep track of the current status on the site.

The ongoing digitalization and the establishment of building information modeling (BIM) technologies in the planning of construction projects can facilitate the use of digital methods in the built environment. In an ideal implementation of the BIM concept, all semantic data on materials, construction methods, and even the process schedule are connected. On this basis, it is possible to make statements about costs and the estimated project finalization. Possible deviations from the schedule can be detected and following tasks are easy to identify.

This technological advancement allows new methods in construction monitoring. As described in (Braun et al. 2015a) the authors propose a system for automated progress monitoring using photogrammetric point clouds. The main idea is to use common camera equipment on construction sites to capture the current construction state ("as-built") by taking pictures of the building from a number of different perspectives. When enough images from different points of view are available, a 3D point cloud can be produced with the help of photogrammetric methods. This point cloud represents one particular timestamp of the construction progress and is then compared to the geometry of the BIM ("as-planned"). Details on the comparison algorithms can be found in (Tuttas et al. 2014; Tuttas et al. 2015).

In order to visualize the comparison results and the detected elements, and to verify the used algorithms, all gathered data is stored in a database that is accessible to the *progressTrack Viewer*. This tool displays all building element information as well as process data. The detected elements are highlighted for an easy identification. Figure 1 shows one of the construction sites

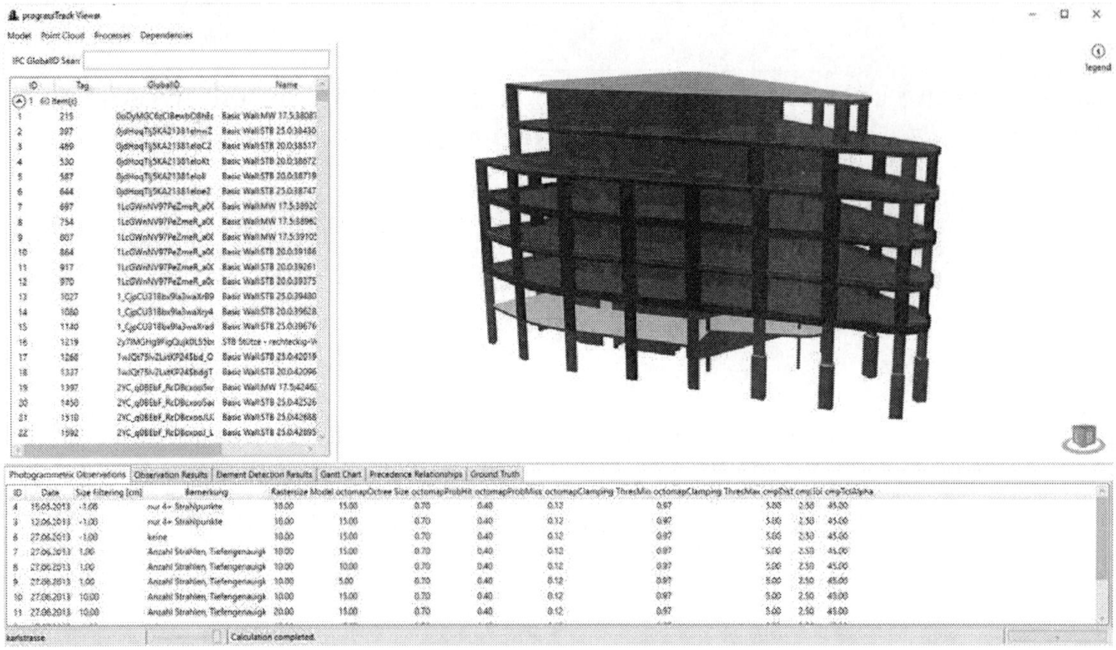

Figure 1: progressTrack Viewer: detected elements for construction site "A". Yellow elements are built, but not detected, green elements are built and detected

that were used for the case studies during this research. The building mainly consists of in-situ concrete elements that were cast using formwork on site. In the figure depicted here, one individual capturing event is selected and all detected elements are highlighted. Green coloring represents elements that have been built and are correctly detected and confirmed through the point cloud. All yellow elements are actually built but were not confirmed through the point cloud.

There are several reasons, why some of those elements were not detected:

Among of the main reasons are occlusions. During construction, large amounts of temporary structures like scaffoldings, construction tools, and construction machinery obstruct the view on the element surfaces. Limited acquisition positions further reduce the visible surfaces and hence the overall quality of the generated point clouds. As introduced in (Huhnt 2005), technological dependencies can help to formalize the schedule sequence. A precedence relationship graph (PRG) can hold this information and help to identify the described occluded elements (Braun et al. 2015b).

Another reason for weak detection rates is building elements which are currently under construction. As those elements count towards the overall progress, they must not be missed and play a crucial role in defining the exact position in the current process. Challenging parts are in general all construction methods, whose temporary geometry differs largely from the final element geometry. This accounts e.g. for reinforcements or formwork. On the one hand, formwork may obstruct the view of the element, making it impossible to be detected. On the other hand, the plane surface of a formwork for a slab might be detected as the surface of the slab itself and thus lead to false positives.

Due to these challenges, further enhancements to the comparison and detection algorithms are needed. Since information on construction methods are already provided by the BIM, the knowledge can be incorporated into the overall detection process and thus refine the detection results.

2. Related work

Process monitoring has become a heavily researched topic recently. Capturing the as-built construction status is mainly achieved by laser scanners or cameras using photogrammetric methods. For the comparison with the as-planned state (BIM 3D geometry), three methods are currently established:

i) Comparison of the as-built point clouds with points from the transformed as-planned geometry.
These methods compare point clouds that are acquired by laser scanners (Bosché 2010; Turkan 2012) or photogrammetric methods and derived point clouds from as-planned surfaces (Kim et al. 2013). This is mainly done by Iterative Closest Point (ICP) algorithms.

ii) Feature detection in the acquired images from the as-built state.
Using feature detection algorithms like SIFT and RANSAC, construction elements are directly identified from the acquired images (Golparvar-fard et al. 2012).

iii) Matching the as-built point cloud onto the as-planned geometry surfaces.
this approach matches relevant points from the point cloud directly onto triangulated surfaces of the as-planned model (Tuttas et al. 2015).

Monitoring with laser scanners or cameras proved to be helpful according to these studies. It is possible to identify individual elements for each use case. In fact, most publications focus on identifying one particular element. All of these approaches lack the possibility to clearly identify building elements under construction. A first attempt to solve the problem of elements under construction is published by (Han et al. 2015). However, Han focusses on visibility issues. E.g. when an anchor bolt for a column is invisible as it is embedded into the concrete, it still must be present since the column on top of it requires the anchor bolt for structural reasons.

Process planning is often executed independently from conceptual and structural design phases. Current research follows the concept of automation in the area of construction scheduling. Binding process information and the underlying building information model provides additional information that can be used in the context of progress monitoring.

Tauscher describes a method that allows automating the generation of the scheduling process at least partly (Tauscher 2011). He chooses an object-oriented approach to categorizing each component according to its properties. Accordingly, each component is assigned to a process. Subsequently, important properties of components are compared with a process database to group them accordingly and assign the corresponding tasks to each object. Suitable properties for the detection of similarities are for example the element thickness or the construction material. With this method, a "semi - intelligent" support for process planning is implemented.

In (Huhnt 2005) a mathematical formalism is introduced that is based on the quantity theory of the determination of technological dependencies as a basis for automated construction progress scheduling. In (Enge 2010) a branch-and-bound algorithm is introduced to determine optimal decompositions of planning and construction processes into design information and process information.

Another important aspect for the as-planned vs. as-built comparison is dependencies. Technological dependencies represent which element is depending on another element, meaning, that it cannot be built after the first element is finished. These dependencies can be defined by precedence relationships (Wu et al. 2010). A solution to store these dependencies in graphs is discussed in (Szczesny et al. 2012). The approach in relation to progress monitoring is presented in (Braun et al. 2015a).

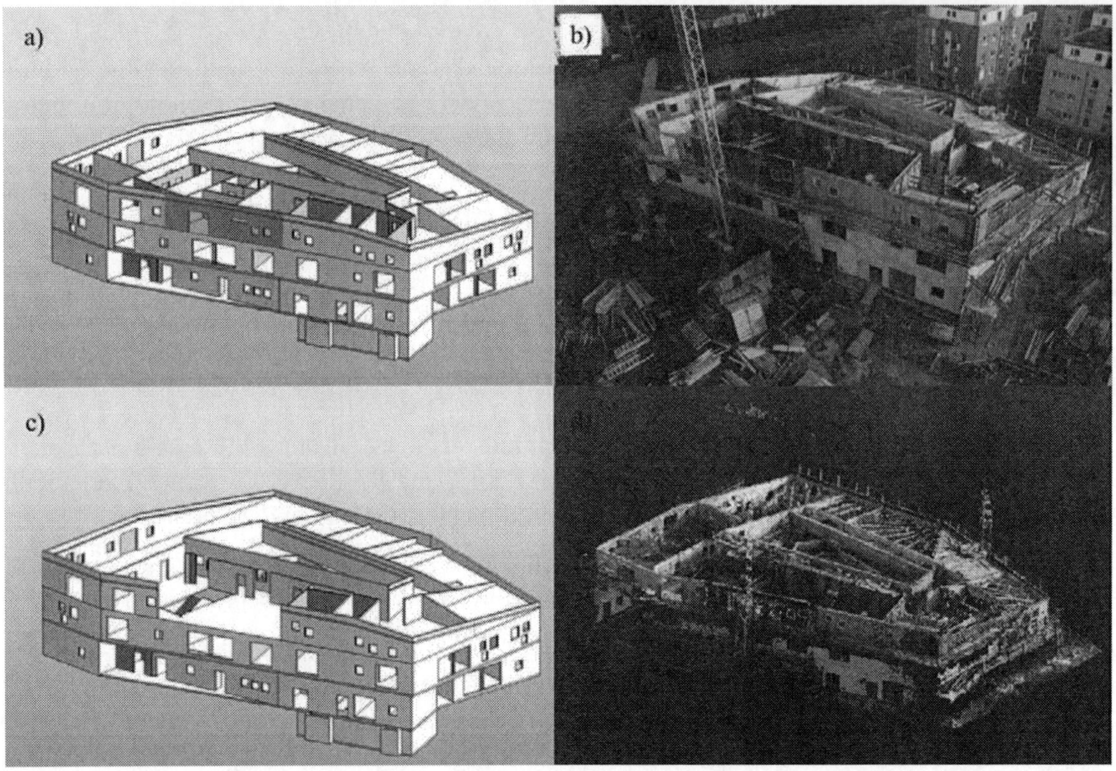

Figure 2: Process modeling problem depicted by a) as-planned modeling, b) as-built photograph, c) as-build modeling, d) as-built point cloud on construction site "C".

3. Challenges

The main goal of this research is to identify suitable construction methods for building elements that can be detected during the comparison process. The focus lies on German construction sites and methods with solid constructions based on in-situ concrete using formwork. However, this does not limit this concept to one particular country as the general construction procedure is similar in almost all sites using concrete elements.

The detection of built elements reveals different challenges:

3.1 Occlusions

As stated, the as-built progress is represented by a 3D point cloud that holds n points with their respective coordinates and corresponding detected color information. The amount n depends on many factors such as lighting conditions, feature detection from different points of view and largely from the amount and resolution of the pictures taken. A point cloud from one timestamp on our construction test site "C" can be seen in Figure 2 d). Scaffoldings and formwork are clearly visible, also various holes in the point cloud that exist due to occlusions or insufficient image quality for a reconstruction. In general, this point cloud is not perfect, but in the expected quality from a construction site that has changing visibility conditions due to working equipment and so on.

3.2 As-planned modeling vs. as-built construction

The as-planned model is represented by a 4D building information model (Figure 2 a)). Each construction element is linked to its belonging process which makes it possible to make statements about the desired construction state at a given timestamp from an as-built point cloud. The corresponding geometry holds 3D information just as the point cloud and since model and point cloud are aligned to the same coordinates, an initial detection algorithm could start the comparison.

However, the as-planned model does not necessarily equal the actual as-built process. To clarify this variance, Figure 2 depicts the BIM from test site "C", a corresponding aerial image taken by a UAV and the generated point cloud (a), b) and d)). The red marked part of the wall on the second is floor currently under construction (as seen in b) and d)), meaning there is formwork installed but no concrete filled yet. On the other hand, the BIM (as seen in a)) has one continuous wall modeled for the same wall, that is constructed on the site in several steps. Therefore, the modeling does not represent the correct construction sequencing. This problem is also described in (Huhnt & Enge 2007; Tulke 2010).

In comparison, Figure 2 c) shows the correct corresponding as-planned model for the current timestamp, with all, subsequently following elements hidden in the view. This "as-built" model is currently modeled iteratively to match the actual construction processes.

4. Identified tasks during construction

During construction, several tasks are required to construct in situ concrete elements or similar elements. The following listing shows the identified tasks on the construction sites, monitored during this research.

4.1 Varying dimensions during construction

With the PRG introduced in Section 5.1, it is possible to identify elements that might possibly be under construction and thus are considered for further investigation.

In situ concrete

In concrete construction, formwork for in situ concrete is the most common construction method. Several different methods are depicted in Figure 2 b) and d). To detect formwork, all possible elements under construction (see Section 4.1) are taken into account.

In general, elements are counted as detected, when a certain amount of points with a distance of less than 2 cm is matched on the surface of the element (Tuttas et al. 2015). If the expected elements are not detected, the threshold for the maximum distance can be adjusted to take into account that the formwork with a thickness of around 0.20m might be currently in place. If this iteration brings positive results, the element can be marked as "under construction".

Composite elements

Modern construction technologies usually use thermal insulation systems for reduced cooling and heating requirements during usage of the finished building. These composite elements consist of several layers, e.g. concrete and rock wool thermal insulation. Depending on the exact element type, these compounds are delivered as precast elements or are manufactured in situ. The latter one is a common and often used method.

In construction modeling, these elements are modeled as one single element consisting of several layers. Due to the thickness of the insulation of around 0.20m, such a wall is not detected, when only the concrete layer is present in the BIM model. Usually, all concrete parts of a building are completed before the thermal insulation is attached, resulting in a very low detection rate. In order to solve this issue, also, single layers of the elements are considered for detection.

4.2 Color detection

In general, formwork for walls and columns consists of a wooden, smooth plate on the concrete side and a steel structure for stability on the backside. This steel structure is often painted yellow, red or orange and differs largely from the gray concrete. Formwork for slabs usually consists of elevated wooden plates that have the same color range as the steel structure mentioned. This color difference can be measured and help to further improve the detection quality of formwork.

The HSV color space provided useful data for the color detection (Sural & Pramanik 2002). HSV stands for hue, saturation and value. With the HSV color space, it is possible to detect color as perceived by humans but also saturation and brightness (value). Each value has a range from 0 to 1.

4.3 Formwork for horizontal elements

Besides the color information mentioned in Section 4.3, slabs and other horizontal elements have another characteristic to identify them under construction. Automated monitoring methods for large construction sites usually observe the site from outside or above. Hence, objects are usually only visible from the side or above. Thus, a slab who's downwards facing surface is detected during the matching seems unusual. This case usually takes effect when the formwork for the element is installed, but the concrete is still missing.

4.4 Reinforcement

The detection of reinforcement depends on the quality of the point cloud itself. In our case, the results vary and make it difficult to identify these thin structures.

5. Concept

The following concept presents possible solutions to tackle the mentioned challenges by incorporation additional information on construction techniques into the comparison algorithms.

5.1 Process sequencing

Automated progress monitoring with photogrammetric methods or laser scanning always captures one particular moment at the current observation time. It is not possible to automatically determine the exact point in a process plan at which the construction progress is currently located.

For an automated handling of dependencies, a precedence relationship graph (PRG) is introduced (Braun et al. 2015a). This graph formalizes technological dependencies between individual elements. One possible graph for the depicted Gantt chart is shown in Figure 3. The correct graph is depending on the real model and not clearly recognizable from the Gantt diagram.

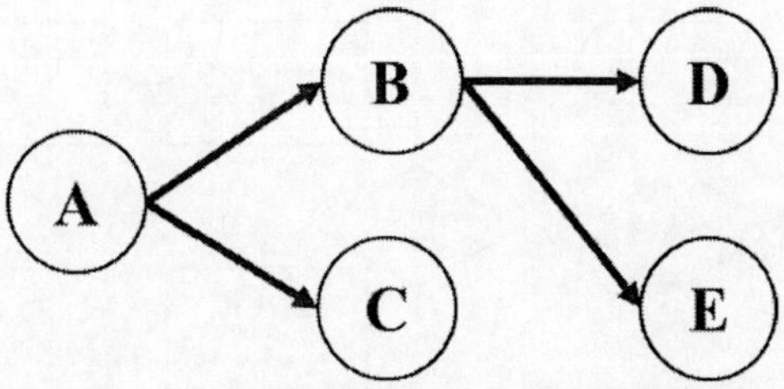

Figure 3: possible precedence relationship graph for the sample in Figure 3

Figure 4 depicts an as-planned Gantt chart visualizing five tasks *A* to *E* where *B and C* as well as *D and E* can run in parallel but are depending on their respective preceding tasks. In this simplified schema, one task represents one building element.

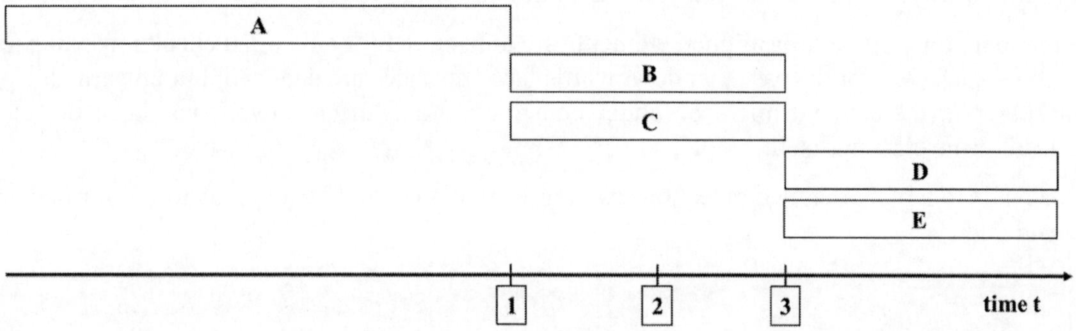

Figure 4: Gantt chart depicting uncertainties for process dependencies and belonging observation time steps

The numbers *1* to *3* symbolize three as-built data acquisitions. For the case that all processes are on time, it is difficult to determine a difference between observation *1* and *2* since the exact construction method is unknown and in most scenarios, construction workers run parallel tasks slightly asynchronous, meaning there might be some work done on task *B* whereas none on task *C*. This gets even more difficult when delays occur, resulting in rearranged process plans.

The PRG will be used to identify objects that are possibly under construction right now. A possible delay of task *A* could result in a detection of parts of the constructed element belonging to task *A* and *B* on observation *2* but no detection of the element belonging to task *C*. As a conclusion, this graph makes it possible to make further assumptions on following tasks when one particular element is detected and forms the basis for the following steps of this concept.

5.2 Workflow

With the PRG introduced in Section 5.1, it is possible to identify elements that might possibly be under construction and thus are considered for further investigation.

The basic flowchart depicted in Figure 5 shows the proposed workflow for the enhanced detection. In general, elements, that are expected to be built, but are not verified by the current detection, run through an extended detection algorithm.

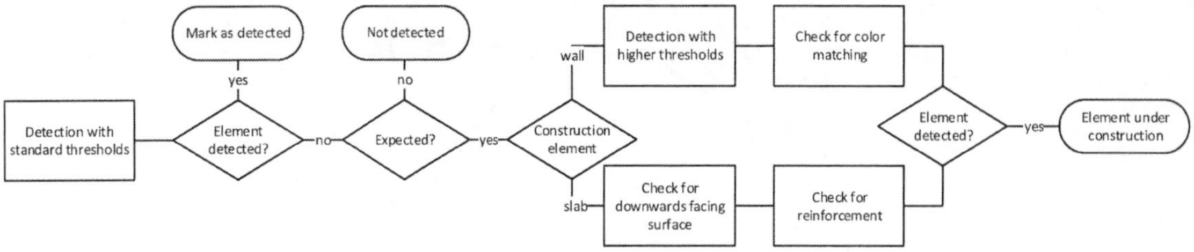

Figure 5: basic flowchart, depicting the workflow for the detection of elements under construction

Depending on the material and type of element, different steps follow. As elaborated, walls and other vertically erected elements are considered for an extended threshold in order to identify possible formwork. Additionally, a color matching for bright red or orange colors is carried out.

In comparison, horizontally aligned elements are considered for a detailed check regarding the detected surfaces. For the case that downwards faced surfaces are detected, but upwards facing surfaces not, the element might be under construction and the formwork has been detected instead of the element itself.

This leads to a more detailed detection result as even elements that are close to be finished are considered.

6. Case Study

To validate the introduced concept, three different construction sites were monitored with different observation methods (Braun et al. 2015b; Tuttas et al. 2016).

6.1 Varying dimensions

Figure 6 depicts a part of a snippet of a point cloud, generated from one time step during observation. It is overlaid with the corresponding 3D geometry, visualized in green color, to symbolize the as-planned as well as the as-built status. Based on this example, the general workflow for elements under construction is shown. As depicted, the front wall is already finished and the concrete surface is visible. The wall in the second row is currently under construction and the formwork is present and registered in the point cloud.

Figure 6: Point cloud of a finished, plain wall and formwork overlaid with the corresponding 3D geometry

During detection, it is expected, that the first row of walls will be detected. Due to the threshold of max. 1 cm, the second row should not be detected due to the formwork. Figure 7 a) shows the expected result, with an additionally set threshold of 1000 points per square meter (green color). Triangles marked in yellow have matching points but do not qualify for the set thresholds while elements marked red have no qualifying points at all.

The walls in the second row are expected to be in progress. As presented in the concept in Section 5.2 the detection is therefore carried out with a larger threshold. In this case, the accepted point to surface distance is increased to 10 cm which leads to the depicted results in Figure 7 b).

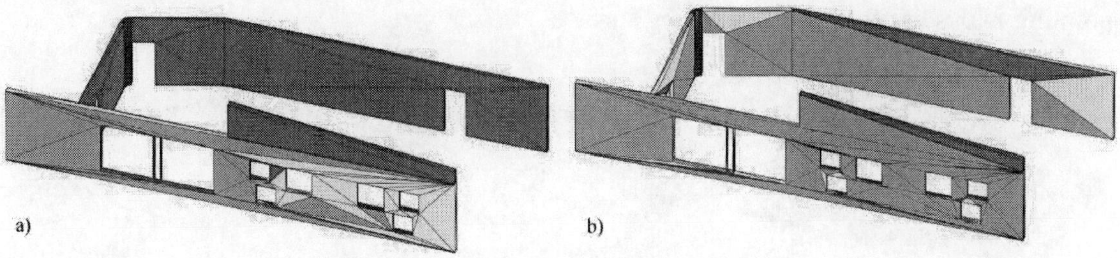

Figure 7: detected triangles during the time step shown in Figure 6. a) with distance 1cm and $\varrho > 1000$ pts/m², b) with distance 10cm and $\varrho > 1000$pts/m²

The increased threshold leads to the expected higher point density on the wall under construction, as the formwork is considered, too. According to the introduced workflow, the wall is now marked as "under construction", leading to a further detailed automated progress monitoring.

6.2 Color detection for formwork and reinforcement

As elaborated in Section 4.2, taking colors into account can improve the detection of formwork or reinforcements due to their significantly varying colors in comparison to the grey colors of the concrete. In order to proof this statement, color values of different elements were compared.

Table *1* shows the calculated mean values for different elements under different lighting conditions.

Table 1: Case study: HSV values for concrete surfaces and formwork

Type	Hue	Saturation	Value
Concrete wall	0.5973	0.0947	0.5690
Concrete wall 2	0.9109	0.0568	0.7040
Formwork 1	0.3880	0.2188	0.3979
Formwork 2	0.1141	0.2850	0.6638
Formwork 3	0.1294	0.7171	0.7078

All points relevant to an element and their color information are taken into account to calculate the mean HSV values. The results show, that the brightness (value) varies largely which is due to the lighting conditions itself. Therefore, this value has no significance. However, the hue values for formwork fall into the correct range for warm, red colors, whereas the concrete walls are based on "colder" colors. Additionally, the saturation differs for at least factor 2.3. This leads to the conclusion, that automated color interpretation is possible and applicable in this context.

6.3 Horizontal elements

Downward facing surfaces are identified by the normal values of their belonging triangulated elements. A normal with negative z-coordinates in a coordinate system with an upwards pointing z-axis has a downwards facing surface.

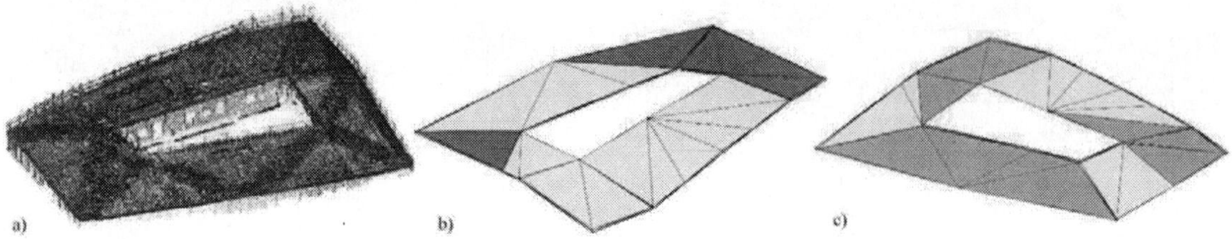

Figure 8: a) point cloud of roof under construction b) detected triangles (top view) c) detected triangles (bottom view)

Figure *8* a) shows the part of a point cloud during construction monitoring. In this case, the roof of one of our test sites is shown. It is currently under construction with the formwork in place. Additionally, parts of the reinforcement are already in place. Figure *8* b) shows the triangulated top surface of the corresponding roof. As visible, only few triangles have matching points that are not sufficient for marking the overall element as "detected". Figure *8* c) shows the downwards facing surface of the roof, that has a significantly higher point density. In this case the available points, representing reinforcement and formwork, matched the corresponding triangles of the roof.

Embedded in the proposed concept, the roof would not be detected as "built" due to the too low point density over the complete surface. However, the downwards facing elements have a sufficient density when considered individually. Thus, the element can be marked as "under construction".

7. Summary

Automated progress monitoring facilitates the need to keep track of construction progress. However, not all elements can be detected with current methods. The presented concept proved helpful to identify elements under construction. Color detection and/or a higher threshold for elements with possible formwork in place can identify additional elements that were not considered as built before. Of course, these methods should not be applied independently from the overall matching process. The methods were tested on three different construction sites.

However, the list of possible construction methods is not complete. Further knowledge on construction methods will help to evolve the system. Especially varying or different construction methods need to be observed and implemented into this concept to help refine the process and detect the construction process for even more elements.

8. Acknowledgements

This work is supported by the German Research Foundation (DFG) under grants STI 545/6-1 and BO 3575/4-1. We like to thank Leitner GmbH & Co Bauunternehmung KG and Kuehn Malvezzi Architects (Test Site A), Staatliches Bauamt München, Baugesellschaft Brunner + Co and BKL (Baukran Logistik GmbH) (Test Site B) as well as Baureferat H5, Landeshauptstadt München, Baugesellschaft Mickan mbH & Co KG, h4a Architekten, Wenzel

+ Wenzel and Stadtvermessungsamt München (Test Site C) for their support during the case studies.

We thank the Leibniz Supercomputing Centre (LRZ) of the Bavarian Academy of Sciences and Humanities (BAdW) for the support and provisioning of computing infrastructure essential to this publication.

References

Bosché, F., 2010. Automated recognition of 3D CAD model objects in laser scans and calculation of as-built dimensions for dimensional compliance control in construction. *Advanced Engineering Informatics*, 24(1), pp.107–118.

Braun, A. et al., 2015a. A concept for automated construction progress monitoring using BIM-based geometric constraints and photogrammetric point clouds. *ITcon*, 20, pp.68–79.

Braun, A. et al., 2015b. Automated progress monitoring based on photogrammetric point clouds and precedence relationship graphs. *Proceedings of the 32nd International Symposium on Automation and Robotics in Construction and Mining*, pp.274–280.

Enge, F., 2010. *Muster in Prozessen der Bauablaufplanung*.

Golparvar-fard, M., Peña Mora, F. & Savarese, S., 2012. Automated Progress Monitoring Using Unordered Daily Construction Photographs and IFC- Based Building Information Models. *Journal of Computing in Civil Engineering*, p.147.

Han, K.K., Cline, D. & Golparvar-Fard, M., 2015. Formalized knowledge of construction sequencing for visual monitoring of work-in-progress via incomplete point clouds and low-LoD 4D BIMs. *Advanced Engineering Informatics*.

Huhnt, W., 2005. Generating sequences of construction tasks. In *Conference on Information Technology in Construction*.

Huhnt, W. & Enge, F., 2007. Consistent information management for structuring construction activities. *Bringing ITC Knowledge to Work, Proceedings of ....*

Kim, C., Son, H. & Kim, C., 2013. Automated construction progress measurement using a 4D building information model and 3D data. *Automation in Construction*, 31, pp.75–82.

Sural, S. & Pramanik, S., 2002. Segmentation and histogram generation using the HSV color space for image retrieval. In *Proceedings. International Conference on Image Processing*. IEEE, pp. II–589–II–592.

Szczesny, K., Hamm, M. & König, M., 2012. Adjusted recombination operator for simulation-based construction schedule optimization. In *Proceedings of the 2012 Winter Simulation Conference*. pp. 1219–1229.

Tauscher, E., 2011. *Vom Bauwerksinformationsmodell zur Terminplanung - Ein Modell zur Generierung von Bauablaufplänen*.

Tulke, J., 2010. Kollaborative Terminplanung auf Basis von Bauwerksinformationsmodellen.

Turkan, Y., 2012. *Automated Construction Progress Tracking using 3D Sensing Technologies*. University of Waterloo.

Tuttas, S. et al., 2014. Comparison of photogrammetric point clouds with BIM building elements for construction progress monitoring. In *The International Archives of the Photogrammetry, Remote Sensing and Spatial Information Sciences, Volume XL-3*.

Tuttas, S. et al., 2016. Evaluation of acquisition strategies for image-based construction site monitoring. In *The International Archives of the Photogrammetry, Remote Sensing and Spatial Information Sciences*. Prague, Czech Republic.

Tuttas, S. et al., 2015. Validation of Bim Components By Photogrammetric Point Clouds for Construction Site Monitoring. *ISPRS Annals of Photogrammetry, Remote Sensing and Spatial Information Sciences*, II-3/W4(March), pp.231–237.

Wu, I.C. et al., 2010. Bridge construction schedule generation with pattern-based construction methods and constraint-based simulation. *Advanced Engineering Informatics*, 24, pp.379–388.

Augmented reality supported work instructions for onsite facility maintenance

Matthias Neges[a] and Christian Koch[b]
[a] Ruhr-University Bochum, Germany
[b] University of Nottingham, United Kingdom
matthias.neges@itm.rub.de (Lead author email address)

Abstract. During the operation and maintenance phase of buildings operators need to perform onsite maintenance activities to prevent functional failures of technical equipment. As this phase is the longest and most expensive one respective improvements can significantly reduce the overall life-cycle budget. Based on their previous work, in this paper the authors present an Augmented Reality (AR) based concept and implementation to support mobile and onsite maintenance activities by (1) preparing and generating AR work order instructions based on Product Lifecycle Management (PLM) information, (2) using these to aid the actual onsite maintenance job using hybrid 3D tracking, and (3) creating enhanced and context-related maintenance service reports to be fed back to the PLM system. Preliminary results reveal the potential of the proposed solution, but also leave room for future improvements.

1. Introduction

The operation and maintenance phase is the longest and most expensive period within the life-cycle of a building or a facility. During this period operators need to perform onsite maintenance tasks to prevent functional failures of technical equipment. Improving current onsite maintenance procedures can significantly reduce the overall life-cycle budget, since it is estimated that more than 85% of the entire life-cycle costs are actually spent on facility management (Teicholz 2004).

Although computer-supported systems have been utilized, it has been reported that still 50% of the onsite maintenance time is solely spent on localizing inspection targets and navigating indoors. (Lee, Akin 2011). Moreover, Hou et al. (2015) have recently concluded that a context-sensitive Augmented Reality (AR) based onsite maintenance procedure for a complex piping system can reduce (1) the total work time by 55% and (2) the error by 50%.

In order to digitally support facility maintenance operators in performing their daily onsite jobs, the authors have previously proposed and tested an Augmented Reality based framework that integrates Building Information Models, natural AR markers and IMU data to support indoor navigation (Neges et al. 2015; Koch et al. 2014). In this paper, however, we present a complementary part of the overall research framework that is related to preparing AR based maintenance instructions offline, using them to support the actual onsite maintenance job, and finally create service reports.

2. Background

Leading projects for AR-based maintenance tasks were ARVIKA (ARVIKA 2003) and STARMATE (Schwald et al. 2001). They focused on AR prototypes and their usability in automotive and aircraft construction as well as machinery and plant manufacturing. The main challenges, however, were the technical possibilities for developing usable and powerful mobile device and robust tracking functionalities. A fundamental finding of the follow-up project ARTESAS (ARTESAS 2004) is the need for IT-based support for the generation of AR maintenance work instructions (Wohlgemuth, Friedrich 2007). Therefore, Saske (2008) focused on the integration of AR maintenance orders in Product Lifecycle Management (PLM) systems for the purpose of generating AR maintenance work instruction based on PLM product structures and available wireframe object models. However, a major drawback is that the overlay of the wireframe object models with real maintenance objects has to be done manually by the user. Mader and Urban (2010) provided an approach for textual work instructions with a specific formularized structure to overlay the maintenance objects with specific visual information, e.g. the work instruction, the used tool and direction indicators for the disassembly process. They used 2D marker tracking and neglected the visualisation of 3D models. The limitation of hardware performance on mobile device led to approaches for outsourcing the tracking and visualisation of 3D models to servers. Following this up, Fründ (2007) provided an approach for AR on mobile devices. The rapid development of high performance smart devices, like phones and tables, enables new approaches for AR solutions. Therefore, existing AR frameworks offer robust 3D tracking functionalities. This combination of modern AR frameworks and up-to-date smart devices is highly promising.

The usability of AR for maintenance task is not limited to the mobile AR software. Rather, an intuitive authoring tool to generate AR specific work instructions is crucial (Steindecker et al. 2014). Some standard 3D-CAD software tools support the generation of work instructions (Wang et al. 2013). Based on the 3D model, the generation of different work steps is very intuitive. However, these instructions are administered specifically to the program and can only be exported as static animations. For that reason, an integration in a dynamic and interactive step-by-step AR work instruction is not possible. In fact, the structure of the work instructions has to be similar to what is presented by Mader and Urban (2010) to actually support an interactive maintenance task. It is conspicuous that AR solutions are limited to visualisation of information and 3D models as an overlay to the real world. Thereby, AR enables new interaction concepts, e.g. intuitive identification of defect parts or position related photos for advanced service reports.

Analysing current approaches the authors have identified seven main requirements for AR work instructions:

1. Use of product information (e.g. product structures and 3D models) from PLM system
2. Intuitive generation of single work steps based on the 3D model
3. Visualisation of affected parts (e.g. screws to unscrew) for the specific work steps on the 3D model
4. Addition of visual hints (e.g. direction indicators for disassembly parts)
5. Flexible structure format of the work instruction
6. Advanced service reports based on interaction in AR
7. Robust tracking of the maintenance object

In summary, there are several existing approaches for AR in maintenance tasks, which all focus on different aspects and meet several, but not all requirements. Currently, an overall approach to generate interactive maintenance work instructions based on product information and to overlay real maintenance objects by using 3D tracking functions is missing.

3. Evaluation of a current standard Augmented Reality framework

In order to fulfil the last requirement (robust tracking) the authors have evaluated existing tracking methods implemented in standard AR frameworks. Neges (2015) has identified six conditions to guarantee the usability of AR in maintenance process. There are five conditions aiming at the robustness of the tracking method, e.g. light conditions, defilement or damages on the surface. Furthermore, the operation under real conditions requires the tracking of the real maintenance objects without the need for additional and artificially placed markers.

Table 1: Evaluation of tracking methods implemented in standard AR frameworks

Tracking methode / condition	ID marker	Borderless markers	Point based tracking	Edge based tracking	Hybrid 2D / 3D tracking	Hybrid 3D tracking (point and edge based)
No need for artificial placed markers	-	O	+	+	O	+
Robustness: damages	-	-	+	O	-	O
Robustness: light conditions	+	+	-	+	+	+
Robustness: pollution	-	-	-	+	-	+
Robustness: various perspectives	-	-	+	O	-	+
Robustness: various distances	O	O	+	O	O	+

Legend for symbols: - poor/negativ O average + good/positiv

As the evaluation shows, a hybrid 3D tracking method is recommended. In this method, the tracking initialisation is based on a virtual edge model, generated automatically from the CAD file. After the initialisation, a Simultaneous Localization and Mapping (SLAM) algorithm detects the environment of the real object and a 3D point cloud map will be generated in the background of the tracking process. This point cloud will be continuously extended and enables the user to move freely around the maintenance object. There is no need to hold a specific point or element in the camera view to keep the tracking going. This hybrid 3D tracking function is only available in one current standard AR framework, the metaioSDK.

3.1 Verification of 3D tracking functions

To guarantee the operation under real conditions, a mobile prototype is implemented on an iPad Air and the Metaio SDK 5.5. The maintenance demonstration object is a smoke detector (Figure 1), which is installed in the buildings of the Ruhr University of Bochum.

a) Real smoke detector b) Virtual CAD model c) Edge model for 3D tracking

Figure 1: Demonstration object to verify the hybrid 3D tracking

The executed tests have shown, that the hybrid 3D tracking has high potential for the operation of maintenance tasks under real conditions. Figure 2 shows an excerpt from the comprehensive results. The defilement was simulated by different grades of graffiti painting (Figure 2a), which can be found frequently in reality. The edge based tracking initialisation was even successful with a high grade of defilement (Figure 2b and c). Furthermore, the combination of edge base tracking initialisation and point based tracking enables the progressive disassembly of the real object (Figure 2d, e and f).

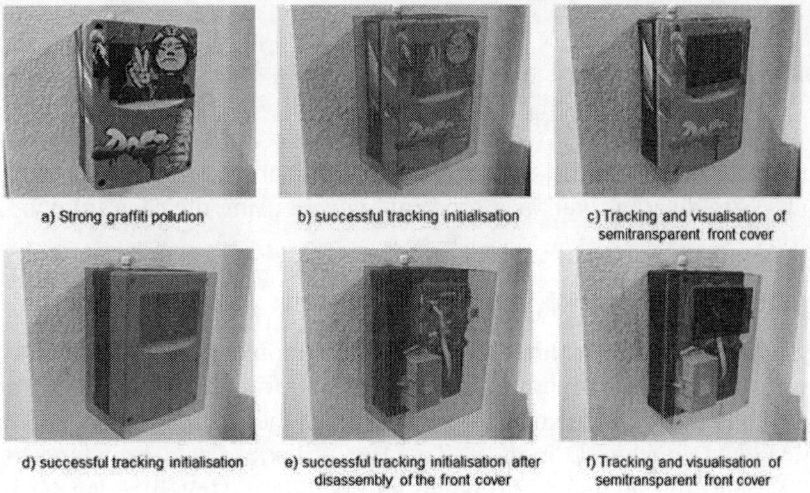

Figure 2: Verification of the hybrid 3D tracking under real conditions

4. Proposed Approach

Figure 3 depicts the authors' overall research framework that mainly consists of three parts: (1) digital work order preparation (local), (2) onsite indoor navigation (mobile), and (3) onsite maintenance support (mobile). The digital work order preparation is the collection and integration of all required information based on digital building and product models. Therefore, a web based AR Maintenance (ARM) management system is needed. On the one hand, 3D building models are usually created within the Building Information Modelling (BIM) approach in the AEC domain. On the other hand, product models, e.g. for technical equipment and installations, are created and managed in Product Life-cycle Management (PLM) systems in the mechanical engineering domain. The second part encompasses BIM based route calculation and AR supported indoor navigation using natural markers and IMU data. Details on this part of the framework can be found in (Neges et al. 2015; Koch et al. 2014).

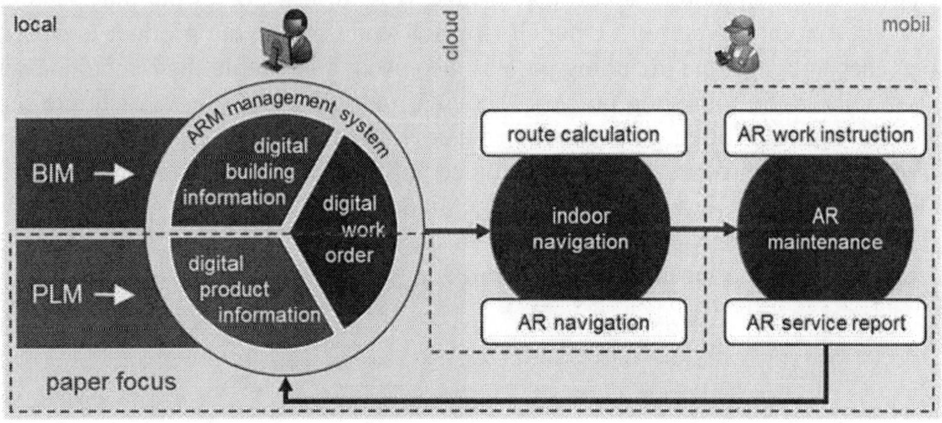

Figure 3: Overall research concept with paper focus emphasised

This paper focusses on the third part of the overall framework, which is AR supported onsite maintenance support (as highlighted in Figure 3). The proposed approach mainly comprises the following three main sub task:

- Creating AR based maintenance instructions and generating a digital maintenance work order (local, offline)
- AR supported onsite maintenance (mobile, online), and
- Creating maintenance reports (mobile, online)

Focusing on these sub tasks, the subsequent sections present the developed concepts and visualization tools in detail as well as a proof of concept using the case study of maintaining a smoke detector.

4.1 Product information from PLM-System

The PLM-System contains all required product information, e.g. the 3D models of the product including parts, the product structure and metadata information. This information can be distinguished into two groups: textual information like the product structure or metadata and geometrical information, the 3D models. To offer a flexible data exchange to the provided management system, the textual information can be administrated by an XML scheme file (Figure 4). Each element (product, part, assembly) has a unique PLM ID that ensures the consistent relationship between the PLM system and the ARM management system.

```
<PRODUCT name="Name of the product" PLM_ID="ID from PLM-System">
//optional block for each assembly/part of the structure
 <MetaDatenBlock>
    <DATA name="Name of the data" Value="Value of the data"/>
    ........ //freely expandable
  </MetaDatenBlock >
  <PART name="Name of the part" PLM_ID=" ID from PLM-System "/>
  <ASSEMBLY name="Name of the assembly" PLM_ID=" ID from PLM-System">
    <PART name="Name of the part" PLM_ID=" ID from PLM-System"/>
    <ASSEMBLY name ="Name of the assembly" PLM_ID=" ID from PLM-System">
      <PART name="Name of the part" PLM_ID=„ ID from PLM-System "/>
    </ASSEMBLY>
  </ASSEMBLY>
  ........ //freely expandable for more parts and assemblies
</PRODUCT>
```

Figure 4: Formalized format for product structure and metadata

The format of the 3D models depends on the used CAD authoring tool. CAD file formats are proprietary and have to be converted to neutral viewing formats, such as JT or STEP. In the field of visualisation on mobile smart devices, the Wavefront OBJ format plays a central role because of the similar structure to OpenGL for 3D rendering. If the product is stored in one CAD file, a separation of the including parts is also needed to enable the interaction with each part individually in the following process. The OBJ data structure allows a simple separation of the parts by batch scripting. Therefore, a conversion of the CAD data to the OBJ format can be realised by a batch process on a conversion server. Within this conversion, the OBJ model is used for the automatic derivation of the edge model, which is needed for the recommended hybrid 3D tracking (see section 3). As a result, a second OBJ, which implies the edge model is generated. The XML and the OBJ files are stored in a container file (Figure 5).

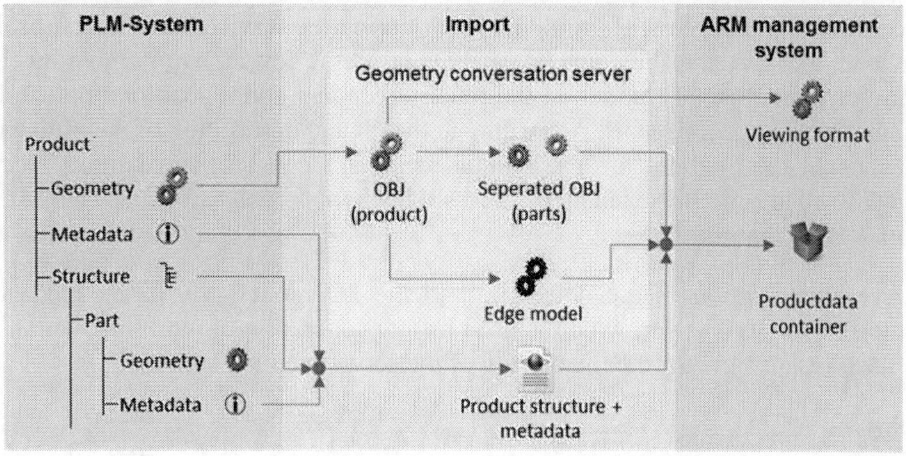

Figure 5: Concept of the product information integration in the ARM management system

4.2 AR based maintenance work instruction

The use of OBJ files for the 3D representation offers the opportunity to realize a generation of maintenance work instructions based on a standard 3D viewing system. This standard 3D viewing system has to be extended with functionalities to create single work steps (Figure). Within each step, a work instruction is needed. This textual information will be extended with several visual information. Each first work step refers to specific parts of the product. For example, in the first work step the four screws on the front panel have to be removed and these screws will be highlighted in the later AR application. Therefore, three different activities are required, (a) highlight a part, (b) disassemble a part and hide it in the next work steps and (c) assemble a part and show it in the virtual model. In addition, the concept considers a library for visual hints, which is available in the viewing system and the mobile application. The library offers all available hints and each hint gets a unique ID. A visual hint can be direction indicators for disassembly parts or textual information about the defined tool used for this work step. This ID minimizes the required data exchange, because no geometrical information has to be transferred. Each hint can be loaded from the local library, within the viewing system or on the mobile application, based on its unique ID. Therefore, all information can also be stored in a corresponding XML scheme file (Figure 6).

```
<WORDINSTRUCTION name= "Description">
<WORKSTEP name="Name of this work step">
    <INSTRUCTION>Description of the work instruction for this step</INSTRUCTION>
    <PART name="Name of the affected part" activity="Activity for this part in this step"/>
    ........ //freely expandable
     //optional hints block
     <HINT ID="ID of the hint">
       <POSITION X="X-Coordinate" Y="Y-Coordinate" Z="Z-Coordinate"/>
       <ROTATION RX="Rotation in X" RY="Rotation in Y" RZ="Rotation in Z"/>
       <SCALE="Scale factor"/>
     </HINT>
     ............//freely expandable
   </ WORKSTEP >
   .........//freely expandable
</ WORDINSTRUCTIOM >
```

Figure 6: Formulized format for AR maintenance work instruction

4.3 AR based service report

As already mentioned, the presented approach is not limited to AR passive visualisation. AR offers new interaction concepts and can be used to enhance the information flow in reports as feedback from service process. If problems occur during the service process, e.g. broken cable or screw head, the service technician can easily identify the correct part number by clicking on the overlay of the virtual 3D model on the touchscreen and add a position related photo with redlining marks to a service report. According to the textual description of the problem and this additional visual information, further maintenance tasks can be planed more precisely and faster. As with all information exchange processes in our approach, a formalized XML structure is used for service reports.

The correct identification of the defect part in the 3D model is a direct feedback to the visualisation in the 3D Viewer, which is used for the generation of work instructions. The 3D viewer is also responsible for the illustration of the service reports (Figure 7).

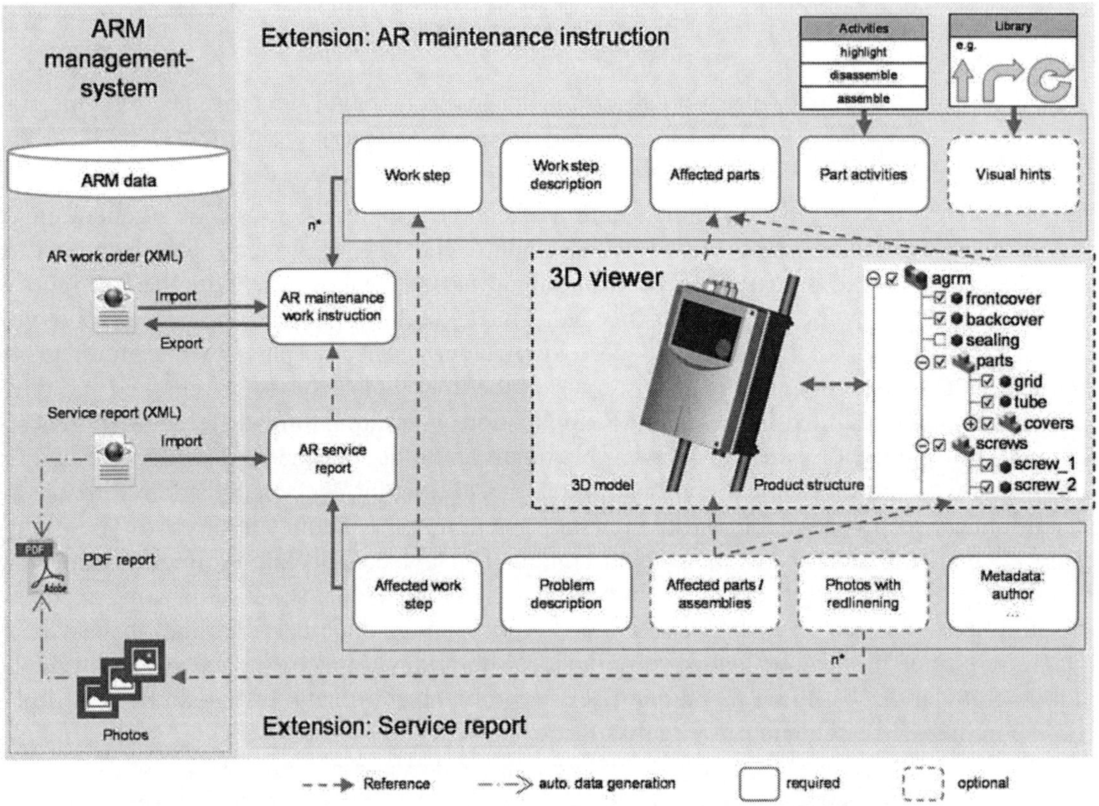

Figure 7: Concept of maintenance work instructions and service reports

5. Preliminary results

In order to test and verify the proposed method, software prototypes have been designed and implemented. The viewer for generation of maintenance work steps (local, offline) is implemented as a 3D PDF template using Adobe Acrobat Professional X and JavaScript (8).

The mobile prototype is implemented on an iPad Air (CPU: 1.4GHz dual-core A7, camera resolution: 1920x1080px), and the AR framework metaio SDK 5.5 (Figure 9).

Figure 10 shows the additional steps during the creation of service reports. The service technician can easily and intuitively add defective parts by touching the overlay of the virtual model (Fig. 10a), without knowing any details about the part itself. Furthermore, position related photos with redlining marks can be added (Fig. 10 b).

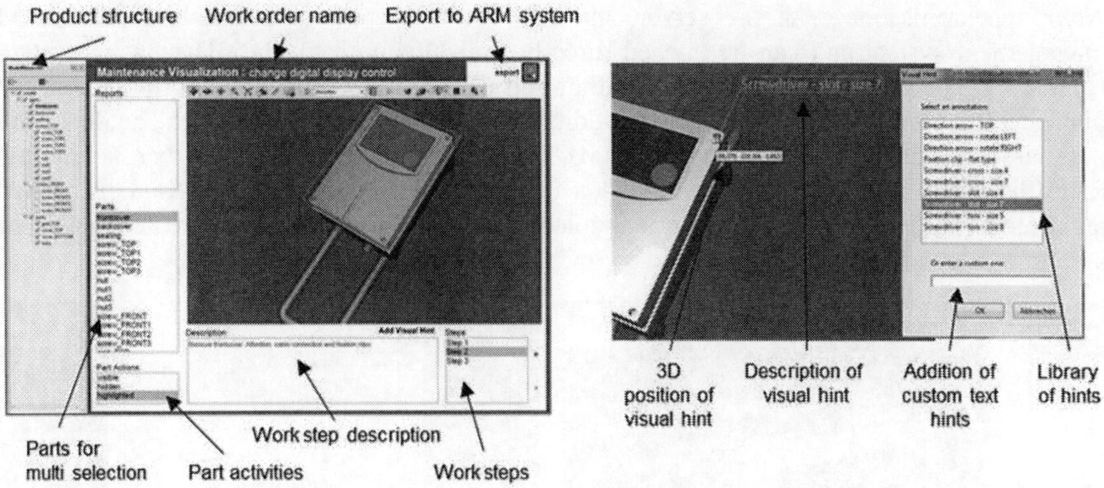

Figure 8: Screenshot of the prototype (offline) - Creating maintenance instructions

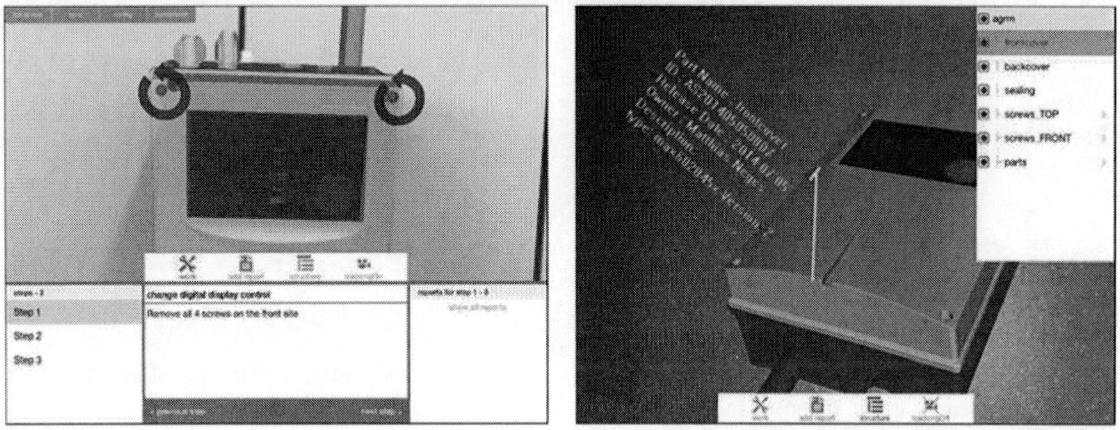

a) AR visualisation of work steps and visual hints

b) Visualisation of meta data from PLM system

Figure 9: Screenshot of the prototype (online) - AR based visualisation of maintenance instructions

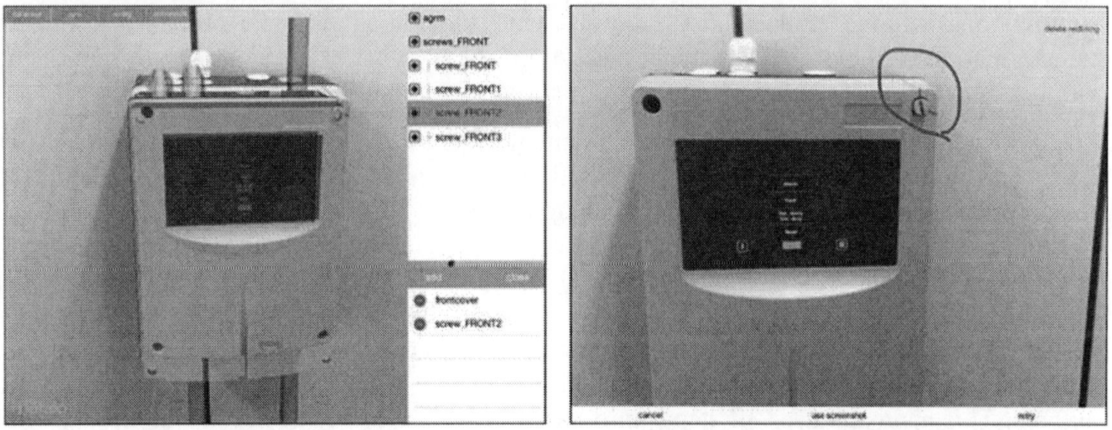

a) Addition of defect parts to service reports by touching the virtual model overlay

b) Position-related photos of real object with redlining

Figure 10: Screenshot of the prototype (online) – Addition of AR based service reports

After synchronisation with the server, the new service report is available in the ARM management system and can be opened directly from this point in the 3D viewing system (Figure 1). The problem metadata, e.g. author and date of the report, the description and the photo with redlining marks are added as additional pages within the PDF file. The deposited part names are direct links to the virtual parts. The illustration of service reports as additional PDF files has further advantages: if needed, service reports can easily be saved and distributed and from now on be opened in the free available Adobe PDF Reader without ARM management system connection.

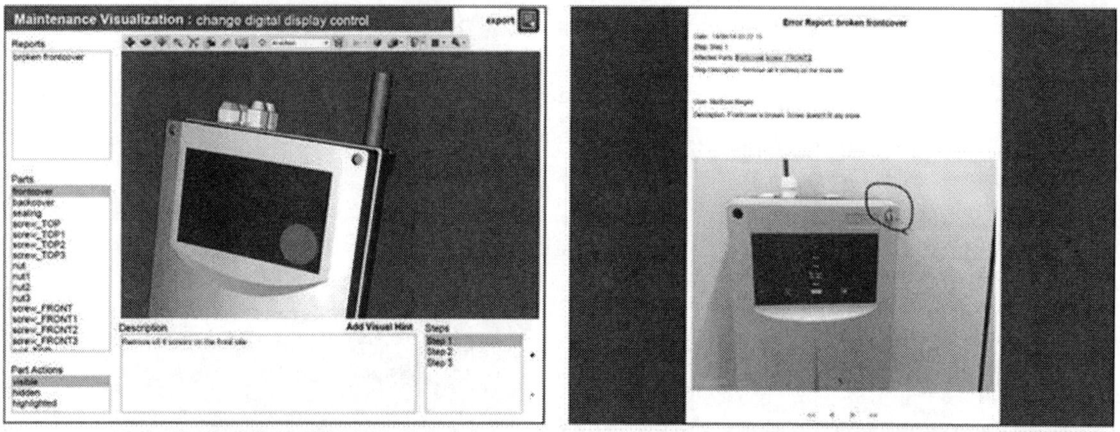

a) Visualisation of deposited defect parts

b) Service report as additional PDF pages

Figure 11: Screenshot of the prototype (online) – Visualisation of service reports

6. Conclusion and future work

The presented AR based approach on the offline generation and the online usage of maintenance instructions as well as the online reporting are a significant part in the authors' overall concept for AR based onsite facility maintenance. The implemented prototype was successfully verified in a controlled, but real environment. Through the consistent use of formulised information exchanges based on the XML format, this approach is universally suitable to different PLM systems and CAD file formats. The developed ARM management system is a web based solution and will be extended with the viewing functionalities. The aim is a complete transformation of the 3D viewer functions within the web-based environment to reduce the number of software systems, e.g. only need for Adobe Acrobat Professional.

The hybrid 3D tracking method has high potential to be used in maintenance processes. After the successful initialisation, the point based tracking is robust and fulfils the identified requirements. However, the edge based tracking works for maintenance objects, which are very close to the virtual models. This approach is a very good choice for mechanical engineering, but contains weaknesses in civil engineering or shipbuilding. In these disciplines the real manufactured parts have rougher tolerances, which leads to a non-fitting of the ideal CAD edge model with reality objects. Therefore, a new approach based on parametric master models, which are directly adjusted in the real environment, are currently being developed by the authors. This approach uses 3D depth information from the smart device within the tracking initialisation process to adapt the virtual model. The metaioSDK, which is currently being used for implementation, will be replaced in order to realise this function.

References

ARTESAS (2004): BMBF-Leitprojekt ARTESAS. Advanced Augmented Reality Technologies for Industrial Service Applications. Available online at http://www.artesas.de/, updated on 8/17/2004, checked on 7/31/2014.

ARVIKA (2003): BMBF-Leitprojekt ARVIKA. Augmented-Reality für Entwicklung, Produktion und Service. Available online at http://www.arvika.de, updated on 8/1/2003, checked on 7/31/2014.

Fründ, Jürgen (2007): Eine Architekturkonzeption für eine skalierbare mobile Augmented Reality Anwendung für die Produktpräsentation. Dissertation. Universität Paderborn, Paderborn, Deutschland. Heinz Nixdorf Institut.

Hou, L.; Wang, X.; Truijens, M. (2015): Using Augmented Reality to Facilitate Piping Assembly: An Experiment-Based Evaluation. In *Journal of Computing in Civil Engineering* 29 (1), p. 5014007. DOI: 10.1061/(ASCE)CP.1943-5487.0000344.

Koch, Christian; Neges, Matthias; König, Markus; Abramovici, Michael (2014): Natural markers for augmented reality-based indoor navigation and facility maintenance. In *Automation in Construction* 48, pp. 18–30. DOI: 10.1016/j.autcon.2014.08.009.

Lee, Sanghoon; Akin, Ömer (2011): Augmented reality-based computational fieldwork support for equipment operations and maintenance. In *Automation in Construction* (4), pp. 338–352. DOI: 10.1016/j.autcon.2010.11.004.

Mader, Steffen; Urban, Bodo (2010): Creating Instructional Content for Augmented Reality based on Controlled Natural Language Concepts. In Bruce H. Thomas, Hirokazu Kato (Eds.): Proceedings of 20th International Conference on Artificial Reality and Telexistence. ICAT'10. Adelaide, Australia, 1.12.-3.12.2010. University of South Australia. Adelaide, Australia: University of South Australia, pp. 9–13.

Neges, Herms-Matthias (2015): Smart Augmented Reality Lösung für die Indoor-Navigation und Instandhaltung. Bochum, Deutschland: Bochumer Universitätsverlag.

Neges, Matthias; Koch, Christian; König, Markus; Abramovici, Michael (2015): Combining visual natural markers and IMU for improved AR based indoor navigation. In *Advanced Engineering Informatics*. In press. DOI: 10.1016/j.aei.2015.10.005.

Saske, Bernhard (2008): Augmented Reality in der Instandhaltung. Konzept zur effizienten Nutzung und Integration in das Product Lifecycle Management. Dissertation. Technischen Universität Dresden, Dresden, Deutschland. Institut für Maschinenelemente und Maschinenkonstruktion.

Schwald, B.; Figue, J.; Chauvineau, E.; Vu-Hong, F.; Robert, A.; Arbolino, M. et al. (2001): STARMATE: Using augmented reality technology for computer guided maintenance of complex mechanical elements. In Brian Stanford-Smith (Ed.): E-work and E-commerce. Novel solutions and practices for a global networked economy. Amsterdam, Netherlands: IOS Press, pp. 196–202.

Steindecker, Erik; Stelzer, Ralph; Saske, Bernhard (2014): Requirements for Virtualization of AR Displays within VR Environments. In Randall Shumaker, Stephanie Lackey (Eds.): Proceedings of the 6th International Conference on Virtual, Augmented and Mixed Reality. VAMR'14, vol. 8525. Heraklion, Crete, Greece, June 22-27, 2014. International Conference on Human-Computer Interaction. Berlin, Germany: Springer Verlag (LNCS sublibrary. SL 3, Information systems and application, incl. Internet/Web and HCI, 8525), pp. 105–116.

Teicholz, Eric (2004): Bridging the AEC/FM technology gap. In *Journal of Facilities Management* 2, pp. 1–8. Available online at http://www.graphicsystems.biz/gsi/articles/Bridging%20the%20AEC_FM%20Gap_r2.pdf, checked on 6/23/2014.

Wang, Xu Ping; Chen, Xiao Hu; Yao, Chun Jiang; Ding, Yao; Gao, Shu Xiang (2013): Desktop Virtual Maintenance Training Platform Based on NGRAIN. In *AMR - Advanced Materials Research* 765-767, pp. 1546–1549. DOI: 10.4028/www.scientific.net/AMR.765-767.1546.

Wohlgemuth, W.; Friedrich, W. (2007): Advanced Augmented Reality Technologies for Industrial Service Applications: ARTESAS. BMBF-Leitprojekt ARTESAS; zusammenfassender Schlussbericht: Siemens AG. Available online at http://books.google.de/books?id=8qPDtwAACAAJ.

Nonlinear sensor fault diagnosis in wireless sensor networks using structural response data

Kosmas Dragos, Kay Smarsly
Chair of Computing in Civil Engineering
Bauhaus University Weimar, Germany

Katrin Jahr
Chair of Computational Modelling and Simulation
Technical University Munich, Germany
katrin.jahr@tum.de

Abstract. This paper introduces a novel approach towards sensor fault diagnosis in wireless structural health monitoring systems. As compared to traditional fault diagnosis approaches, a number of innovations are reported in this paper. First, by embedding fault models and algorithms directly into wireless sensor nodes, sensor faults can be self-detected by the nodes in a distributed-cooperative fashion. Second, no redundant sensor installations are required for fault diagnosis, because the wireless sensor nodes exploit the redundant information of correlated sensors already installed in the monitored structure ("analytical redundancy"). Third, instead of using raw time series of sensor data for analytical redundancy, the sensor data is first transformed from the time domain into the frequency domain on-board the sensor nodes, entailing significantly reduced data traffic. Fourth, nonlinearities in the data sets (e.g. due to measurement factors) are handled by implementing the analytical redundancy approach in terms of feedforward backpropagation neural networks embedded into the wireless sensor nodes. Fifth, due to the adaptation abilities of the embedded neural networks, sensor fault diagnosis remains efficient and accurate even if the monitored structure is subject to structural changes (or damage) as reflected in the sensor data. Sixth, no a priori knowledge about the structure or about the sensor instrumentation is required because the neural networks, representing a purely data-driven approach, take previously collected sensor data as the sole basis for fault diagnosis. This paper presents the fault diagnosis methodology, followed by the implementation into a fault-tolerant wireless structural health monitoring system prototype. Validation experiments on a laboratory test structure demonstrate the efficiency and accuracy of the proposed approach.

1. Introduction

Structural health monitoring (SHM) is increasingly employed for assessing the condition of civil engineering structures. In the field of SHM, wireless sensor networks have been gaining growing popularity over conventional cable-based systems, due to the advantages of easy and cost-effective installation of wireless sensor nodes. Moreover, the on-board processing power of wireless sensor nodes has been utilized in many research approaches for embedding algorithms that execute various monitoring tasks (Dragos and Smarsly, 2015).

Wireless SHM systems, operating in harsh environments over long periods of time, are vulnerable to sensor faults and sensor miscalibrations. Sensor faults affect the reliable and accurate operation of SHM systems, resulting in errors (manifestations of sensor faults), which lead to failures detectable in sensor outputs. The detection and isolation of sensor faults, hereinafter for simplification referred to as "fault diagnosis", has been a topic of ongoing investigation since about 40 years (Willsky, 1976). Fault diagnosis approaches usually rely on residuals between predicted and actual sensor outputs, typically structural response data (Smarsly and Petryna, 2014). The comparison between predicted and actual sensor outputs is performed either by installing redundant sensors ("physical redundancy") or by using the redundant information obtained by existing sensors ("analytical redundancy"). In both cases, the calculation of predicted outputs is based on the inherent correlations in the structural response data obtained from different locations of the structure (Kraemer and Fritzen, 2007). According to the available information on the properties of the structure, the correlations in the structural response data is derived either from physics-based models (e.g. finite element models) or from data-driven models (e.g. artificial neural networks).

Sensor fault detection based on artificial neural networks (ANNs) has been a topic of extensive research. For instance, the detection of process failures (e.g. sensor faults) using various neural network topologies has been proposed by Venkatasubramanian et al. (1990). Obst (2009) has introduced a sensor fault detection schema employing a distributed recurrent neural network. In their fault detection approach, Basirat and Khan (2009) have presented an ANN-based method for distinguishing faulty sensor data from non-faulty sensor data. The use of analytical redundancy in the correlations between sensor outputs for detecting sensor faults in wireless SHM systems has been proposed by Smarsly and Law (2014) by mapping both the characteristics of the structure and the correlations among the sensors.

In the approaches reported so far, fault diagnosis, performed either in a centralized or decentralized manner, entails a non-negligible wireless communication load due to the utilization of raw sensor data. This paper presents a novel approach towards fault diagnosis in wireless structural health monitoring systems based on processed structural response data, enabling wireless sensor nodes to self-diagnose sensor faults and miscalibrations. The diagnosis of sensor faults is performed by exploiting correlations among Fourier amplitudes of acceleration response data from different sensors, at peaks of the corresponding frequency spectra indicative of structural modes of vibration. More specifically, for a given structural condition, predictions of Fourier amplitudes for each sensor node are obtained using the Fourier amplitudes of other sensor nodes as input data. Residuals between the predicted and the actual Fourier amplitudes, obtained from the transformation of newly collected acceleration response data, exceeding a predefined threshold are indicative of sensor faults. While in theory Fourier amplitudes of acceleration response data from different locations of the structure are linearly connected, in practice, due to several factors, deviations from linearity are observed. The fault diagnosis approach presented in this study is nonlinear and entirely data-driven, requiring no knowledge on the characteristics of the structure. To this end, for the derivation of predicted Fourier amplitudes, ANNs are employed. Laboratory experiments are conducted for validating the proposed approach, demonstrating the efficiency of the approach in detecting sensor faults.

First, the background of the fault diagnosis approach is illuminated, and the implementation into a wireless SHM system is described. Second, the validation tests of the proposed approach are presented. Finally, results of the validation tests as well as potential future research directions are discussed.

2. Mathematical background

In this section, the mathematical background of the proposed methodology is elucidated, followed by the design principles developed for implementation of the methodology into a fault-tolerant wireless SHM system prototype.

2.1 Spectral density

In signal processing, spectral density represents the amount of energy carried by a signal. Considering a continuous function $f(t)$ of time, the spectral density S is defined as

$$S = \int_{-\infty}^{+\infty} |f(t)|^2 dt \quad (1)$$

It can be proven that spectral density is directly related to the autocorrelation of a signal. Indeed, according to Parseval's theorem, if the Fourier transform of the signal (the transformation of the signal into the frequency domain) exists, the spectral density and the Fourier transform are related as shown in Eq. 2.

$$\int_{-\infty}^{+\infty} |f(t)|^2 dt = \int_{-\infty}^{+\infty} |F(\omega)|^2 d\omega \qquad S(\omega) = \lim_{T \to \infty} \mathbf{E}|F(\omega)|^2 \quad (2)$$

In Eq. 2, **E** denotes the expected value and ω is the eigenfrequency. For a time lag τ, Eq. 2 is transformed as follows:

$$S(\omega) = \lim_{T \to \infty} \mathbf{E}\left[\int_{-T}^{+T} f(t) e^{i\omega t} \overline{f(t+\tau) e^{-i\omega(t+\tau)}} dt\right] = \int_{-\infty}^{+\infty} R(\tau) e^{-i\omega\tau} d\tau = R(\omega) \quad (3)$$

where $R(\omega)$ is the autocorrelation function of signal $f(t)$ at time lag τ. The overbar denotes complex conjugate. If two different signals are used in Eq. 3, the cross spectral density is obtained, which is essentially the cross correlation function of the two signals. If the signals in Eq. 1, Eq. 2, and Eq. 3 represent acceleration response data sets, the correlations among the response data sets can be extended to the transformed response data sets, i.e. to the corresponding frequency spectra. It has been also proven that these correlations in the frequency domain are stronger at the peaks of the frequency spectrum indicative of structural modes of vibration – a feature used for modal identification (Brincker et al., 2000).

2.2 Fault diagnosis using the correlations among Fourier amplitudes

As shown in Figure 1, four fault types can be distinguished: bias, drift, complete failure, and precision degradation (Qin and Li, 1999). Bias is the deviation by a constant value between sensor output and actual structural output. Drift is the incrementing deviation between sensor outputs and actual structural outputs. In case of complete failure, the sensor outputs remain constant regardless of changes in the actual structural outputs, while in precision degradation the sensor outputs are contaminated with a white noise function.

All fault types affect the amplitudes of the frequency spectrum; however, it should be noted that the effect of each fault on the Fourier amplitudes, at the peaks used for fault diagnosis, varies. For example, sensor faults usually introduce unwanted frequency components into the frequency spectrum, but the contamination of the frequency spectrum is not uniform at all frequencies. Hence, if the effects of a sensor fault on the amplitudes at potential modal peaks used for fault diagnosis are small, the respective fault might be undetectable.

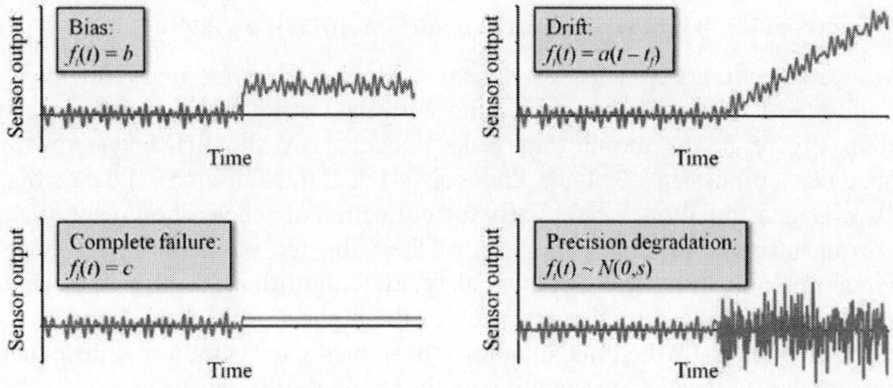

Figure 1: Categories of sensor faults in SHM systems

From structural dynamics, it is proven that the relationship among the Fourier amplitudes of acceleration responses from different locations of the structure at modal peaks is linear. However, in experimental dynamics, due to measurement factors, a deviation from linearity among the Fourier amplitudes of acceleration response data from different sensors is observed. For example, if a mode is not well excited, the Fourier amplitudes at the respective peak correspond to an "operating deflection shape", rather than the exact mode shape, and the linear relationship among the amplitudes does not hold. Furthermore, "round-off" errors (also referred to as "quantization errors" or "quantization noise"), following the analog-to-digital conversion, also introduce nonlinearities in the relationships among Fourier amplitudes. Finally, similar effects on frequency spectra are observed due to the presence of ambient noise. Figure 2 illustrates the nonlinearities (deviations from linear regression lines) introduced into the relationships among Fourier amplitudes, due to the aforementioned factors, for an arbitrary structure subjected to *N* different excitations.

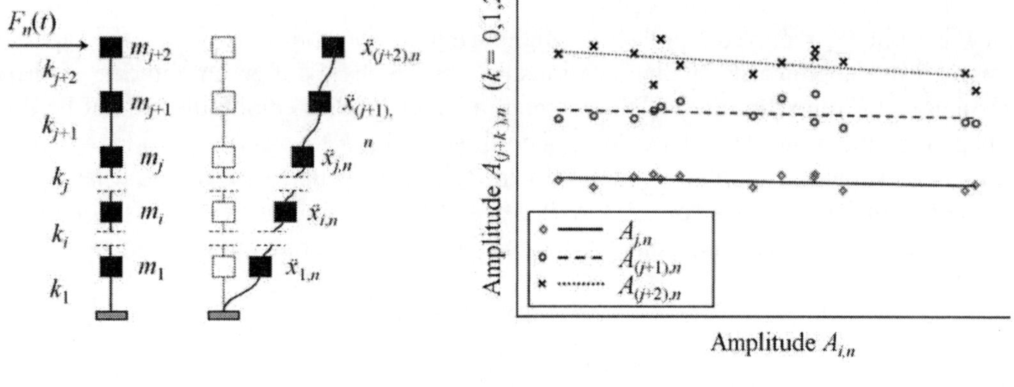

Figure 2: Relationships between Fourier amplitudes of acceleration response data from different locations of a structure deviating from linearity

3. Implementation of the fault diagnosis approach into a wireless SHM system

A wireless SHM system prototype is employed to implement the proposed fault diagnosis approach. In this section, the components of the SHM system are described and the embedded software is presented, with particular focus on the fault diagnosis tasks.

3.1 Components of the wireless structural health monitoring system

The SHM system comprises wireless sensor nodes, a gateway node (denoted as "base station"), and a host computer communicating with the sensor nodes via the base station. As illustrated in Figure 3, the monitoring tasks executed by the SHM system are: 1) data acquisition, 2) data processing, 3) fault diagnosis, 4) data transmission, 5) data storage, and 6) data analysis. Data acquisition is essentially the collection of acceleration response data, while data processing involves the transformation of the collected acceleration response data into the frequency domain, using the Cooley-Tukey FFT algorithm (Cooley and Tukey, 1968). Data processing is completed by the detection of the highest peak of the frequency spectrum, typically corresponding to the fundamental (first) mode of vibration. Subsequently, fault diagnosis is conducted through cooperative analysis among the sensor nodes. Tasks 1, 2, and 3 are executed on-board the sensor nodes. The processed data is wirelessly communicated to the host computer through the base station (task 4), where the data is stored and analyzed (tasks 5 and 6).

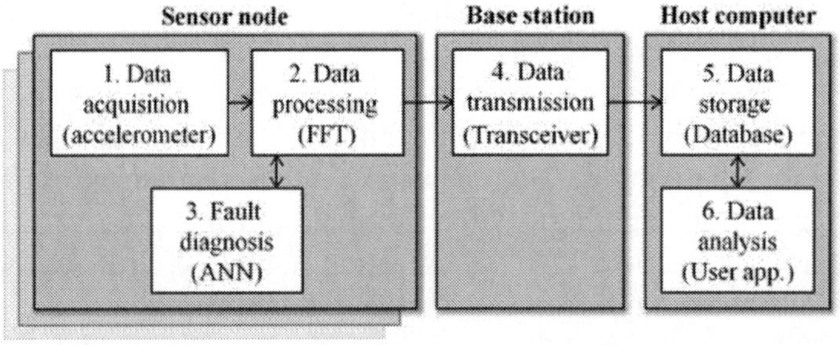

Figure 3: Monitoring tasks supported by the fault-tolerant wireless SHM system

The proposed fault diagnosis approach follows the concept of analytical redundancy, implemented in terms of ANNs embedded into the wireless sensor nodes. The embedded ANNs consist of several neurons structured in three layers. Considering an arbitrary sensor node *j* of the SHM system, the topology of the embedded ANN is given in Figure 4. The actual *k* amplitudes received from 1…*k* neighboring sensor nodes are fed to the input layer. Because of the nonlinearity in the relationship among the Fourier amplitudes of different sensor nodes, the output of the ANN (i.e. the predicted Fourier amplitude) cannot be directly obtained from the input data. Therefore, according to the ANN theory, a hidden layer of *m* neurons is added to accommodate the nonlinear relationship between the input layer and the output layer. In the output layer, the predicted amplitude of sensor node *j* is obtained. The synapses, i.e. the neuron connections, define the data exchange rate between the neurons.

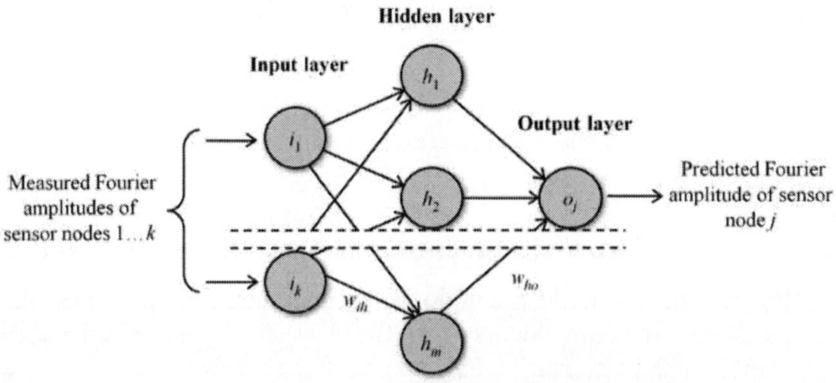

Figure 4: Artificial neural network embedded into sensor node *j*

The ANNs are trained by adjusting the weights of the synapses until the desired predicted Fourier amplitude of sensor node *j* is obtained. In a final step, the ANN properties, i.e. the topology (the number of neurons per layer) and the behavior of the neurons (the functions connecting the output of each neuron to the input of the next neuron), are defined.

3.2 Architecture of the embedded software

For operating the SHM system, embedded software is written in Java programming language. In particular, two packages have been developed, one for managing the tasks of the sensor nodes (package "`sensornode`") and one for handling the tasks of the host computer (package "`server`").

In the `sensornode` package, Java classes that perform the three sensor node tasks, as described in Figure 3, as well as the wireless communication to the base station, are included. The classes `AccelerationSampler` and `Sample` are responsible for data acquisition; the class `FFT` handles data processing, while the class `Communication` is used for establishing wireless communication links to the base station. Fault diagnosis is performed by the classes `NetworkTraining` and `MainNode`. For the implementation of ANN tasks, the external ANN library SNIPE is used (Kriesel, 2010). An extract of the `sensornode` package is provided in Figure 5.

The package `server` contains Java classes to perform the server tasks. For example, the class `MainBase` handles the communication between the base station and the sensor nodes. The `Sample` class manages the information received by the sensor nodes, converting it to the desired form to be stored into the database. Finally, the class `DatabaseHandler` is used to connect to a MySQL database, where the information packaged by the `Sample` class (eigenfrequencies and amplitudes calculated by the sensor nodes, sensor IDs, and fault diagnosis assessment) is stored.

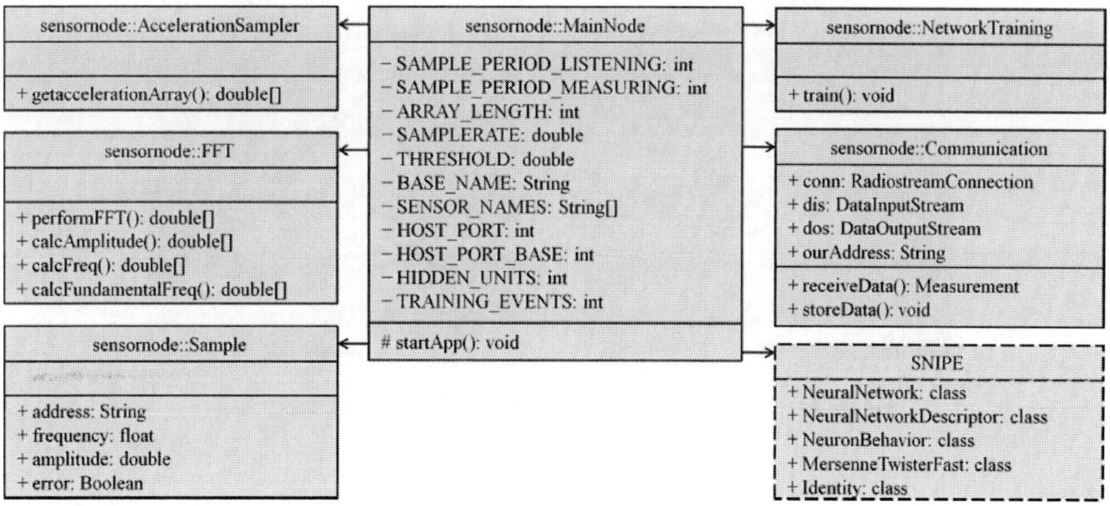

Figure 5: Extract of the "sensornode" package

4. Validation tests

Validation tests for the proposed fault diagnosis approach are conducted for demonstrating the ability of the approach to detect faults at a given structural condition. In this section, the validation tests are described, including the definition of the (case-specific) ANN properties and the application of the approach on a laboratory test structure.

4.1 Laboratory test setup

For the validation tests conducted in this study, Oracle Sun SPOT sensor nodes are employed (Oracle Corp., 2010). A sensor node includes an integrated digital output MEMS accelerometer, type MMA7455L, with a measurement range from ±2g to ±8g. The test structure employed for the validation tests is a 4-story steel frame structure. Each story slab is a steel sheet of 250 mm × 500 mm × 0.8 mm (length × width × thickness) dimensions, resting on four M5 steel threaded rods representing the columns of the structure. The frame structure is fixed at the column bases into a solid block (Figure 6).

In this study, two common fault types are exemplarily simulated: bias and precision degradation. Bias faults often occur when there is partial loss of connectivity of the sensor to the structure. For simulating the bias, sensor node B is rotated by 45° with respect to the initial position, as shown in Figure 6b. The ANN properties are first defined and the selected ANNs are trained by collecting acceleration response data from the unfaulty state (Figure 6a). Fault diagnosis is performed by using acceleration response data from the two faulty states: for the bias fault, acceleration response data from the state depicted in Figure 6b is used, while for precision degradation, the collected acceleration response data from the unfaulty state is contaminated by excessive variance white noise.

Figure 6: (a) Laboratory test setup and (b) simulated sensor fault

4.2 Definition of artificial neural network properties

The definition of the ANN properties depends on the structural properties (i.e. it is case-specific) and is based on prediction accuracy, i.e. the deviations between the predicted Fourier amplitudes (F_{pred}) and the actual Fourier amplitudes (F_{act}) (Eq. 4), and on performance, i.e. the time used to derive the output. Since the training of the ANNs also requires the adjustment of the weights until the desired output is obtained, the definition of the ANN properties essentially coincides with the ANN training.

$$\varepsilon_{RMS} = \sqrt{\frac{\sum_{i=1}^{N} F_{pred,i}(\omega_1)^2 - F_{act,i}(\omega_1)^2}{N}} \tag{4}$$

In Eq. 4, ε_{RMS} is the root mean square error between F_{pred} and F_{act}, at iteration i of the ANN training, ω_1 is the fundamental eigenfrequency, which characterizes the structural condition, and N is the number of samples, i.e. sets of input and output values. In this study, the data set used for selecting the ANN properties contains 100 Fourier amplitudes at the fundamental eigenfrequency derived on-board the sensor nodes from collected acceleration response data under free vibration. Each data set is divided into a training set for adjusting the neuron weights, a validation set for monitoring the training process, and a test set for confirming the predictive power of the ANN. Several ANN topologies and neuron behaviors are tested, the results of which are summarized in Table 1. Based on the results shown in Table 1, an ANN with 3-2-1 topology and interlayer backpropagation neuron behaviour is selected, considering a reasonable trade-off between the selection criteria, i.e. low prediction error as well as low computation time.

Table 1: Definition of ANN properties based on prediction accuracy and performance

Neuron behavior	Topology	Neurons/node	Computation time (s)	ε_{RMS} (-)
Interlayer, backpropagation	3-1	4	6.6	0.149
	3-2-1	**6**	**13.0**	**0.096**
	3-3-1	7	17.2	0.144
	3-5-1	9	25.0	0.081
	3-7-1	11	32.2	0.063
	3-2-2-1	8	21.0	0.092
	3-5-5-1	14	46.6	0.137
Interlayer and supralayer, backpropagation	3-3-1	7	15.2	0.147
	3-5-1	9	22.6	0.132
	3-2-2-1	8	19.4	0.137
Interlayer, resilient backpropagation	3-3-1	7	113.0	0.153
	3-5-1	9	172.4	0.143
	3-2-2-1	8	120.6	0.208

4.3 Operation of the fault-tolerant SHM system

Using the defined ANN properties, the operation of the SHM system is performed at the two faulty states. First, the bias fault type is simulated on sensor node B, as shown in Figure 6b. The test structure is excited by imposing a deflection at the top story and by removing the deflection force. Acceleration response data is collected under free vibration and, on-board the sensor nodes, transformed into the frequency domain. The embedded peak detection algorithms on the nodes pick the amplitudes that corresponds to the fundamental eigenfrequency, in an attempt to verify that the structural condition remains unaltered with respect to the ANN training stage. Subsequently, 30 sets of acceleration response data are collected and the corresponding Fourier amplitudes are calculated by all sensor nodes. Then, the amplitudes from sensor nodes A, C, and D are fed into the ANN of sensor node B as input data, and the predicted Fourier amplitude of the sensor node is derived. Finally, the root mean square error ($\varepsilon_{RMS,30}$) of the residual between the predicted Fourier amplitude and the actual Fourier amplitude of sensor node B is calculated for the Fourier amplitudes of the 30 acceleration response data sets. For precision degradation, a similar testing procedure is followed. However, the test is conducted using the setup shown in Figure 6a, because the fault is injected into sensor node B by adding white noise in terms of random values to the collected acceleration response data.

Drawing from the benchmark ε_{RMS} values of Table 1 for non-faulty operation, the threshold for fault diagnosis is set to τ = 0.150. The results of the operation of the SHM system are summarized in Table 2.

Table 2: Fault diagnosis of simulated sensor faults, indicated by root mean square error.

Root mean square error (30 data sets)	Non-faulty operation	Faulty operation	
		Bias	Precision degradation
$\varepsilon_{RMS,30}$	0.102	0.264	0.372

From Table 2, it can be seen that for non-faulty operation the $\varepsilon_{RMS,30}$ is 0.102, a value which complies with the ANN properties definition and ANN training values shown in Table 1. For faulty operation, the values of the $\varepsilon_{RMS,30}$ are 0.264 for bias and 0.372 for precision degradation. Since the $\varepsilon_{RMS,30}$ values for both sensor faults exceed the predefined threshold, it is concluded that both faults are efficiently and accurately diagnosed by the proposed fault diagnosis approach.

5. Summary and conclusions

To ensure the reliable and consistent performance of SHM systems, sensor faults must be accurately and efficiently detected. Common fault diagnosis approaches, in both cable-based and wireless SHM systems, use raw structural response data for fault diagnosis. However, in wireless SHM systems, the wireless communication of raw data entails considerable power consumption. In this paper, a fault diagnosis approach using processed structural response data and the concept of analytical redundancy has been presented. In the proposed approach, fault diagnosis is based on the correlations among Fourier amplitudes of structural response data derived from different sensors at a given structural condition. The Fourier amplitude at the peak corresponding to the fundamental eigenfrequency is predicted at each sensor node, using the Fourier amplitudes of other sensor nodes as input data and implementing artificial neural networks (ANNs) in an entirely data-driven approach. Deviations between the predicted Fourier amplitude and the actual Fourier amplitude calculated from newly collected acceleration response data are indicative of faulty sensor operation.

Validation tests of the fault diagnosis approach have been conducted on a 4-story laboratory frame structure. A fault-tolerant wireless SHM system prototype has been implemented to validate the proposed approach. The wireless SHM system has been installed on the laboratory frame structure. First, the ANN properties have been defined based on prediction accuracy and performance criteria. Then, two fault types, bias and precision degradation, have been considered for testing the wireless SHM system under faulty sensor operation. The results from the faulty sensor operation have shown that the residuals between the predicted Fourier amplitudes and the actual Fourier amplitudes are indicative of sensor faults. It is clear that the efficiency of the proposed fault diagnosis approach depends on the effect of the sensor fault on the amplitude at the selected peak of the frequency spectrum. Importantly, if the eigenfrequency is altered, the embedded ANNs are able to retrain and adapt to the new structural condition. Future research will focus on the applicability limits of the proposed approach, as well as the suitability of the approach to diagnose other various fault types.

Acknowledgments

The authors would like to gratefully acknowledge the support offered by the German Research Foundation (DFG) under grant GRK 1462 ("Evaluation of Coupled Numerical and Experimental Partial Models in Structural Engineering"). The financial support is gratefully acknowledged. Any opinions, findings, conclusions or recommendations expressed in this paper are those of the authors and do not necessarily reflect the views of DFG.

References

Basirat, A. H. and Khan, A. I. (2009). "Graph neuron and hierarchical graph neuron, novel approaches toward real time pattern recognition in wireless sensor networks". In: Proc. of the 2009 International Conference on Wireless Communications and Mobile Computing. Leipzig, Germany, 21/06/2009.

Brincker, R., Andersen, P. and Zhang, L. (2000). "Modal identification from ambient responses using frequency domain decomposition". In: Proc. of the 18th International Modal Analysis Conference (IMAC), San Antonio, TX, USA, 07/02/2000.

Cooley, J. W. and Tukey, J. W. (1965). "An algorithm for the machine calculation of complex Fourier series". Mathematics of Computation, Vol. 19, No. 90, pp. 297-301.

Dragos, K. and Smarsly, K. (2015). "A comparative review of wireless sensor nodes for structural health monitoring". In: Proc. of the 7th International Conference on Structural Health Monitoring of Intelligent Infrastructure. Turin, Italy, 01/07/2015.

Jahr, K., Schlich, R., Dragos, K. and Smarsly, K. (2015). "Decentralized autonomous fault detection in wireless structural health monitoring systems using structural response data". In Proc. of the 20th International Conference on the Applications of Computer Science and Mathematics in Architecture and Civil Engineering (IKM). Weimar, Germany, 22/07/2015.

Kraemer, P. and Fritzen, C.-P. (2007). "Sensor Fault Identification Using Autoregressive Models and the Mutual Information Concept". Key Engineering Materials, Vol. 347, pp. 387-392.

Kriesel, D. (2007). "A brief introduction to neural networks". Available at: http://www.dkriesel.com.

Obst, O. (2009). "Distributed fault detection using a recurrent neural network". In: Proceedings of the 2009 International Conference on Information Processing in Sensor Networks. Washington, DC, USA, 13/04/2009.

Oracle Corp. (2010). "Sun SPOT eDEMO Technical Datasheet, 8th edition". Sun Labs, Santa Clara, CA, USA, 2010.

Qin, S. J. and Li, W. (1999). "Detection, identification, and reconstruction of faulty sensors with maximized sensitivity". Journal of American Institute of Chemical Engineers, Vol. 45, No. 9, pp. 1963-1976.

Smarsly, K. and Petryna, Y. (2014). "A Decentralized Approach towards Autonomous Fault Detection in Wireless Structural Health Monitoring Systems". In: Proc. of the 7th European Workshop on Structural Health Monitoring. Nantes, France, 08/07/2014.

Smarsly, K. and Law, K. H. (2014). "Decentralized fault detection and isolation in wireless structural health monitoring systems using analytical redundancy". Advances in Engineering Software, Vol. 73, pp. 1-10.

Venkatasubramanian, V., Vaidyanathan, R. and Yamamoto, Y. (1990). "Process fault detection and diagnosis using neural networks – 1. Steady-state processes". Computers & Chemical Engineering, Vol. 14, No. 7, pp. 699-712.

Willsky, A. S. (1976). "A survey of design methods for failure detection systems". Automatica, Vol. 12, pp. 601-611.

Smart Sensor Based Real Time Monitoring for Prediction and Prevention of Coastal Dike Failure

Ralf Becker, Stefan Herle, Jörg Blankenbach
RWTH Aachen University, Germany
ralf.becker@gia.rwth-aachen.de

Abstract. Coastal dikes protect people and economic values against flooding caused by temporally high water levels. The influences of wind, waves as well as the current stability of the dike construction should be considered more closely for a meaningful prediction of dike failure and early warning. The research project "EarlyDike" has been started to conquer this problem. It consists of multiple monitoring and simulation tools. They require different kinds of real-time spatially related data. Therefore, small sensor nodes were developed, which are set up in a Wireless Geo Sensor Network (WGSN). All observed sensor data are transmitted over the WGSN. Hence, a novel lightweight communication protocol, GeoMQTT, is developed, which extends the Message Queue and Telemetry Transport (MQTT) protocol by adding spatio-temporal information. Central data access and visualization tool for all data is the dike GeoPortal, a web portal enabling data access at any time, place and from multiple clients using.

1. Introduction

Coastal dikes protect people and economic values against flooding caused by temporally high water levels triggered by tide, wind, waves and their accumulation. In Germany the North Sea coast with its hinterland of Lower Saxony, Schleswig Holstein and the metropolitan region of Hamburg embodies such a region. More than 2,400,000 people and an area of more than 12,000 km^2 are protected by more than 1,200 km of sea and estuarine dikes. For example, in the city of Hamburg the protected value by estuarine dikes is more than 10 billion of euros, in Schleswig-Holstein more than 47 billion of euros (Schüttrumpf 2008).

Predictions of the different influencing parameters such as the tidal effects to the water level and or the wind strength and direction are accomplished and published e.g. by German Weather authority (DWD). However, in particular the influences of wind and waves as well as the current stability of the dike construction should be considered more closely for a meaningful prediction of dike failure and early warning. The overlapping effects of tide, wind and waves are not sufficiently examined in today's forecasting systems. Furthermore, automatic processing chains from the computation of dike's stability up to flooding simulation and alerting should be improved. It is required to establish an early warning system, which takes all parts of the causal chain into account. Combining different sensors and third party data, prediction models, marine data infrastructures and smart technologies into a risk-based approach could facilitate the assessment of stability of coastal defence mechanisms. It should operate in real time, allows access to all data and results at any time and any place and has to be compliant to international standards for data definition and exchange.

In June 2015 the joint research project "EarlyDike" has been launched to conquer this problem. It is funded by the German Federal Ministry of Education and Research (BMBF) and consists of multiple monitoring and simulation tasks.

2. State-of-the-Art

"Early" warning systems are not entirely new technologies. Since humans built dikes to protect values, early detection of dike breaches and warning of affected inhabitants is of major importance in coastal areas. Starting with the riding dike reeves as described in the novella "Der Schimmelreiter" by T. Storm (1888), the early warning facilities has evolved with technological progress.

2.1 Early Warning Systems

Current early warning systems are based on water level observations and predictions. It is well understood, that wind, waves, currents and the resistance of sea dikes towards wind and waves play also a pivotal role in dike safety.

Initiated by the EU-flood directive, the risk of flooding was investigated in various national and international projects (e.g. EU-Floodsite, BMBF-HoRisk, BMBF-XtremRisk). They focussed on themes such as probabilistic determination of design water levels, failure mechanisms and probabilities, resulting probability of flooding and expected economic, ecological and socio-economic damages. Results of the projects are improved risk analysis, risk assessment and risk mitigation methods. Thus, a number of tools, data and information are available to assess the risk in respect to storm surges. All these tools, data and information are rather used in a prospective fashion than for real time evaluation of coastal risks. The EU-Urban-Flood project for river dikes implements computational models in flood early warning systems. However, not all relevant sensor data is considered and, additionally, the system was not developed for more vulnerable coastal areas (Pengel et al. 2013).

Other fields of disaster management such as earthquakes (Zambrano et al. 2015), landslides (BMBF-TaMIS) or flooding caused by heavy precipitation (BMBF-EVUS) make also essential use of early warning. In the EVUS project, accumulation effects of urban groundwater and crowd sourcing data for rainfall should be taken into account. BMBF-TaMIS has been initiated since hillside structure data is missing to make reasonable landslide predictions. In both projects the need of suitable sensor and communication technology has been identified.

2.2 (Wireless) sensor technology

(Wireless) sensor technology has rapidly developed in the past years and fosters interests in different disciplines. Current sensor platforms can be equipped with multiple sensors for measuring environmental parameters (e.g. air temperature, air pollution, water quality, etc.). Due to the ongoing technological improvements, geo sensor networks (GSN), often wireless (WGSN) are increasingly utilized to monitor the Earth's environment. Examples are disaster management, environmental monitoring, public security or urban flooding (Zambrano et al. 2015, Iyengar 2012, Akyildiz 2010, Pengel et al. 2013). Especially WGSN have evolved heavily over the last two decades since new communication protocols were invented and introduced by different organizations to create personal area networks with small, low-power digital radios. ZigBee, Z-Wave, 6LoWPAN or Bluetooth low energy are, for instance, some communication protocols competing in this segment.

No matter which communication technologies used, sensor data captured by (W)GSN should be stored and connected to the World Wide Web (WWW) to be accessible in a standardized way. This concept is called the "Sensor Web". The Sensor Web Enablement Initiative (SWE) of the Open Geospatial Consortiums (OGC)[1] has developed standards for accessing sensor data (Grothe & Kooijman 2008). SWE compliant services are already occasionally used in recent projects, such as the EU-OSIRIS-project utilized for different use cases (e.g. air pollution monitoring) (Jirka et al. 2009), SLEWS for landslide early warning (Walter & Nash 2009) or FluGGS for river basin management (Spies & Heier 2010).

2.3 Bridging WGSN and the Sensor Web

The Sensor Web standards issued by the SWE initiative use mainly Hypertext Transport Protocol (HTTP) and XML which is reasonable to retrieve sensor data by end users in an easy and reliable manner. Broering et al. (2010) argue that the SWE standards focus more on interacting with the upper application level, because they are designed from an application-oriented perspective. For sensing instruments and especially small devices in WGSN inserting data with HTTP and XML has some drawbacks such as the large overhead of XML documents.

One approach for bridging WGSN and the Sensor Web, implemented by Broering et al. (2010), is to introduce an intermediary layer, a so-called sensor bus, It uses the message bus pattern to establish a communication infrastructure through a publish/subscribe mechanism. They apply Twitter, XMPP, JMS or IRC for the underlying messaging technology to achieve a push-based communication style.

For bridging WGSN and the Sensor Web services, the publish/subscribe pattern has some advantages in comparison with the request/response mechanism of HTTP. Especially, it facilitates scaling between different entities in the system because the strength of the event-based scheme lies in the full decoupling in time, space and synchronization between producers and consumers of data (Eugster et al. 2003).

However, protocols such as XMPP or IRC are not suitable in our setting since they are too heavyweight due to XML payload and/or rely on Transmission Control Protocol (TCP) as a transport layer which cannot be used in WGSN. Therefore, Bandyopadhyay & Bhattacharyya (2013) suggest to use lightweight protocols such as Constrained Application Protocol (CoAP) and Message Queue and Telemetry Transport (MQTT) which can be used to connect sensing devices to the Web. We use the idea of the sensor bus and incorporate an adapted version of the MQTT protocol to bridge the WGSN and the Sensor Web (see 4.2).

2.4 Spatial Data Infrastructures and GeoPortal

Data networks for spatial information (Spatial Data Infrastructures, SDI) are currently built up worldwide improving the availability and the exchange of geospatial data (Groot 2003, Bocher & Neteler 2012, Harvey et al. 2012). Generally, a SDI provides user access to many voluminous geospatial datasets via a consistent infrastructure (Schleyer et al. 2014). In Europe it is particularly followed by the INSPIRE directive (INSPIRE 2007) for "establishing an infrastructure for spatial information in Europe to support Community environmental policies, and policies or activities which may have an impact on the environment"[2]. Data structures defined by the INSPIRE directive and its subsequent specification documents make use of the OGC-standards[3], in particular the OGC web service interface standards (e.g. Web Map Service, WMS, Web Feature Service, WFS) (Benedict 2005) or the OGC data encoding

[1] http://www.opengeospatial.org/
[2] http://inspire.jrc.ec.europa.eu/
[3] http://www.opengeospatial.org/standards

standards (e.g. Geography Markup Language, GML, Observations and Measurements, O&M, WaterML). SDIs are currently established in different levels of governments in the EU member states (Craglia & Annoni 2006, Thomas 2013) and for different themes. A current state report of the German spatial data infrastructure (Geodateninfrastruktur Deutschland, GDI-DE) is published by the "Lenkungsgremium" GDI-DE (BKG 2013). Regarding waterbodies and coastal protection, the marine spatial data infrastructure Germany (MDI-DE) was established (Rüh & Bill 2012, Lehfeldt & Melles 2011) (fusing former Nord-Ostsee-Küsten-Informations-System, NOKIS[4] and Spatial Data Infrastructure at the Federal Maritime and Hydrographic Agency, GDI-BSH[5]), which integrates data resources for coastal engineering, marine environment, and maritime conservation from different federal states and national agencies.

Web portals are often deployed to discover, view, access, and query geospatial information via the WWW (Bernard et al. 2005). The so-called geo portals serve as central access points to SDIs, e.g. the GEOportal.NRW[6] or the portals of the metropolitan areas of Hamburg[7] and Berlin[8]. Besides, geo portals increasingly provide INSPIRE-compliant access to spatially related information (geoinformation) to different subjects like energy, land use, etc.

3. EarlyDike – System Architecture

EarlyDike as a prediction and prevention tool combines several factors influencing respectively causing dike failures and their consequences. Such factors are the tides, storm surges, wind and waves and the inner structure of the dike. It also simulates the flooding of the hinterland in case of a dike failure. The different factors of the project are subdivided into work packages (WP 1-4).

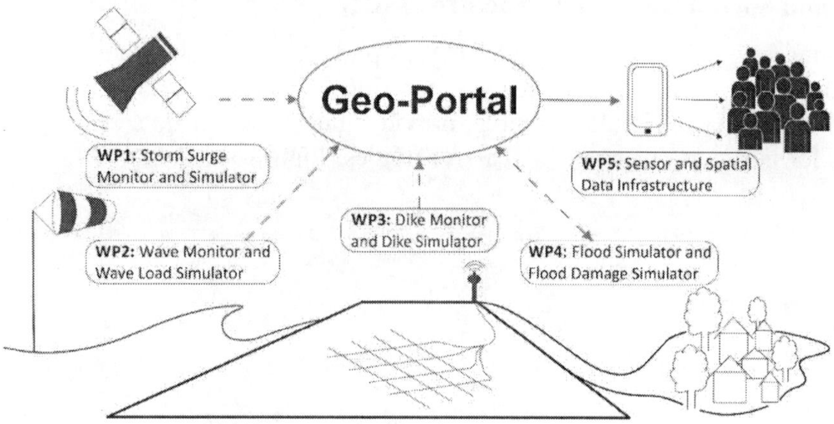

Figure 1: Packages of EarlyDike-project

The "Storm Surge Monitor and Simulator" package covers the development of a statistical storm surge model by using observation and model data as a basis for a storm surge simulation (WP 1). Based on observations of wind, water levels and the influence and behaviour of waves, a wave simulator using a statistical wave model is developed (WP 2). In

[4] http://projekt.mdi-de.org/services/nokis.html
[5] http://www.bsh.de/de/Meeresdaten/Geodaten
[6] https://www.geoportal.nrw.de
[7] http://geoportal.metropolregion.hamburg.de/
[8] http://www.stadtentwicklung.berlin.de/geoinformation/

the third package the dike construction itself will be monitored in real-time by sensors for soil temperature, soil moisture and by innovative "smart geotextiles". Taking into account the influences of soil temperature and soil moisture, the geotextile will be able to identify stress and deformation (strain) (WP 3). Finally, the "Flood Simulator" computes predictions of inundation areas in the case of an expected dike failure on the basis of the simulation results of the prior packages (WP 4) (Figure 1). The different monitors and simulator depend on each other as it is exemplary shown in the processing chain of Figure 2.

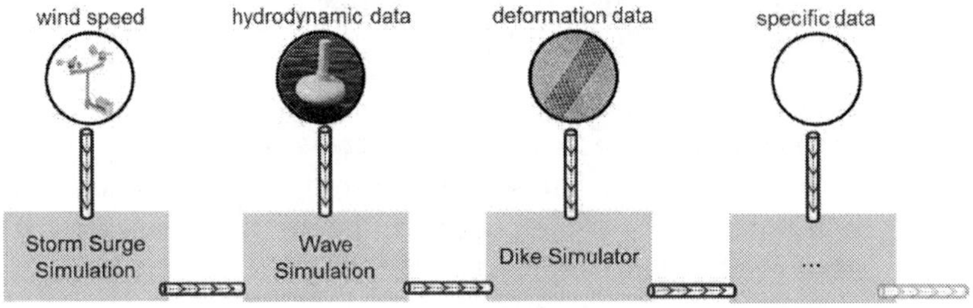

Figure 2: Real-time processing chain

For collecting in-situ data, especially of the inner structure of the dike, a suitable GSN is required. Additionally, needed data should be accessed from third parties such as the DWD and MDI-DE. For visualization of data and simulation results a GeoPortal will be set up. GSN, data transfer as well as the GeoPortal are bundled in the package "Sensor and Spatial Data Infrastructure" (WP 5).

4. Sensor and Spatial Data Infrastructure (SSDI)

The interconnecting core element combining all previous mentioned parts is the Sensor and Spatial Data Infrastructure (SSDI). It is responsible for access, storage and provision of all data. The SSDI affiliates simulation tools, provides interfaces for data requests, visualization and is basis for information channels to alert services (Figure 3).

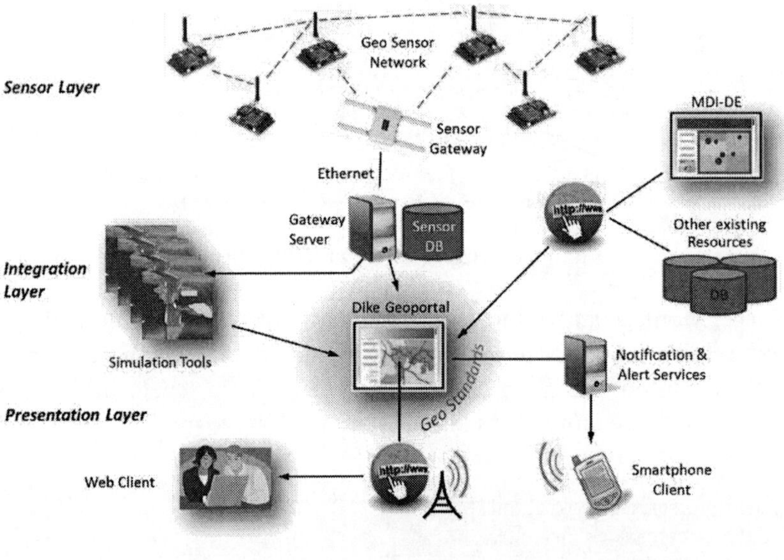

Figure 3: Sensor and Spatial Data Infrastructure

Summarized, the SSDI including the GSN and the GeoPortal has to implement the following aspects

- Capturing and processing of in-situ data,
- Integration of external data sources,
- Integration of tools for monitoring and simulation,
- Providing and visualization of the data (raw data, simulation results etc.),

4.1 Wireless Geo Sensor Network (WGSN) for in-situ data

The simulators of the influencing factors require different kinds of real-time data. In particular, environmental data and information about the current dike structure are crucial for resilient simulations. As mentioned, many types of data (e.g. weather data and forecasts) are already provided by third parties. Thus, it is not necessary to measure respectively compute these data independently. However, current data of the structure and of environmental data in the surroundings (e.g. soil moisture) have to be measured in-situ by assembled sensors.

Therefore, small energy efficient sensor nodes were developed for real-time parameter sensing on site. Different sensors, such as soil temperature and soil moisture sensors are connected to sensor nodes. For monitoring the structure of the dike, a geo textile sensor for measuring deformation is to be developed by one of the project partners. Due to the vast size of coastal dikes the sensor nodes are placed along the whole dike line and set up in a WGSN. All observed sensor data are transmitted over the WGSN to be stored in a geo sensor database.

4.2 Middleware for coupling sensors, services and simulations

The system should be compliant with the idea of the Sensor Web mentioned earlier. Therefore, standards of the SWE such as the Sensor Observation Service (SOS) should be used to access the WGSN as well as the data. The main challenge is to connect the low-level sensor networks with the high-level services of the SWE in a sophisticated way. Simultaneously, the simulations according to the processing chain in Figure 2 should be invoked automatically if new measurements are available. So, in the system there are multiple producers of data such as the sensor nodes and multiple consumers of this data such as storage services or processes. Some additional requirements like the data exchange in real-time, the notification of consumers in a push-based manner or the limited resources of system components narrow down the alternatives of suitable information exchange mechanism. First, since there are multiple producers and consumers, the messaging paradigm of choice is the publish/subscribe pattern. Consumers may specify their interest in messages while producers are able to publish information to specific interests. The distribution of notifications in publish/subscribe systems is accomplished by a central component, the so-called broker, which stores subscriptions of interest and forwards messages accordingly. Second, the used mechanism has to be efficient in terms of real-time messaging and feasible for constraint environments such as WGSN. As mentioned before (see 2.3), we propose the use of an adapted version of the lightweight MQTT protocol. With its extension MQTT for Sensor Networks (MQTT-SN), it is also applicable in non-TCP environments such as ZigBee networks.

4.2.1 MQTT

MQTT is a topic-based publish/subscribe system. Consumers register their interests with topic filters at the broker and producers publish their information with topic names. In a subscribe message, either the topic filter is set to the topic name or wildcards are used to express interest in multiple topic names. Since topic names in MQTT have a hierarchical structure whose tiers are divided by a forward slash, a single-level ("+") or a multi-level ("#") wildcard can be applied in the topic filter. For instance, the topic filter *room/+/temperature,* whose second tier denotes a wildcard for the room number, subscribes to the topic names *room/422/temperature* and *room/423/temperature* as well as all temperature data of other rooms which uses this topic structure. The central broker manages all subscriptions and forwards incoming messages to the subscribed clients according to the evaluation of topic names against topic filters. MQTT has some additional convenient features which are specified in the standard (OASIS 2014).

4.2.2 GeoMQTT

Within the project, the MQTT protocol is enhanced by a spatio-temporal extension, so that every message consists of a timestamp and a geospatial location besides of the topic name. This so-called *GeoMQTT* extension is fully compliant to MQTT meaning that the new introduced message do not interfere the original protocol. With the added metainformation to every message issued by producers, new subscription mechanisms which consider the timestamp and geospatial location information are possible. Consumers are able to subscribe to specific time intervals, locations and topics. With this novel protocol a real-time spatial notification and data stream transfer mechanism can be established. We call this concept *GeoPipes*.

In detail, the protocol introduces three additional message types: *GeoPublish*, *GeoSubscribe* and *GeoUnsubscribe*. Like the publish message type in MQTT, the GeoPublish message consists of a topic name and a payload but it also expects a time stamp in ISO8601 or Unix time format and a location by specifying the latitude and longitude in World Geodetic System 1984 (WGS84). The *GeoSubscribe* message inherits the topic filter mechanism from the MQTT subscribe message and adds an interval filter as well as a geometry filter. The interval filter consists of a start and an end timestamp in ISO8601 or a combination of a Cron expression and an interval length to specify repetitive periods. The geometry filter expects geometries in Well-known text (WKT) format. The broker evaluates for every incoming *GeoPublish* message if its timestamp is within the specified interval and if its location is within the geometry of the stored geo subscriptions. The topic name is also checked against the topic filter. Only if all three filters are satisfied the *GeoPublish* message is forwarded by the broker to the subscribed clients. The *GeoUnsubscribe* message enables the clients to unsubscribe from existing geo subscriptions by intersecting interval and geometry filters.

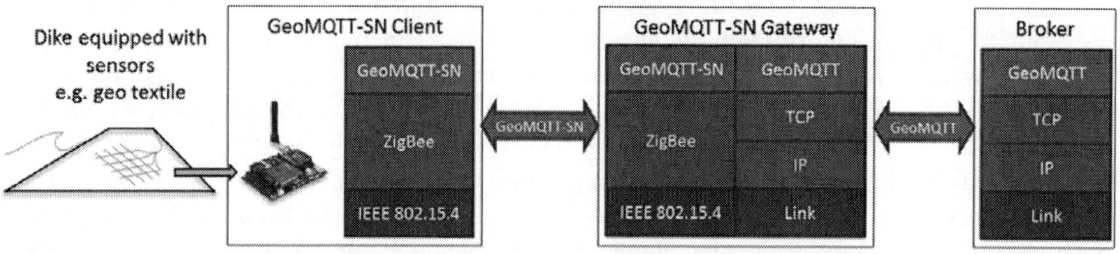

Figure 4: GeoMQTT(-SN) architecture and layer stacks

For the sensor nodes in the WGSNs, a GeoMQTT-SN client is implemented on top of the transport layer, which uses the communication protocol ZigBee[9]. A gateway serves as the translator between GeoMQTT-SN and GeoMQTT (Figure 4).

By utilizing the GeoMQTT protocol as a middleware, it is effortless to implement the idea of a sensor bus like presented in Broering et al. (2010). This facilitates to bridge the low-level protocol of the ZigBee based WGSN and the high-level services of the Sensor Web. High-level services are subscribed to the messages issued by the sensor nodes, so that e.g. the collected data is stored persistently in our SOS database. Pushing this idea of the sensor bus further, an *Event Bus* can be established connecting all kinds of different components (Figure 5). Not only measured sensor data are distributed in real-time by this mechanism to subscribers but also processes can publish their events on that bus.

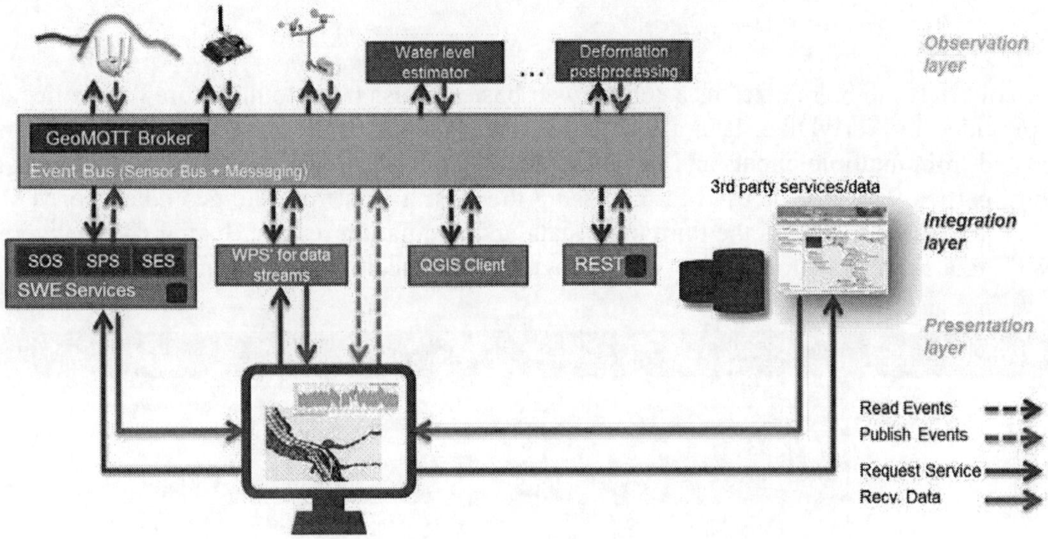

Figure 5: Event bus as an intermediary layer of EarlyDike architecture

This middleware solution enables the system to react on the latest measured data available and simultaneously offers the capability of constructing real-time processing chains between different instances acting on this data. The different simulators developed in this project can easily be integrated and, thus, the processing chain in Figure 2 can be established.

An additional beneficial feature of MQTT and, therefore, GeoMQTT is the use of the WebSocket protocol. Thus, users may login to the event bus via browser and receive the notifications in their session which can be used, for instance, in long-lasting processing chains to receive intermediate results.

4.3 Third Party Data

Mandatory third party environmental data such as water levels, weather, topography and bathymetry are provided by national authorities and institutions. Several third party providers are identified: e.g. DWD for climate data and weather forecast, the German Federal Maritime and Hydrographic Agency (BSH) for bathymetric data, geo information authorities of the federal states for Topographic and cadastral data and the German Federal Institute of Hydrology (BfG) for water level data.

---

[9] http://www.zigbee.org/

The data will be accessed by the standardized up-to-date web services WMS and WFS of the OGC if possible. Otherwise the mandatory data is provided for download in formats like Comma-separated values (CSV), Network Common Data Form (NetCDF)[10] and GRIdded Binary (GRIB)[11]. Worldwide often used are geographical coordinates of WGS84 and the spherical Mercator projection (Google Maps, Bing-Maps)[12]. The German authorities for geoinformation decided to use the European Terrestrial Reference System 89 (ETRS89) with the Universal Transverse Mercator (UTM) projection, because it uses the best fitting ellipsoid for Germany. Thus, the most suitable projection has to be chosen. For fusing data provided in different projections, transformation parameters are needed. They have to be analyzed for sufficient suitability and reliability. Thus, WFS data can be easily transformed into the project-specific projections. However, WMS data, if not originally provided in the required projection, unfortunately has to be transformed pixel by pixel image by image.

4.4 GeoPortal

The GeoPortal is to be realized as a central web-based access point to the entire data collected and provided by EarlyDike. It is a web portal that enables data access at any time, in any place and from multiple clients and provides visualization of in-situ measured as well as data of third parties. The SOS is used for accessing the in-situ data from the geo database. WMS and WFS are used to access the third party data and simulation results. Spatial data delivered by WFS requests is transformed into the map viewer's projection if necessary.

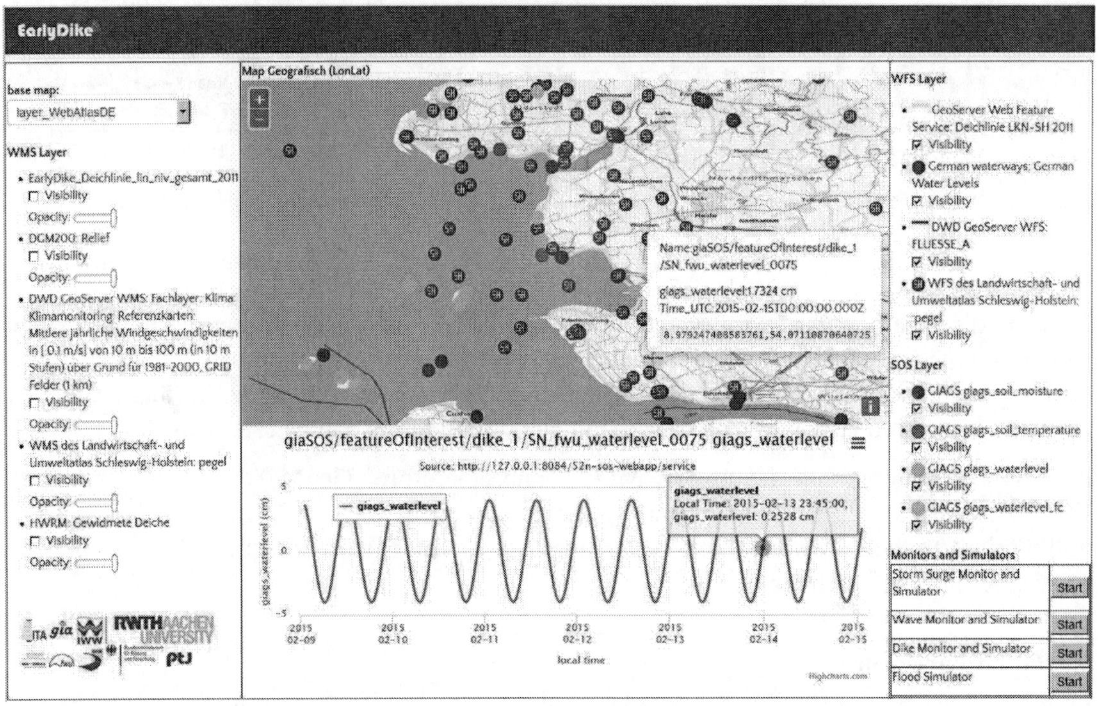

Figure 6: EarlyDike GeoPortal in the current stage of development

Furthermore, the GeoPortal can also be used for invoking simulation processes of the participating working groups using OGC's Web Processing Service (WPS) standard. The

[10] http://www.unidata.ucar.edu/software/netcdf/

[11] http://www.wmo.int/pages/prog/www/WDM/Guides/Guide-binary-2.html

[12] https://alastaira.wordpress.com/2011/01/23/the-google-maps-bing-maps-spherical-mercator-projection/

results of the simulation processes will be visualized not only by tables and graphs, but also by geo-referenced thematic maps and overlays of existing cartographic context like topographic maps or orthoimages. For maximizing the information effectiveness all connected data (sensor data, external data and simulation results) will be presented together in one coherent and geo-referenced matter.

The GeoPortal is implemented by using open JavaScript frameworks and components based on OpenLayers[13] allowing the binding of geo web service interfaces. This approach enables the seamless integration of all data from the integration layer. Thus, the web portal delivers descriptions (metadata), provides access, and enables the map-based visualization of all information. Besides the current situation also the state in the past can be observed using in-situ measured as well as third party data, e.g. time series to analyze even sudden changes over time. The third party data sources accessible by common geo services as well as the SOS service for sensor data are integrated in the GeoPortal (Figure 6).

5. Summary and Conclusions

First prototypes are set up, which show the feasibility of the described methodology. The tripartite architecture with sensor, integration and presentation layer seems to be a reasonable pattern which fits the projects requirements. The event bus using the adapted GeoMQTT protocol as well as common geo web services are the integrative components in this approach. Sensor nodes assembled in the WGSN prove to be suitable when using lightweight transfer protocols like GeoMQTT for communicating with other subsystems. The simulation processes consume the incoming data as soon as it becomes available and republish their results so that consecutive processes can make use of them. The prototyped GeoPortal accesses and combines data of different providers using the OGC SOS and OGC WMS, respectively WFS for feature data. Using international standards of OGC and modern web techniques enable access to existing data and decrease the necessity of data measuring to a minimum.

The described approach promises a sound basis for real-time monitoring and simulation of dikes. In case of a predicted but unavoidable dike failure, the consequential flooding is simulated enabling early warning for protecting people and economic values.

Acknowledgements

The EarlyDike project (http://www.earlydike.de/) is funded by the German Federal Ministry of Education and Research (BMBF) within the GEOTECHNOLOGIEN programme (03G0847A).

References

Akyildiz, I.F.; Vuran, M.C. (2010): Wireless Sensor Networks. John Wiley, West Sussex, UK.

Bandyopadhyay, S.; Bhattacharyya A. (2013): Lightweight Internet Protocols for Web Enablement of Sensors using Constrained Gateway Devices. In: International Conference on Computing, Networking and Communications, Workshops Cyber Physical System.

Benedict, K. (2005): The Open Geospatial Consortium Web Map, Web Feature and Web Coverage Service Standards – an Overview. ESIP Federation Meeting, Mexico.

---

[13] http://openlayers.org/

Bernard, L.; Kanellopoulos, I.; Annoni, A. (2005): The European geoportal – one step towards the establishment of a European Spatial Data Infrastructure. Computers, environment and urban systems, 29(1).

Bocher, E., Neteler, M. (2012): Geospatial Free and Open Source Software in the 21st Century, Dordrecht.

Broering, A., Foerster, T., Jirka, S., Priess, C. (2010): Sensor Bus: An Intermediary Layer for Linking Geosensors and the Sensor Web. In: Proceedings of the 1st International Conference on Computing for Geospatial Research and Application, COM.Geo'10, 21-23 June, Bethesda, MD, USA; ACM: New York pp.1-8.

Craglia, M., Annoni, A. (2006): INSPIRE: an innovative approach to the development of spatial data infrastructures in Europe. In: Proc. of GSDI World Conference, Santiago, Chile.

BKG (2013): Federal Agency for Cartography and Geodesy: Ad hoc reporting by INSPIRE AG to the GDI-DE Steering Committee (LG GDI-DE): INSPIRE Infrastructure for Spatial Information in Europe. Member State Report: Germany.

Groot, R. (2003): Geospatial Data Infrastructure: Concepts, Cases, and Good Practice, Oxford, UK.

Grothe, M., Kooijman, J. (eds.) (2008): Sensor Web Enablement. Netherlands Geodetic Commission, Netherlands, 2008.

Harvey, F.; Iwaniak, A.; Coetzee, S; Cooper A.K. (2012): SDI Past, Present and Future: A Review and Status Assessment. In: Proc. of GSDI 13 World Conference, Quebec, Canada.

INSPIRE (2007): Directive 2007/2/EC of the European Parliament and of the Council of 14 March 2007 establishing an Infrastructure for Spatial Information in the European Community (INSPIRE), http://eur-lex.europa.eu/legal-content/EN/ALL/?uri=CELEX:32007L0002.

Iyengar, S. S.; Brooks, R. R. (2012): Distributed Sensor Networks. CRC Press: Boca Raton, USA.

Jirka, A; Bröring, A.; Stasch, C. (2009): Applying OGC Sensor Web Enablement to Risk Monitoring and Disaster Management. In: Proc. of GSDI 11 World Conference, Rotterdam, Netherlands.

Lehfeldt, R., Melles, J. (2011): Die Marine Dateninfrastruktur Deutschland MDI-DE. In: Karl-Peter Traub, Jörn Kohlus und Thomas Lüllwitz (Hg.): Geoinformationen für die Küstenzone. Norden Halmstad: Points Verlag (3), S. 107–116.

OASIS (2014): MQTT Version 3.1.1 OASIS Standard, 29 Oct 2014.

Pengel, B. et al. (2013): Flood Early Warning System: Sensors and Internet. In: IAHS Red Book N 357, Floods: From Risk to Opportunity. IAHS Publ. 357. (Eds), pp. 445-453, January 2013. ISBN 978-1-907161-35-3.

Rüh, C; Bill, R. (2012): Concepts, Models and Implementation of the Marine Spatial Data Infrastructure in Germany (MDI-DE). In: Proc. of ISPRS Congress, Sydney, Australia, 2012.

Schleyer, A.; Luckhardt, T.; Thiel, F.,Welzel, R.-W. (2014): Geodateninfrastruktur. In: Kummer et al. (2014): Das Deutsche Vermessungs- und Geoinformationswesen – Band 2015. Wichmann Verlag, Heidelberg, S. 829-871, ISBN 978-3-87907-547-8.

Schüttrumpf, H. (2008): Aktuelle Entwicklungen im internationalen Küsteningenieurwesen - International Conference on Coastal Engineering. In: Korrespondenz Wasserwirtschaft : KW. - Hennef : GFA. - ISSN: 1616-430X, 1865-9926. - 1 (2008) 12, S./Art.: 664-665.

Spies, K.-H.; Heier, C. (2010): Sensor Web Enablement in der Wasserwirtschaft – Von der Hydrologie über das Monitoring zum Management. In: Schilcher (Hg.): Geoinformationssysteme: Beiträge zum 15. Münchner Fortbildungsseminar. abcverlag, Heidelberg.

Storm, T. (1888): Der Schimmelreiter. Novelle. Paetel Berlin, 1888.

Thomas, R. (2013): European Directive (2007/2/EC) INSPIRE - Update on INSPIRE Directive. UN Expert Group on Resource Classification, Fourth Session, 23- 26 April 2013. https://www.unece.org/fileadmin/DAM/energy/se/pp/unfc_egrc/egrc4_april2013/25_april/5_Thomas_INSPIRE.pdf.

Walter, K., Nash, E. (2009): Coupling Wireless Sensor Networks and the Sensor Observation Service – Bridging the Interoperability Gap. In: Proc. of 12th AGILE International Conference on Geographic Information Science, Hannover, Germany.

Zambrano, A. M., Pérez, I., Palau, C.E., Esteve, M. (2015): Sensor Web Enablement Applied to an Earthquake Early Warning System. In: Di Fatta, G., Fortino, G., Li, W., Pathan, M., Stahl, F., Guerrieri, A. (Eds.) Internet and Distributed Computing Systems, 8th International Conference, IDCS 2015, Windsor, UK, September 2-4, 2015. Proceedings, pp. 51-62.

Mobile Augmented Reality Implementation for Teaching Structural Analysis

Y. Turkan[a], A. Karabulut-Ilgu[a], R. Radkowski[a], A. Chen[a], A.H. Behzadan[b], C.T. Jahren[a]
[a] Iowa State University, USA
[b] Missouri State University, USA
yturkan@istate.edu

Abstract. In this paper, augmented reality (AR) technology is used to design and launch a mobile application to visualize structural components, and their behavior under loading, which will help students transfer their abstract knowledge into real world situations. To validate results, a set of example problems are used that include questions concerning structural component behavior under loading. For these examples, 3D models are developed and overlaid on top of the book images to help students see the effect of loads on structures in action. For assessment, both control and experimental groups are deployed and students' learning is measured in order to investigate the design characteristics of an effective pedagogy involving AR to teach structural analysis, how AR impacts students' learning, the role of AR in creating an inclusive learning environment that caters to various learning styles, and enhancing students' adaptive flexibility, and how AR impacts students' engagement in the learning process.

1. Introduction

Structural Analysis is an introductory core course which is taught in undergraduate civil engineering programs, and in most architectural and construction programs. It incorporates applied mechanics, materials science, and mathematics to compute a structure's deformations, internal forces, stresses, and support reactions under external loads. Despite its critical role in the curriculum, most students do not appear to have a sound understanding of fundamental concepts such as load effects, and load path; and in general, they lack the ability to visualize the deformed shape of simple structures, a necessary skill to comprehend structural behavior beyond theory. In particular, students have difficulty relating basic structural members (trusses, beams, frames) to more complex structural systems (buildings, bridges). This deficiency can be largely attributed to the ineffectiveness of the traditional instructional techniques that puts much effort on the analysis of discrete members, and less emphasis on studying the members in a 3D structural context.

Several methods have been proposed to improve student learning such as using a physical teaching lab, and cyber teaching tools (Davalos et al., 2003, Yuan and Teng, 2002). There are both cons and pros to these methods. For example, it was reported that students could use "hands-on" laboratory exercises to better grasp fundamental structural behavior concepts (Davalos et al., 2003). However, the cost associated with the development, implementation, maintenance, and staffing, as well as unavailability of space are major impediments to this approach. While flexible and affordable graphical tools can address these limitations, most such tools are still not taking advantage of 3D capabilities and lack features that allow better spatial perception and orientation.

Although the aforementioned methods can supplement existing curriculum to improve teaching and learning, little work has been done on the instructional delivery aspects, which have remained unchanged for a long time in structural analysis. Students join engineering programs because they want to learn how to design and build buildings, towers, bridges, and aircrafts (Matusovich et al., 2010). Yet, limitations of the traditional teaching methods, disconnections between classroom implementations and real-life practice, and lack of opportunities for hands-on experiences have to a large extent prevented them from understanding their profession on a larger, application-based scale.

In order to address these challenges, the authors designed and tested a new pedagogy using mobile augmented reality (AR) and advanced 3D technology for structural analysis instruction. AR superimposes the physical world with 3D digital information (Behzadan et al. 2015), and enables the visualization of structural members thus allowing students to contextually relate these members to real world structures. This is an important and timely topic because recent technological advancements have made it possible not only to model structures in 3D but also to interact with them in a cost-efficient, risk-free, and accessible manner. 3D design and AR applications have also become the forefront of civil engineering in areas such as 3D Building Information Modeling (BIM) that is rapidly expanding to other domains such as building mechanical systems (Bosché et al. 2013), and bridge and road design and inspection (Tang and Akinci 2012). Despite this, there is still a major gap between the way structural engineering is taught and the demand from the industry. It is thus imperative that existing curriculum be revised to fill this gap.

In the research presented in this paper, AR technology is used to enhance the contents of an existing structural analysis textbook by visualizing structural components, and creating 3D animations illustrating how they behave under loading. For selected problems in the book, 3D models are developed and overlaid on top of the book images, in order to help students see the effect of loads on structures in action, and thus better relate their abstract classroom knowledge to real world situations. For example, when working on a problem concerning a beam under loads, students can interactively change the load and parameters of the virtual beam, and observe how it affects the beam deformation. In order to assess the pedagogical impact of the work, control and test groups are deployed, and students' learning and performance are measured. This approach allows for a complete investigation of the design characteristics of the developed pedagogy involving AR to teach structural analysis; how AR impacts students' learning; the role of AR in creating an inclusive learning environment that caters to various learning styles, and enhancing students' adaptive flexibility; and how AR impacts students' engagement in the learning process.

2. Development of the Augmented Reality (AR) Tool for Structural Analysis

In this study, a self-developed marker-based AR application was designed for IOS-based tablet systems. This application uses fiducial template markers to register virtual contents over the views of the real world as observed by users (i.e. students). This section introduces the application design and the software architecture.

2.1 Application Interface Design and Interaction

Figure 1 shows the software interface of the AR application. As shown in this Figure, the application screen follows a typical border layout in landscape orientation with a center area and adjacent borders. The main part of the view is reserved for the AR view. Additional graphical interaction widgets are placed on the borders. The notion behind this layout is to keep a major portion of the view free of clutter, usually caused by widgets and other elements. The AR view shows a video image (in the background) which is superimposed with virtual objects (rendered in the foreground). For this application, the virtual image shows a 3D model of a truss (similar to that shown in Figure 1), beam, or another type of structural element. In addition, 3D arrows are used to indicate the load exerted on the structural elements as well as to show the reaction forces. For instance, the truss in Figure 1 is subjected to a uniformly distributed load and a point load, both indicated by arrows. The arrows are animated and their lengths can change to indicate a change in the magnitude of the loads, thus allowing the user to obtain a quick overview of the current loading situation. The application is interactive; the user can and is supposed to change the load using stepper and slider widgets. The stepper widgets are placed at the left and right borders of the application view. Users can easily access them in landscape mode with their thumbs when holding the iPad on the left and right border. The steppers allow one to change the load in discrete steps only. All reaction forces as well as deflections of the truss elements are instantly calculated in real-time. Thus, the user sees an immediate response.

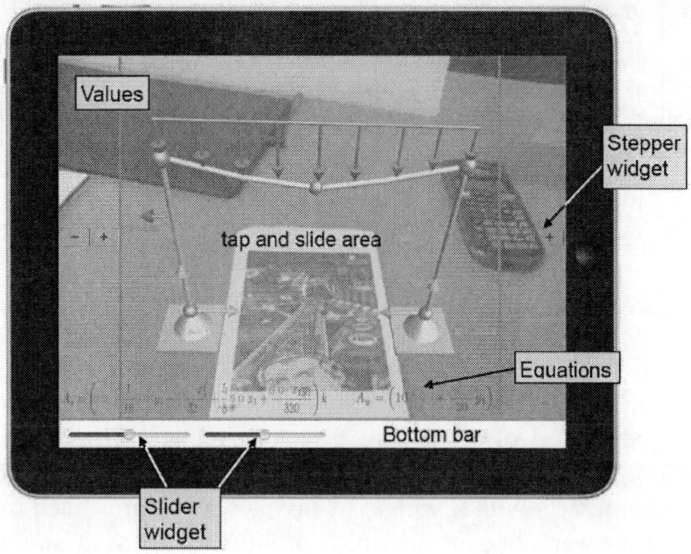

Figure 1: User Interface of the Designed AR Application

The interaction widgets are hidden from the user, in the regular view mode, a mode, in which the user only views the result in an uncluttered scene and does not intend to interact (e.g. to change the load). To reactivate the stepper elements on the right and left sides, the user must tap the screen a single time anywhere on the main view. The stepper elements disappear automatically after 5 seconds' idle time. Slider widgets, on the other hand, will appear with an upward swipe gesture with two fingers, and a downward swipe gesture hides them again.

The application is locked in landscape orientation since this orientation offers the best view to the scene while interacting. A portrait orientation in border layout would further shrink the available view space when placing widgets on left and right borders. As previously mentioned, the designed AR application is marker-based, template markers in particular (see Section 2.4). The 3D models for a particular problem appear when the user places a maker in front of the camera.

2.2 Software Architecture

The designed AR application is based on the iOS SDK and follows its prevalent model-view-controller (MVC) architecture. Figure 2 shows an overview of the software architecture including all subcomponents and their functions. The main software components are an interface/view component, an application controller, a rendering component, and a tracking component. The interface is mainly implemented using Apple's Cocoa touch SDK, written in Objective-C. The rendering module is based on OpenGL ES 2.0 and written in C++. The tracking module uses the ARTookit library and is also implemented in C++. The controller module is implemented using Objective-C as well as C++.

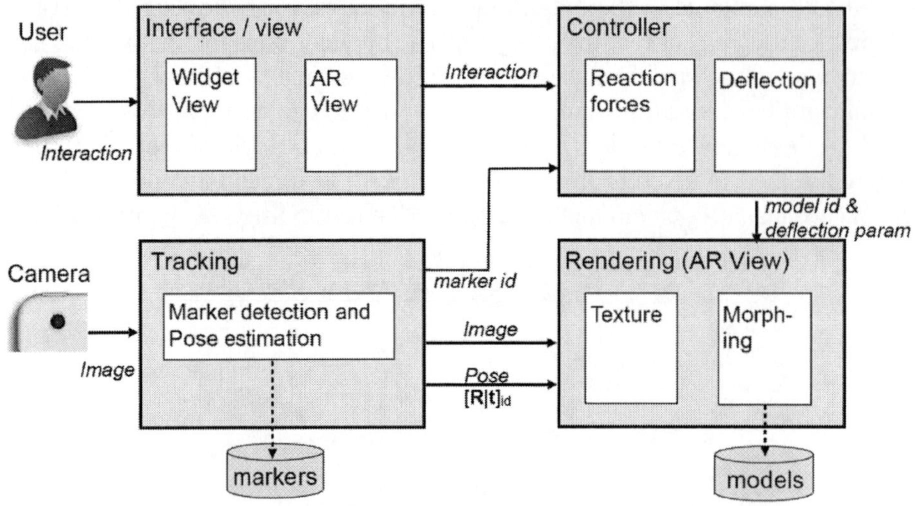

Figure 2: Software Architecture of the Designed AR Application

The main function of the *interface/view component* is to maintain the data structures and algorithms for all interaction widgets, the interaction processing, as well as for the AR view. The widget view is composed of a standard Cocoa *UIViewController* class along with the corresponding *UIView*. All interface widgets are part of the view. The view controller receives events when the user interacts with a widget or invokes a gesture. Each received interaction event is processed and forwarded to the controller. Following the MVC architecture pattern, no further processing is carried out in the view. The AR view is essentially implemented using the same two mentioned classes, with new instances. However, this instances only act as wildcards which allow access to the underlying graphics resources. The view object, especially its resource handle is replaced by an OpenGL handle.

The *controller component* implements the application logic. From the application's point-of-view, the main task is to manage the computations required to solve the structural analysis problem. In addition, the controller also controls the appearance/disappearance of all widget elements and selects the 3D models that need to be displayed for a given task.

The management process is twofold: first the controller identifies the current problem and selects the associated equations. Next, it calculates the deflection and reaction forces.

The application can manage multiple structural analysis problems/tasks using a template pattern (Vlissides et al., 1995), further denoted as problem template. The problem template basically implements the reaction force equations and deflection calculations. Each structural analysis problem is an instance of a problem template, denoted as problem object, which is associated with a unique problem ID. Every problem ID is further associated with a marker ID that relates that problem to an AR marker. Given a structural analysis problem, the task of the controller component is to maintain a list with all associations and to activate the problem object when the related marker is visible. Only one problem object, thus, one set of equations can be activated and processed at any given time. Thus, only one structural analysis problem can be solved at a time. The marker ID is decoupled from the problem ID to prevent sudden problem object swaps. The tracking component sends the marker ID continuously, at each frame in which it detects a marker. Nevertheless, a marker can disappear for one or two frames as a result of random noise, shadows, user interaction, or other events that cause the tracking component to stop submitting the marker ID. Without further insertions, the application would stop processing the current structural analysis problem. To a user, this will translate visually into the

3D models starting to flicker on the screen. To bypass this issue, the controller component observes the marker ID and only disables or replaces the subsequent equations when the marker disappears for more than 5 frames.

The second task of the controller component, besides managing equations, is actually to compute the reaction forces and deflections, as previously described. The reaction force calculation, the equilibrium equations in particular, are currently implemented in C++ and are part of a problem object. The deflection information is pre-computed and loaded from a file. A minimum of two models are required for one load: a nominal model of a truss, and a model with maximum deflection for a given load. The nominal model represents a structure under zero loading, and the maximum deflection model represents the same structure under full loading. For any given loading situation, these two models are blended linearly resulting in a blend weight ω to accommodate that particular load situation; the blending is processed by the rendering component. For each additional load, an additional maximum deflection model is required.

The next module is the *tracking component*. The class of AR application used in this research is commonly referred to as marker-based AR, which relies on continuous object tracking (i.e. marker) in video frames. This function is carried out by the tracking component. In particular, this component fetches images from the video camera of the iPad, processes them to identify markers and to calculate the position and orientation of each marker. Subsequently, the marker ID is forwarded to the controller component and the marker pose is sent to the rendering component. Further tracking details are explained in Section 2.4. The largest component of the designed AR application is the *rendering component*. It generates the AR view, which incorporates the video background and the virtual objects. Technically, the video background is implemented as a 2D texture the content of which being the image from the video camera. All 3D objects are rendered into a second image, which is superimposed on the video image. In this research, OpenGL ES 2.0 was used to implement all rendering functionalities.

2.3 Three Dimensional (3D) Content and Deflection

The 3D content of the scene consists of a truss model which is implemented as a morphed triangle mesh. Morphing results in a visual deflection of the 3D model. In the designed application, blend shape morphing is used (Akenine-Moller et al. 2008). Blend shape morphing is an interpolation technique that interpolates the position for each vertex of a triangle model between a nominal model and one or more transformed/morphed models (Alexa 2002). The basic idea is explained in Figure 3 on one point of a beam.

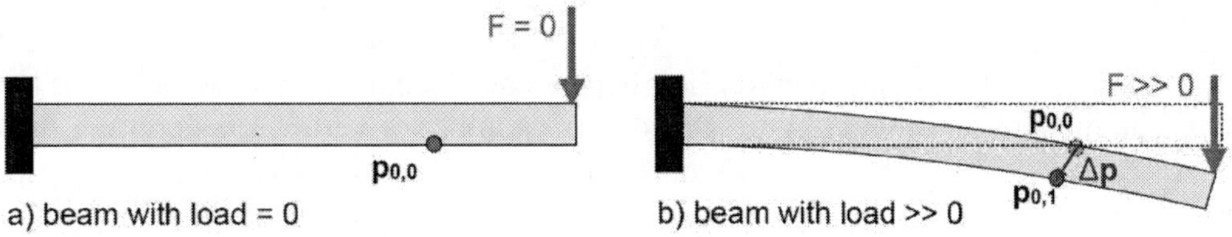

Figure 3: Blend shape morphing Based on Difference Vectors between (a) Nominal, and (b) Morphed Shapes

In this Figure, consider the point $\mathbf{p}_{0,0} \in R^3$ as a nominal vertex point. The nominal model shows the shape in its original, unloaded situation or under minimal load. A second model shows the model in its deflected situation under full load, with a vertex point $\mathbf{p}_{0,1} \in R^3$. Each additional model shows another load situation. During application initialization, a delta vector is calculated for each point, given the location in both models k=0 (nominal model) and $k+1$, as,

$$\Delta p_i = p_{i,0} - p_{i,k} \quad (1)$$

with i, the point index, and k, the index of the deflected models. All models are loaded from .obj files. During runtime, the final, deflected model is calculated for each point i as,

$$p_i = p_{i,0} + \sum_{k=1}^{N} w_k p_i \quad (2)$$

with w_k a weight values ranging from 0 to 1. A changing weight value changes the shape of the final model. A value $w_k = 0$ results in the nominal model, and a value $w_k = 1$ results in the maximal deflected model. The equation to calculate w_k depends on the load situation and the shape of the structural element. In this study, elastic behavior of the structure is considered. Therefore, structural deflections are proportional to external loads. For instance, given the loading situation (an axial load P and a uniform load u) applied to the truss shown in Figure 4,

$$w_k = \frac{1}{\delta_{max}}\left[\frac{P}{P_{max}}\delta_P + \frac{u}{u_{max}}\delta_u\right] \quad (3)$$

with δ_{max}, the maximum deflection at a point i from model k, δ_P, the current deflection from load P, δ_u, the current deflection from load u, and P_{max}, u_{max}, the maximum forces. The last two are fixed parameters, which are calculated using complex structural analysis methods. The weight value obtained from equation 3 is calculated separately for the x- and y-directions. This calculation is also part of the controller component.

Results are shown in figure 4. Figure 4(a) is the nominal model, Figure 4(b) is the morphed model with a maximal load P, and Figure 4(c) adds the uniform load u to the point load P. Although the situation shown in Figure 4(b) only needs a blended model, the situation in Figure 4(c) requires to gradually blend two models with a nominal model when the forces increase.

Figure 4: Blend Shape Morphing Results with Different Load Situations: a) Nominal Model, b) Truss Subjected to a Point Load, c) Truss Subjected to a Point Load and a Uniform Load

Although blend shape morphing is an easy to use technique which facilitates real-time rendering, a disadvantage of this method is its dependency on known point associations between models. The method essentially requires a constant number of vertex points during the entire morphing process, thus, the overall shape of an object must remain somehow unchanged. Having said that, for the intended purpose of the designed application (visualizing small structural deflections), blend shape morphing is deemed suitable since only slight changes in the shape of the structural element are expected.

2.4 Object Tracking in AR Application

As discussed earlier, AR relies on tracking which means to identify an object (i.e. an AR marker) and to calculate its pose (position and orientation) in the image with respect to the camera, in each video frame. The position and orientation allows one to align a virtual object with the physical object, which is shown in the video image, thus giving a user the impression that the virtual object is blended into the physical world.

In this research, the ARToolkit tracking system was used for object identification and pose estimation (Kato and Billinghurst 1999). The ARTookit works with black-and-white template markers (Figure 5) to identify a marker in a video image and to calculate its pose. The marker's black border facilitates locating the marker in the video image and calculating its pose. The pattern inside the boarder is required to identify a marker, and to determine marker ID. The ARToolkit library returns this ID along with the pose as transformation matrix [**R**|**t**] in a homogenous coordinate system. More than one marker can be tracked at any time. The maximum number is governed by the processing power of the CPU.

In the presented work, a multi-marker tracking approach is adopted to increase robustness. A multi-marker combines several physical markers into one logical marker. To maintain tracking, ARToolkit must detect at least one marker in the video image. Occasionally, a user may unintentionally cover one or more markers when using the application or when moving around the sheets of paper (on which the markers are printed). Using more than one marker in a multi-marker approach increases the chance that at least one marker always remains visible, thus guaranteeing robustness of marker tracking process.

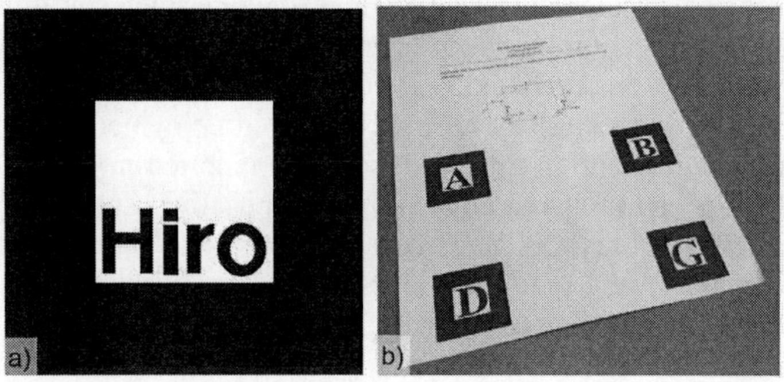

Figure 5: a) An ARToolkit Marker, b) ARToolkit Multi-Marker Sets Are Used to Increase the Tracking Robustness

In the experiments conducted in this research using structural analysis problems, the markers are placed at the corners and/or borders of the paper that the students receive (Figure 5). A marker ID is associated with each structural analysis problem or vice versa, every structural analysis problem is associated with one logical marker. As soon as the ARToolkit detects this marker, it sends its ID to the controller component, which automatically selects the proper models, the interaction widgets, and the reaction force equations. If two or more multi-marker sets are in the field-of-view, the ARToolkit will report all of them to the controller component.

3. Pilot Study: Assessment of the Augmented Reality (AR) Application

In order to measure the effectiveness of the designed AR application in teaching structural analysis concepts to students, a quasi-experimental design is adopted in this research. In this assessment study, data sources included a pre-test, a post-test, and a survey. Students were given a quiz, as the pre-test, during the lecture to capture their baseline knowledge. In this quiz, students were asked to sketch a deflection diagram of a frame given its bending moment diagram and other parameters. Responses were graded out of 10 points based on the accuracy of the deflection directions and curvatures. Next, students were placed in the experimental and control groups based on their enrolled recitation sections. Even though attendance in these recitations are not required, it is strongly recommended. In the control group the course teaching assistant solved a deflection example problem using a traditional board and chalk approach. The experimental group, on the other hand, observed the deflection behavior of the frame by manipulating different variables in the AR application. Both groups then took another quiz, which was designed to be the post-test. The post-test quiz was similar to the pre-test quiz so that the learning gain could be accurately measured; however, it was slightly changed (i.e. the direction and the magnitude of the force) in order to avoid learning by mimicry. Out of the entire student population who was enrolled in the course, only students who took both the pre-test and post-test quizzes were included in this study. Table 1 displays detailed information about the participants.

Table 1: Participant information

Control Group N= 19				
Gender		Year of Study		
Male	Female	Junior	Senior	Grad
16	3	12	7	-
Experimental Group N=22				
18	4	7	16	1

The experimental group also completed a survey investigating student attitudes toward learning structural analysis in an AR environment. The survey was adapted from Wojciechowski and Cellary (2013) and based on Technology Acceptance Model (Davis, 1989). The survey measured interface style, perceived usefulness, perceived enjoyment, perceived ease of use, attitude toward using, and intention to use. Results are reported in Table 2. The survey also included two open-ended questions asking positive and negative aspects of learning via an AR application. Descriptive statistics was used to analyse the results. In particular, means, standard deviations and percentages were reported (See Section 4 for further details). Qualitative data was coded to identify recurring themes and categories.

4. Experimental Results

The pre-test and post-test results indicated that there was an increase in mean scores for both groups. However, the results of one-way ANOVA test indicated no statistically significant difference both within (pre-test and post-test) and between (experimental vs. control) groups, as shown in Table 2. Given the experimental nature of this pilot study and potential opportunities for improving the designed methodology and assessment regime, the following is an abridged list of possible reasons why this result was obtained:

- The structural analysis topic that was targeted had been already covered in the class prior to the pilot study. The tool, therefore, was used for review purposes rather than for teaching a new topic.
- Only one structural analysis example problem was used. Results could be different and more representative had multiple problems been used in the pilot study.
- The designed AR application was not fully integrated into the curriculum (it was rather a short-term add-on to the existing instructional method), thus limiting the ability to deploy it for an extended period of time during the semester. On a similar note, some students did not fully understand the added value of the application, thus falling short in reflecting on what they observed using the application and explaining the underlying theoretical concepts. It seemed like in some cases, students did not go beyond playing with application features and tweaking load parameters.

Table 2: Results of one-way ANOVA test

Source	DF	Sum of Squares	Mean Square	F Ratio	Prob > F
Condition	1	3.60324	3.60324	0.4110	0.5252
Error	39	341.88457	8.76627		
C. Total	40	345.48780			

Even though there was no statistically significant improvement in student scores following the AR application exercise, the survey results indicated that the tool has the potential to improve student experience in learning structural analysis concepts. As can be seen in Table 3, students in the experimental group positively rated the interface style, usefulness, ease of use, enjoyment, attitude, and intention to use. The only items that were rated lower than 4 (agree) were the items 14 and 18. The relatively low rating for the AR was boring item might have resulted from the reversed nature of the item. Some students might have rated everything positively without paying close attention to what the item was asking. Being able to solve structural analysis problems was also relatively rated low compared to other features. This indicated that AR application cannot replace the instructor. Rather, the instructor needs to meaningfully integrate the tool into instruction and help students understand the theoretical concepts behind observed physical behaviour of structures.

Table 3: Student attitudes toward using AR for learning structural analysis (N=26)

Survey Item	M	SD
Interface Style (IS)		
1. Navigating the AR application is easy	4.54	0.71
2. Using an AR application on an iPad is a good idea	4.35	1.12
3. I could easily control the course of the structural deflection using the AR application	4.42	0.76
Perceived Usefulness (PU)		
4. The use of AR improves learning in the classroom	4.04	0.92
5. Using the AR application would facilitate understanding of certain concepts	4.54	0.58
6. I believe the AR system is helpful when learning	4.08	0.85
Perceived Ease of Use (PEU)		
7. I think the AR system is easy to use	4.31	0.68
8. Learning to use the system is not a problem	4.35	0.80
9. Operation with the AR system is clear and understandable	4.23	0.99
Perceived Enjoyment		
10. I think the AR system allows learning by playing	4.46	0.76
11. I enjoyed using the AR system	4.08	1.16
12. Learning with an AR system is entertaining	4.19	0.94
Attitude Toward Using (ATU)		
13. The use of an AR system make learning more interesting	4.32	0.75
14. Learning through the AR system was boring (reversed item)	3.80	1.23
15. I believe that using an AR system in the classroom is a good idea	4.23	0.90
Intention To Use (ITU)		
16. I would like to use the AR system in the future if I had the opportunity	4.27	0.83
17. Using an AR system would allow me to solve Structural Analysis problems on my own	3.92	1.02
18. I would like to use the AR system to learn Structural Analysis and other engineering subjects.	4.15	0.78

The qualitative findings from the open-ended questions also provided insights on the benefits and challenges of using an AR application for learning. The visualization and interactive features of the tool were considered to be beneficial for learning. For example, one student mentioned the visual aspect of the tool as a contributing factor as he pointed, "*for a visual learner like myself, this allows you to see how the individual parts come together to affect the entire structure*". Another student said "*I liked how you could increase the forces to see how the structural numbers were affected*". Students also highlighted some deficiencies of the tool which will help the team to improve it for future use. Having only one example problem was apparently a limitation as pointed out by several students. For example, one student pointed out "*there was only so much you could do. After you achieve it, it was a bit boring. If we had more structures to visualize, it would have been more interesting*". Holding the iPad from a reasonable distance to be able to see the 3D image was another hassle for students, as stated by one student "*I had to hold [the device] in the air while sliding it, which becomes tiresome after an extended period of time*".

5. Conclusions and Future Work

The work presented in this paper aimed at transforming the current methods in teaching structural analysis using advanced interactive 3D visualization techniques. Despite the fact that structural analysis is a critical part of the curriculum and is taught widely in almost all civil engineering programs, and in most architectural and construction programs, most students do not appear to have a sound understanding of fundamental concepts such as load effects, and load path; and in general, they lack the ability to visualize the deformed shape of simple structures, a necessary skill to conceptualize structural behavior beyond theory. In this paper, a new pedagogy using mobile augmented reality (AR) was introduced for structural analysis instruction. In particular, a self-developed marker-based AR application was designed for IOS-based tablet systems. This application used fiducial template markers and blend shape morphing to register and render virtual contents over the views of the real world as observed by users (i.e. students). In addition, to measure the effectiveness of the designed AR application in teaching structural analysis concepts to students, a quasi-experimental design was adopted which consisted of a pre-test, a post-test, and a survey.

References

Akenine-Möller, T., Haines, E. and Hoffman, N., 2008. Real-time rendering. CRC Press.

Alexa, M. (2002). Recent advances in mesh morphing. In Computer graphics forum (Vol. 21, No. 2, pp. 173-198). Blackwell Publishers Ltd.

Behzadan, A. H., Dong S., Kamat V.R. (2015). Augmented reality visualization: A review of civil infrastructure system applications. Advanced Engineering Informatics, 29(2), 252-267.

Bosché, F., Guillemet A., Turkan Y., Haas C. T., Haas R. (2013). Tracking the built status of MEP works: Assessing the value of a Scan-vs-BIM system. Journal of Computing in Civil Engineering, 28(4), 05014004.

Davalos, J. F., Moran, C. J., & Kodkani, S. S. (2003). Neoclassical active learning approach for structural analysis. In Proceedings of the 2003 American Society for Engineering Education Annual Conference & Exposition.

Kato H. and Billinghurst M. (1999). Marker tracking and hmd calibration for a video-based augmented reality conferencing system. In the 2nd International Workshop on Augmented Reality, 1999, San Francisco, CA, USA.

Matusovich, H. M., Streveler, R. A., & Miller, R. L. (2010). Why do students choose engineering? A qualitative, longitudinal investigation of students' motivational values. Journal of Engineering Education, 99(4), 289–303.

Wojciechowski R. and Cellary W. (2013). Evaluation of learners' attitude toward learning in ARIES augmented reality environments. Computers & Education, 68, 570-585.

Tang P. and Akinci B. (2012). Formalization of workflows for extracting bridge surveying goals from laser-scanned data. Automation in Construction, 22, 306-319.

Vlissides, J., Helm, R., Johnson, R. and Gamma, E., (1995). Design patterns: Elements of reusable object-oriented software. Reading: Addison-Wesley, 49(120), p.11.

Yuan, X. F. and Teng, J. G. (2002). Interactive Web-based package for computer-aided learning of structural behavior. Computer Applications in Engineering Education, 10(3), 121–136.

Auto-detection and assignment of unexpected tasks in embedded systems design process

Adam Górski, Maciej Ogorzałek
Jagiellonian University, Poland
a.gorski@uj.edu.pl

Abstract. In this paper we propose a new methodology for auto-detection and assignment of unexpected tasks in embedded systems design process. Unlike other solutions unexpected tasks are not given to the system but are detected by the system itself. It is achieved when the system cannot execute one task. In such a situation system creates a list of problems and tries to find a solution by dividing all predicted tasks on maximum number of subtasks and connecting them into new tasks. The methodology is divided on four levels. In three of those levels optimization can be made.

1. Introduction

Distributed embedded systems e.g. Górski et al. (2014a) are systems consisted of two kinds of resources: Processing Elements (PEs) and Communication Links (CLs). Those systems are able to execute some tasks (like measuring temperature, measuring the speed of a car, recording a program by a DVD recorder, etc.) due to embedded software. Therefore we can describe embedded systems as hardware with software. Today embedded systems can be found in many areas like: modern cars e.g. Srovnal et al. (2010), mobile phones e.g. Sun et al. (2010), digital cameras e.g. Wolf et al. (2002), etc. PEs can be divided on two groups: Programmable Processors (PPs) and Hardware Cores (HCs). PPs are universal resources able to execute more than one tasks. Using PPs can decrease the cost of the system but increases a time of execution the tasks. HCs are resources dedicated to execute only one task. Those resources decrease the time of execution the tasks but increase the overall cost of the system. CLs are used to provide communication between PEs.

Most of papers e.g. De Micheli et al. (1997) concentrate on three phases of embedded systems design process: modeling, implementation and validation e.g. Ko et al. (2008). Modeling provides a hardware/software model of a system. Implementation is a hardware representation of the system. Validation checks if requirements are satisfied and if the system works properly.

Cosynthesis e.g. Jozwiak et al. (2010) is a process which automatically generates the architecture of embedded systems. It can be divided on: allocation – choice of number of PP, HCs and CLs, assignment – assignment of tasks to PEs and task scheduling. There are two basic kinds of existing solutions: constructive e.g. Dave et al. (1997) and iterative improvement algorithms Górski et al. (2014b). Constructive methodologies build system step by step choosing PE for each task separately. Those algorithms have one disadvantage – they can stop in local minima of optimizing parameters. The disadvantage can be reduced by using evolution algorithms like genetic algorithms e.g. Guo et al. (2007) or genetic programming e.g. Deniziak et al. (2008). Iterative improvements algorithms start from designed, suboptimal solution (mostly from the fastest) and build the system architecture by making local changes (allocating/deallocating PEs, moving tasks between PEs). However the results are still suboptimal.

The target architecture of embedded system must satisfy some requirements. The requirements can be obtained using scenarios e.g. Gheorghita et al. (2009). Scenarios can be also used to obtain the system's architecture (software e.g. Douglass (2004) and hardware e.g. Paul et al. (2006)). However scenarios must contain all of possible interactions between user and the system.

The behavior of embedded system can be described using graph (task graph, conditional task graph e.g. Eles et al. (1998) or extended task graph e.g. Klaus et al. (2001)), matlab e.g. Banerjee et al. (2000) or c-code e.g. Venkataramani et al. (2004). We decided to use graph representation of embedded system in this paper.

One of very practical problems in embedded systems design process is a problem of unexpected tasks e.g. Górski et al. (2016). The problem assumes that besides tasks, that need to be executed by the system, new (unexpected) tasks can appear. The system was not originally designed to execute those tasks. What is more the architecture of the system cannot be modified or such modification are too expensive. The situation is different than in many papers which assume unexpected behaviour e.g. Mise et al. (2006), but understand it as faults e.g. Kovalev et al. (2014).

In existing solutions unexpected tasks were given to the system. Therefore the assignment process was not fully automated. The system needed to be controlled by a human to work dependable. What is more in existing algorithms unexpected tasks do not modify the order of original tasks.

In this paper we propose a novel approach to auto-detection and assignments of unexpected tasks in embedded systems design process. In the approach understanding of the scenario is modified. It is understood rather as a target tasks. Thus it can be described using singles tasks and inserted in the task graph as a different node. This possibility can also help in detection of unexpected tasks by the system itself. Unlike in other approaches unexpected tasks can appear in any part of task graph. Therefore the original task graph can be dynamically modified. What is worth to underline for us unexpected tasks are not faults but extension of possibilities of embedded systems which can make the system more universal. The system can also react in situation when other options are impossible.

2. Representation of embedded system

Behavior of embedded system is described using an acyclic, directed graph G = {T, E}, which shows dependencies between system's activity. In most of papers the activity means tasks that have to be executed by the system. However our methodology needs some modifications on that representation. We decided to use mixed scenario and task graph. Very simple tasks, that can be executed only in one way are marked on the graph as a single tasks (for example measuring a temperature, moving the arm of a robot). Activities which can be executed in different ways are marked as scenarios. Therefore moving to location "A" by a robot can be described as "reach the location "A"". There is no information about resources used by the system to execute the scenario. Such a description indicates that reaching the selected location can require execution of some number of unexpected tasks. What is more it indicates that there is not only one possibility to execute the scenario. Figure 1. presents an example of a task/scenario graph.

The graph is consisted of seven nodes which consist five tasks and two scenarios. T0, T1, T2, T3, and T4 are tasks, S1 and S2 are scenarios. The edges describe amount of data e_{ij} that needs to be transferred between connected tasks/scenarios.

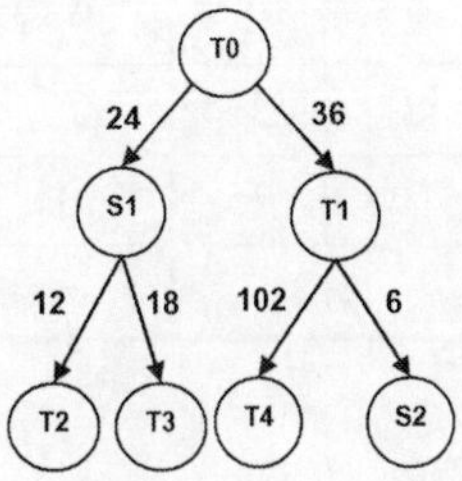

Figure 1: Example of a task/scenario graph. Letter "T" indicates on tasks, letter "S" on scenarios

The transmission time D is described by the formula below:

$$D = \frac{e_{ij}}{b} \tag{1}$$

Each scenario in the graph has predefined solution consisted of tasks. The solutions does not include any information about possible hardware implementation. An example of scenario's solution is presented on Figure 2.

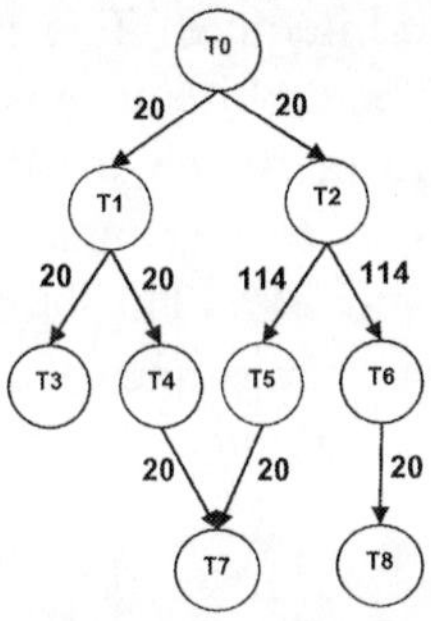

Figure 2: Example of a scenario's solution

The scenario includes nine tasks: T0, T1, T2, T3, T4, T5, T6, T7 and T8. Generally scenario does not have to be consisted only of tasks. It can include some other scenarios.

In table 1 an example of database for the system from figure 1. is given. It includes three PEs: two PPs one HC and one CL.

Table 1: Example of database for a system described by task/scenario graph from figure 1.

Task/Scenario	PP1 C=200		PP2 C=250		HC1	
	t	c	t	c	t	c
T0	100	12	103	10	30	100
T1	45	18	50	20	3	60
T2	90	9	86	8	10	95
T3	35	5	40	8	2	40

T4	22	1	30	3	2	55
S1	87	23	60	34	5	93
S2	190	25	150	30	25	150
CL1 (b=6)	c=3		c=2		c=10	

C is the cost of the resource. t is a time (in seconds) of execution a task. c is a cost of execution a task. Costs of execution tasks assigned to HC include a cost of the resource. The overall cost of the system (C_f) is a sum of: costs of all PP in the system, cost of execution of all the tasks and cost of CLs. The cost can be described by the following formula:

$$C_f = \sum_{i=1}^{p} C_{PP_i} + \sum_{j=1}^{n} C_j + \sum_{k=1}^{m} \sum_{l=1}^{P_k} C_{CL_k, PC_l} \qquad (2)$$

The target system consist of p programmable processors, n tasks and m communication links connected to P_k of PEs.

3. Methodology

The algorithm starts from a ready architecture. The architecture cannot be modified. It is consisted of p PPs, h HCs and l CLs. The architecture is also characterized by two parameters: overall cost of the system and a time in which all the tasks finish theirs executions. The behavior of the system is described using task/scenario graph. Every scenario has predefined solution. All the tasks are assignment to PEs. The methodology is divided on three phases: execution/simulation, analyze and inserting unexpected tasks to the graph, finding the solutions of the problems and task assignment. The scheme of the methodology is presented on figure 3 below.

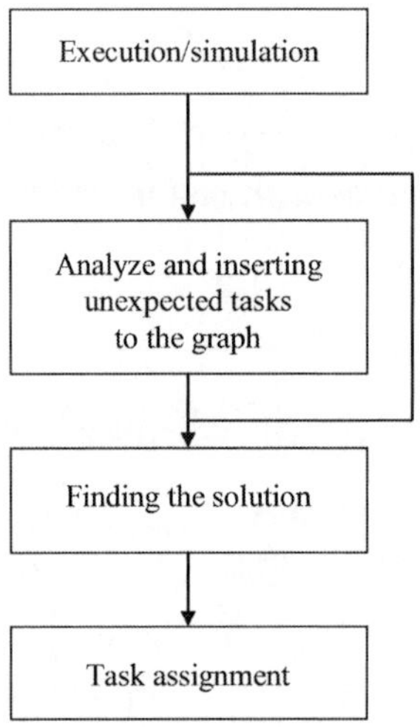

Figure 3: Scheme of the methodology. It is consisted of four sequential phases

At the beginning every tasks and scenarios are executed or simulated. Most of tasks required some data before they can start theirs execution. If the data is not received that indicates on some barriers between the task and its predecessor. Therefore between the nodes which correspond to the tasks a new node is inserted. The node is marked as unexpected target task. It can be easily observed that the structure of original task/scenario graph can be modified. Unexpected tasks can appear in any moment of operation process of the system.

The next phase is an analyze of possible problems. The system must make a list of all possible problems which make the task impossible to execute. The list includes only simple information for example: too large distance, lack of energy, existence a barrier, etc. The system checks if the data is received by next task after one problem would be solved. If not the combination of two or more problems is investigated. In this situation another node or nodes are added to the graph. Every new node describes unexpected task or scenario.

The system must find solutions of the problems marked on task/scenario graph. It is made by searching the combination of all defined tasks. However simple combination of defined earlier tasks could be not enough. All the tasks should be divided on a maximum possible number of subtasks. Then the combination of those subtasks can be solution of the problems. Unexpected tasks must be characterized by time of execution and cost of execution on every possible PE. Therefore in this phase not only solutions are proposed. In the phase unexpected tasks are also described by the values.

The last phase is unexpected task assignment. All unexpected tasks must be assigned to PEs. Because unexpected tasks can appear after every task the task assignment of predefined tasks can be changed. The tasks assigned to HCs cannot be reassigned because HCs are dedicated only to execute those tasks and any other tasks cannot be executed by those resources. We decided to proposed iterative improvement methodology for tasks assignment. This group of algorithms has the largest representation in task assignment process. Those methodologies starts usually from the fastest possible architecture. Therefore all unexpected tasks and tasks previously allocated to PPs are assignment to theirs fastest implementations. The system must meet time constrains. Next for the tasks the value of following function F_i is calculated for every PP:

$$F_i = c_{ip} * t_{ip} \quad (3)$$

In formula above c_{ip} is the cost of execution the task i for PP number p, t_{ip} is time of execution of the task for the PP number p. The tasks are assigned on PP on which the F_i value is the lowest only if such assignment exceeded the constrains. Finally overall cost of the solution and time of execution of all the task is calculated.

4. Example

To test the efficiency of presented methodology we decided to use benchmark proposed by Górski and Ogorzałek. The benchmark describes an autonomous robot working on planet mars. The benchmark was obtained after modification of autonomous robot proposed by Klaus et al. (2001) In the benchmark task graph was used to describe behavior of the system. We assume that some of the tasks can be replaced by scenarios. Task/scenario graph for investigating system was presented on figure 1.

The methodology starts from ready system. The cost of the system is 1011 and time when the last task (or scenario) finishes its execution is 89. The time constrain was set on 100. The system contains two PPS: PP1 (executes T3) and PP2 (executes T4). The rest of tasks are executed by HCs. At the beginning all the tasks are executed. We assume that, after execution/simulation, tasks T1 and T4 cannot be executed. Therefore between T1 and T0, and before T4 new nodes are added. The nodes are marked as unexpected target tasks. The task/scenario graph after such operations is presented on figure 4.

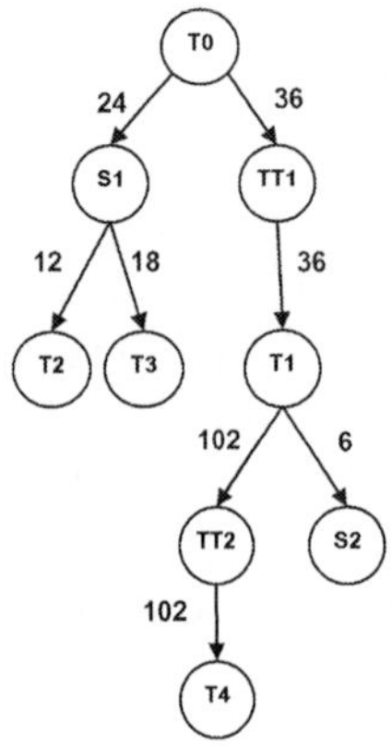

Figure 4: Task/scenario graph after adding unexpected target tasks. TT1 is unexpected target task 1, TT2 is unexpected target task 2

Table 2: Database for all the subtasks. t is time of execution of a subtask, c is a cost of the execution

Tasks	PP1		PP2	
	t	c	t	c
T0a	30	3	28	2
T0b	35	3	37	3
T0c	25	4	27	3
T0d	10	2	11	2
T1a	20	8	19	8
T1b	25	10	31	12
T2a	30	3	32	2
T2b	30	3	33	3
T2c	30	3	33	3
T3a	10	1	15	3
T3b	10	1	5	1
T3c	15	3	20	4
T4a	7	0	12	1
T4b	15	1	18	2

The graph is now consisted of nine nodes. The next step is finding the solutions. To achieve this all the tasks are divided on possible number of subtasks. The database for all the subtasks is given in table 2 above.

The list of problems is constructed. It is defined as the information of what data missing to execute the next task. In general case the system can also have some predefined propositions of the problems to solve. The system choose the problem from the list to solve. We assume that the list in the example is consisted of seven problems for TT1 and six problems for TT2. The solution is proposed by connecting two or more subtask. In this example we decided to choose first problem from the list and try to solve it. If the solution of the problem does not give any result the next problem is investigated. In some cases it is necessary to investigate more than one problem. The first solution of a problem which enable the next task to receive the data is detected unexpected task (or scenario consisted of two or more tasks). The example of solution for problem 1 for TT1 can be consisted of comparison the subtasks: T0a/T3c/T4b. The example solution of a problem 2 for TT1 is: T0a/T1b, of a problem 3: T1b/T2c/T4b, of a problem 4: T1b/T4b, of a problem 5: T0b/T4a, of a problem 6: T0d/T3b/T4b, of a problem 7: T0c/T3c/T4a. The example solution for TT2 of a problem 1 is: T2a/T4a, of a problem 2: T1b/T3a of a problem 3: T0d/T1b/T2c of a problem 4: T0d/T2a of a problem 5: T1a/T3a of a problem 6: T2c/T4a. In table 3 below parameters of time and cost for investigated problems are presented. The parameters are given for all PPs.

Table 3: Example of database for solutions of investigated problems.

Task/Scenario	PP1 C=200		PP2 C=250	
TT 1	t	c	t	c
SProblem1	75	10	66	8
SProblem2	65	13	59	14
SProblem3	70	14	82	17
SProblem4	45	14	49	14
SProblem5	42	3	49	4
SProblem6	40	7	34	5
SProblem7	47	7	59	8
TT 2				
SProblem1	37	3	34	3
SProblem2	35	11	46	15
SProblem3	50	6	59	8
SProblem4	40	5	43	4
SProblem5	30	9	34	11
SProblem6	37	3	45	4

After simulation of the solutions it was found that TT1 can be represented as two unexpected tasks: solution of problem 3 and problem 7. It means that TT1 was unexpected scenario consisted of two tasks. TT2 can be replaced by one unexpected task – solution of a problem 1. The final task/scenario graph is presented on figure 5.

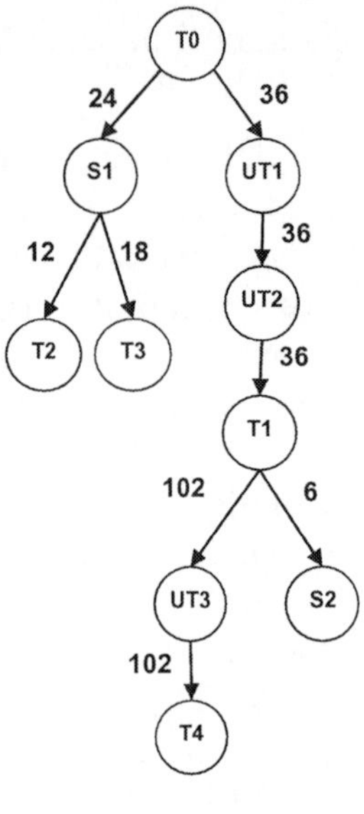

Figure 5: The final task/scenario graph. UT1, UT2 and UT3 are unexpected tasks.

Next the system makes task assignment. We assume that time constrains was extended to 330. All the tasks assigned to PPs and all unexpected tasks are assigned to the fastest PPs. Every task which tame of execution does not exceed the constrains are reassigned to the PP with the lowest value of function F_i. UT1 and UT2 are assigned to PP1, UT3 is assigned to PP2. Task T4, which was previously located on PP2, was assigned to PP1 The final cost of the system is 1035. The time of execution of all the tasks is 321. The final task assignment was presented on figure 6 below.

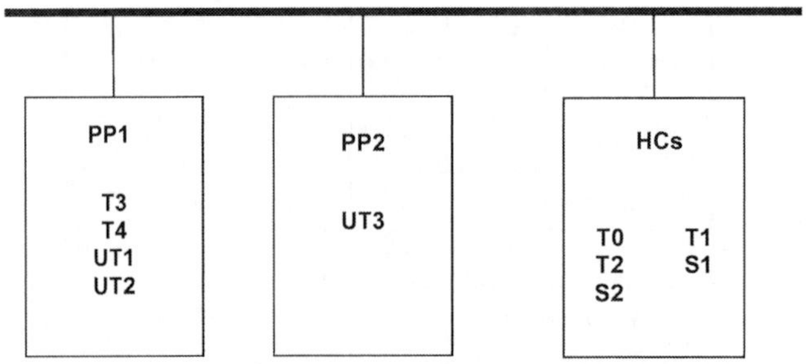

Figure 6: The final task/scenario assignment.

5. Conclusions and future work

In this work we presented a methodology for auto-detection and assignment of unexpected tasks in embedded systems design process. Unlike other methodologies we decided to extend graphs which describe a behaviour of the systems by scenarios. The definition of scenario was modified. Therefore the system was able to detect unexpected tasks and propose a solution. That implies that system is more universal and design process is cheaper because some parts of the process can be independent from people.

Providing solutions in this area can allow the system to react when other possibilities are impossible. Understanding the scenario as a connection of two or more tasks indicates that the same unexpected scenario can be consisted of different unexpected tasks. it means that there exists more than one way to reach the target. Therefore this methodology indicates that there are three fields in which optimization can be made: 1. deciding which problems from the list should be solved, 2. deciding which subtasks should be connected to provide the solution of the problems, 3. unexpected tasks assignment. It is also possible to make concurrent optimization of two or three phases. In such a optimization results from one phase have influence on results of another phase. In second and third phase it is possible to optimize time and cost. In first phase it is possible to optimize for example number of problems to solve.

Future work will concentrate on examining new methodologies to assign of unexpected tasks and new approaches to expand scenarios. We will also analyze another possibilities of appearing unexpected tasks.

References

Górski, A., and Ogorzałek, M. (2014a). Adaptive GP-based algorithm for hardware/software co-design of distributed embedded systems. In Proceedings of the 4th International Conference on Pervasive and Embedded Computing and Communication Systems, 2014, Lisbon, Portugal.

Sun, L., Zhang, D., Li, B., Guo, B. and Li, S.. (2010). Activity recognition on an accelerometer embedded mobile phone with varying positions and orientations. In Zhiwen Yu, Ramiro Liscano, Guanling Chen, Daqing Zhang and Xingshe Zhou, Ubiquitous Intelligence and Computing, Lecture Notes in Computer Sciences, volume 6406, Springer-verlag, pp. 548-562. Xi'an, China.

Wolf, W., Ozer, B., and Lv, T. (2002). Smart cameras as embedded systems. In Computer, vol. 35, no. 9, pp. 48–53.

De Micheli, G., Gupta, R., (1997). Hardware/software co-design. In Proceedings IEEE 95.3 (Mar). IEEE.

Ko, H. F., Kinsman, A. B., and Nicolini, N. (2008). Distributed Embedded Logic Analysis for Post-Silicon Validation of SOCs. In Proceedings of the IEEE International Test Conference.

Jozwiak L., Nedjah N., and Figueroa, M. (2010). Modern development methods and tools for embedded reconfigurable systems – a survey. In Integration, VLSI Journal, pp.1-33.

Dave, B., Lakshminarayana, G., Jha, N., 1997. COSYN: Hardware/software Co-synthesis of Embedded Systems. In Proceedings of the 34th annual Design Automation Conference (DAC'97).

Górski, A., and Ogorzałek, M.J. (2014b). Iterative improvement methodology for hardware/software co-synthesis of embedded systems using genetic programming. In Proceedings of the 11th Conference on Embedded Software and Systems (Work in Progress Session), 2014, Paris, France.

Guo, R., Li, B., Zou, Y., and Yhuang, Z. (2007). Hybrid quantum probabilistic coding genetic algorithm for large scale hardware-software co-synthesis of embedded systems. In Proc. of the IEEE Congres on Evolutionary Computation, pp. 3454-3458.

Deniziak, S., and Górski, A. (2008). Hardware/Software Co-Synthesis of Distributed Embedded Systems Using Genetic Programming. In Lecture Notes in Computer Sciences, volume 5216, Springer-verlag pp. 83-93.

Gheorghita, S. V., Palkovic, M., Hamers, J., Vandecappelle, A., Mamagkakis, S., Basten, T., Eeckhout, L., Corporaal, H., Catthoor, F., Vandeputte, F., and De Bosschere, K. (2009) System-scenario-based design of dynamic embed-ded systems," ACM Trans. on Design Automation of Electronic Systems, vol. 14, no. 1, pp. 1–45.

Douglass, B. P. (2004). Real Time UML: Advances in the UML for Real-Time Systems. Addison Wesley Publishing Company, Reading, MA.

Paul, J. M., Thomas, D. E., and Bobrek, A. (2006). Scenario-oriented design for single-chip heterogeneous multiprocessors. In IEEE Transations on Very Large Scale Integration (VLSI) Systems, 14, 8, pp. 868–880.

Eles, P., Kuchcinski, K., Peng, Z., Doboli, A., and Pop, P. (1998). Scheduling of Conditional Process Graphs for the Synthesis of Embedded Systems. In Proceedings of Design, Automation and Test in Europe, pp. 132-138.

Klaus, S., and Huss, S. A. (2001). Interrelation of specification method and scheduling results in embedded system design. In Proceedings of the IEEE International Forum on Design Languages.

Banerjee P., Shenoy, N., Choudhary, A., Hauck, S., Bachmann, C., Haldar, M., Joisha, P., Jones, A., Kanhare, A., Nayak, A., Periyacheri, S., Walkden, M., and Zaretsky D. (2000). A MATLAB compiler for distributed, heterogeneous, reconfigurable computing systems. In Proc. of the 8th IEEE Symposium on Field Programmable Custom Computing Machines, pp. 39-48.

Venkataramani G., Budiu, M., Chelcea, T., and Goldstein S., C. (2004). C to asynchronous data-flow circuits: an end-to-end tool-flow. In Proc. of the International Work- shop on Logic Synthesis, pp. 501-508.

Górski, A., Ogorzałek, M. (2016). Assignment of unexpected tasks in embedded systems design process, Microprocessors and Microsystems, DOI:10.1016/j.micpro.2016.01.001.

Mise, T., Shinyashiki, Y., Nakatani, T., Ubayashi, N., Katamine, K., and Hashimoto, M. (2006). A Method for Extracting Unexpected Scenarios of Embedded Systems. In Proceedings of the Knowledge-Based Software Engineering, pp. 41-50.

Kovalev, S., and Sukhanov, A (2014). Anomaly detection based on Markov chain model with production rules. Prgrammnye produkty i sistemy, no3 pp. 40-44.

Enhanced Differencing and Merging of IFC Data by Processing Spatial, Semantic and Relational Model Aspects

Simon Daum, André Borrmann
Chair of Computational Modeling and Simulation
Technische Universität München, Germany
simon.daum@tum.de

Abstract. Building Information Modeling promotes collaborative work in which models are edited and enhanced in parallel by domain experts. In this environment, revised and extended datasets have to be combined to an overall database. To perform this merging, duplicates have to be identified. This paper describes a novel, comprehensive approach for detecting equivalences in datasets of the Industry Foundation Classes (IFC), an open and full-fledged schema for building models. In contrast to available methods, the presented approach is independent of object identifiers. Instead, the detection of duplicates is performed on entity level considering spatial, semantic and relational aspects of the IFC data.

1. Introduction

The paradigms of Building Information Modeling (BIM) promote the use of comprehensive digital building representations. Instead of previously adopted approaches, which focus on pure geometric data, a BIM comprises not only the 3D shapes of elements and enclosed spaces, but also type information and the relationships between elements. Therefore, a BIM has the potential to serve as a data pool used by all participants involved in the design, construction and operation of a building. Despite the benefits of a BIM-based planning, there are still open questions in the field. In this contribution, we delve into methods of combining several submodels to an overall BIM model.

The terminology we use is borrowed from textual comparison tools. For instance, these tools are employed for the management of source code which is concurrently edited by several developers. In this context, the process of creating one integrated dataset from changed files is referred to as *merging*. Here, textual data has to be classified as original, newly added or modified. Hence, the textual comparison tools can show all differences (also known as *diffs*) between two files.

In a BIM environment, merging takes place as part of a distributed planning in which various project participants separately enhance their sections of the building model (Weise et al., 2004). The workflow of one participant can be summarized as submodel extraction, model enhancement und submodel integration (Figure 1).

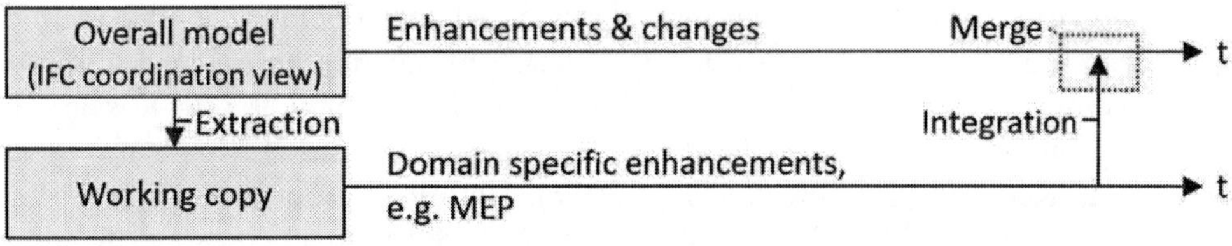

Figure 1: Merging in a multi-disciplinary BIM-based planning process.

The last step of the workflow comprises the necessary merging of the current overall model with the modified submodel. As the working copy contains original elements, some of them will be represented twice, once in the overall model and once in the working copy. This is critical as these duplicates lead to erroneous computations in downstream application, e.g. in quantity take-offs or simulations.

In the currently applied tools, the support for merging BIM data is limited. A manual solution is to tag the original entities at the time when domain specific enhancement starts. But this annotating demands a great amount of discipline of all involved editors, leads to recurrent manually work, is error-prone and hampers the editors in their actual tasks.

On the other hand, the support of a high quality merging process for BIM data is important because of the specific conditions of collaboration in the construction industry. Despite the former aspiration of one central BIM model, the reality shows that even in midsize projects several interrelated models are produced. Additionally, projects are developed during complex design and planning phases, in which models are often significantly changed. Finally, there are a large number of contributors involved in the ongoing detailing of a model. Here, each domain focuses on different views of the model whereas the used subsets of entities intersect.

The paper is structured as following. In the next section, related work is discussed. In Section 3 it is explained why a textual merging is not feasible. Instead, an entity-based approach is presented in Section 4, showing how doublets can be found by spatial, attributive and relational aspects of a model. The following section describes the prototypical implementation of the developed approach and presents a case study. Section 6 concludes this contribution and gives an outlook for further research.

2. Related Work and State of the Art

There are various applications for differencing and merging textual data. One of the best known tools is *diff3* which is used e.g. in revision control systems (Smith, 1988; Khanna et al., 2007). For textual merging, algorithms are facilitated which compute the *longest common subsequence* to identify unchanged parts between documents (Hunt and MacIlroy, 1976).

For differencing and merging of more structured data, various proposals are available in literature. In the domain of model-driven engineering, methods for merging are developed for the general Meta-Object Facility (MOF) and demonstrated for data of the Unified Modeling Language (UML) (Alanen and Porres, 2003). For documents written in the Extensible Markup Language (XML), various merging algorithms are available which process the tree structure of this encoding (Lindholm, 2004; La Fontaine, 2002). An algorithm for merging graph-like structures is discussed in Zündorf et al., (2001).

In the domain of 3D modelling, a system is presented that operates on the identifiers of meshes (Doboš and Steed, 2012). Also the BIM Server has the ability to check for duplicated entities by examine their object identifiers (Beetz et al., 2010). Later in this article, it is explained why this is not reliable if BIM-data is processed. More BIM-specific approaches are presented in Koch and Firmenich (2006, 2011). Here it is proposed to store all steps of operations in the model. This is beyond the scope of the current schemas and would require an extensive redesign of the transfer formats and all applied applications. In contrast, the approach which is described in this contribution can deal with the currently available Industry Foundation Classes (IFC).

To verify the spatial quality of BIM data, clash detection is employed (Tommelein and Gholami, 2012). Here, intersecting geometric representations of entities are reported. The implementation of clash detection is based on the identification of triangle intersections (Möller, 1997). Indeed, finding intersections can be used to identify doublings. But clashes do not indicate spatial duplicates by necessity as intersections can also occur in touching constellations. Thus, another geometrical examination is needed.

Appropriate strategies for a reliable geometrical matching can be found in the field of mechanical engineering. Here, the identification of similar 3D shapes in a database of components is an ongoing research topic. To efficiently select parts in this repository, the user introduces a lookup mesh. In the query, similarities between the lookup mesh and the stored shapes are computed and the most similar entities are returned (Rea et al., 2005; Tangelder and Veltkamp, 2008).

3. Textual Versus Entity-based Differencing

Whereas textual comparison tools match paragraphs and search for added and removed words and tokens, the merge process in a BIM environment requires a different strategy. As BIM data is based on identifiable entities of the considered Universe of Discourse (UoD), the differencing and merging has to be performed on entity level. In this contribution, entities are represented as instances of the IFC4 schema (Liebich, 2013).

To perform the merging, the changed entities of the current submodel have to be integrated in the overall model whereas certain entities supersede other entities. Three sets of IFC entities can be classified in the emerging overall model:

1. Some entities are represented twice and match each other exactly. This comprises the entity's attribute values, its use in relations as well as its geometric representation.
2. Some entities are represented twice but do not match each other exactly as some or all of the following aspects have changed.
    a. The geometric representations of the entity pair differ.
    b. The attribute values of an examined entity pair differ.
    c. The use of the entities in relations differs.
3. Some entities are added to the datasets independently and therefore have no matches.

The recognition of spatial, attributive and relational differences between the datasets enables for a fine-grained merging during model integration. In the first case, which represents a complete match, duplicates can be eliminated automatically. This is also the group of entities we focus on in this contribution. The second and third cases may call for intervention by the end user, e.g. if conflicts emerge because of simultaneous editing.

To extract the three types of differences, the identification of entities is required. In the IFC, entity identification is based on the *GlobalId* attribute with holds a unique string. However, there is a high risk of losing the GlobalId of an entity during processes of import, export and conversion.

As an example for the weak support of consistent GlobalId handling, a minimalistic IFC file is exported from Autodesk Revit 2015 by use of the extended IFC exporter plug-in (Autodesk, 2016). In the first case, a single wall with an opening forms the dataset. For the second export, the opening is deleted and the plain wall is exported. A textual differencing of the two files shows that the GlobalIds of the associated relationships get lost, although the entities reflect the identical, unchanged information (

Figure 2). Note, that the textual comparison can only help to identify differences in these minimalistic IFC files which approximately comprise 250 lines of code. Files in realistic productive scenarios contain about 10.000 – 1.000.000 lines of code and are thus by far too large for textual comparison.

```
#209= IFCRELDEFINESBYPROPERTIES('3uhd6lbe190x2omI6GDmTm',#41,$,$,(#110),#207);
#217= IFCRELAGGREGATES('1F0zP3_s91Sgv41B5mmR_6',#41,$,$,#91,(#201));
-----------------------------------------------------------------------------
#209= IFCRELDEFINESBYPROPERTIES('1qNfZoYpf52vnboENcp0uY',#41,$,$,(#110),#207);
#217= IFCRELAGGREGATES('1OeBRZBMj68B3HEWkiN2IR',#41,$,$,#91,(#201));
```

Figure 2: Varying GlobalIds of unchanged entities in two IFC exports.

To demonstrate the inadequacy of a textual comparison, a common IFC sample file is imported in Allplan 2016 and exported again (KIT, 2008). As the original file contains about 50.000 IFC entities, the exported one is made of about 150.000 entities. The multiplication of entities can be explained because of the duplication of geometrical elements, e.g. IfcCartesianPoint instances. A textual comparison of the two files does not detect any identical part of the two datasets. Nevertheless, from the view of a domain expert, both sets represent the identical model.

Thus, the matching of IFC files on a textual basis is not feasible. Furthermore, identifying entities by their GlobalIds is considered as unreliable. Other approaches for finding duplicates are necessary. To close this technology gap, a novel approach for matching IFC entities is presented next.

4. An Entity-Centric Matching Approach

All versions of the IFC schema are defined by use of the EXPRESS modelling language. The most central modelling elements of the language are the *Entity* and the *Type*. The first can be seen as a full-fledged object description, the latter depicts more simple types. Furthermore, there are elements for representing containers such as list and sets, enumerations and selection types. A detailed discussion of EXPRESS-based modelling is available in Schenck and Wilson (1994).

Although the IFC contains about 650 different entity declarations, only subclasses of IfcRoot have an unambitious identity. Other entities must be referenced by rooted instances and cannot be stored independently. This modelling approach leads to an elementary consequence for the matching of IFC datasets. Searching duplicates of non-rooted objects is not feasible as these instances attain their semantics solely by references from rooted objects. Therefore, the matching between entities must start at rooted objects, which are traversed for all referenced entities.

IfcRoot splits up in three subclasses. These are IfcObjectDefinition, IfcRelationship and IfcPropertyDefinition. The first one represents semantically described objects or processes on instance and type level. IfcRelationship is used to express entity-to-entity connections by explicitly instantiated objectified relationships. For example, this can indicate the spatial assignment of a wall to a storey or that a floor is covered by a specific coating. The

IfcPropertyDefinition stands in for pre- and user-defined semantically related sets of properties. Again, the concept of objectified relationships is used to establish the connection between an entity and a property set. A set can dynamically be attached to an entity by an IfcRelDefinesByProperties instance, subclass of IfcRelationship. Finally, a common type of some building element can be represented in the IFC schema by an IfcTypeObject object. The type comprises property sets and geometric representations which are reused by the linked entities. To establish the connection between elements and their IfcTypeObject, the IfcRelDefinesByType relationship is used.

For the user, the concepts of types, property sets and objectified relationships are quite abstract. The most tangible objects are IfcObjects, subclass of IfcObjectDefinition which stand in e.g. for building elements, processes and actors. For a domain expert, these objects and their mutual relations represent the primary informative content of the model.

Thus, from a user's point of view, a differencing algorithm for IFC data should be based on comparing IfcObjects. Other entities e.g. instances of IfcPropertyDefinition, IfcRelationship and IfcTypeObject are examined indirectly by their interactions with IfcObjects. This is demonstrated in Figure 3. Property sets which are connected to an entity or its type object are considered as original entity attributes (a, b). Objectified relationships, subclasses of IfcRelationship are processed as attributes which holds between a pair of IfcObjects (c).

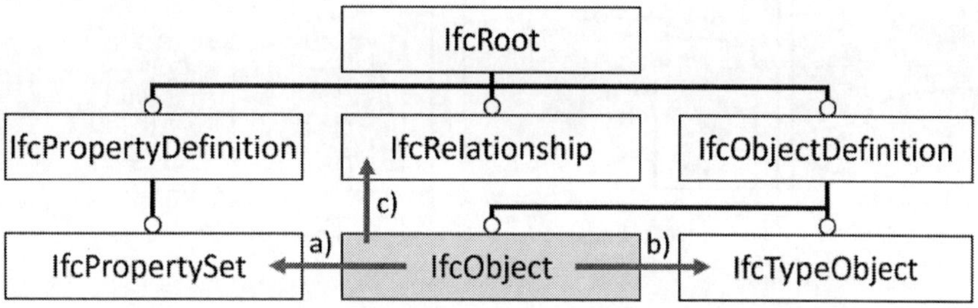

Figure 3: IfcObject instances interact with property sets, type objects and inter-entity relations which makes the class the appropriate starting point in the developed matching algorithm.

In the following the developed matching approach is presented. It comprises two steps. In the first one, the comparison of geometric representations is used to identify duplicates. In the next step, a semantical matching can find attributive modifications of already matched geometrical entities. The semantical matching is also necessary to recognise doublets of non-geometrical entities such as tasks or processes.

4.1 Geometrical Matching

In a BIM dataset, the semantics of an entity are strongly influenced by the entity's geometric representation and the resulting interactions with other spatial objects. Therefore, processing geometric shapes is an essential part in the proposed IFC differencing and merging.

The geometry of IFC entities can be expressed through several modelling approaches. There are data structures for procedural geometry such as lofts and sweeps. In addition, constructive solid geometry (CSG) can be facilitated. Finally, for static and unmodifiable spatial entities, an explicit boundary representation (B-Rep) can be used. A B-Rep structure can also be produced from procedural geometry and CSG. Thus, a matching for all variants of geometric modelling in the IFC can be based on processing the B-Reps of entities.

However, the creation of B-Rep structures from procedural geometry and CSG is ambiguous in concern of their tessellations. This means that various triangle meshes can be produced from one procedural geometry or CSG. Thus, a geometry-based identification must be independent from the actual triangulation which can differ in each BIM tool. Only the permanent information about the entity's boundary should be considered.

Therefore, approaches for 3D database lookup are adjusted for a spatial BIM matching. In contrast to geometric database lookups, the comparison of shapes should not be invariant to linear transformations such as transition, rotation and scaling. These operations change the semantics of entities in a building model. Instead, the shape matching is performed on globally oriented representations.

In the suggested processing, sample points are distributed on the surface of an entity. For each sample point, the minimal distance to another meshes is computed (Figure 4). To speed up this computation, an upper bound of distance d_{max} is introduced and the triangles of entities are indexed in R*-Trees (Beckmann et al., 1990). By extending the bounding box of an entity with d_{max}, corresponding candidate meshes can be found (a). In the next step, an extended triangle box is used in the candidate's tree to identify triangle candidates (b). These triangles are then examined for distances to the sample points on the original triangle (c). Finally, the minimal distance found for each sample point is stored.

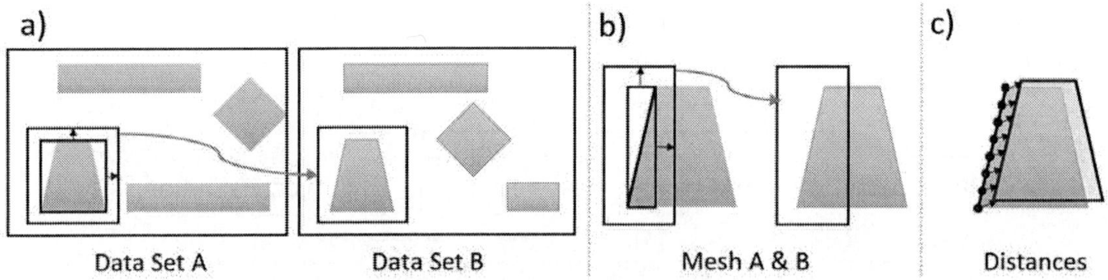

Figure 4: Matching geometric representations by using sample points and computations of minimal point/triangle distance (2D view for simplicity).

If all sample points are verified for lying on triangles of the second mesh, a geometric duplicate is identified. In contrast to clash detection, the presented method matches all surface areas of two entities. In addition, the method can identify the most similar shape in a group of candidates. The number of used sample points can be adjusted which enables for a trade-off between the robustness of the algorithm against its runtime.

The presented matching on geometry level is performed for all IfcObject instances which offer a geometric representation. During a pre-processing step, the necessary B-Rep structures are computed. After the geometric matching has been executed, the semantic matching is invoked. Accordingly, in the semantic matching, links to geometric representations are not considered.

4.2 Semantic Matching

In computer science, two equality comparisons are common. The first one is called *value equality*, also known as *equivalence*. This means that the actual values of two variables are equal. The second equality determines if two variables point to the same address in memory. This type of equality check is called *reference equality*, or *identity* (Albahari and Albahari, 2012).

In IFC modelling, the worldwide unique GlobalId value forms the identity of an entity and thus can be used for checking a specific kind of reference equality between two instances. If this kind of equality would be robust, it would be an appropriate basis for matching and differencing between IFC datasets. Actually, it had the potential for extracting a change history for entities. But, as explained in Section 3, GlobalIds are often handled inconsistently during import/export steps. A hypothesis of this contribution is that differencing and matching on reference level is not necessary for an IFC merge. Instead, an approach based on the former described spatial comparison in combination with equivalence checks is proposed.

In the following subsection, the algorithmic approach for semantic matching is depicted. The algorithm for finding duplicates on the semantical level iterates through all IfcObjects of the two IFC datasets under examination. For each IfcObject pair the ValueEquality function is called. In this process, attributes with simple types and references to other entities are recursively compared. The two overloaded ValueEquality functions are stated in Figure 5.

```
Algorithm bool ValueEquality (Entity entityA, Entity entityB)
    if TypeOf(entityA) != TypeOf(entityB)
        return false
    foreach attributeA of entityA.AttributesWithoutGlobalId
        attributeB = entityB.FindAttribute (attributeA)
        if ! ValueEquality(attributeA, attributeB)
            return false
    foreach referenceA of entityA.References
        referenceB = entityB.FindReference (referenceA)
        if ! ValueEquality(referenceA, referenceB)
            return false
Algorithm bool ValueEquality (Attribute attributeA, Attribute attributeB)
    if TypeOf(attributeA) != TypeOf(attributeB)
        return false
    return attributeA == attributeB
```

Figure 5: The two overloads of the ValueEqual function.

For example, an IfcBuilding is a subclass of IfcObject and accordingly an evaluated entity. Figure 6 shows two IfcBuilding instances. The recursive ValueEquality function traverses both object structures and yields a difference in the *Description* attribute of the IfcOrganization entity.

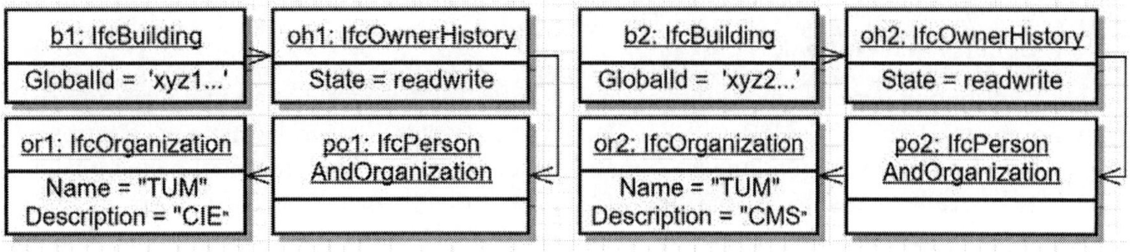

Figure 6: Two IfcBuilding instances which are not value equal because of a difference in the referenced IfcOrganization entity.

5. Prototypical Implementation and Case Study

The presented approach of an IFC merging is evaluated in a C# implementation. As a case study, two data sets of an office building are compared (Figure 7). The original data is taken from KIT (2008). The first set comprises 458 spatial building elements and 17732 IFC entities in total (a). In the second set, 283 instances of IfcDoor and IfcWindow are added which extends the number of IFC entities to 22982 (b). In the initial geometrical matching, all duplicates of the doubled building elements are identified. Figure 7c shows the resulting diff between data set a) and b).

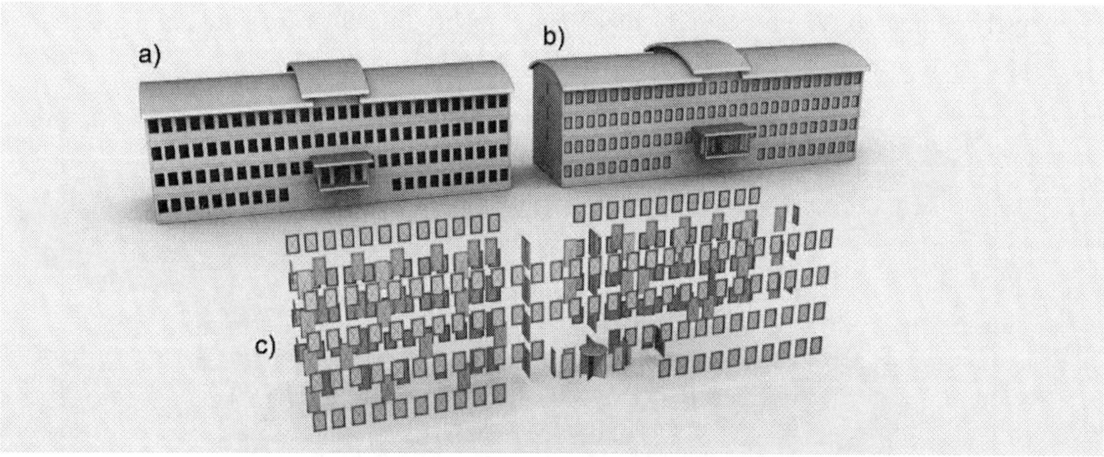

Figure 7: Two IFC data sets and their computed geometrical differences.

The following semantic processing matches entities without geometry representations. In the sample data, these are instances of spatial structures such as IfcSite and IfcBuildingStorey. In addition, correlating type objects such as IfcWallType and IfcRailingType instances are recognised.

The prototype showed that the computational accuracy of the geometrical matching is high. The divergences between actual matching entities were in the range of 1E-4 and 1E-6 millimetres. The computation of the example takes about 25 seconds in the single threaded prototype on a standard workstation.

6. Summary and Outlook

This contribution demonstrates a novel approach for file based collaborative work in a BIM environment. Here, submodels with overlapping entity sets have to be merged to an overall model. Instead of relying on the matching of object identifiers, the presented method is based on a two-level processing. In the first step, geometrically matching entities are identified. Then, a sematic matching is used to link entities which are equivalent. Instead of a time consuming and error-prone manual investigation of model differences, the method helps to produce high quality overall models more efficiently.

There are various research questions emerging. The most centric one is dealing with a matching algorithm based on a similarity metric. This is necessary when entities without geometrical representation have changed slightly. Here, the presented approach will not find duplicates. With a metric, the semantically most similar entity can be identified. Finally, more research is necessary to extend the method and handle more complex scenarios such as a three way diff with simultaneous modifications, additions and deletions in the entity sets.

References

Alanen, M. and Porres, I. (2003) *Difference and union of models.*

Albahari, J. and Albahari, B. (2012) *C# 5.0 in a Nutshell: The Definitive Reference*, O'Reilly Media, Inc.

Autodesk (2016) *IFC for Revit: .NET code for the Revit 2012-2016 IFC open source* [Online]. Available at https://sourceforge.net/projects/ifcexporter/.

Beckmann, N., Kriegel, H.-P., Schneider, R. and Seeger, B. (1990) *The R*-tree: an efficient and robust access method for points and rectangles*, ACM.

Beetz, J., van Berlo, L., Laat, R. de and van den Helm, Pim (2010) 'Bimserver. org-an Open Source IFC model server', *Proceedings of the CIP W78 conference.*

Doboš, J. and Steed, A. (2012) '3D Diff: an interactive approach to mesh differencing and conflict resolution', *SIGGRAPH Asia 2012 Technical Briefs*, p. 20.

Hunt, J. W. and MacIlroy, M. D. (1976) *An algorithm for differential file comparison.*

Khanna, S., Kunal, K. and Pierce, B. C. (2007) 'A formal investigation of diff3', in *FSTTCS 2007: Foundations of Software Technology and Theoretical Computer Science,* Springer, pp. 485–496.

KIT (2008) *Office Building: Office Building ArchiCAD 11 IFC 2x3* [Online]. Available at http://iai-typo3.iai.fzk.de/www-extern/index.php?id=1184&L=1.

Koch, C. and Firmenich, B. (2006) 'A novel diff and merge approach on the basis of operative models', *Proc. of the 11th Int. Conf. on Civil and Building Engineering (ICCCBE-XI).*

Koch, C. and Firmenich, B. (2011) 'An approach to distributed building modeling on the basis of versions and changes', *Advanced Engineering Informatics*, vol. 25, no. 2, pp. 297–310.

La Fontaine, R. (2002) 'Merging XML files: a new approach providing intelligent merge of XML data sets', *In Proceedings of XML Europe 2002.*

Liebich, T. (2013) *IFC4 specification* [Online], no. 4. Available at http://www.buildingsmart-tech.org/ifc/IFC2x4/rc4/html/index.htm.

Lindholm, T. (2004) 'A three-way merge for XML documents', *the 2004 ACM symposium.* Milwaukee, Wisconsin, USA, p. 1.

Möller, T. (1997) 'A fast triangle-triangle intersection test', *Journal of graphics tools*, vol. 2, no. 2, pp. 25–30.

Rea, H. J., Sung, R., Corney, J. R., Clark, D. E. R. and Taylor, N. K. (2005) 'Interpreting Three-Dimensional Shape Distributions', *Proceedings of the Institution of Mechanical Engineers, Part C: Journal of Mechanical Engineering Science*, vol. 219, no. 6, pp. 553–566.

Schenck, D. and Wilson, P. R. (1994) *Information modeling: the EXPRESS way*, Oxford University Press New York.

Smith, R. (1988) *GNU diff3: Version 2.8. 1* [Online], distributed with GNU diffutils package.

Tangelder, J. W. H. and Veltkamp, R. C. (2008) 'A survey of content based 3D shape retrieval methods', *Multimedia Tools and Applications*, vol. 39, no. 3, pp. 441–471.

Tommelein, I. D. and Gholami, S. (2012) 'Root causes of clashes in building information models', *Proceedings of IGLC20: 20th Annual Conference of the International Group on Lean Construction.*

Weise, M., Katranuschkov, P. and Scherer, R. J. (2004) 'Managing long transactions in model server based collaboration', *eWork and eBusiness in Architecture, Engineering and Construction: Proceedings of the 5th European Conference on Product and Process Modelling in the Building and Construction Industry-ECPPM 2004, 8-10 September 2004, Istanbul, Turkey*, p. 311.

Zündorf, A., Wadsack, J. P. and Rockel, I. (2001) 'Merging graph-like object structures', *Proceedings of the Tenth International Workshop on Software Configuration Management, May*, pp. 12–19.

A CA-based Crowd Model for the Generation of Alternative Evacuation Routes in case of Hazardous Circumstances

Isaac Koumis[1], Ioakeim G. Georgoudas[1], Jarosław Wąs[2], Georgios Ch. Sirakoulis[1]
[1] Laboratory of Electronics, Department of Electrical and Computer Engineering
Democritus University of Thrace GR-671 00 Xanthi, Greece
[2] Department of Applied Computer Science
AGH University of Science and Technology
gsirak@ee.duth.gr (corresponding author)

Abstract. Crowd modelling and simulation has been thoroughly investigated in the recent years. The development of advanced modelling methods along with the impressive upgrade of computational resources boosted particular crowd modelling. This paper approaches modelling of crowd movement with the use of Cellular Automata (CA) aiming at the appropriate management of evacuation processes. Thus, simulation results are further elaborated in order proper metrics to be calculated and obscure spatial points during evacuation to be disclosed. More specifically, static and dynamic potential fields of simulation scenarios are depicted, the relationship of flow with respect to density is graphically described and evacuation times are calculated. Thus, spots within the area of evacuation are indicated that disturb the process either by triggering congestion nor generating queues. Finally, the case of evacuating Building B, of the Department of Electrical Engineering of the Democritus University of Thrace is investigated.

Keywords: Crowd Evacuation, Cellular Automata, Flow, Density

1. Introduction

Modelling of crowd movement constitutes an issue of thorough scientific research for activities both indoors and outdoors as well as for transport networks. The development and continuous optimisation of relative mathematical patterns along with the enhancement of available computational resources boosted the corresponding research and simulation potentialities. Thus, significant and applicable knowledge has been consolidated especially regarding design and assessment of public venues.

Models that approach mass egress effectively have been presented in literature, proposing theoretical and applicable solutions in the area of crowd evacuation. Results prove that people under panic tend to lose their individuality, display herding behaviour and it is possible to misuse means of emergent evacuation (Hirai and Tarui (1977)). Moreover, abrupt behaviours of the crowd could cause more injuries or losses compared to the actual cause of the disaster (Chertkoff and Kushigian (1999)). Such behaviours, also called "non-adaptive" (Law et al. (2005)), refer to the destructive actions that a crowd may experience during a disaster, such as stampede, pushing others out of the way, knocking others down or trampling on others.

Adopting an approach that treats crowd as consisting of discrete individuals requires a large number of computations. Modern computer power and the adoption of Cellular Automata (CA) as the dominant computational tool of the simulation process meet this operational requirement. CA are featured by massive parallelism and they are very effective in simulating physical systems, because they can capture the essential features of systems where global behaviour arises from the collective effect of simple components which interact locally (Feynman (1982)). On the other hand, evacuation process is a multi-parameterised process, thus inherently complex and its response cannot be easily estimated. Thus, evacuation could be defined as a non linear problem with many factors affecting it. A system of Partial Differential Equations (PDEs) could effectively approach it. But this would lead to a system of PDEs very difficult to handle, which would also be demanding in terms of computer power and computation time. CA can act as an alternative to PDEs (Karafyllidis and Thanailakis (1997), Toffoli (1984)). These equations contain much more information than it is usually needed, because variables may take an infinite number of values in a continuous space and PDEs are used to compute values of physical quantities at points in continuous time. But the values of physical quantities are usually measured over finite volumes at discrete time steps. CA are used to compute values of physical quantities over finite areas (CA cells) at discrete time steps.

Literature review indicates that CA-based models have been thoroughly applied in order to investigate crowd behaviour under various circumstances and from different points of view. CA based methods model human behaviours, such as inertial effects, unadventurous effect and group effect (Aube and Shield (2004), Vihas et al. (2013)) or treat pedestrians as particles subject to long-range forces (Yuan and Tan (2007)). Others use walkers leaving a trace by modifying the underground on their paths (Burstedde et al. (2001)). Taking into account technical aspects of CA-based modeling an interesting combination of CA with navigation graph was presented in (Kneidl et. al (2013)), whilst a prototype of combination of CA with macroscopic approach was introduced in (Borrmann et. al (2013)). Furthermore, the impact of environmental conditions (Varas et al. (2007)) and proxemics (Was (2010) and Was et al. (2012)) have been studied with the use of CA as well as interactions among pedestrians and herding behaviour (Georgoudas et al. (2007), Bandini et al. (2007)).

This paper approaches pedestrian movement modelling from the viewpoint of the effective computational tool of CA, applied with the use of the Matlab software package. The theoretical background of the model is inspired by the concept of the dynamic floor field that exerts forces to the members of the crowd in order to direct them towards the exits (Burstedde et al. (2001), Kirchner and Schadschneider (2002)). The floor field is considered as a 2-dimensional array of CA cells that corresponds to the area under study and each cell is assigned a value according to its distance from the exit.

In the context of the present work, various evacuation scenarios are investigated. Based on the corresponding results, proper metrics are calculated and the evacuation processes are studied thoroughly. More particularly, evacuation curves are drawn, flow as a function of density is calculated and the corresponding evacuation durations are extracted as the response of the model. In addition, Building B of the Department of Electrical and Computing Engineering of the Democritus University of Thrace, in Xanthi, Greece, is designed and the most appropriate evacuation route is derived according to pedestrian movement principles and the operation of the venue. Applying various evacuation scenarios, useful information is collected that is further elaborated in order crowd movement attributes to be studied thoroughly. Based on the derived results, the process of evacuation is described. The main aim of this work is to focus on the significant contribution of such simulation approaches to the efficient design and operation control of public venues in cases of massive evacuation. Thus, within the venue are pointed out certain areas that evoke congestion, queue generation and accidents.

In the following, the fundamental concepts of the proposed CA-based evacuation model are explained. In Section 3, simulation scenarios and respective results are thoroughly presented and discussed, thus further clarifying the operational attributes of the model and evaluate its efficiency. Finally, in section 4, conclusions are drawn along with directions of future work.

2. The Principles of the Model

The proposed model is CA based and its theoretical background derives from a dynamic floor-field model (Helbing et. al (2000), Gwizdałła (2015)). Thus, its aim is to form a field underneath that generates forces that they themselves drive pedestrians towards the exits. Each cell of the two-dimensional CA can be occupied by one individual and it is dynamically assigned a value according to its current distance from the closest exit point. Based on literature, the size of each cell is assumed equal to 0.4cm×0.4cm (Burstedde et al. (2001)). The array F of the floor field is initialised with all of its elements equal to zero. Cells that represent exits are assigned the lowest value $F_{Fdoor} = 1$, whereas the values of obstacles and walls are not elaborated at all and they remain equal to zero, i.e. $F_{Fwall} = 0$.

The generating mechanism of the field is driven by a rule, according to which each cell is looking for its neighbouring cell with the lowest non-zero value:

$$F_{F\_\min} = \min(n, w, e, s) > 0 \tag{1}$$

$$F_{F\_\min} = \min(nw, n, ne, w, e, sw, s, se) > 0 \tag{2}$$

In case that $State\_cell_{i,j} \neq wall$ then if

$$F_{F\_\min} \neq 0 \Rightarrow F_{F\_cell\_i,j} = F_{F\_\min} + 1, \quad F_{F\_cell\_i,j} > F_{F\_\min} \quad or \quad F_{F\_cell\_i,j} = 0 \tag{3}$$

More specifically, the parallel processing of array F commences and during a time step, each cell is affected by its neighbourhood, and it evolves with time according to the transition rule. The latter evolves in a two-steps stage; during the first step, each cell is searching its neighbouring one with the lowest, non-zero value. During the second step, in case that the value of the reference cell is zero or in case that the value of the neighbouring cell at the first step is lower that the value of the reference cell, then the reference cell is assigned the value that has been detected during the first step increased by one unit. Otherwise, its value remains the same. The array is updated continuously, until all cells (apart from those that represent walls) are assigned a certain value (Gwizdałła (2015)).

The adopted neighbourhood is a combination of Moore neighbourhood and von Neumann one, thus achieving a more realistic floor-field formation (Figure 1 (a)). In case of a Moore-only neighbourhood, people tend to generate rectangular arches around the exit cell (Figure 1 (b)), whereas in case of a von Neumann-only neighbourhood the corresponding arches are triangular (Figure 1 (c)). Moreover, normalising coefficients (weights) have also been introduced in order to further smooth the generated field.

Figure 2 depicts the corresponding virtual fields that are generated in case that the renowned metrics of distance are implemented; Manhattan distance (Figure 2(a)) and Euclidean distance Figure 2(b). The corresponding equations are:

$$d_1 = \sum_{i=1}^{n} |x_i - y_i| \text{ (Manhattan)} \tag{4}$$

$$d_2 = \sqrt{\sum_{i=1}^{n} |x_i - y_i|^2} \tag{5}$$

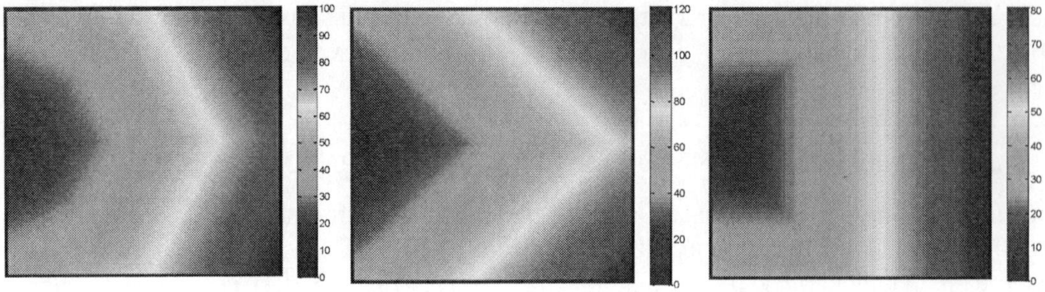

(a) (b) (c)

Figure 1: The response of the field a) as a result of the combination of the two types of neighbourhoods, in case of b) Moore-only neighbourhood and c) von Neumann-only neighbourhood. The exits are located at the middle of the left wall

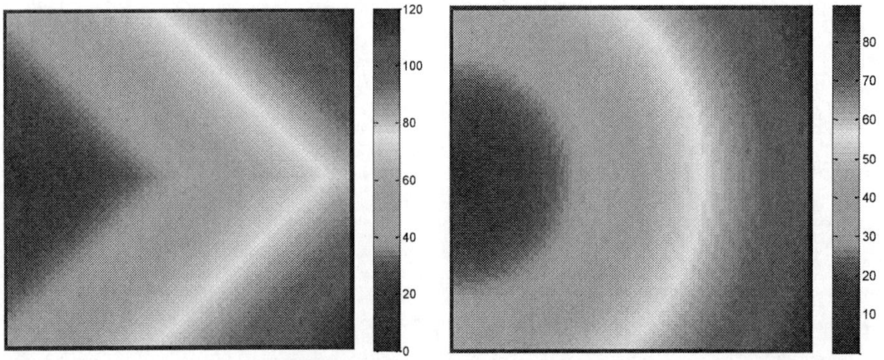

(a) (b)

Figure 2: The response of the field a) Manhattan distance b) Euclidean distance. The exits are located at the middle of the left wall

Figure 2(a) depicts that Manhattan field is similar to the one that is generated by the evolution of the floor field in case of von Neumann neighbourhood. This is explained by the fact that macroscopically the calculation mode is similar for both cases. Euclidean case ideally represents the distance of every single point from the exit. Though, it can be hardly adopted due to intrinsic issues of digital accuracy. On the other hand, the assumed scenario of Moore-von Neumann combined neighbourhood adequately converges Euclidean case, thus affirming the validity of the applied method.

Furthermore, the width of the exits influences the values of the floor field. Thus, in cases of wider exits, the feature of attenuating attraction is introduced. More specifically, the exit could be assumed as a non-uniform unit of attraction. Thus, for instance, in case that the width of the exit is three cells long, then the central cell is assigned a lower value than the two others (left and right). Taking a closer look, the cells that form the former 3-tuple could not be assigned the same value. The cell in the middle should have a lower (better) value, since it incorporates three options to reach the exit (straight, left and right). On the other hand, the two other cells provide only two options (straight and left (or right)). Moreover, suppression of any algorithmic case like the one in Figure 3(b), in which the central cell of an exit is not to be chosen for abandoning the area should be considered.

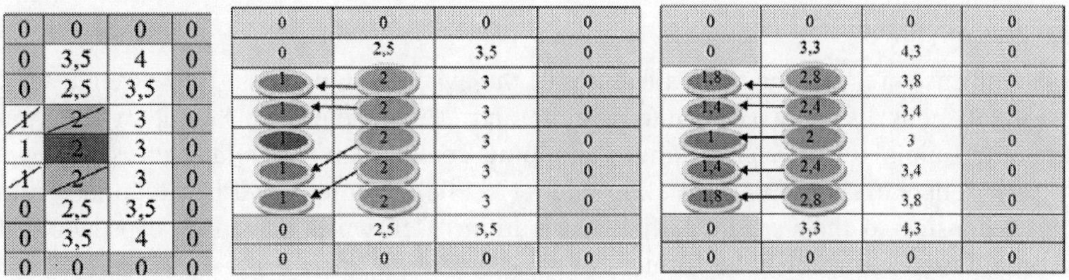

(a) (b) (c)

Figure 3: The impact of the central cell of an exit. (a) Red-coloured cell can see three cells of exit, whereas the orange ones can only see two; (b) to supress any inconvenience regarding the choice of central cell due to the initial algorithmic confrontation, (c) the model is updated by introducing attenuating attraction.

Thus, following the method introduced by Fu et al. (2013), two more variables are adopted; the distance of the CA cell of the exit from the geometrical centre of the exit and a coefficient of attenuating attraction β. The central cells is assigned value equal to one, whereas the rest of the cells are assigned values according to their distance from the central cell of the exit (Figure 3(c)). The aim the attenuating attraction is exactly to introduce a more rational simulation approach by favoring the choice of the central exit cell as experimental data indicate.

3. Simulation Process and Results

Various simulations are taking place in order the response of the proposed model to be calibrated properly and validated effectively. The calibration process refers to flow-density response of the model and respective comparison with diagrams from literature (Johansson et al. (2008), whereas the validation process could be enriched in the future with real data responses. Hence, evacuation scenarios including one, two, three or four exits are simulated, where people that move with different speeds co-exist, with the presence of obstacles or not and for different layouts. Finally, a more realistic scenario is performed that is evolving in Building B, of the Department of Electrical Engineering of the Democritus University of Thrace. In the following, the most characteristic cases are presented and discussed.

3.1 First scenario

The first case that is presented is taking place in a room with a single exit and obstacles. The dimensions of the room are 16m×16m (40×40 cells) and include 125 individuals. In the middle of the room a V-shaped type obstacle exists. The form of the obstacle introduces more difficulties in the process of overcoming it. Thus, the motivation is to prove the effectiveness of the adopted obstacles' avoidance mechanism. The width of the exit is 1.2m (3 cells). Pedestrians are divided into two groups; the first one includes common people that move with a speed of 1.5 m/sec and the second one is an elderly group that moves with half the previous speed (0.75 m/sec). The speed of common people derives from literature (Bandini et al. (2014)) and thus each time step corresponds to 4/15 sec. The position of elderly is updated once every two time steps, whereas that of common people once every time step. The complete evacuation takes place in 52 time steps (almost 14 secs) and the response is better compared to scenario that only elderly people exist within the room. Figure 5 depicts (a) the static floor field of the area, (b) a snapshot of the evacuation process and (e) the corresponding evacuation diagram with respect to time.

3.2 Second scenario

The second case presents the main attributes of the evacuation process from a venue of 20m x 20m (50x50 cells) with two separated rooms and 229 people. The layout of the venue is artificial and aims at partly emulating a shopping center with two retail stores, across from each other. There exist two exits of 1.2m width (3 cells) and the crowd is categorised into two groups according to their speed. Initial distribution of crowd is driven by a pseudo-random generation function aiming at uniformly covering the whole area.

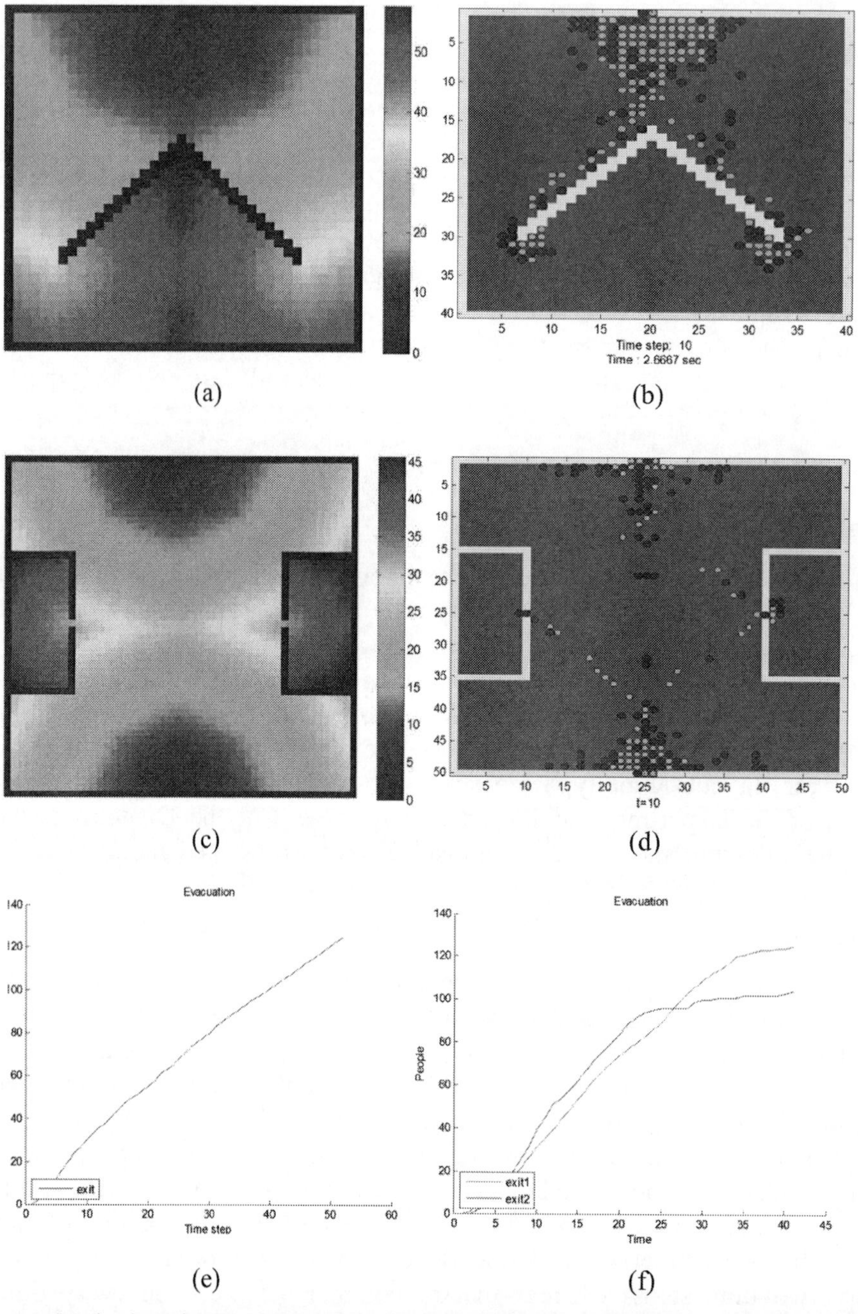

Figure 5: Case of a single exit and obstacle located in the room: (a) the static floor field of the area, (b) a snapshot of the evacuation process. Case of two separated rooms: (c) the static floor field of the area, (d) a snapshot of the evacuation process. (e) and (f) depict the corresponding evacuation diagrams of the aforementioned two cases with respect to time.

The graphical representation of the evacuation process depicts that during the evacuation 125 people left the area from exit one after 41 time steps whereas 104 people left the area from exit two after 41 time steps (Figure 5). The evacuation process is terminated after 11 secs.

3.3 Evacuation of Building B

In the following, the evacuation of Building B is described as a characteristic complicated scenario of emergent evacuation, for inhomogeneous crowd groups. Building B comprises three floors (the basement and two floors) and for the modeling of the evacuation process in Matlab, the corresponding floor plans have been adapted in the programming environment. According to the adopted scenario, the evacuation of the whole building is studied in case of emergency. The elaboration starts from the second floor, then continues with the first floor and it is terminated on the ground floor. The reason is that for the simulation of the first floor the people from the first floor are also included and accordingly for the simulation of the ground floor the people from the two upper floors are also needed to be taken into consideration. People are categorised into two groups (common and elderly) and speed characteristics follow the same attributes that have been defined above, as far as values and update process concerns.

The people that exist on the second floor at the beginning of the evacuation are supposed to be 61 and the stairs are assumed to be the unique outlet that all people will utilise to abandon the area. In order to approach a more realistic simulation of the usage of the stairs a slowdown is incorporated, as a time-penalty of 4 secs, for each individual that changes a floor through the stairs. The value of the additional time has been determined after conducting real measurements. On the first floor there are 83 people and there should be also taken into consideration the 61 people of the second floor. That is 144 people in total are evacuating floor 1; 83 that were already there and 61 that moved from the second floor using the stairs.

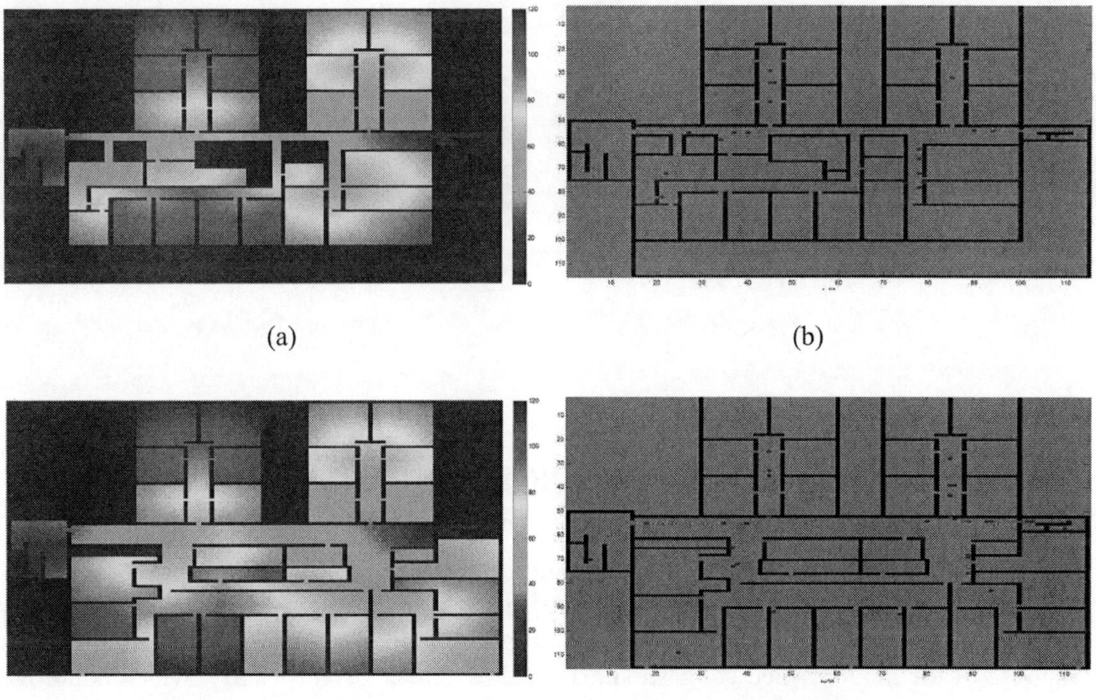

(a) (b)

(c) (d)

Figure 6: Static fields and a snapshot of the evacuation process for (a-b) floor 2, (c-d) floor 1

From the 83 people of the first floor, 23 leave the building from the emergency exits that exist within the offices of the first floor and 60 use the stairs. The duration of the evacuation of the first floor is 123 time steps and the delay compared to the evacuation of the second floor is due to the delay that people from the second floor introduce to the system. Finally, there are 130 people at the basement. The 121 individuals of the second and first floor should also be taken into consideration. It is assumed that apart from the stairs people can also use the emergency exits that exist within the three south offices. The corresponding static fields are depicted in Figure 6, along with a snapshot of the evacuation process. Totally 251 evacuate the basement (130 already there and 121 that enter the basement from stairs of the first and second floor). From the 130 that already exist, 7 use emergency exits from within the offices, 125 use the east exit and 119 the west exit. The whole evacuation duration is 145 time steps that is almost 40 secs. Figure 7 depicts the corresponding evacuation diagrams with time.

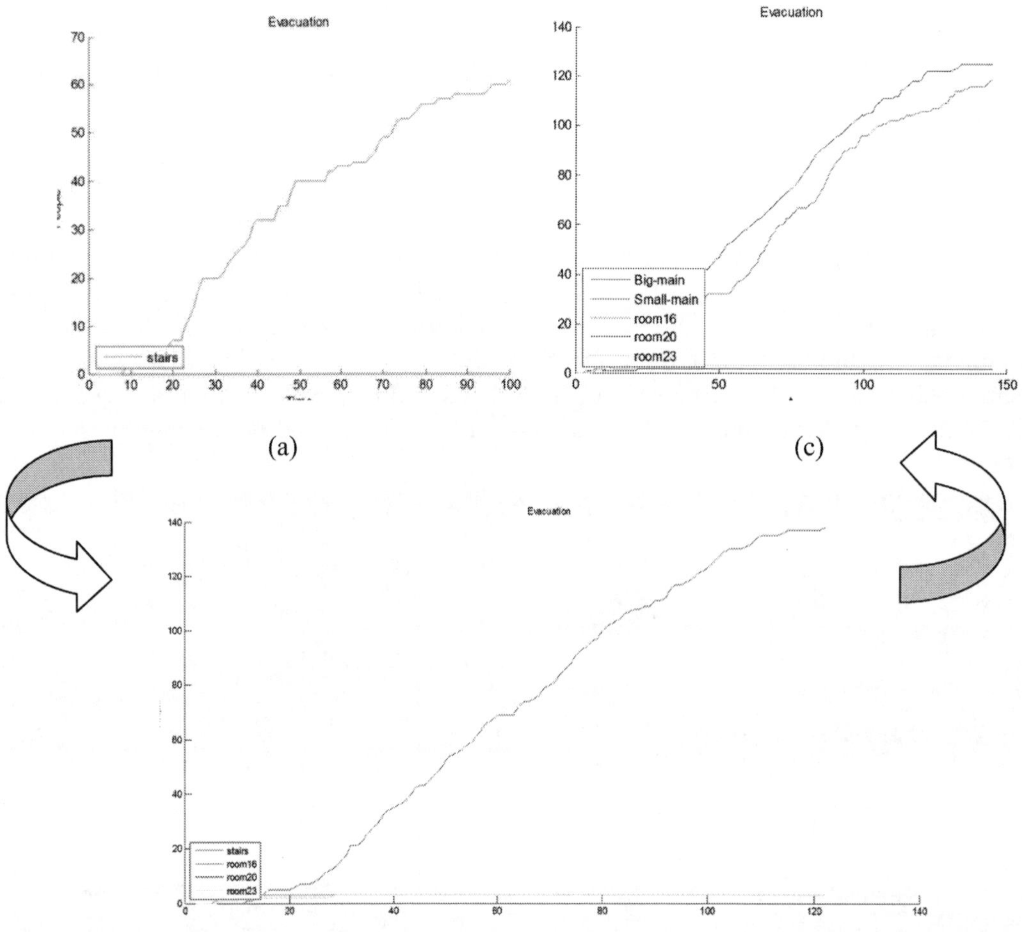

(b)

Figure 7: Evacuation with time for floor 2 (a), floor 1 (b), basement (c)

The study of the crowd dynamics is always interesting. The corresponding speed-density and flow-density diagrams are drawn. The study focuses on the area of the east exit, where congestion phenomena arise. Results reveal some remarkable phenomena that validate the response of the model; when congestion arises, flow reduces significantly, which could lead to stop-and-go waves, whereas further increase of the density could lead to dangerous phenomena. Therefore, the operational crowd density of public venues should stay lower enough from its maximum value. Practically, mean density is calculated by measuring all people within the area of interest and then dividing with the surface of that area. Speed is calculated by calculating the mean value of the speeds of all people within the area of interest and flow is defined by the product of mean density times the mean speed or by dividing the number of people that cross an imaginable line per time unit with the length of that line. It should be noted that mean local speed in exits never becomes zero. This does not mean that people never stop but rather that this stop is very short (Johansson et al. (2008)). The fundamental diagrams refer to the area of interest (east exit), where more congestion is investigated (Figure 8).

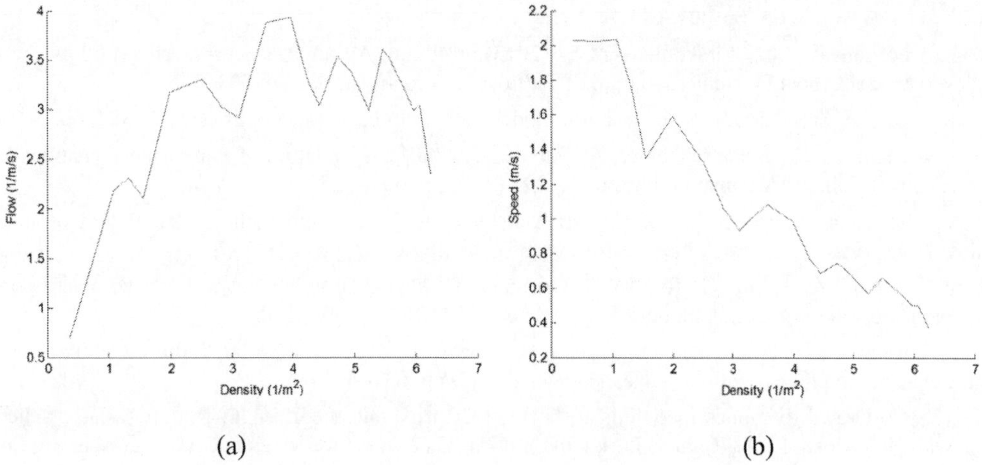

Figure 8: (a) Flow-density and (b) speed-density diagrams

4. Conclusions and Future Work

This paper models crowd movement with the use of CA aiming at the appropriate management of evacuation processes. Various simulation scenarios are taking place in order to enlighten the impact of spatial arrangements to the evolution of the evacuation. Static and dynamic potential fields of simulation scenarios are depicted, the relationship of flow with respect to density is graphically described and evacuation times are calculated. Thus, within the area of evacuation are indicated areas that disturb the process. The case of evacuating Building B, of the Department of Electrical Engineering of the Democritus University of Thrace is investigated.

Regarding further perspectives, more attributes can be assigned to the model and also the case of simultaneous fire spreading can be taken into consideration. Thus, the floor can be considered as morphologically non-uniform, introducing, for example, different levels within the area of evacuation. Furthermore, a real-data based validation process could take place in order to reinforce the evaluation method of the model and its efficiency. The efficiency of CA to represent such phenomena and the efficiency of the contemporary computational systems enables the elaboration of more complex conditions.

References

Hirai, K. and Tarui, K. (1977). A Simulation of the Behavior of a Crowd in Panic, Systems and Control, Japan.

Chertkoff, J. and Kushigian, R. (1999). Don't Panic: The Psychology of Emergency Egress and Ingress. London, UK: Praeger.

Law, K., Dauber, K., Pan, X. (2005). Computational Modeling of Nonadaptive Crowd Behaviors for Egress Analysis: 2004-2005 CIFE Seed Project Report, CIFE Technical Report #162. Stanford University, USA: October 2005.

Feynman, R. P. (1982). Simulating physics with computers, International Journal of Theoretical Physics, 21 (6/7), pp. 467–488.

Karafyllidis, I. and Thanailakis, A. (1997). A model for predicting forest fire spreading using cellular automata, Ecological Modelling, 99, pp. 87–97.

Toffoli, T. (1984). Cellular automata as an alternative to (rather than an approximation of) differential equations in modeling physics. Physica D, 10 (1-2), pp. 117–127.

Aubé, F., and Shield, R. (2004). Modeling the Effect of Leadership on Crowd Flow Dynamics, Lecture Notes in Computer Science, vol. 3305, pp. 601–611.

Vihas, C., Georgoudas, I.G., Sirakoulis, G.Ch. (2013). Cellular Automata Incorporating Follow-the-Leader Principles to Model Crowd Dynamics, Journal of Cellular Automata, 8(5-6), pp. 333–346.

Yuan, W.F. and Tan, K.H. (2007). An evacuation model using cellular automata, Physica A, 384, pp. 549–566.

Burstedde, C., Klauck, K., Schadschneider, A., Zittartz, J. (2001). Simulation of Pedestrian Dynamics Using a Two-dimensional Cellular Automaton, Physica A, 295 (3-4), pp. 507–525.

Kneidl A., Hartmann D., Borrmann A. (2013). A hybrid multi-scale approach for simulation of pedestrian dynamics. Transportation Research Part C: Emerging Technologies 37, pp. 223–237.

Borrmann A., Kneidl A., Köster G., Ruzika S., Thiemann M. (2012) Bidirectional coupling of macroscopic and microscopic pedestrian evacuation models, Safety Science 50 (8), pp. 1695–1703.

Varas, A., Cornejo, M.D., Mainemer, D., Toledo, B., Rogan, J., Munoz, V., et al. (2007). Cellular automaton model for evacuation process with obstacles, Physica A 382, pp. 631–42.

Was, J., (2010). Crowd dynamics modeling in the light of proxemic theories. In: Rutkowski, L., Scherer, R., Tadeusiewicz, R., Zadeh, L. A., Zurada, J. M. (Eds.), ICAISC (2), Lecture Notes in Computer Science, Springer, 6114, 683–688.

Was, J., Lubas, R., and Mysliwiec, W. (2012). Proxemics in discrete simulation of evacuation. In Georgios Ch. Sirakoulis and Stefania Bandini, (Eds.), ACRI, Lecture Notes in Computer Science, Springer, 7495, pp. 768–775.

Georgoudas, I.G., Sirakoulis, G.Ch., and Andreadis, I.Th. (2007). An Intelligent Cellular Automaton Model for Crowd Evacuation in Fire Spreading Conditions. In Proc. 19th IEEE International Conference on Tools with Artificial Intelligence (ICTAI 2007), vol. 1, pp. 36–43.

Bandini, S., Manzoni, S., Mauri, G., and Redaelli, S. (2007). Emergent pattern interpretation in vegetable population dynamics, Journal of Cellular Automata, 2 (2). pp. 103–110.

Kirchner, A., Schadschneider, A. (2002) Simulation of evacuation processes using a bionics-inspired cellular automaton model for pedestrian dynamics, Physica A, 312, pp. 260–76.

Helbing, D., Farkas, I., Vicsek, T. (2000). Simulating Dynamical Features of Escape Panic, Nature 407 (6803), pp. 487-490.

Gwizdałla T. (2015). Some properties of the floor field cellular automata evacuation model, Physica A 419, pp. 718-728.

Fu, Z., Yang, L., Chen, Y., Zhu, K., Zhu S. (2013). The effect of individual tendency on crowd evacuation efficiency under inhomogeneous exit attraction using a static field modified FFCA model, Physica A 392 (23), pp. 6090–6099.

Bandini, S., Crociani, L., Vizzari G. (2014) Heterogeneous Speed Profiles in Discrete Models for Pedestrian Simulation. 93rd Transportation Research Board annual meeting, Washington, January 2014 - Committee number AHB45 - TRB Committee on Traffic Flow Theory and Characteristics.

Johansson, A., Helbing, D., A-Abideen, H. Z., Al-Bosta, S. (2008). From crowd dynamics to crowd safety: A video-based analysis, Advances in Complex Systems 11 (4), pp. 497–527.

A geometrical Description of a Motion Sensor in a Building Model for Identifying Construction Site Activities

Michael Kluge, Wolfgang Huhnt
Computing in Civil Engineering – Technische Universität Berlin, Germany
m.kluge@tu-berlin.de

Abstract: An automated non-intrusive monitoring is a quality assurance approach accepted in many other industry disciplines, e.g. transportation, automotive or aircraft industry. At present time, equivalent approaches are not state of the art in the construction industries. Research takes place in this field. Results are partly used; but further research is still required. The use of a specific motion sensor for identifying construction site activities is addressed in this paper. A geometrical description of the sensor devices is a mandatory initial step towards an integration of these sensing devices into a building information model as a second step. The geometry in the building information model serves as a basis for a detailed project schedule for the execution phase of a project. An integration of a motion sensor into the building geometry delivers information about visibility of building elements represented by their surfaces. The sensor detects motions; these motions are assigned to construction site activities which are planned to take place at the surfaces of building components. As a consequence, an automated detection of construction site activities is supported. The paper presents the geometrical description which is the basis for upcoming steps in our research. It ends with an outlook describing our planned next steps.

1. Introduction

The construction industry lacks an automated way of aggregating performance data from construction sites. Multi-purpose sensors are common in daily life, i.e. built-in sensors in smartphones. They are used for several purposes, e.g. for a public transportation arrival time estimation and comparison against schedules (Gerlich et al. 2011). Other approaches use gps and gyro sensor data from a mobile sensor network as input data to detect anomalies and monitor road surface conditions (Mohan et al. 2008 & Eriksson et al. 2008). The devices used were motion sensors in usual smartphones carried by taxi drivers.

The lack of acceptance among work crews, foremen and other involved personnel is a challenge for any monitoring on-site. Tracking with wearable sensors often represents an intrusion for the workers. Many advances in wearing a sensor device are proved by other researchers in areas such as user localization in indoor construction environments (Khoury and Kamat 2008), construction ironworker's education and training in safety and productivity (Teizer et al. 2013) and automated trajectory and path planning analysis on-site (Cheng et al. 2011 & Cheng and Teizer 2013). Even installing additional sensors in construction equipment (Akhavian and Behzadan 2015) is a possible way to get valuable knowledge about the processes on a construction site.

Vision-based approaches use multiple cameras for a video interpretation for productivity analysis of construction sites (Gong & Caldas 2011). Another vision-based research focus is to exactly detect construction workers in video frames (Park and Brilakis 2012). (Kim & Caldas 2013) extended this approach and combined activity and object recognition of construction workers during the execution of specific activities. It's possible to extend vision-based approaches by integrating point clouds from laser scans (Brilakis et al. 2010). In (Braun et al. 2015) progress data is obtained by analyzing differences between photogrammetric point clouds.

(Kluge 2012) presented an approach to store data continuously in a monitoring device named "Construction Site Black Box" as a metaphor for a storage of various time synced data from a construction site. The overall aim of all these detection, tracking and in the end monitoring systems is obtaining a detailed body of knowledge about processes on a construction site, based on monitored data instead of assumptions. The advantages of that research towards a monitor-able construction using with mobile sensors in general were introduced (Kluge and Huhnt 2013).

Due to the described restrictions a non-intrusive monitoring seems from the author's perspective the most promising way to detect actual anomalies or prove from another perspective the correctness of a planned schedule execution. A motion sensor and a light barrier were selected as example mobile monitoring devices. This paper is focused on a motion sensor.

Section 2 of this paper presents an introduction to the sensor, a geometrical description of the motion sensor device, and the integration into the geometry of a building model. The following section 3 describes the algorithm to determine the visibility of surfaces inside a building information model. Results from a follow up test setup with sensors influenced this algorithm in terms of the minimal monitor able size of objects. These results are presented in section 4. Section 4 also includes results of the geometrical algorithms. The construction site deployment of the sensor should verify the potential to monitor scheduled activities and compute mean values for the duration of specific activities. These issues are addressed in section 5 of this paper. The paper ends with conclusions and an outlook.

2. Motion sensor and it's geometrical description

2.1 Motion Sensor

The chosen non-intrusive motion sensor PIR-STD-LP (Figure 1) is a system available in the consumer market to deliver reliable results for security or facility management purposes. It is very small with a footprint of 24 mm x 24 mm. The area of visibility of such a sensor is influenced by the lens and the used circuit. The circuit is placed directly underneath the lens. The Fresnel lens in our example ensures a regular signal distribution in the field of view of 120° up to a range of 12 m from the sensor itself.

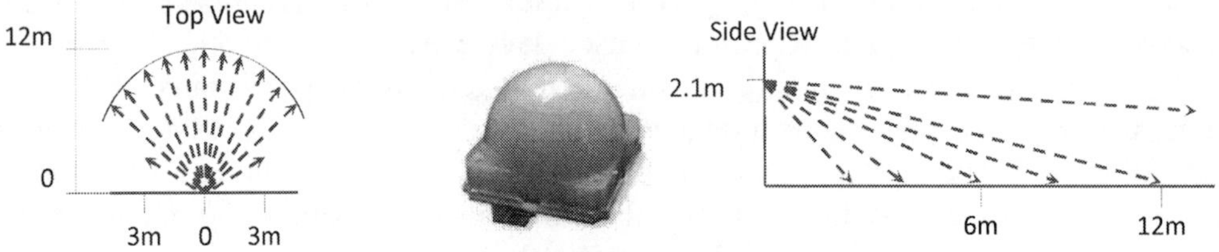

Figure 1: Motion sensor (B+B 2015) and corresponding field of view

An attached wireless sensor node connected to the internet ensures the delivery of data to a cloud based data storage.

2.2 Geometrical description

The visible volume of a motion sensor is in the focus of our research. It is defined by the manufacturer's specifications from the sensor itself towards the maximum visible range of 12 m around a centered axis with 60° angle to both sides.

The visible volume is represented by a cone. The sensor itself is the apex of the cone; and the visible volume ends at a specific maximum distance from the apex of the cone.

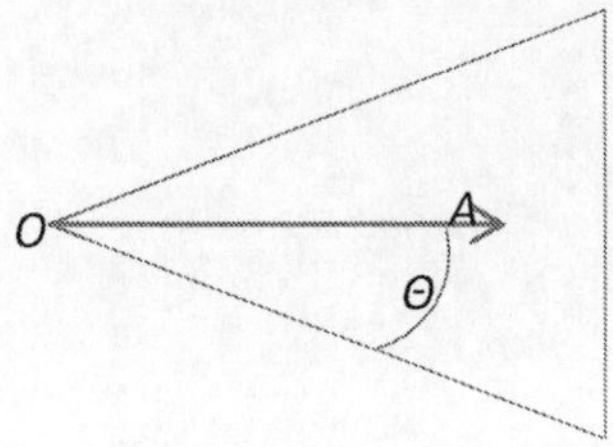

Figure 2 The acute cone

The cone is defined by a vertex O, an axis direction vector A and an angle θ between the axis and the outmost edge. The definition of $\theta \in \left(0, \frac{\pi}{2}\right)$ is necessary for an acute cone to satisfy $\cos\theta > 0$. The location of the motion sensor e.g. at a wall or a ceiling corresponds for the cone in vertex O. The direction vector A represents the outwards oriented centered axis of the motion sensor. The outer edges of the cone represent the border of the field of view around the centered axis.

2.3 Motion sensor in a building

The motion sensor represented by the cone should monitor activities which are executed at building elements. These building elements must be accessible inside a building model with a corresponding geometry. The geometry of building components is defined by its boundary (boundary representation model). The boundary of a building element can be triangulated. This is a typical result for tools which are used in the field of Building Information Modeling such as Autodesk Revit®.

For our research we assume:

- all scheduled activities are represented by tuples of activities and corresponding surfaces of building elements where the activity shall be executed
- all surfaces have an internal attribute describing their corresponding building element
- a single activity occurs on a part of the visible surface of a building element (the sensor cannot detect activities hidden behind another surface)
- an activity occurs inside a monitor able volume between the origin of the cone and a monitor able surface of a building element
- the appropriate space necessary for a workman to work on a surface of a building element isn't checked

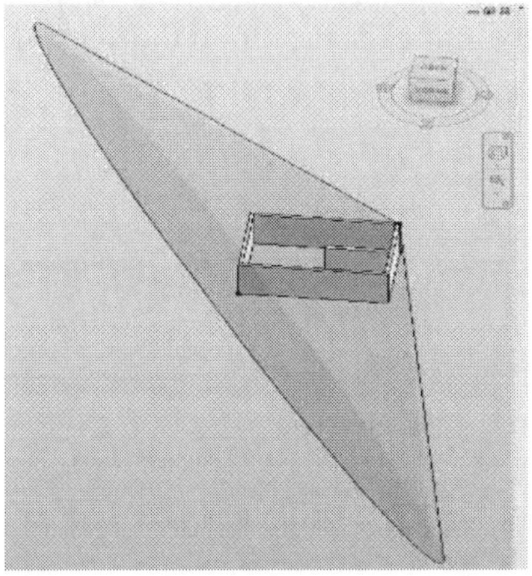

Figure 3 Cone representing the visible volume of a sensor shown in an Autodesk™ Revit model

3 Geometric tests for activity visibility

3.1 Building elements in the building information model

In several aspects, there are analogies of our problem with problems in computer graphics, especially in game design (Eberly 2005). In this field, they introduced a very fast intersection test between a cone and a triangle for graphic applications, e.g. frustum culling of triangles from a view. They assumed that it is sufficient to exclude a triangle from further computational steps if an intersection with a cone is impossible. Their approach is especially useful if many of the triangles T of a model, which should be tested, are located partly or complete inside the cones volume. Each triangle T_i is defined by its vertices $V_{i,0}, V_{i,1}, V_{i,2}$ and references a corresponding building element BE_X.

$$T = \{T_1, T_2, \dots, T_N\}$$ *triangles in the model*

$$T_i : \{V_{i,0}, V_{i,1}, V_{i,2}, BE_X\}$$ *triangle with vertices and building element*

3.2 Filtering of backward surface triangles

In a first step it is computed whether the surfaces of these triangles are part of a backward surface of a building element. Following this precondition, we want to eliminate these surfaces from the result set of triangles. The orientation of these triangles is therefore computed. If that test is positive, these front surface triangles are stored in a set of triangles T_{vis} visible from the origin O of the cone.

$$T_{vis} = \{ T \mid \text{face normal of } T \text{ is pointing towards cone origin } O \}$$

3.3 Filtering of triangles intersecting the cone

The implementation of the intersection test is following the avoidance strategy of costly computations. It uses as much as possible quick exits if a test is successful. It was presented by (Schneider and Eberly 2004).

Stepwise intersection tests were implemented in the following order:

- intersection between each vertex of the triangle and the cone
- intersection between the edges of the triangle and the cone
- intersection between the cone axis A and the plane of the triangle itself

The intersection points, intersecting line segments or intersecting curves with the cone are not computed; only the answer is given whether an intersection exists. The result is a set of triangles T_{int} creating intersections with the cone.

$$T_{int} = \{ T_{vis} | \text{ is visible and intersecting the volume of the cone } \}$$

We are aware that a blocking situation is still possible. A backwards oriented surface might block a clear line of sight to other visible building element surfaces. We assume that this condition during a monitoring process will not occur. It would imply an installation inside a building element (e.g. a wall, a ceiling).

3.4 Filtering and sorting monitorable triangles

As a last step, we apply an intersection test between a ray R and these finally intersecting triangles T_{int}. During that test we send rays from the cone origin O towards the far clipping plane of the cone at 12 m distance from O and compute the exact location L in space at which an intersection occurs. The shortest intersection distance between $L_{i,j}$ and O is stored per ray. In addition, we store per ray $R_{i,j}$ the id for the building element which is visible.

$$\mathcal{R}_{i,j} = O + t\, \hat{a}_{i,j} \quad | \text{ i = ring index, j = segmentation index}$$

This algorithm is equivalent to usual z-buffering as described e.g. in (Pahl et al. 2006). The amount of rays send out from the cone origin O for this test is significant for that test. The required segmentation (defining i and j) of the clipping plane was investigated. The results are presented in section 4.1.

That ray triangle intersection test is applied to all visible triangles T_{int} and results in a set of monitorable triangles T_{mon}.

$$T_{mon} = \{ T_{vis} | \text{ is visible and monitorable inside the volume of the cone } \}$$

Each of these triangles is a part of the surface of a building element and references this building element. As a consequence, T_{mon} covers surfaces of all building elements which are visible from the sensor.

3.5 Scheduled activities on monitorable building elements

Each activity can take place at a subset of a surface of a building element. If activities are assigned to rooms, the geometry of the surfaces of the enclosing building elements must be computed. In our research, we assume that each activity is assigned to surfaces of building elements where it shall take place. In the case that the entire building element is affected by an activity, the complete surface of the building element has to be referenced.

A motion detected by a sensor must be assigned in a first step to all scheduled activities at the visible surfaces of building elements of that sensor. A motion takes place during a specific time frame. The schedule provides the planned activities for that time frame.

An intersection of both sets gives all activities that are planned to take place in the visible volume of the sensor. In the case that the intersection covers more than one building element, further information is necessary. The integration of further information is beyond the scope of this paper. It will be addressed in future publications.

3.6 Accuracy

We accept in that geometrical context a minor inconsistency. In reality the sensor device has a volume of a housing which has a size of 8 cm * 8 cm * 7 cm. Assuming a proper placement in a corner of a room creates a minor acceptable error compared to the calculated position of the cones origin O.

4 Verification of the accuracy of the sensor devices

4.1 Verification of the hardware devices

As already mentioned, the segmentation of the far clipping plane was initially set to a starting value. Because of the major impact of that value for computation, a specific research (Bachelor thesis of Tal Zaif, 2015) was started to determine exactly if that value is acceptable for the outer edges of the cone. That research was started using 2 motion sensors and a light barrier. A test environment together with test scenarios for angle, orientation and distance inside a monitorable volume were prepared.

As a result of that bachelor thesis a verification of the initial values of an outer segmentation of the clipping plane of 40 cm by 40 cm was acceptable. With that minimum monitorable size for a motion sensor at maximum distance a value could be defined which is much smaller compared to a usual size of a worker and secures our confidence in values obtained from a construction site.

4.2 Verification of the test algorithms

We make use of the geometry of building components that have been modeled using Autodesk™ Revit™. Triangulated surfaces of building components are exported from Revit™ using the application programming interface (API). The data structure of a set of triangles exported from Revit™ contains the belonging building element identification as additional data.

During an initial test the following geometry with 4034 building elements and 2153769 triangles was provided by Autodesk Revit.

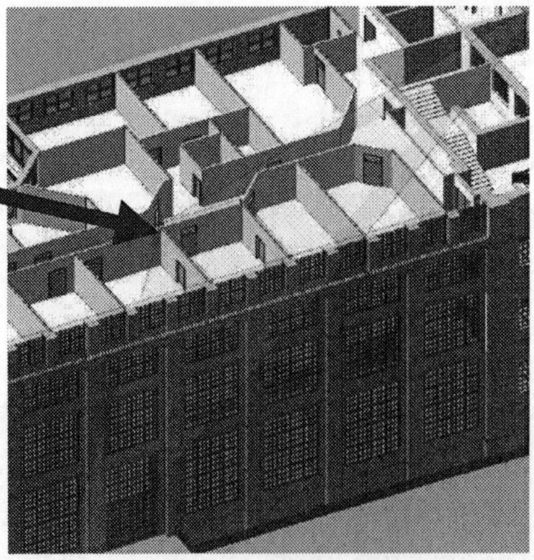

Figure 4 perspective view into the planned outfitting area with marked cone origin

In the next step, the backward face filtering reduced the amount to 4019 building elements with 1080498 triangles. After a second filtering with the help of the intersection test it could be reduced to an amount of 499 building elements and 212058 triangles inside the volume of the cone. After the final filtering and sorting only 54 triangles of 10 building elements were provided, which could be monitored from the current position of the sensor.

5 Planned next steps

Our plan is now to test our approach by monitoring outfitting processes inside of our university building. The construction site processes, e.g. dry wall demolition, dry wall construction, finishing and painting of dry wall constructions will be monitored. Sensor data is captured continuously for a later analysis. The progress on the construction site itself will be additionally captured using a photo documentation.

The obtained data will be analyzed to verify whether single durations of scheduled activities can be detected. In further steps, mean values can be computed in the case that several projects with equivalent activities are evaluated. These mean values can be used to generate more accurate schedules based on actual monitored duration data instead of using standard data from databases.

6 Conclusion and outlook

Non-intrusive monitoring represents a new way to obtain temporal data from a construction site. A geometrical representation was introduced for the use of sensor devices inside a building information model. Test algorithms verified the possibility for a linkage between the sensor and visible building elements modeled in a building information model. Detailed monitoring on an existing construction site will deliver real data in upcoming steps of our ongoing research.

A pre-computation of specific locations of sensors is also on our agenda to reduce the number of sensors in such a way that with a small amount of sensors all relevant activities can be monitored.

7 References

Akhavian, R. & Behzadan, A. H. (2015), 'Construction equipment activity recognition for simulation input modeling using mobile sensors and machine learning classifiers', Advanced Engineering Informatics 29(4), 867--877.

B+B Thermo-Technik GmbH (2015), www.bb-sensors.com Website, https://shop.bbsensors.com/out/media/Bedienungsanleitung_Passiv-Infrarot_Bewegungsmelder_low_power_PIR-STD-LP.pdf, accessed February 2016.

Braun A, Tuttas S, Borrmann A, Stilla U (2015) A concept for automated construction progress monitoring using BIM-based geometric constraints and photogrammetric point clouds, ITcon Vol. 20, Special Issue ECPPM 2014 - 10th European Conference on Product and Process Modelling , pg. 68-79, http://www.itcon.org/2015/5

Brilakis, I.; Lourakis, M.; Sacks, R.; Savarese, S.; Christodoulou, S.; Teizer, J. & Makhmalbaf, A. (2010), 'Toward automated generation of parametric BIMs based on hybrid video and laser scanning data', Advanced Engineering Informatics 24(4), 456--465.

Cheng, T.; Venugopal, M.; Teizer, J. & Vela, P. A. (2011), 'Performance evaluation of ultra wideband technology for construction resource location tracking in harsh environments', Automation in Construction 20(8), 1173-1184.

Cheng, T. & Teizer, J. (2013), 'Real-time resource location data collection and visualization technology for construction safety and activity monitoring applications', Automation in Construction 34, 3-15.

Eberly, D. (2005). 3D game engine architecture: Engineering real-time applications with Wild Magic. Amsterdam [u.a.]: Elsevier [u.a.].

Eriksson, J.; Girod, L.; Hull, B.; Newton, R.; Madden, S. & Balakrishnan, H. (2008), The Pothole Patrol: Using a mobile sensor network for road surface monitoring, in 'MobiSys'08 - Proceedings of the 6th International Conference on Mobile Systems, Applications, and Services', pp. 29-39.

Gerlich, T.; Biagioni, J.; Merrifield, T. & Eriksson, J. (2011), Demo: Tracking Transit with EasyTracker, in 'Proceedings of the 9th ACM Conference on Embedded Networked Sensor Systems', ACM, , pp. 401--402.

Gong, J. & Caldas, C. H. (2011), 'An object recognition, tracking, and contextual reasoning-based video interpretation method for rapid productivity analysis of construction operations', Automation in Construction 20(8), 1211-1226.

Huhnt, W. (2012). A digital environment for managing processes in civil engineering. In Abstract Volume, 14th International Conference on Computing in Civil and Building Engineering (14th ICCCBE), V. TELICHENKO, A. VOLKOV and I. BILCHUK (Editors), Moscow 27–29 June, Moscow State University of Civil Engineering (National Research University), Publishing House "ASV",p.24, ISBN 978-5-93093-877-7

Kim, J. Y.; Caldas, C. H.; Kim, J. Y. & Caldas, C. H. (2013), 'Vision-based action recognition in the internal construction site using interactions between worker actions and construction objects', 2013 Proceedings of the 30th ISARC, Montreal, Canada, 661--668.

Kluge, M. (2012). Construction site black-box ConBBox – data monitoring for construction sites. In Abstract Volume, 14th International Conference on Computing in Civil and Building Engineering (14th ICCCBE), V. TELICHENKO, A. VOLKOV and I. BILCHUK (Editors), Moscow 27–29 June, Moscow State University of Civil Engineering (National Research University), Publishing House "ASV",p. 484, ISBN 978-5-93093-877-7

Kluge, M. and Huhnt, W. (2013) Sensor based monitoring of construction site activities, Proc. of the EG-ICE 2013 Vienna, Austria

Mohan, P.; Padmanabhan, V. N. & Ramjee, R. (2008), Nericell: rich monitoring of road and traffic conditions using mobile smartphones, in 'Proceedings of the 6th ACM conference on Embedded network sensor systems', ACM, , pp. 323--336.

Pahl, P. J.; Damrath, R.; Enseleit, J.; Laabs, A. & Huhnt, W. (published online 2006), Objektorientierte Analyse und Visualisierung zeitabhängiger physikalischer Zustände dreidimensionaler Körper, Wiley-VCH Verlag GmbH & Co. KGaA, pp. 139--170.

Park, M. ..; Makhmalbaf, A. & Brilakis, I. (2011), 'Comparative study of vision tracking methods for tracking of construction site resources', Automation in Construction 20(7), 905-915.

Schneider, P., & Eberly, D. (2004). Geometric tools for computer graphics (2. [print.] ed.). Amsterdam [u.a.]: Morgan Kaufmann.

Teizer, J.; Cheng, T. & Fang, Y. (2013), 'Location tracking and data visualization technology to advance construction ironworkers' education and training in safety and productivity', Automation in Construction.

Zaif, T. (2015) Planung und Durchführung einer Messreihe mit mobilen Sensoren, Bachelor Thesis, Technische Universität Berlin, November 2015, Germany

Image-based Window Detection – An Overview

Marcel Neuhausen*, Christian Koch**, Markus König*
*Ruhr-University Bochum, **The University of Nottingham
marcel.neuhausen@ruhr-uni-bochum.de

Abstract. Automated segmentation of buildings' façade and detection of its elements is of high relevance in various fields of research as it, e. g., reduces the effort of 3 D reconstructing existing buildings and even entire cities or may be used for navigation and localization tasks. In recent years, several approaches were made concerning this issue. These can be mainly classified by their input data which are either images or 3 D point clouds. This paper provides a survey of image-based approaches. Particularly, this paper focuses on window detection and therefore groups related papers into the three major detection strategies. We juxtapose grammar based methods, pattern recognition and machine learning and contrast them referring to their generality of application. As we found out machine learning approaches seem most promising for window detection on generic façades and thus we will pursue these in future work.

1. Introduction

In recent years, the Building Information Modelling concept of using 3 D building models for construction and maintenance purposes has increasingly developed towards models of entire cities as civil engineering goes beyond the scope of single buildings. Moreover, models of buildings are required in other application areas such as virtual and augmented reality, navigation or simulation.

By now, 3 D city models often are publicly available by services like Google Earth or can be requested from land-registries. However, since such models are commonly released as coarse block models, they often lack details, such as the shape of roofs, façades, and façade elements, which are essential in some civil engineering tasks. For most applications these models are insufficient since façade elements constitute the major part of a building. In building recognition as often used for navigation and localization, e. g., tourist guidance (Ali et al., 2007), façade elements and windows in particular play a major role. The same applies to other tasks as simulations of the stability of buildings. Especially mechanized tunnelling projects may benefit from more detailed models as they ease risk assessment of settlement-induced damages inflicted to urban structures (Obel et al. 2016). In particular, the so-called wall-openings coefficient, meaning the ratio of openings to wall, is a crucial factor in risk assessment. Openings within a solid wall decrease its stiffness and thus increases the vulnerability to settlements. Windows, in this regard, account for the major part of wall-openings.

Façade reconstruction including window detection is, hence, a crucial issue which is by far not solved (Musialski et al., 2013). In this paper, we present an overview of the major strategies for automated window detection on façades and discuss their advantages and limitations regarding tunneling projects.

2. Related Work

In the past decades an extensive body of literature arose concerning building reconstruction and particularly façade reconstruction. The approaches made in this field of research are highly diverse and manifold. However, some effort to categorize existing methods has already been made. Usually approaches are mainly differentiated by the type of input data. Baltsavias (2004),

Brenner (2005), and Haala and Kada (2010) provide surveys focussing on airborne imagery and laser scans. Although rudimentary building reconstruction is possible, this data source is certainly not well suited for façade elements recognition. The papers of Baltsavias (2004) and Brenner (2005), hence, concern the detection of large structures like buildings and streets and the reconstruction of simple buildings' shapes, respectively. On the contrary, Haala and Kada (2010) also include approaches using terrestrial laser scans to gain more detailed geometrical information. They also present approaches developing façade's texture mapping to reconstructed 3 D models of buildings. In the comprehensive survey of approaches on building and façade reconstruction of Musialski et al. (2013), the authors cover both airborne and terrestrial imagery and laser scans. Additionally, they differentiate between automatic and semi-automatic approaches. Although they discuss approaches of pattern detection, matching as well as façade parsing, the paper focuses on reconstruction, while façade element detection is only briefly mentioned.

3. Approaches

In the following we concentrate on approaches based on terrestrial imagery, as we focus on window detection in this paper. Indeed laser scan generated point clouds simplify the detection of façade elements and especially windows (van Gool et al., 2007). However, the acquisition is very time-consuming and expensive as for risk assessment in tunnelling projects models of entire cities or at least of areas along the tunnelling alignment are required. Façade images, contrariwise, are mostly publicly available from Google Street View and other services or may be easily gathered manually or even semi-automatic by drone flights as Freimuth and König (2015) showed.

Most approaches using ground view imagery can roughly be categorized by three main strategies, although some combine multiple strategies, which interdicts a clear disjunction in general. However, for comparison reasons the following partition by strategies facilitates a contrasting juxtaposition. We, therefore, classify multiple strategy approaches by their prominent method.

The remainder is structured as follow: section 3.1 gives an overview of approaches applying grammars to façade images. Section 3.2 summarizes pattern recognition approaches and section 3.3. relates to window detection using machine learning techniques. Accordingly, in section 4 we discuss the limitations of these strategies with respect to their generality of application. Finally, section 5 concludes our findings and makes proposals for further research.

3.1 Grammar Based Approaches

The most prominent methods in grammar based façade reconstruction are shape and splitting grammars. These grammars make use of assumptions to symmetry such as grid-like arrangement of façade elements or their usually rectangular shapes. In the context of several comprehensive publications Ripperda and Brenner (2009) proposed an approach to apply a formal grammar to façades for automatic reconstruction. Exploiting the assumptions mentioned above, Ripperda (2008) designed a context-free grammar splitting a façade into its symmetric and repeating areas, respectively. To optimize the grammar's segmentation of a façade, the authors proposed a *reversible-jump Markov chain Monte Carlo* (rjMCMC) method sampling over numerous runs (Ripperda and Brenner, 2006). Thus, façade elements are automatically derived. To improve their approach, Ripperda and Brenner (2007) extended their approach by a data driven rule extension. Müller et al. (2007) proposed an approach which splits the façade into floors and tiles by means of symmetry information. Ensuing, it subdivides the tiles further into smaller rectangular regions and clusters them into groups. The extracted architectural elements can then be matched with 3 D objects of a database. For façade reconstruction the windows' depth information has to be explicitly specified via interaction with users. Compared to the former, Teboul et al. (2010) defined a more detailed shape grammar that not only splits a façade into rectangles but models sematic relationships of façade parts and their elements, e. g., the relationship of attic to roof or window. The authors understand façade segmentation by use of a grammar as finding a specific sequence of rules. Thus, they use an energy minimization scheme determining the best fitting manifestation on particular images. In a last step, they classify each segmented part of the image by a randomized decision forest which labels each pixel according to its probability of class affiliation. In a subsequent approach, Teboul et al. (2013) are content with a simple shape grammar that only allows iteratively splitting rectangles in smaller ones in order to focus on improving the parsing of facades. The parsing is then done by a reinforcement learning algorithm. As the one of Ripperda and Brenner (2006), many approaches fall back on sampling algorithms like MCMC for the optimization of parse trees. Riemenschneider et al. (2012) pointed out that sampling such a large solution space holding a complex structure is not a sufficient method. For this reason they propose the *Cocke-Younger-Kasami algorithm* (CYK) for efficiently parsing context-free grammars. In their approach the authors define a grammar allowing for irregular lattices splitting the façade into rectangular regions of different sizes. Similar to Teboul et al. (2010) they assign the most probable label of class affiliation to each pixel using a merit function that describes the likelihood of each pixel belonging to a class.

To stochastically sample parse trees or finding the most probable parse tree of an ambiguous grammar for a given input, probabilistic grammars provide the method of choice. In contrast to deterministic grammars these extend former by stochastic components. Each production rule in a grammar's set of rules additionally possesses a likelihood of appearance that, as consequence, induces a probability distribution on the generated output. Assuming façades to be structured highly regular and symmetric like it can be found at large office buildings, Alegre and Dellaert (2004) developed a stochastic context-free grammar which only contains horizontal and vertical splits of the façade. This is used to derive a Bayesian stochastic model which depicts a hierarchical partitioning of disjoint blocks of façade images. For approximating the posteriors of partitions the authors apply MCMC sampling. Tyleček and Šára (2012) propose a novel approach by relinquishing to specify a grammar with an explicit set of production rules. Instead of this they develop a stochastic model in a tree-like structure acting as grammar. For optimizing the grammar's manifestation they use a general rjMCMC framework.

3.2 Pattern Recognition

As windows are mostly assumed to be rectangles arranged in a grid-like manner parallel to the façade's contour, some approaches detect windows by patterns of horizontal and vertical edges in façade images. Lee and Nevatia (2004) proposed an approach to window detection on rectified façade images which was later resumed by Meixner et al. (2011) for interpreting façade elements. In the image, they project horizontal and vertical edges, respectively, and interfered resulting histograms with each other. At emerging peak's location window candidates are supposed and finally verified based on the beforehand extracted edges. Since this method only detects rectangular shaped windows, Lee and Nevatia (2004) extended their approach to arch windows by allowing the detected window's top edge to become curved and again verifying it with the image's edges. To apply window detection to more irregular facades, Recky and Leberl (2010) picked up Lee and Nevatia's (2004) concept. They deduce a subdivision of the facade into levels from vertical edge projection of the façade image and subsequently applied a horizontal edge projection separately on each level to further divide the levels into blocks. By applying a *k*-Means clustering by color to these blocks, Recky and Leberl (2010) identify if a block belongs either to the façade or to a window. Final window detections are obtained by joining adjacent window blocks. Korah and Rasmussen (2008) discussed a method that focuses more on the grid-like alignment of windows on a façade. Therefore they hypothesize rectangles from all pairs of parallel edges in the image resulting in a large quantity of hypotheses. As windows are supposed to be aligned in a grid, a best possible lattice of a subset of the extracted rectangles is constructed by means of a MCMC optimization procedure.

Instead of explicitly assuming the shape of windows to be rectangular, the *implicit shape models* (ISM) introduced by Leibe et al. (2004) combine the recognition and segmentation of objects in one process. These models consist of a codebook prototypically defining local features and a probability distribution determining their spatial positions. Reznik and Mayer (2008) applied ISM for window detection. Interest points in combination with their geometric arrangement around the window's center constitute the ISM which is then learned from a manually labelled training set. They generate window hypotheses by cross correlating image patches around interest points with the training data. Retrieved good hypotheses are used in a self-diagnosis manner to validate weak hypotheses. For refinement of the windows' alignment, model selection is done based on the assumption that windows are arranged in rows and columns.

Usually façade elements occur recurrently on facades. Thus, elements' alignment on facades can be understood as repeating patterns. An approach to window detection as a subtask of façade reconstruction, relying on repetitions on the façade is proposed by van Gool et al. (2007). They tackle the problem by a bifid strategy approach depending on the quality of the input images. As for their method of fully automatic reconstruction, sufficient perspective effects in the images are required elsewise they switch to the approach of Müller et al. (2007) (see section 3.1). If sufficient perspective is available, interest points occurring repeatedly over the façade are computed and grouped to infer the camera's calibration. Window detection is then done by energy minimization using graph-cut optimization. In a concluding refinement step van Gool et al. (2007) use shape priors for vertical and horizontal alignment.

3.3 Supervised Machine Learning

In supervised machine learning in the context of computer vision object recognition is achieved by training a classifier using image features of a labelled data set. By training, classifiers learn a function to separate object classes. In this field *support vector machines* (SVM), building a kind of algorithms able to cope with high dimensional inputs, are widely deemed to yield good classification results (Yang et al., 2012). Inspired by Lee and Nevatia (2004) and Recky and Lerberl (2010), Haugeard et al. (2009) utilize the fact that windows mostly are aligned to floors and, thus, they split facades into floors by thresholding vertical edge histograms. On each floor they project horizontal edges to a histogram to infer window candidates. Edges of these candidates are extracted from the image and represented in a graph. Windows are then classified by a SVM using a kernel operating in inexact graph matching such that windows emerge as a sub-graph of the graph of all contours extracted from the façade image (Musialski et al., 2013).

Bag-of-visual-words (BoW) approaches offer another way to handle multiple different image features at once by integrating them into sparse vectors of feature occurrences. These can then be fed into a classifier. Csurka and Perronnin (2008) described a method making use of BoW for a pixel-wise semantic segmentation of façade images into façade elements. The approach relies on the detection of image patches out of which local image features are extracted and combined to a BoW representation. Classified by sparse logistic regression, the results are assigned back to the level of pixels. Fröhlich et al. (2010) improved this method. Instead of extracting image patches they compute local color features obtained by dense sampling.

Classification is then done by feeding the gained feature vectors into a randomized decision forest.

The previously described classification approaches aim on high dimensional vectors as input. Feature responses have to be explicitly arranged in vector shape. Boosting algorithms contrariwise allow for deriving a strong classifier directly from image features. Originally designed for face detection, Viola and Jones (2001) illustrate a boosted cascade of simple features as a method for object detection which uses image features as classifiers. Features are treated as weak learners and fused by boosting in a way that they form a strong classifier. Ali et al. (2007) applied the approach of Viola and Jones (2001) to detect windows on facades. Divers thresholded Haar-like features (Oren et al., 1997) on different positions within the image act as a pool of weak learners out of which an adapted AdaBoost algorithm (Freund and Schapire, 1997) selects a subset and arranges them in cascading stages to form a strong classifier. For detection a search window is slid over the image and resulting patches are presented to the classifier. To enable detection of different façade elements Drauschke and Förstner (2008) describe an approach similar to the one of Ali et al. (2007) which also builds a strong classifier by AdaBoost. Though, the novel idea is serving different kinds of image features at once to the AdaBoost algorithm. Since the detection and classification of façade elements using supervised learning algorithms are highly dependent on which features are used, Yang et al. (2012) proposed an empirical study on feature evaluation in this context. For region-wise labelling the façade's elements they used randomized decision forests based on different features as classifiers. Martinović et al. (2012) present a similar approach like Yang et al. (2012) but in order to substantiate classification results they augment the decision tree's output with further processing results. In their three layered approach they make use of an oversegmentation of a building's façade image. In a first step a recursive neural network merges oversegmented regions into objects. These hypotheses are then combined with the classification results of a decision tree of integral channel features (see Dollar et al., 2009) learned by discrete AdaBoost. Finally they refine detections by exploiting weak architectural principles, e. g., vertical and horizontal alignment or co-occurrence of objects.

It may be necessary to detect more than one single object class. In terms of façade element recognition this could mean distinguishing between windows, doors, and maybe even more categories. Fidler et al. (2006) established an approach to multiple class categorization based on hierarchical models reducing the computational complexity which such a task usually implicates. Mačák and Drbohlav (2011) adapted the generic approach given by Fidler et al. (2006) for the use of window detection. They applied a difference of Gaussians to extract edge features forming the lowermost layer of a hierarchical window model. From there on they learn following layers such that the respectively superior layer is a composition of instances in local neighborhoods of the underlying layer. The resulting model is then used to detect windows in façade images.

4. Discussion

To apply window detection approaches to buildings of different architectural style or even to cities in various countries the methods should well generalize as facades' and windows' appearance vary in both geographical region and year of construction. In the following we discuss the assumptions and limitations of the methods presented above.

Grammar Based Approaches. For all grammar based approaches an optimization of the parse tree is inevitable for each presented façade which is a time-consuming procedure if applied on a high quantity of façade images as it is the case in our research. Optimization may either be done by sampling over all possible trees or by relying on special parsing algorithms like CYK. Especially sampling methods limit the field of application as they are, on the one hand, only applicable to grammars consisting of small rule sets and, on the other hand, potentially get stuck in local optima (Riemenschneider et al., 2012). This mostly leads to simple shape grammars consisting of less rules which only split façade images into rectangles as windows and other façade elements often are assumed to be of rectangular shape. On the other hand, defining more complex grammars may be highly dependent on expert knowledge about building construction. This seems advantageous as there are explicit universal constructions rules. The aesthetic sensibility, however, differs in country which complicates deducing general rules. Moreover, the more a grammar's set of rules is refined the stronger it gets biased from specific façade types and thus is no longer generally applicable as architectural style varies not only among country but also among geographical regions and even among year of the buildings' construction (Haala and Kada, 2010). However, in case of simple shape and splitting grammar as well as in case of complex grammars these approaches only achieve a rough segmentation of façade images. This has to be processed in further steps to both gain proper object contours and determine the objects' class using either image processing or machine learning techniques. Since mostly also a pre-processing of the images is required to obtain symmetry or edge information the grammar and the sampling algorithm, respectively, can be applied to, it is questionable if a detour over grammars yields to be a promising solution.

Pattern recognition. Approaches focusing on pattern recognition usually rely on a couple of assumptions. Assumptions on the distribution of pixels' intensities, meaning that windows are darker than the surrounding façade, often yield erroneous results (Musialski et al., 2013). However, other approaches make assumptions referring to both the windows' shape and their alignment on the façade. More precisely, like in the approach of van Gool et al. (2007) it is often assumed that windows occur on facades as multiple elements of the same type, i. e. same size and shape, and repeat in fixed displacements in both horizontal and vertical direction. This practice yields remarkable good results as long as facades are, on the one hand, highly regular structured and, on the other hand, broad enough such that façade elements form the presumed patterns. This may be valid for structures like large office buildings but it does not hold for the majority of structures in typical European inner city areas and adjacent regions. In apartment buildings the windows of staircases often deviate in size from residual windows and also hardly break the pattern spanned by them. Detection of such asymmetric patterns cannot be well handled as van Gool et al. (2007) and Meixner et al. (2011) pointed out. Furthermore, most buildings are rather small resulting in less repetitions which also complicates detection. Another drawback Reznik and Mayer (2008) highlighted is that the images' resolution and potential partially occlusions of windows by trees, traffic signs and similar highly impacts the detection's quality. This comes into account right then if publicly available images are used, such as ones of Google Street View, as they are, firstly, usually taken from the street sight such that occlusions occur unavoidably and, secondly, undistorted whereby block artefacts may arise and lower the resolution.

Supervised Machine Learning. In contrast to the aforementioned strategies, supervised machine learning approaches rely neither on assumptions of the windows' alignment on the façade as they detect an object by its own characteristic instead of the interplay with other objects, nor do they need explicit prior knowledge about construction details. This is advantageous as both result in a loss of universal applicability. Nevertheless, the detection rate of machine learning algorithms is, amongst others, constrained by the type of image features whose responses are fed in. Features extracted from the input images, thus, should be significant and relevant. This constitutes a challenge in itself, as windows are usually rather poor of outstanding features, except for their frames. However, there are already approaches like Yang et al. (2012) to cope with this issue. Certainly, for training a supervised machine learning algorithm a labelled set of training images is required which definitely is time-consuming in gathering and setting up correctly. Since these algorithms, however, are able to generalize well, this procedure has only to be made once to detect windows in facades of different construction years or architectural styles.

5. Conclusion

We highlighted the meaning of window detection to improve existing 3D city models for the use in civil engineering tasks such as tunnelling. By comparing several approaches of different strategies, we discussed application limitations and concluded that there is, by now, no adequate approach for universal use. Though we showed that machine learning techniques may yield promising results in future since they avoid restricting assumptions and offer an excellent ability of generalization.

We, thus, will focus on machine learning techniques to detect windows in our future work. Particularly, we believe that the approach of Ali et al. (2007) may be developable. An extension of this approach by a pre-processing of the image easing the feature extraction and unifying the windows' characteristics as well as a post-processing to reject misclassification may increase the detection rate. Moreover, we will adapt the approach by substitution of Voila and Jones' (2001) detector by a Soft Cascade detector (Bourdev and Brandt, 2005) as this may also increase the detection rate. For training and testing issues we recommend the eTRIMS data set (Korč and Förstner, 2009) as it provides extensive samples and is already used in several approaches which supports the comparability.

By now, for windows detection mostly edges features are used, in other respects windows seem to be poor of features. Additionally to Yang et al.'s (2012) work, we consider a further evaluation of image features to be desirable since in most facades there are other objects providing even stronger responses on edge features (Recky and Leberl, 2010). Thus, finding sets of features which significantly describe the windows' characteristics is a major task. Features found in this context can also contribute to improve the results of the above mentioned approach.

In recent years, *deep neural networks* (DNN) attract more and more attention in computer vision for object classification tasks. Szegedy et al. (2013) proposed a method to not only classify objects but also locate them within an image. As such approaches often outperform classical computer vision algorithms, it would be desirable further pursue former and apply them to window detection.

Acknowledgement

Financial support was provided by the German Research Foundation (DFG) in the framework of the Collaborative Research Center SFB 837 "Interaction Modelling in Mechanized Tunnelling".

References

Alegre, F., Dellaert, F. (2004). A Probabilistic Approach to the Semantic Interpretation of Building Facades. In CIPA International Workshop on Vision Techniques Applied to the Rehabilitation of City Centers.

Ali, H., Seifert, C., Jindal, N. and Paletta, L. (2007). Window Detection in Facades. In Proceedings of the IEEE Computer Society Conference on Image Analysis and Processing, pp. 837-842.

Baltsavias, E. P. (2004). Object extraction and revision by image analysis using existing geodata and knowledge: current status and steps towards operational systems. In ISPRS Journal of Photogrammetry and Remote Sensing 58, pp. 129–151.

Bourdev, L., Brandt, J. (2005). Robust Object Detection Via Soft Cascade. In Proceedings of the IEEE Computer Society Conference on Computer Vision and Pattern Recognition, pp. 236-243

Brenner, C. (2005). Building reconstruction from images and laser scanning. In International Journal of Applied Earth Observation and Geoinformation 6 (3–4), 187–198.

Brenner, C., Ripperda, N. (2006). Extraction of Facades using rjMCMC and Constraint Equations. In Proceedings of the ISPRS Symposium on Photogrammetric Computer Vision, pp. 155-160.

Csurka, G., Perronnin, F. (2008). A Simple High Performance Approach to Semantic Segmentation. In Proceedings of the British Machine Vision Conference, pp. 22.1-22.10.

Dollar, P., Tu, Z., Perona, P. and Belongie, S. (2009). Integral channel features. In Proceedings of the British Machine Vision Conference, pp. 91.1-91.11.

Drauschke, M., Förstner, W. (2008). Selecting Appropriate Features for Detecting Buildings and Building Parts. In Proceedings of the Congress of the International Society for Photogrammetry and Remote Sensing, pp. 447-452.

Fidler, S., Berginc, G. and Leonardis, A. (2006). Hierarchical statistical learning of generic parts of object structure. In Proceedings of the IEEE Computer Society Conference on Computer Vision and Pattern Recognition, pages 182–189.

Freimuth, H., König, M. (2015). Generation of Waypoints for UAV-Assisted Progress Monitoring and Acceptance of Construction Work. In Proceedings of the International Conference on Construction Applications of Virtual Reality. Available from: http://www.convr2015.com, accessed February 2016.

Freund, Y. and Schapire, R.E. (1997). A desicion-theoretic generalization of on-line learning and an application to boosting. In Journal of Computer and System Science 55, pp. 119-139.

Fröhlich, B., Rodner, E. and Denzler, J. (2010). A Fast Approach for Pixelwise Labeling of Facade Images. In Proceedings of the IEEE Computer Society International Conference on Pattern Recognition, pp. 3029-3032.

van Gool, L., Zeng, G. van den Borre, F. and Müller, P. (2007). Towards Mass-Produced Building Models. In Proceedings of Photogrammetric Image Analysis Conference, pp. 209-220.

Habib, A. F., Zhai, R. and Kim, C. (2010). Generation of Complex Polyhedral Building Models by Integrating Stereo-Aerial Imagery and Lidar Data. In Photogrammetric Engineering & Remote Sensing 76 (5), pp. 609-623.

Haala N., Kada, M. (2010). An update on automatic 3D building reconstruction. In ISPRS Journal of Photogrammetry and Remote Sensing 65, pp. 570-580.

Haugeard, J., Philipp-Foliguet, S., Precioso, F. and Lebrun, J. (2009). Extraction of Windows in facade using Kernel on Graph of Contours. In Proceedings of the 16th Scandinavian Conference on Image Analysis, pp. 646–656.

Korah, T., Rasmussen, C. (2008). Analysis of Building Textures for Reconstructing Partially Occluded Facades. In Proceedings of the European Conference on Computer Vision, pp. 359-372.

Korč, F., Förstner, W. (2009). eTRIMS Image Database for interpreting images of man-made scenes. Technical report, Department of Photogrammetry, University of Bonn.

Lee, S.C., Nevatia, R. (2004). Extraction and Integration of Window in a 3D Building Model from Ground View images. In Proceedings of the IEEE Computer Society Conference on Computer Vision and Pattern Recognition, pp. 106-113.

Leibe, B., Leonardis, A. and Schiele, B. (2004). Combined Object Categorization and Segmentation with an Implicit Shape Model. In Proceedings of the Workshop on Statistical Learning in Computer Vision, European Computer Vision Conference, pp. 17-32.

Mačák, J., Drbohlav, O. (2011). Hierarchical shape model for windows detection. In Proceedings of the ÖAGM/AAPR Workshop. Available from: http://oagm2011.joanneum.at, accessed February 2016.

Martinović, A., Mathias, M., Weissenberg, J. and van Gool, L. (2012). A Three-Layered Approach to Facade Parsing. In Proceedings of the European Conference on Computer Vision, pp. 416-429.

Meixner, P., Leberl, F. and Brédif, M. (2011). Interpretation of 2D and 3D Building Details on Facades and Roofs. In Proceedings of the ISPRS Conference on Photogrammetric Image Analysis, pp. 137-142.

Müller, P., Zeng, G., Wonka, P. and van Gool, L. (2007). Image-based procedural modeling of facades. In ACM Transactions on Graphics 26 (3), pp. 85.1-85.9

Musialski, P., Wonka, P., Aliaga, D.G., Wimmer, M., van Gool, L. and Purgathofer, W. (2013). A Survey of Urban Reconstruction. In Computer Graphics Forum 32 (6), pp. 146-177

Obel, M., Mark, P., Neuhausen, M., König, M. and Schindler, S. (2016). Settlement risk assessment by means of categorized surface infrastructure. In Proceedings of the International Conference on Structural Analysis of Historical Constructions. [Accepted]

Oren, M., Papageorgiou, C., Sinha, P., Osuna, E. and Poggio, T. (1997). Pedestrian detection using wavelet templates. In Proceedings of the IEEE Computer Society Conference on Computer Vision and Pattern Recognition, pp 193-199.

Recky, M., Leberl, F. (2010). Windows Detection Using K-means in CIE-Lab Color Space. In Proceedings of the IEEE Computer Society International Conference on Pattern Recognition, pp. 356-360.

Reznik, S., Mayer, H. (2008). Implicit Shape Models, Self-Diagnosis, and Model Selection for 3D Facade Interpretation. In Photogrammetrie, Fernerkundung und Geoinformation 3, pp. 187-196.

Riemenschneider, H., Krispel, U., Thaller, W., Donoser, M., Havemann, S., Fellner, D. and Bischof, H. (2012). Irregular lattices for complex shape grammar facade parsing. In Proceedings of the IEEE Computer Society Conference on Computer Vision and Pattern Recognition, pp. 1640-1647.

Ripperda, N. (2008). Grammar Based Facade Reconstruction using rjMCMC. In Photogrammetrie Fernerkundung Geoinformation 2, pp. 83-92.

Ripperda, N., Brenner, C. (2007). Data driven rule proposal for grammar based facade reconstruction. In Proceedings of the ISPRS Conference on Photogrammetric Image Analysis, pp 173-178.

Ripperda, N., Brenner, C. (2009). Application of a Formal Grammar to Facade Reconstruction in Semiautomatic and Automatic Environments. In Proceedings of the AGILE Conference on Geographic Information Science. Available from: http://www.agile-online.org accessed February 2016.

Szegedy, C., Toshev, A. and Erhan, D. (2013). Deep Neural Networks for Object Detection. In Advances in Neural Information Processing Systems 26, pp. 2553-2561.

Teboul, O., Kokkinos, I., Simon, L., Koutsourakis, P. and Paragios, N. (2013). Parsing Facades with Shape Grammars and Reinforcement Learning. In IEEE Transactions on Pattern Analysis and Machine Intelligence 35 (7), pp. 1744-1756.

Teboul, O., Simon, L., Koutsourakis, P. and Paragios, N. (2010). Segmentation of Building Facades Using Procedural Shape Priors. In Proceedings of the IEEE Computer Society Conference on Computer Vision and Pattern Recognition, pp. 3105-3112.

Tyleček, R., Šára, R. (2012). Stochastic Recognition of Regular Structures in Facade Images. In IPSJ Transactions on Computer Vision and Applications 4, pp. 63-70.

Viola, P., Jones, M. (2001). Rapid Object Detection Using a Boosted Cascade of Simple Features. In Proceedings of the IEEE Computer Society Conference on Computer Vision and Pattern Recognition, pp. 511-518.

Yang, M, Förstner, W. and Chai, D. (2012). Feature Evaluation for Building Façade Images - An Empirical Study. In International Archives of the Photogrammetry, Remote Sensing and Spatial Information Sciences, Volume XXXIX-B3, pp. 513-518.

Simplifying Building Energy Performance Models to support an Integrated Design workflow

Sundaravelpandian Singaravel, Philipp Geyer
KU Leuven, Belgium
sundar.singaravel@kuleuven.be

Abstract. Detailed building performance simulation (BPS) is suited for verification of a design. Increasing needs to develop net-zero energy buildings, demands for passive, active and renewable energy design strategies to be aligned from the early design stage. This gives rise to simplified Building Performance Simulation (BPS) to be integrated at early design stage. This paper aims to identify the required BPS model level of detail with minimum error using parametric simulation models and Design of Experiments (DoE). Results indicates oversimplification in occupancy can produce huge error percentage of the simplified BPS model compared to detailed BPS model; followed by HVAC system, building form and so on.

1. Introduction

European Union is striving to achieve net-zero energy building by 2018 for offices and 2020 for residential buildings (Kreinera, Passera and Wallbaumb, 2015). The challenge in developing buildings with these sustainability requirements is that design elements cannot be directly associated with the requirements; it is the result of interactions between various design elements, local weather conditions, human behavior and so on (Weck, Roos and Magee, 2011).

The current design and development process equals more a linear process than an integrated process (Negendahl, 2015). Design information exchange takes place only for finalized or updated design (British Standard Institution, 2007). This situation limits the number of design options evaluated at early design stages. However, at these stages, chief decisions are made concerning the performance of the design. Therefore, a holistic approach is preferred, as it provides insight on interactions with other stakeholders and design element; such an approach allows to weigh all the pros and cons of a design decision (Kreinera, Passera and Wallbaumb, 2015). The term holistic approach refers to making decisions by considering both architectural and engineering design elements.

Technology for informed decisions is available: The design process uses Building Performance Simulation (BPS), which provides insight in performance of various design variants; Building Information Modelling (BIM) allows to share geometric and technical data with all stakeholders. The application of BPS causes modelling effort and computational load with respective delays – a fact that is aggravated by many variants or the systematic design space exploration (DSE). Common data formats like gbXML, IFC and visual programming languages like Dynamo enables easy data exchange between BIM and BPS facilitating the reduction of BPS modelling effort. Although BIM has the potential to ease the BPS modelling process, its application in early design stage is limited (Negendahl, 2015). Furthermore, it does not reduce time for detailed performance model definition as well as computation.

Simplified BPS models can reduce delay-causing efforts. Such models directly model dependency on chief design parameters and variables, such as occupancy, HVAC systems, lighting systems, building form, window to wall ratio, and material properties etc. However, depending on the kind of simplification, such models generate results that may or may not coincide with a detailed BPS model potentially steering the design in a wrong direction. This risk poses the question "What is the minimum required level of detail for BPS model's to predict energy with accuracies similar to a detailed BPS model?"

This paper examines the required level of detail for a simplified BPS model to predict energy with sufficient accuracy but adequate effort and proposes an alternative metamodeling method for pure simplification of physical BPS. Depending on the metamodel implementation strategy, these models could become complimentary or competitive to early stage BPS models which is discussed further in the conclusion section.

2. Conceptual analysis

Early stage building design process

To determine, examine and propose possible model simplifications, it is necessary to know about the available information at early design stages. RIBA Plan of work 2013 and AIA outline the objectives of design stages and BIM model element's Level of Development (LOD) (RIBA, 2013, Hamedani and Smith, 2015). Based on the definitions from RIBA and AIA, we transfer the LOD concept to the whole building as "component" and divide early design it into two stages, namely, preparation stage with LOD 100 and conceptual design stage with LOD 200:

Preparation stage with LOD 100	*Concept design with LOD 200*
- Quality objectives - Project outcomes - Sustainability aspiration - Budget - Other constrains	- Architectural design - Structural design - Building services systems and outline specifications - Cost

The increase of LOD relates the accumulation of information by planning activity and inherent decision making. Key design decisions taken at LOD 100 and 200 have major impact on the performance of the actual building (Piccoa, Lollini and Marengo, 2014).

Performance gap and prediction gap

The difference between the monitored energy consumption and the predicted energy demand is referred as performance gap (Niu, Pan and Zhao, 2015). Reasons for performance gap are erroneous design assumptions, fundamental errors within modelling tools and their application as well as deviations and misbehaviour in building operation. Design assumptions include simplification of models and idealistic design inputs (Menezesa et al., 2012).

Early stage usually simplifies analysis and typically focuses on either architectural design elements (Hamedani and Smith, 2015) or building systems (Seo, Ooka, Kim, & Nam, 2014). Depending on focus of the analysis model, different areas of BPS model are simplified. In analogy, we call the potential error of model simplification compared to a detailed BPS model in this paper as 'prediction gap'.

Hierarchy of a building's energy performance and BPS

Energy performance of a building depends on building characteristics, building systems and building operation (Kalkman, 2012). Figure 1 shows the layers of a detailed BPS model that contribute to the building energy predictions. The more layer a BPS model has the more detailed it is and vice versa. The number of layers in each BPS model area is referred as its level of detail (please note the distinction to level of development, LOD). Realistic representation of these BPS model areas reduces the performance gap (Murphy and Castleton, 2015, Beltrami et al., 2015).

When areas of building characteristics are dynamic in nature, like the use of smart window or movable overhangs these areas are moved to building systems and operations levels. The reason is that these design elements form a system, whose performance not only depends on interaction between design elements buts also other stakeholders. Therefore, selecting a suitable simplification method becomes a key factor. Level of details is reduced by considering higher hierarchy levels within the model resulting in a simple BPS model with less layers. The impact of an area, which is later in the paper determined, is key information for deciding about this simplification. Simplification is done using a simple BPS tool or using detailed BPS tool with assumptions on unknown parameters. Hence, knowing the required minimum level of detail for a holistic BPS model helps in making effective choice between a simple or detailed tool.

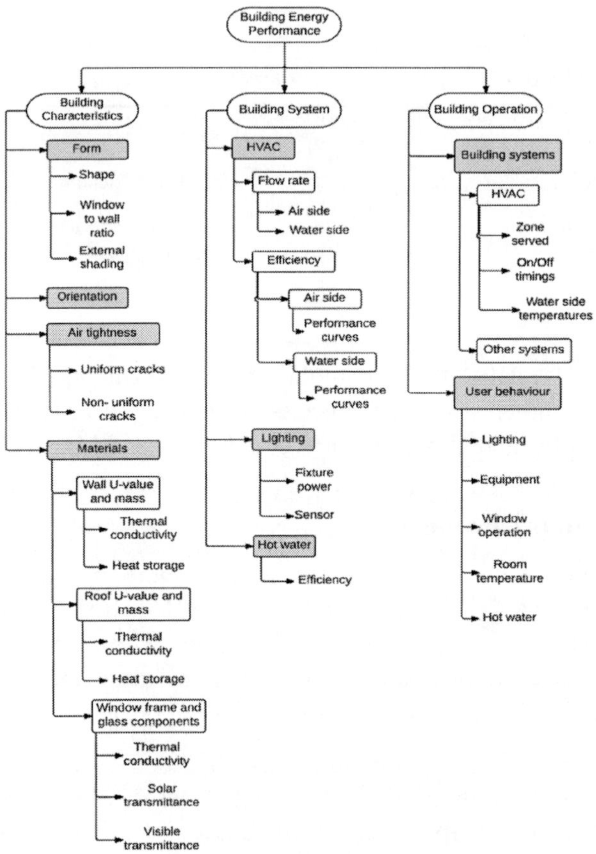

Figure 1: Hierarchy of building energy performance

Design of Experiments (DoE)

In this paper, DoE is used to identify the required level of detail for a BPS model. Typically, application of DoE serves to get insights on the variables, that have the most impact on the performance with a minimum number of experiments, i.e., simulations in this case (Antony, 2003). DoE is typically used because it provides information about all main effects and interactions. Main effects are the individual effects of a variable on the performance while interactions are the effects of a variable on performance depending on the state of another variable.

Plackett-Burman (P-B) design, which is a fractional factorial design technique, is applied to evaluate the required level of detail for a simplified BPS model. This design technique is suitable this study, as it can identify the parameters which have the highest impact in a process with minimum experiments. This means only main effects are evaluated through this technique. The P-B design is based on Hadamard matrices which has experimental runs in multiples of four. P-B design matrix indicates the variations of a parameter in each experiment (Antony, 2003). Variation of a parameter is defined as the different parameter values used in each experiment. Variations in this study refers to simple and detailed modelling methods.

Metamodelling simulation

The chosen metamodelling approach provides a black box surrogate model to approximate expensive simulation experiments. Forrester et al. (2008) gave a general introduction on the use of metamodelling in engineering. Simpson et al. (2001) provided a comparison of such techniques. Simpson et al. (2001) and Jin et al. (2001) examined the influence of design types and size for computer experiments and different methods of metamodelling. Bletzinger and Lähr (2006) applied RSM in the context of an agent-based decision environment. Chlela et al. (2009) and Jaffal et al. (2009) applied traditional RSM to the setup of a metamodel for the thermal performance of a building. Gholap and Khan (2007) used metamodelling for component-level optimization of a heat exchanger in a refrigerator. They built a component metamodel for optimization but did not use it further for design and simulation. Furthermore, a metamodel traces relationships observed within the reference data (Liu, Huang and Stouffs, 2015). Metamodels developed with specific datasets makes them applicable in limited situations only; this makes it complimentary to BPS. In contrary, the hypothesis of this paper is that models developed with diverse datasets could result in generic metamodels which could substitute BPS in certain situations and makes them competitive with BPS.

3. Identifying the required level of detail

Objective of the experiments

The objective of the experiment is to identify level of detail for a simplified BPS models. A P-B design with 16 runs is performed in IES VE software. The BPS model represents a schools located in an urban environment in Abu Dhabi. Please note that the DoE outcomes for other weather files can be different and is not dealt in this paper.

Variations of the level of detail

Table 1 shows the variation of BPS model's level of details. The P-B design matrix, generated through Matlab using the command "hadamard", consists of the combination of variations within the BPS model for each experiment, i.e., simulation run.

Figure 2: IES VE models

The following variations are considered:

1. *The building form* at – 1 and +1 levels have the same built-up area. The complexity is increased by changing the shape of the building to better represent the real form.
2. *Variations for orientation, shading and airtightness* do not have the same values at -1 and +1. These parameters are present to induce noise in the experiments.
3. The *thermal mass* modelled for walls at -1 and + 1 levels are the same. However, the roof is modelled with two different thermal masses. This is done to observe possible errors in energy predictions with wrong assumption.
4. *Detailed occupancy* is modelled by creating rooms within the model and assigning three different profiles (see Figure 3) in an alternating manner varying occupancy and equipment load but not lighting. Lights are assumed to be turned on while the building is occupied.
5. *Simple HVAC system* is modelled by means of the Apache systems in IES VE and *detailed HVAC system* is modelled by means of Apache HVAC.
6. *Simple airtightness* is modelled with constant infiltration of 0.25 ACH and *detailed airtightness* is modelled by defining cracks in IES VE's MacroFlo module.

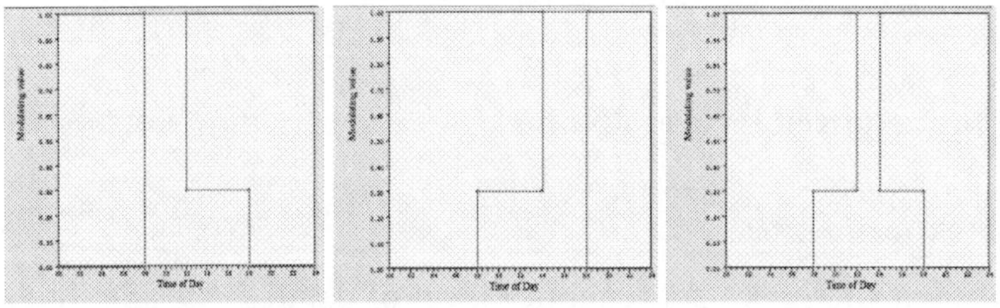

Figure 3: Occupancy and equipment usage profile

Table 1: Variations in BPS model's level of detail

BPS model areas	Value	Variations in BPS model level of detail	
		-1	1
Building form		Square	L-shape

Orientation		0	230
Shading		No shading	External fixed overhang
Window to wall ratio	40%	Single window	Multiple windows
Wall properties	0.32 W/m^2K and light weight	Single layer construction	Layer by layer construction
Roof properties	0.1 W/m^2K	Single layer construction (very light construction)	Layer by layer construction (light construction)
Windows properties	1.14 W/m^2K and 0.36 (g-value)	Single layer	Layer by layer
Airtightness		0.25 ACH	Crack length 7% of openable perimeter and crack flow coefficient of 0.150 l/(s m Pa^0.6)
Lighting	10 W/m^2	On/Off	Daylight sensor
HVAC	Chiller COP – 6.3 Boiler efficiency – 0.81	Peak and seasonal efficiencies	VAV-reheat with EWC chiller and HW boiler
Occupancy		8:00 to 18:00	3 profile for occupancy and equipment. Lighting operated between 8:00 to 18:00

Analysis results

The level of detail within a BPS model, which has the most impact on energy performance predictions are shown in Figure 4. It can be noted that level of detail for occupancy has the highest impact on the predicted building energy. This is followed by HVAC system, building form, lighting, airtightness and so on.

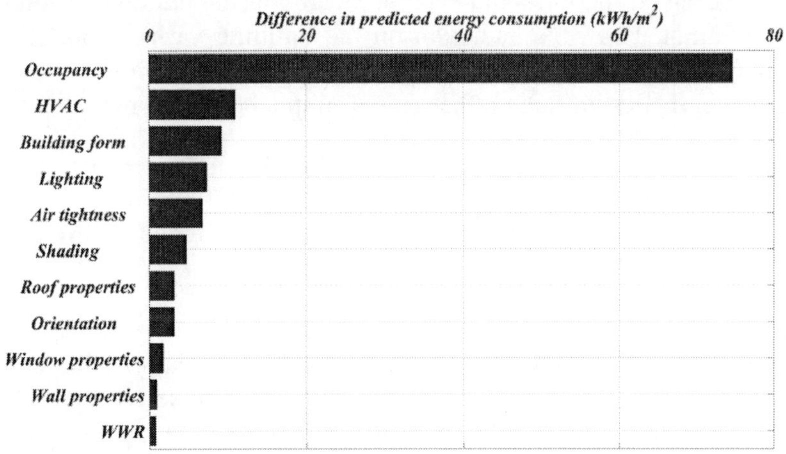

Figure 4 Pareto graph of effects for varying BPS model level of detail

Interpretation and discussion of results

In general, BPS model areas with high main effects require high level of detail. In contrast, low level of detail is sufficient for areas with low main effects.

Occupancy. The results indicates that wrong assumptions or over-simplification in occupancy will result in a high prediction error, which could lead to a wrong energy strategy. Therefore, modelling occupancy as detailed as possible is crucial. Some possibilities for occupant modelling are:

- Acquire occupancy related data from similar building in the region via platforms like CarbonBuzz.
- Use statistical methods to model occupancy and predict energy for various occupancy scenarios as suggested in CIBSE TM54.

HVAC system. Figure 5 shows the HVAC chiller efficiency used to calculate energy consumption with a detailed HVAC model. Colour of the points in Figure 5 shows the chiller COP varying between 4 to 13 under varying chiller load and ambient temperature. This illustrates that modelling only peak and seasonal efficiencies is not sufficient, as lot of data essential for accurate energy prediction is absent in an oversimplified HVAC model.

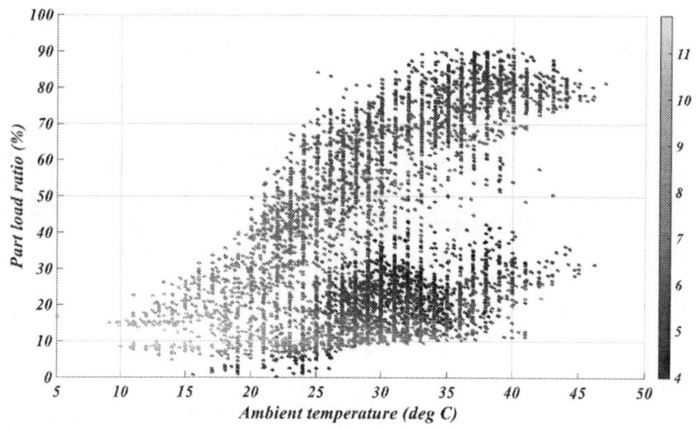

Figure 5: Chiller COP as a function of part load ratio (%) and ambient temperature (deg C)

Building form. Depending on the form and external neighbouring building shading, the solar radiation profile, i.e., amount of solar radiation on the building varies. This in turn has an impact on the buildings energy performance. Therefore, it is crucial to model various building form and urban area at early design stage rather than a simple box building.

Lighting. Lighting system design that uses daylighting dimming sensors requires to be modelled in detail. However, the impact of lighting design's level of detail may not be observed in locations where majority of the days are cloudy. Hence a simplified lighting model would be sufficient for these regions.

Material properties. In the study, roof material properties have more impact on accuracy than wall or window. This is the result of a difference in thermal mass in the roof material's level of detail. Therefore, it is important to capture thermal conductivity and heat storage capacity for wall and roof accurately. Modelling it through a single layer or layer by layer method has less impact on energy predictions. A similar observation is made for window properties. Capturing the solar heat gain value accurately is more important than the method of modelling. However, these methods may play more importance in predictions of other requirements.

Window to wall ratio. Modelling a simple window will be sufficient to predict energy accurately.

4. Simplification by metamodelling

Detailed models are not suitable for early design stage due to high simulation and development time. Furthermore, conventional detailed simulation approaches do not focus on the design parameters that are important in early design phases, e.g., window-to-wall ratio. Metamodels built on simulation results can be very beneficial in this situation. There are two different kinds of the application of metamodels to reduce the simulation time:

(1) to build metamodels for the whole simulation model;
(2) to develop meta-models of building components, which are integrated into other models, in our case the BPS model.

Whereas the first method focuses on the specific case, the second method has the potential to produce more general models. The aim of such general models is the reuse if the conditions match. Besides detailed BPS model, meta-models can also be generated based on measurement data.

Meta-models are models that imitate the behaviour of a physical simulation model or a real object based on measurement data. Figure 6 shows the surface generated through MATLAB's curve fitting tool with thin-plate spline interpolants method for the simulation results of the chiller shown in Figure 5. Thin-plate spline interpolation method fits a smooth surface over the available data-points which also extrapolates in a good manner. However, predicting values in extrapolated regions may be inaccurate. This surface can be used to predict the COP of the chiller for various chiller load and ambient temperature. For different chiller types or design COP, more data have to be generated and a further model needs to be fitted. Inputting these (or similar curves) efficiency into a BPS model to predict energy performance could reduce the prediction gap, when replacing peak and seasonal chiller COP. Figure 7 shows the proposed interaction between BPS and chiller metamodel. The first few simulation steps are called preconditioned simulation, where BPS model provides COP dependent on cooling load and ambient temperature for the metamodel. The resulting metamodel is then used to predict energy consumption during annual simulation. Once stability in this process is achieved, actual simulations begins.

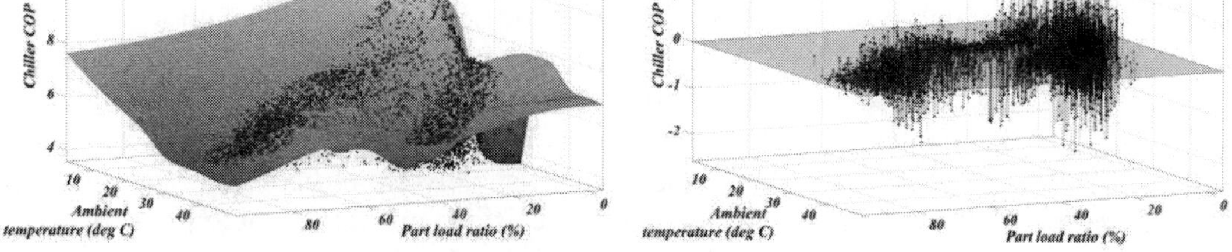

Figure 6: Interpolated surface model (top) and residuals plot (bottom) of chiller COP Vs Ambient temperature and part load ratio

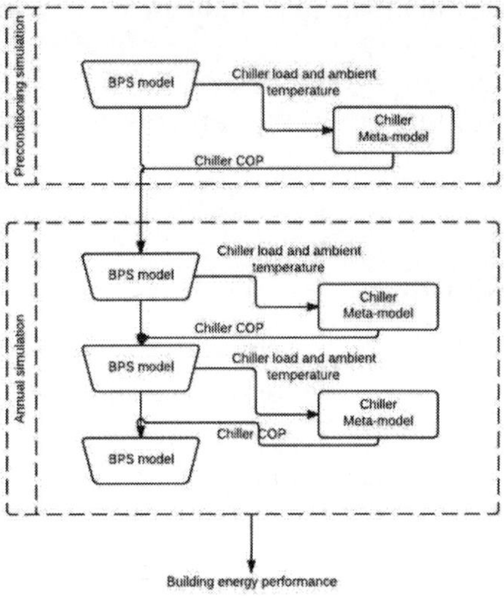

Figure 7 Integrating meta-modelling into BPS for model simplification

The effectiveness of this simplification method has to be researched further. Some possible advantages of this method are:

1. Generalized metamodels deliver the detailed performance of a component without tedious detailed modelling and simulation. However, one has to pay attention that the parameters are within the bounds of the model.
2. Modelling limitations of a BPS can be compensated by metamodels. For example, modelling capabilities of upcoming complex technologies like smart windows, organic solar cells or PCM are limited in most of the whole building simulation tool. Metamodels of these technologies can be integrated into BPS so that they can be evaluated in early design stage. Besides simulation-based metamodels, also empirical data from laboratory can be used.

Next steps in research are the implementation of the metamodel in a dynamic simulation environment and test its accuracy. Metamodels will be developed in such a way that the prediction error is low for new datasets, i.e., datasets different from the reference dataset. High prediction error on new datasets requires changes in the metamodel configuration or more reference data. Decision on modifying the metamodel or gathering more data will be made based on observations in the following graphs (1) prediction error vs dataset size (2) prediction error vs model complexity (Richert and Coelho, 2013).

5. Conclusion and discussion

Developing simple quick-responding BPS models for early design stages with low prediction gap is crucial in our mission to reduce the performance gap and effective development of net-zero energy building. This paper highlights the areas of BPS models, which requires high- and low level of detail. Enabling, early design stage BPS model simplification that caters to the requirements of both architects and engineers. A holistically simplified BPS model creates a common platform, upon which early-stage-design decisions on passive, active and renewable energy systems can be based and respective strategies are developed in synergy.

Integrating metamodel component, which captures all the interactions of a detailed BPS model area, within a simple BPS model could result in a model with low prediction gap. This arrangement also allows evaluation of innovative technologies or complex systems, which are typically difficult to model in simple BPS models. Metamodels that can be applied to a wide range of situation makes it competitive to detailed BPS models for early design stage. While metamodels developed for a specific case make it complementary to BPS.

The quality of inputs within the BPS model plays an import role in reducing the prediction and performance gaps. Quality here represents the closeness of these inputs towards reality or as-built conditions. Predication gap is minimized directly by the presented study. Whereas, performance gap is reduced indirectly: The knowledge about the impact of input parameters by the shown level-of-detail analysis allows to improve the quality of input parameters; the input quality is the main key to reduce the performance gap. Quality inputs could be obtained from databases like CarbonBuzz or by involving various stakeholders like occupants, building system supplier during early design stage for BPS models inputs.

Involving various stakeholders at early design stage results in a shift from a linear design process towards an integrated design process. This shift requires a platform and a structure to communicate information between different stakeholders. We expect future capabilities of BIM to facilitate such communication between design teams and other stakeholders. Increasing BIM capabilities could include integration of tool like life cycle analysis, BPS, etc into the BIM environment. Results from the BPS models can be communicated to various design teams and stakeholders via BIM, which can be used to steer design and information exchange. Information exchange stored within BIM can be used to trace a particular design decision as design progresses or during post-occupancy study.

References

Antony, J. (2003) *Design of Experiments for Engineers and Scientists*, 1st edition, Butterworth-Heinemann.

Beltrami, A., Jones, R.V., Wilde, P.d., Picco, M. and Marengo, M. (2015) 'Towards an integrated decision tool for evaluation of energy performance during building and plant design', Eindhoven.

Bletzinger, K. and Lähr, A. (2006) 'Prediction of interdisciplinary consequences for decisions in AEC design processes', *ITcon 11*, pp. 529-545.

British Standard Institution (2007) *Collaborative production of architectural, engineering and construction information – Code of practice*, 3rd edition, BSI.

Chlela, F., Husaunndee, A., Inard, C. and Riederer, P. (2009) 'A new methodology for the design of low energy buildings', *Energy and Building*, no. 41, pp. 982-990.

Forrester, A.I.J., Sobester, A. and J.Keane, A. (2008) *Engineering Design via Surrogate Modelling : A practical guide*, John Wiley & Sons Ltd.

Gholapa, A.K. and Khanb, J.A. (2007) 'Design and multi-objective optimization of heat exchangers for refrigerators', *Applied Energy*, vol. 84, no. 12, December, pp. 1226–1239.

Hamedani, M.N. and Smith, R.E. (2015) 'Evaluation of performance modelling: optimizing simulation tools to stages of architectural design', *Procedia Engineering*, vol. 118, pp. 774 - 780.

Jaffala, I., Inarda, C. and Ghiausb, C. (2009) 'Fast method to predict building heating demand based on the design of experiments', *Energy and Buildings*, vol. 41, no. 6, June, pp. 669–677.

Jin, R., Chen, W. and Simpson, T. (2001) 'Comparative studies of metamodelling techniques under multiple modelling criteria', *Structural and Multidisciplinary Optimization*, vol. 23, no. 1, December, pp. 1-13.

Kalkman, A. (2012), 25 Apr, [Online], Available: http://www.chri.nl/upload/05 Arie Kalkman.pdf.

Kreinera, H., Passera, A. and Wallbaumb, H. (2015) 'A new systemic approach to improve the sustainability performance of office buildings in the early design stage', *Energy and Buildings*, vol. 109, pp. 385 - 396.

Liu, Y., Huang, Y. and Stouffs, R. (2015) 'Using a data-driven approach to support the design of energy-efficient buildings',.*Journal of Information Technology in Construction (ITcon)*, vol. 20, no. ECPPM 2014, pp. 80-96.

Menezesa, A.C., Cripps, A., Bouchlaghem, D. and Buswell, R. (2012) 'Predicted vs. actual energy performance of non-domestic buildings: Using post-occupancy evaluation data to reduce the performance gap', *Applied energy* , vol. 97, pp. 355-364.

Murphy, E. and Castleton, H. (2015) 'Predicting the actual energy performance of low carbon buildings: a case study approach'.

Negendahl, K. (2015) 'Building performance simulation in the early design stage: An introduction to integrated dynamic models', *Automation in Construction*, vol. 54, pp. 39-53.

Niu, S., Pan, W. and Zhao, Y. (2015) 'A virtual reality supported approach to occupancy engagement in building energy design for closing the energy performance gap', *Procedia Engineering*, vol. 118, pp. 573 - 580.

Piccoa, M., Lollini, R. and Marengo, M. (2014) 'Towards energy performance evaluation in early stage building design: A simplification methodology for commercial building models', *Energy and Buildings*, vol. 76, March, pp. 497-505.

RIBA (2013) *RIBA Plan of work 2013*, [Online], Available: http://www.ribaplanofwork.com/Download.aspx.

Richert, W. and Coelho, L.P. (2013) *Building machine learning systems with Python*, Birmingham : Packt Publishing Ltd.

Simpson, T.W., Lin, D.K.J. and Chen, W. (2001) 'Sampling strategies for computer experiments: design and analysis', *International Journal of Reliability and Applications*, August, pp. 209-240.

Simpson, T.W., Poplinski, J.D., Koch, P.N. and Allen, J.K. (2001) 'Metamodels for Computer-based Engineering Design: Survey and recommendations', *Engineering with Computers*, vol. 17, no. 2, July, pp. 129-150.

Weck, O.L.d., Roos, D. and Magee, C.L. (2011) *Engineering systems : Meeting Human Needs in a Complex Technological World*, Cambridge, Massachusetts: MIT Press.

Multi-agent reinforcement learning for optimizing technology deployment in distributed multi-energy systems

L.A. Bollinger[1,2] and R. Evins[1,2]

[1]Urban Energy Systems Laboratory, Empa, Switzerland
[2]Chair of Building Physics, ETH Zürich, Switzerland

Abstract

Optimal use of distributed renewable sources of energy requires effective and efficient techniques for optimizing technology investment and dispatch in distributed multi-energy systems (DMES). State-of-the-art approaches for optimizing DMES are often formulated as mixed-integer linear programmes, which are limited in terms of their scalability. This paper describes an initial attempt to address DMES optimization using an alternative approach based on multi-agent reinforcement learning. It describes the implementation and results of a multi-agent model implementing two different learning techniques, Q-learning and CACLA. The results indicate that both techniques are able to achieve near-optimal solutions for multi-energy generation dispatch in a DMES without storage. With storage implemented, neither of the multi-agent models reaches a solution close in optimality to that of the equivalent MILP model. Despite this shortcoming, it is concluded that multi-agent reinforcement learning shows promise in addressing specific classes of energy hub problems, especially those dealing with large scales.

1. Introduction

The realization of sustainable urban systems requires optimal use of distributed and renewable sources of energy. By serving as loci for the production, storage and consumption of energy in multiple forms (e.g. electricity, heat, gas), distributed multi-energy systems (DMES) can play an important role in this. Effectively leveraging the flexibility of these systems, however, necessitates intelligent approaches to their design and operation.

Recent work has solidified a set of methods and tools for optimizing technology investment and dispatch in DMES. Such "energy hub" models enable accounting for the techno-economic properties of technologies, network constraints, resource availability and different types of uncertainties (Evins et al., 2014; Mavromatidis et al., 2015; Morvaj et al., 2015). State-of-the-art energy hub models are often formulated as mixed-integer linear programmes (MILP), enabling efficient solution of relatively complex problems. MILP-based energy hub formulations, however, suffer from important drawbacks. Most importantly, they are restricted in terms of the number of integer or binary variables that can be practically included and are difficult to efficiently parallelize. This limits possibilities for optimizing the planning and control of large-scale DMES (e.g. larger than 30–100 buildings). This in turn limits possibilities for effectively comparing the performance of DMES on different scales, and thus fully realizing their benefits.

In fields from transportation to factory scheduling, multi-agent approaches have been shown capable of identifying optimal solutions to difficult, and particularly large-scale, problems (Karageorgos et al., 20013; Kumar et al., 2011). Compared with MILP, multi-agent approaches adopt a distributed approach to optimization, in which computational load is shifted from a central optimizer to a set of "intelligent" agents which collectively arrive at an optimal solution. The intelligence of agents may be manifested in their ability to collectively or individually *learn* over time. This ability may take different computational forms. One common such form is *reinforcement learning*, which has been shown to generate near-optimal solutions on par with conventional operations research approaches (Gabel and Riedmiller, 2007).

This paper represents an initial attempt to address DMES optimization using a multi-agent reinforcement learning approach. The purpose is to evaluate the potential of multi-agent reinforcement learning for energy hub modeling of DMES. We first describe the implementation and results of a multi-agent model of a hypothetical DMES, and then evaluate the efficiency and quality of results obtained and compare them with the results of a MILP-based energy hub formulation for an identical system. We conclude by identifying important advantages and shortcomings of the employed approach, and highlight important directions for future research.

2. The Energy Hub Problem

An *energy hub* is a conceptual model of multi-carrier energy systems used to represent the interactions of multiple energy conversion and storage technologies (Geidl and Andersson, 2007). The energy hub concept serves as a basis for developing models to optimize the operation and design of multi-carrier energy systems at different scales, often with the objective of minimizing total costs or carbon emissions. The energy hub problem refers to the challenge of dimensioning and scheduling the deployment of technologies in a multi-carrier energy system, and determining which technologies should be installed, given known (though possibly uncertain) energy demand and resource availability patterns.

Technologies represented in an energy hub problem include various energy conversion and storage technologies. Energy demand patterns normally represent the (composite) heat and electricity demands of a given set of buildings, and may be pre-calculated using building energy models which account for detailed thermal, electrical and occupancy characteristics of buildings. To calculate a solution, most state-of-the-art energy hub models formulate the energy hub problem as a mixed-integer linear program, which offers an advantageous balance of solution efficiency and accuracy. Other formulations have also been implemented, including bi-level formulations, which link a MILP with a genetic algorithm (Evins, 2015), and nonlinear formulations (Proietto et al., 2014).

The objective of energy hub optimization is normally cost minimization, which generally includes both technology investment and operation costs. Carbon emissions may also be minimized or a multi-objective approach can be applied using the ϵ-constraint method (Brahman et al., 2015). Typical constraints include limitations on the capacity of energy conversion and storage processes, available space (e.g. roof area for solar photovoltaics) and minimum load of energy conversion technologies. Stochastic and robust optimization approaches are sometimes used to account for uncertainties in variables such as energy demand, technology performance and available renewable resources.

3. Multi-agent Reinforcement Learning

Reinforcement learning is a form of machine learning that facilitates the ability of software agents to learn optimal behavior under different conditions. Key concepts in reinforcement learning are *state*, *action*, *reward* and *policy*. The *state* refers to the state of the environment and/or agent at a given point in time. For instance, in the case of an agent navigating a path through a two-dimensional environment, the state might be the physical coordinates of the agent. The *action* refers to the specific action taken by an agent, e.g. the direction and distance of an agent's movement within a given interval of time. The *reward* refers to the feedback signal (often a simple scalar value) given to an agent as a result of a specific action taken within a specific state. The *policy* links the states and actions of an agent, and refers to the action(s) with the estimated highest reward value in any given state. The aim of reinforcement learning is normally to facilitate agents in identifying an optimal policy.

When reinforcement learning is applied in a multi-agent context, each agent acts independently to identify its optimal policy. Under certain conditions, the independently optimized policies of agents may be proven to correspond with the global optimum (Kilic and Arslan, 2002). An important challenge in multi-agent reinforcement learning is the potentially dynamic nature of an agent's environment. In the case of a single agent learning to navigate a defined environment, the relationship between state, action and reward may be entirely deterministic. In the case of multiple agents interacting with (and simultaneously changing) an environment, the relationship between state, action, and reward may change over time, complicating the identification of an optimal policy.

In energy systems research, multi-agent reinforcement learning is most often applied to facilitate the ability of agents to identify optimal policies for bidding in real or hypothetical electricity markets. Existing research in this area has largely focused on two types of problems – *power system control* and *power market design*. Applications of reinforcement learning to power systems control problems range from unit commitment and economic dispatch in large power systems (Raju et al., 2015; Wu et al., 2015) to adaptive control of microgrids including battery storage (Leo et al., 2014; Mao et al., 2015). In many of these cases, emphasis is placed on the identification of optimal control policies considering renewables intermittency. Applications of reinforcement learning to power market design generally focus on identifying the weaknesses of specific market designs (Haring et al., 2012; Yu et al., 2010), or comparing the performance of different market models (Suzuki et al., 2007). In these cases, reinforcement learning enables the representation of realistic market agents that exhibit strategic behavior and effectively exploit market flaws.

4. Learning Techniques

Reinforcement learning may be implemented in many different ways, and a number of techniques have been developed. For the model described in this paper, we implement and test two reinforcement learning techniques, *Q-learning* and *Continuous Actor Critic Learning Automaton (CACLA)*.

In Q-learning, the results of an agent's previous actions are stored in a so-called *state-action table*, with each cell corresponding to the relative value of carrying out a specific action in a specific state. Each time an agent performs an action, the value of the corresponding cell is updated based on the reward received. In selecting an action to perform at a given point in time, the agent uses the table to identify the highest valued action(s) corresponding to the current state. Exploration is enabled insofar as the agent may periodically select a random action instead of the highest valued one.

In mathematical terms, Q-learning involves each agent developing an estimate of an action-value function $Q(s, a)$, where s and a represent the state of the environment and an action taken, respectively. Each time an action is taken, the agent receives a reward and adjusts the function according to the following updating rule:

$$Q_{t+1}(s_t, a_t) = Q_t(s_t, a_t) + \alpha(s_t, a_t) \cdot (R_{t+1} + \gamma \cdot \max_a Q_t(s_{t+1}, a) - Q_t(s_t, a_t)) \quad (1)$$

where: $Q_{t+1}(s_t, a_t)$ is the new Q-value, $Q_t(s_t, a_t)$ is the old Q-value, $\alpha(s_t, a_t)$ is the learning rate, R_{t+1} is the reward, γ is the discount rate, and $\max_a Q_t(s_{t+1}, a)$ is an estimate of the optimal future value.

An important feature of the conventional Q-learning algorithm is that it is applicable only to *finite* Markov decision processes, which implies that the process in question must consist of a finite number of possible states and actions. In cases with continuous state and/or actions spaces (infinite decision processes), two options are available: (1) the state-action space can be artificially partitioned to mimic a finite decision process, or (2) an alternate technique, or a modified form of the Q-learning technique, can be used to accommodate a continuous state-action space. With regard to the latter, a number of alternative techniques can be found in literature. This includes SMC-learning (Lazaric et al., 2008), fuzzy Q-learning (Salehizadeh and Soltaniyan, 2016), wire-fitted neural network Q-learning (in Continuous State and Spaces, 1999) and others.

The Continuous Actor Critic Learning Automaton (CACLA) technique (van Hasselt and Wiering, 2007) is a reinforcement learning technique developed to deal efficiently with continuous state and action spaces. The technique is based on *actor-critic* methods, which entail representing the policy independent of the value function. The CACLA technique builds on the actor-critic structure in a manner that allows for learning in continuous state and action spaces. To enable this, the CACLA technique replaces the tabular representation of the Q-learning technique with parameterized function approximators, which are used to store the value of observed states and extrapolate to as yet unobserved states.

These function approximators are represented in CACLA as neural networks. The knowledge of an agent is thus represented in the form of two neural networks, one representing the policy structure (actor) and one representing the value function (critic). Each time the agent performs an action, the weights of these neural networks are updated to reflect the new information. In selecting an action to perform, the agent passes the current state to the actor neural network, which uses a feed-forward process to identify the estimated optimal action. After each action selection process, the critic "critiques" the policy followed by the actor, which takes the form of a *temporal difference error* (TD-error):

$$\delta_t = r_{t+1} + \gamma V(s_{t+1}) - V(s_t) \quad (2)$$

where: δ_t is the TD-error, r_{t+1} is the reward, γ is the discount rate, and $V(s_t)$ is the outcome of the value function for state s at time t. A positive TD-error suggests to the actor that the tendency for the selected action should be reinforced in the future; a negative TD-error suggests that tendency for the action should be weakened.

5. Description of the model

To explore how multi-agent reinforcement learning may be effectively used to address the energy hub problem, we develop and test a model of a simple, hypothetical DMES. The developed model includes four types of agents – *technology* agents, *building* agents, a *grid* agent and a *market* agent. An overview of the agents and their parameters is provided in Table 1. Technology agents represent different energy conversion and storage technologies with specific techno-economic properties. Building agents represent the demand entities in the DMES, assumed in this case to represent aggregations of buildings with defined demand profiles for heat and electricity. The grid agent represents the external electricity grid to which the DMES is connected, which is assumed to have an infinite supply and demand for electricity. The market agent is responsible for clearing a hypothetical set of linked heat and electricity markets in the DMES. In the initial version of the model described here, two agents of each type are implemented (with the exception of the grid and market agents) in order to ensure a competitive market environment.

Table 1: Overview of the technology agents in the model, their defined parameters and the assigned parameter values.

Agent	**Properties**	**Participates in**
Building	Electricity demand (time series), Heat demand (time series)	Electricity market, Heat market
Heat pump	Capacity (100 kW), COP (3.2), Maintenance cost (0.1 CHF/kWh)	Electricity market, Heat market
Gas boiler	Capacity (100 kW), Efficiency (0.94), Maintenance cost (0.01 CHF/kWh)	Heat market
Combined heat & power (CHP) unit	Capacity (50 kW), Heat-to-power ratio (1.73), Efficiency (0.3), Maintenance cost (0.021 CHF/kWh)	Electricity market, Heat market
Solar PV array	Covered area (200 sq m), Efficiency (0.14), Capacity (0.125 kW/sq m), Maintenance cost (0.06 CHF/kWh)	Electricity market
Solar thermal array	Covered area (200 sq m), Efficiency (0.46), Capacity (0.7 kW/sq m), Maintenance cost (0.12 CHF/kWh)	Heat market
Battery	Storage capacity (100 kWh), Charging efficiency (0.9), Discharging efficiency (0.9), Decay (0.001 / hr), Maximum charging rate (0.1), Maximum discharging rate (0.1), Minimum storage state (0.3)	Electricity market
Hot water tank	Storage capacity (100 kWh), Charging efficiency (0.9), Discharging efficiency (0.9), Decay (0.01 / hr), Maximum charging rate (0.25), Maximum discharging rate (0.25), Minimum storage state (0.0)	Heat market
Grid agent	Electricity price (0.24 CHF/kWh), Feed-in tariff (0.14 CHF/kWh)	Electricity market

An overview of the model structure and interactions is given in Figure 1. Each iteration, agents generate offers and/or requests for electricity and/or heat for each hour within a 24-hour period. These offers and requests are passed to the market agent, which matches buyers and sellers using a pay-as-bid mechanism. After matching buyers and sellers, the market agent passes the market results for each market (heat and electricity) and hour back to technology agents. Based on (1) the amount an agent has been allotted to produce/consume in each hour, (2) the price it has agreed to pay/receive and (3) the agent's variable costs, the agent calculates its profits for the given step. The profit received by an agent in a given step serves as the reward signal for the agent's learning algorithm, and is calculated as follows.

$$X(t) = Q_e(t) \cdot [P_e(t) - C_e(t)] + Q_h(t) \cdot [P_h(t) - C_h(t)] \tag{3}$$

where $X(t)$ is an agent's profit at time t, $Q_e(t)$ and $Q_h(t)$ are the quantity of electricity and heat produced by the agent at time t, $P_e(t)$ and $P_h(t)$ are the offer prices of electricity and heat, and $C_e(t)$ and $C_h(t)$ are the agent's variable costs (per kWh) of heat and electricity production. For purposes of simplicity, fixed costs are currently ignored.

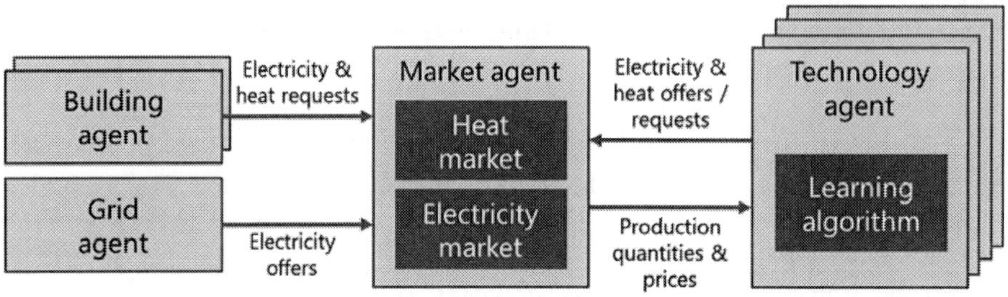

Figure 1: Overview of the model structure and interactions.

We test two different learning algorithms, based on the Q-learning and CACLA techniques. The Q-learning algorithm features an artificial discretization of the state-action space. In selecting an action, the algorithm uses an ϵ-greedy strategy – that is, the agent normally selects the highest valued action in the given state, but ϵ fraction of the time selects a random action to encourage exploration of the state space. The CACLA algorithm features a continuous representation of the state-action space using parameterized function approximators represented as neural networks. To encourage exploration, the action ultimately followed is sampled from a Gaussian distribution with the mean at the action value determined by the actor.

In the case of both of these algorithms, the *state* corresponds to the current hour of day, and varies from 1–24. For the storage technologies (battery and hot water tank), the state variable also includes a second value representing the storage's current state of charge. This facilitates the agent in determining when to offer vs. request energy. For the energy conversion technologies, the *action* corresponds to the prices at which the agent should offer its capacity on the electricity and heat markets. For the storage technologies, the action also includes variables for the quantity to offer and/or request on the electricity and heat markets (for the energy conversion technologies, it is assumed that agents offer their full capacity).

Simulation of the model consists of two distinct periods, an *exploration* period and an *exploitation* period. During the exploration period, the agents' action selection policies include a certain degree of randomness to ensure thorough exploration of the action space. During the exploitation period, the agents always select the highest-valued action, thus exploiting the knowledge they have built up during the exploration period. The length of the exploration period is tailored to the dynamics of the learning process in each case, and is usually of the order of 1,000–2,000 steps. The results shown below constitute the mean heat and electricity production quantities across all steps of the exploitation period.

The degree of optimality of the results of the Q-learning and CACLA implementations of the multi-agent model are determined by comparison with the results of a mixed-integer linear programming (MILP) model representing an identical technical system, which has a guarantee of optimality. The key difference is the manner of solution – where the results of the MILP model are derived from a global optimization (cost minimization), the results of the multi-agent model are determined by the distributed learning processes of the technologies themselves. In each of case, we run the respective models both with and without storage technologies implemented. This allows us to separately gauge the influence of storage on the quality of the results.

The multi-agent model is implemented in Python and makes use of the Mesa agent-based modeling package [1]. The MILP model is implemented in AIMMS and makes use of the CPLEX optimizer. Code for the CACLA algorithm has been adapted from Stahlhut (2014). Code for the developed models can be found online on the Holistic Urban Energy Simulation (HUES) platform[2].

6. Results

Figure 2 shows the heat and electricity dispatch schedules of technologies for each model, for the case in which storage is not implemented. The models give a nearly identical production schedule. The gas boiler is used exclusively to satisfy heat demand, and of a mix of grid electricity and solar PV are used to meet electricity demand – patterns which may be attributed to the lower operational and maintenance costs of these technologies compared with the alternatives. Logically, solar PV production is maximized in the middle of the day when solar insolation is highest. During these hours, some of the excess electricity is exported to the grid.

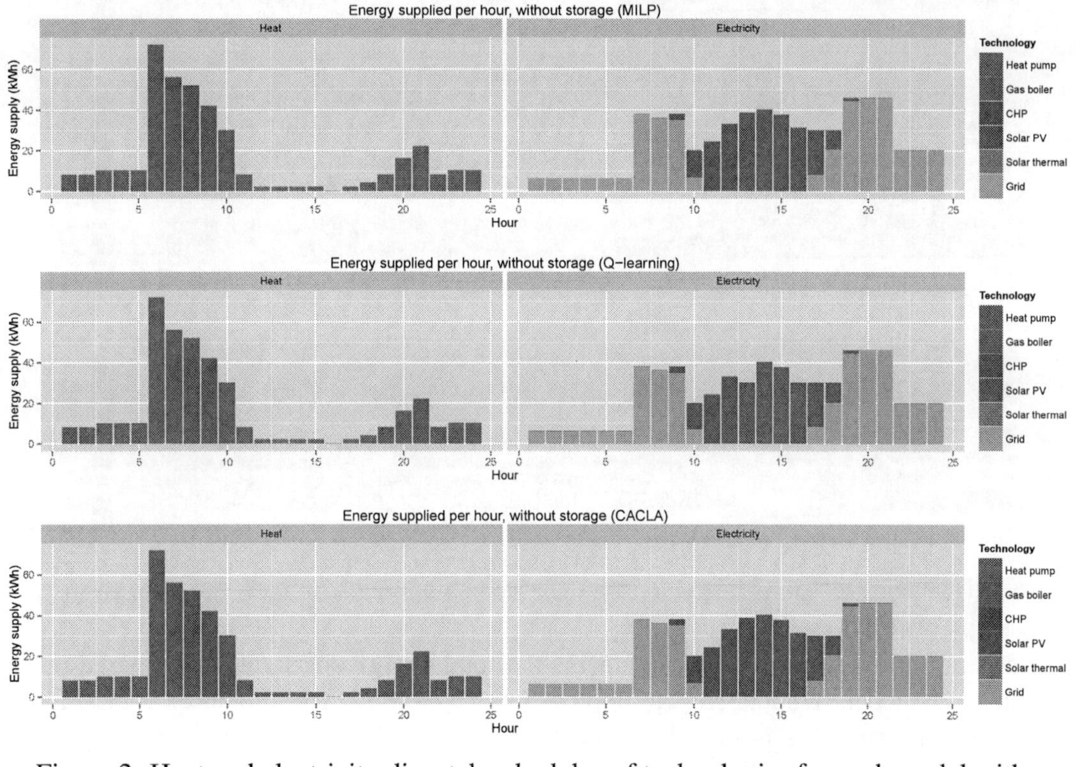

Figure 2: Heat and electricity dispatch schedules of technologies for each model with no storage.

With storage implemented, the dispatch schedule of the three models differs significantly (Figure 3). In the MILP model, the heat and electricity storages are emptied early in the day when solar energy is not available. When the solar PV arrays start producing, their excess production

[1]https://github.com/projectmesa/mesa

[2]https://hues.empa.ch/index.php/Multi-agent_reinforcement_learning-based_energy_hub_model

is used to recharge the battery storage – rather than being exported to the grid – and is subsequently used to meet the buildings' electricity demand later in the day. The storage agents in the multi-agent models prove less strategic in the deployment of their resources. In both of these models, the battery and hot water tank agents produce energy early in the day, as in the MILP model. The battery, however, fails in this case to make use of the excess solar PV production in the middle of the day to recharge itself. In the case of the Q-learning model, the added state and action variables necessary to enable optimal storage scheduling run up against the capabilities of the learning algorithm. In particular, the artificial discretization of the state-action space and the inter-temporal dependencies inherent in storage scheduling challenge the ability of storage agents to successfully optimize their heat and electricity bids. The CACLA algorithm does not suffer from the issue of state-action space discretization, but is unable to deal effectively with the inter-temporal dependencies of storage scheduling.

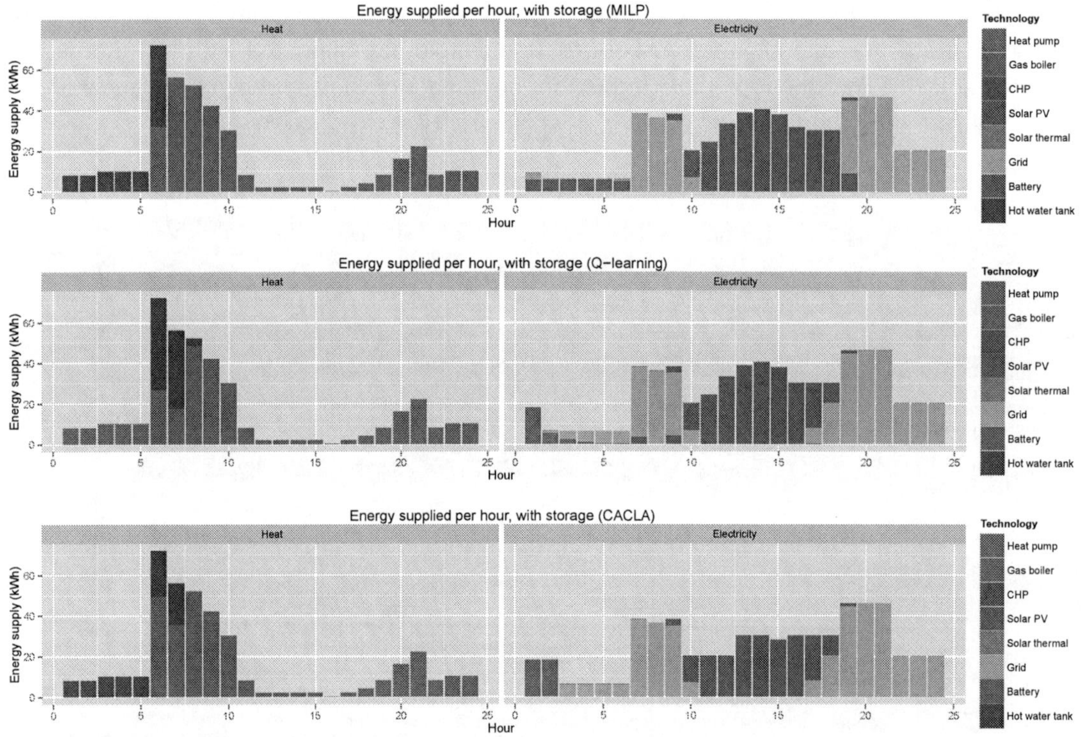

Figure 3: Heat and electricity dispatch schedules of technologies for each model with storage.

Summarizing these results, Table 2 compares the total energy costs calculated based on the results of each model. Without storage implemented, both the Q-learning and CACLA implementations of the multi-agent model generate a technology dispatch schedule with total costs very close to that of the MILP model. Due to the added precision offered by a continuous state-action space, the CACLA model is able to achieve a slightly lower total cost, identical to that of the MILP model. With storage implemented, neither of the multi-agent models is able to achieve a dispatch schedule comparable to that of the MILP model.

In terms of solution efficiency, the MILP model far outperforms its multi-agent counterparts. The MILP model arrives at a solution in 0.01 seconds. The multi-agent models, in their current crude implementation, arrive at a solution from within a few seconds to several minutes, depending on the settings of the learning algorithm and the inclusion of storage.

Table 2: Comparison of the total energy costs based on the results of each model.

Model	Total cost (CHF)	
	no storage	*with storage*
MILP	140.79	114.56
Q-Learning	141.59	124.13
CACLA	140.79	128.91

7. Discussion

This paper has described the approach of multi-agent reinforcement learning and the implementation and results of a multi-agent model dealing with a hypothetical DMES. The application of multi-agent reinforcement learning to energy hub modeling of DMES presents several key challenges, including: (1) simultaneous consideration of multiple energy carriers and the interactions between them, (2) consideration of energy storage and thus inter-temporal trade-offs, and (3) optimization of asset investments.

Via the implementation of technology agents that place linked bids in electricity and heat markets markets and the development of a market agent that sequential clears these markets, the developed model demonstrates an effective approach for addressing the first of these challenges. Additionally, via the implementation of storage agents with the ability to request and offer energy in a manner accounting for real-time state-of-charge and temporal dynamics, we have attempted to address the second of these challenges. However, the results suggest that the implemented learning algorithms are unable to effectively deal with the inter-temporal trade-offs of storage scheduling.

We have not attempted to deal with the third of the aforementioned challenges in the developed model. However, several options are available for accomplishing this via extensions to the current formulation. One possibility is to use a modified version of the bi-level approach implemented by Evins (2015) for MILP models. This would entail exposing the technology agents in the model to an evolutionary algorithm that encourages the replication of successful technologies and the deletion of unsuccessful technologies – with success defined in terms of the financial performance of agents over time.

The initial results presented in this paper suggest that the performance of the multi-agent reinforcement learning approach lags with respect to MILP in terms of both the quality and efficiency of solution. With respect to improving the quality of solution, further refinement of the CACLA technique shows promise. Without implementation of storage, the CACLA model was shown to identify a solution equal in optimality to that of the MILP model. Further testing of the approach suggests that this result is generalizable to other technical system configurations, with certain limitations[3]. Further tuning of the CACLA model's neural network parameters may also enable the identification of an equally optimal solution for the case with storage.

With respect to the efficiency of solution, it is unlikely that a multi-agent reinforcement modeling approach can compete with MILP for solving conventional energy hub problems dealing with small-scale DMES. However, the distributed nature of solution and the adaptive nature of the agent-based approach suggest that the multi-agent approach may be comparatively better suited for specific classes of energy hub problems. This includes, for instance, problems dealing with larger-scale DMES and systems featuring technologies with demand response capabilities. Given the foreseen key role of demand response technologies in future DMES and the reality

[3]One important limitation of the model in its current form is the necessity to have multiple agents of each type in order to ensure a competitive market environment. When this is not the case, optimality cannot be guaranteed.

that DMES may span systems greater than 100 buildings, these types of problems are highly relevant. Furthermore, the most computationally expensive element of a multi-agent reinforcement learning approach is the training of agents. However, once these agents have been trained, they are, in theory, suited for deployment in a range of DMES.

A possible route moving forward, and for applying this approach to real-world engineering problems, is thus to develop a repository of pre-trained agents which could be efficiently deployed to solve a range of energy hub problems. This set of agents could be used to calculate optimal dispatch schedules for real-world DMES or as a basis for optimizing the technological configuration and dimensioning of technologies in DMES. This would necessitate the systematic development of suitable training sets and systematic testing to determine the window of validity – the range of problem types for which (near-)optimal solutions can be expected. As with the case described in this paper, validity can be established via testing on problems with known solutions, established via MILP or other methods. A prerequisite to this is the development of storage agents capable of effectively dealing with the inter-temporal trade-offs of storage scheduling, an important (but likely not insurmountable) shortcoming of the developed models in their current form.

8. Conclusions

This paper has evaluated the potential of multi-agent reinforcement learning for energy hub modeling of distributed multi-energy systems (DMES). The results indicate that both of the tested techniques are able to achieve near-optimal solutions for multi-energy generation dispatch in a DMES without storage. With storage implemented, neither of the multi-agent models reaches a solution close in optimality to that of the equivalent MILP model. Despite certain shortcomings in terms of solution quality and efficiency with respect to MILP, it is expected that a multi-agent based implementation of the CACLA technique may offer advantages in situations characterized by large-scale DMES and systems featuring demand response.

9. Acknowledgements

This research has been financially supported by CTI within SCCER FEEB&D (CTI.2014.0119).

References

F. Brahman, M. Honarmand, and S. Jadid. Optimal electrical and thermal energy management of a residential energy hub, integrating demand response and energy storage system. *Energy and Buildings*, 90:60–75, 2015.

R. Evins. Multi-level optimization of building design, energy system sizing and operation. *Energy*, 2015. doi: 10.1016/j.energy.2015.07.007.

R. Evins, K. Orehounig, V. Dorer, and J. Carmeliet. New formulations of the 'energy hub' model to address operational constraints. *Energy*, 73:387–398, 2014.

T. Gabel and M. Riedmiller. On a successful application of multi-agent reinforcement learning to operations research benchmarks. In *IEEE International Symposium on Approximate Dynamic Programming and Reinforcement Learning*, 2007.

M. Geidl and G. Andersson. Optimal power flow of multiple energy carriers. *IEEE Transactions on Power Systems*, 22:145–155, 2007.

T. Haring, G. Andersson, and J. Lygeros. Evaluating market designs in power systems with high wind penetration. In *9th International Conference on the European Energy Market*, 2012.

Q.-L. in Continuous State and A. Spaces. Chris gaskett and david wettergreen and alex zelinsky. In *Proceedings of the 12th Australian Joint Conference on Artificial Intelligence*, 1999.

A. Karageorgos, N. Mehandijev, G. Weichhart, and A. Haemmerle. Agent-based optimisation of logistics and production planning. *Engineering Applications of Artificial Intelligence*, 16 (4):335–348, June 20013.

A. Kilic and A. Arslan. *Advances in Information Systems*, chapter Minimax Fuzzy Q-Learning in Cooperative Multi-agent Systems, pages 264–272. Springer, 2002.

R. Kumar, D. Sharma, and A. Sadu. A hybrid multi-agent based particle swarm optimization algorithm for economic power dispatch. *International Journal of Electrical Power and Energy Systems*, 33(1):115–123, January 2011.

A. Lazaric, M. Restelli, and A. Bonarini. *Advances in Neural Information Processing Systems*, volume 20, chapter Reinforcement learning in continuous action spaces through sequential monte carlo methods, pages 833–840. MIT Press, Cambridge, 2008.

R. Leo, R. Milton, and A. Kaviya. Multi agent reinforcement learning based distributed optimization of solar microgrid. 2014.

M. Mao, P. Jin, N. Hatziargyriou, and H. Xu. Q-learning algorithm based multi-agent coordinated control method for microgrids. In *9th International Conference on Power Electronics and ECCE Asia*, 2015.

G. Mavromatidis, K. Orehounig, and J. Carmeliet. Climate change impact on the design of urban energy systems. In *CISBAT*, Lausanne, Switzerland, 2015.

B. Morvaj, R. Evins, and J. Carmeliet. Bi-level optimisation of distributed energy systems incorporating non-linear powerflow constraints. In *CISBAT*, Lausanne, Switzerland, 2015.

R. Proietto, D. Arnone, M. Bertoncini, A. Rossi, D. L. Cascia, R. Miceli, E. Sanseverio, and G. Zizzo. Mixed heuristic-non linear optimization of energy management for hydrogen storage-based multi carrier hubs. In *IEEE International Energy Conference*, 2014.

L. Raju, R. Milton, S. Suresh, and S. Sankar. Reinforcement learning in adaptive control of power system generation. *Procedia Computer Science*, 46:202–209, 2015.

M. R. Salehizadeh and S. Soltaniyan. Application of fuzzy q-learning for electricity market modeling by considering renewable power penetration. *Renewable and Sustainable Energy Reviews*, 56:1172–1181, April 2016.

C. Stahlhut. Learning to reach with interactive reinforcement learning. Master's thesis, Universitaet Hamburg, 2014.

S. Suzuki, H. Kita, E. Tanaka, and J. Hasegawa. Evaluation of costs for procuring reserve capacity under deregulated power system using multi-agent model. *IEEJ Transactions on Power and Energy*, 127(3):459–466, 2007.

H. van Hasselt and M. Wiering. Reinforcement learning in continuous action spaces. In *IEEE International Symposium on Approximate Dynamic Programming and Reinforcement Learning*, pages 272 – 279, Honolulu, 2007.

Z. Wu, L. Zhao, W. Jia, C. Wu, and L. Wu. Multi-objective power dispatch based on q-learning algorithm considering reliability of icpr. *Journal of Computational Information Systems*, 11 (13):4665–4672, 2015.

N. Yu, C. Liu, and J. Price. Evaluation of market rules using a multi-agent system method. *IEEE Transactions on Power Systems*, 25(1):470–479, 2010.

Semantic Enrichment and Multimodel Data Exchange Approach for CFD Analysis of Bridges

A. Ismail, Y. Srewil , R. Scherer
Institute of Construction Informatics, TU Dresden, Germany
T. Mansperger
Leonhardt Andrä und Partner VBI AG, Germany
ali.ismail@tu-dresden.de

Abstract. This paper presents an approach and prototype implementation for semantic enrichment and classification method using a reference database for classification and standard property sets for typical elements of BIM models. The research aims to improve the semantic quality of BIM models and link specific domain information from various domains with focus on bridge models based on the IFC standards. The concept and the web-based annotation tool "BIM-Annotator" as prototype implementation is presented. This paper presents also the use of Multimodel approach for linking data among different domains to exchange and analyze the information in a standard way. Recent infrastructure and bridge information modelling efforts and developments are reviewed.

1. Introduction

The research work presented in this paper is a part of the Eurostar project E!7987 BridgeCloud: "Model-Based Aeroelastic Analysis of Long-Span Bridges on the HPC Cloud", which aims to revolutionize bridge design by developing a methodology and producing a corresponding software product for obtaining wind pressure distributions in space and time resulting from fluid – structure interaction, automatically incorporating them into the structural design process. The final product of this project will provide a "virtual and significantly improved wind tunnel laboratory" on the cloud that will enhance the design phase, which will be integrated seamlessly via Building Information Model (BIM) technology in the model based design process, essentially shifting the experimental phase (virtual wind tunnel tests) towards the early stages of the whole design procedure, thus facilitating testing and comparison of alternative bridge typologies, and optimizing bridge design in all design stages.

The availability of good quality and rich semantic BIM models is an important criteria to get the ultimate potential of using these models for different data exchange scenarios during the construction life cycle. The semantic enrichment improves the interoperability between BIM models for different domains like structural analysis and Computational Fluid Dynamic (CFD) software. However, at moment the IFC standard, which is the most common natural vendor-independent format to exchange BIM models, doesn't cover special domains like CFD analysis and has a limited support for infrastructures constructions like roads, bridges and tunnels. The basic idea is to introduce an external tool that allows improving semantic enrichment; classification and data exchange for IFC models based on the current supported IFC version (IFC2X3) taking into account the results of recent developments of IFC4, which include new classes for alignment of infrastructure and the under-development IFC-Bridge extension. This approach aims to enable an open information capture, exchange, sharing, filtering, comparison and storage of BIM models.

2. BIM for infrastructures and bridges

The adoption of BIM methods for infrastructure projects has increased in the last few years; however there are still a lot of challenges to establish it in the practice to the same level of maturity for vertical construction (90% usage in 2014 according to McGraw-Hill construction), here horizontal construction generally refers to road, tunnel and bridge design while vertical construction refers to design of buildings. One of the big challenges is the interoperability issues during data exchange between various software platforms, project functions, and users. In the domain of bridge construction many national and international efforts addressed this problem. One of these efforts is the development of special bridge extension IFC-Bridge (Yabuki and Li (2006), Lebegue, et al. (2012) and Amann, et al. (2015)) to be a part of IFC standards. However, this extension has never been integrated in the official releases of the IFC schema. One of the main reasons was missing broad international commitment and funds, required for acceptance as part of an international standard and the missing of basic data structure of horizontal and infrastructure projects like the horizontal and vertical alignment definitions. The recent development and the release of "IFC alignment" extension as a buildingSMART final standard will support the further development of IFC-Bridge and other extensions.

The ongoing MINnD project "Interoperable Information Model for Sustainable Infrastructures" (http://www.minnd.fr/en/) is committed by the French Ministry of Transport to develop the "P5 IFC bridge" project as an international project. The recent publications of this project refers to the practice problems of using the current IFC schema for bridge modelling through proxy elements and the lack of standard property sets and semantic definition of bridge elements.

In December 2015, the German ministry of traffic and digital Infrastructure published a graduated scheme for digital design and construction (Bramann and May, 2015) which demands digital data models of all new constructions in a neutral data format from the year of 2020. For this neutral data format IFC is proposed. Up to now, no commercial software offers classes of IFC-bridge and although developing activities are going on, it is doubted that satisfying semantic classes and property sets for IFC-Bridge will be available at that time or IFC interfaces of commercial software are fully developed respectively. Hence it is necessary to have a proper tool to improve the semantics of IFC bridge models.

Another recent development is the Bridge Information Modeling (BrIM) project run by the Federal Highway Administration (FHWA) in USA. It introduced a parametric XML-based digital data exchange protocol and tools to facilitate the data exchange of bridge control information and roadway geometry (OpenBrIM, 2016).

Several research works addressed the semantic data enrichment. Lee and KIM (2011) introduced an IFC data schema expansion plan targeting integrated road bridge and tunnel, in which they focused on the enrichment of spatial elements. Ji et al. (2013) proposed an interchanging parametric bridge models as extension to the IFC-Bridge format to deal with its limitation.

In BridgeCloud project the data exchange between BIM design models and CFD tools is the main interest. For fluid dynamic analysis of wind loads on long span bridges a CFD model should be prepared for each model variation during the primary design phase, however the interoperability between BIM and CFD tools is not solved yet. Extending the IFC standard with special classes and property sets in order to carry most needed information to generate the CFD models based on IFC models is possible. However, this process takes long time and needs huge effort of domain experts and enough funding to be done.

In our research we are targeting this problem in a practical way by providing annotation and classification tool for IFC or any 3D models "BIM Annotator", applying a Multimodel data exchange method and developing a set of services, which facilitate the semi-automatic generation of CFD models.

3. Semantic Enrichment of Bridge Models

The review of available design and analysis software on the market shows that bridge designers can use various tools in order to model and analysis bridge models. For bridge design software (e.g. Bentley LEAP Bridge, CSI Bridge Modeler, SOFiSTiK, InfoCAD, Autodesk Revit with bridge extension, Midas Civil) the 3D bridge model is generated quickly through bridge templates, geometrical parameter wizards and component libraries, other general design software like Tekla Structure and Allplan are used also for bridge modelling. It is common practice to define bridge models using proxy elements using names to cope missing classes. These good-looking bridge models however have a very bad semantic information quality and lose most of the design parameters when they are exported as IFC models (in case if the tool has an IFC export interface) and are not exchangeable among different tools using the native formats. The concept of 3D models annotation and a Multimodel data exchange method aim to fill this gap. BIM Annotator is not meant to be a modelling tool for bridges but as an annotation and online collaboration tool in order to improve the semantic quality of bridge models.

The semantic enrichment with BIM Annotator is based on a reference database for classification and standard attributes of typical bridge elements. The IFC-Bridge extension provides the core of semantic description of bridge components and the relationships between them. The additional semantic data model which is provided by the user is stored separately and linked with the corresponding elements of the original IFC model through a special link model. The identification of model elements is based on the unique global ID (GUID) of each element inside the original IFC model or a unique ID if the 3D model has another format. BIM-Annotator allows exporting the original 3D models, semantic models and the link models based on the Multimodel data exchange approach. This approach was developed in the German research project Mefisto (www.mefisto-bau.de 2009-2012) and under further development and dissemination since 2013 by a workgroup of the German chapter of buildingSMART (http://www.buildingsmart.de/kos/WNetz?art=Project.show&id=143).

In order to have a rich semantic model every element in the model should directly describe a specific component. It should be assigned to a specific class and described with a set of properties and relations with other elements. The necessary effort to complete the semantic enrichment depends on the data exchange requirements and the amount of information which have to be assigned to single element or agroup of elements. The result will be a virtual 3D bridge model which consists of components such as piers, beams and abutments and hence partial views and specific information can be extracted through filtering and semantic reasoning.

To ensure a consistent annotation process, a classification of bridge system is needed. This classification facilitates annotation task by equipping bridge components with a correct and compatible description. Also it provides users an accessible and searchable database. The classification method depends on the definition and enumerations available in IFC bridge extension and standards like ASTM standard (Fig.1). According to this classification, each element has a specific function and independently can be used among various bridge system types (e.g. highway, railroad, and pedestrian bridges). Furthermore, it helps users to understand the purpose and application of the different elements and allows creating user-defined properties those are not covered yet by IFC standard.

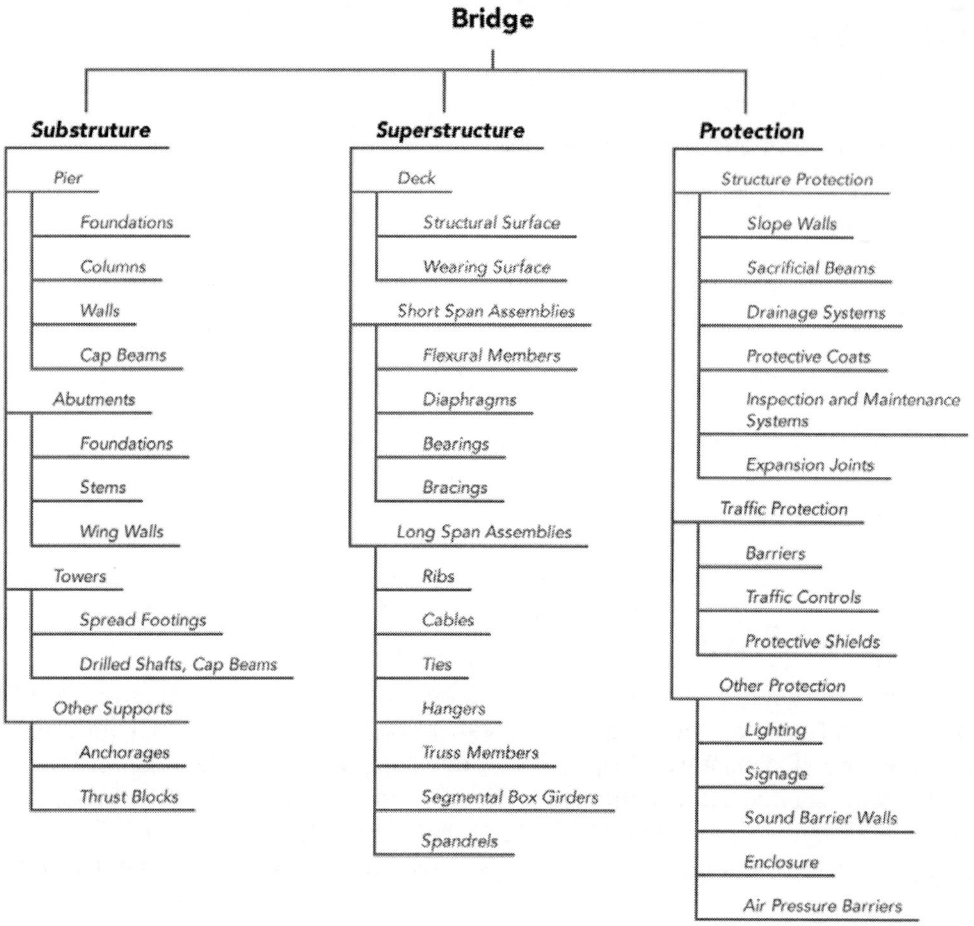

Figure 1: Hierarchical classification of a bridge system according to ASTM standard (2013)

4. Prototype Implementation and annotation workflow

The IFC model annotation and classification tool BIM-Annotator has been implemented as a 3D online viewer with WebGL technology. It offers special functionalities for annotation and Multimodel export interface. It uses the threejs.org java script library for client side rendering and PHP scripting language on the server side. The current implementation allows the user to assign classes of elements, edit, delete and add new property sets, define and organize group of objects hierarchically and assign attributes to them.

The BIM-Annotator uses a reference database which includes a list of components classes and templates for property sets. All IFC classes including extra bridge classes of the IFC-Bridge extension and standard property sets of IFC model have been integrated into the reference database. The structure of this database is based on the XSD schema of Property Set Definition (PSD) of buildingSMART (Fig.2) in order to simplify the process of importing standard property sets and exporting user-defined and non-standard domain specific property sets. The reference database can be managed and extended easily through a simple online GUI. The user can define new domain specific property sets and non-standard classes. All new defined property sets will be available as ready-to-use templates according to the element class of selected object inside the viewer.

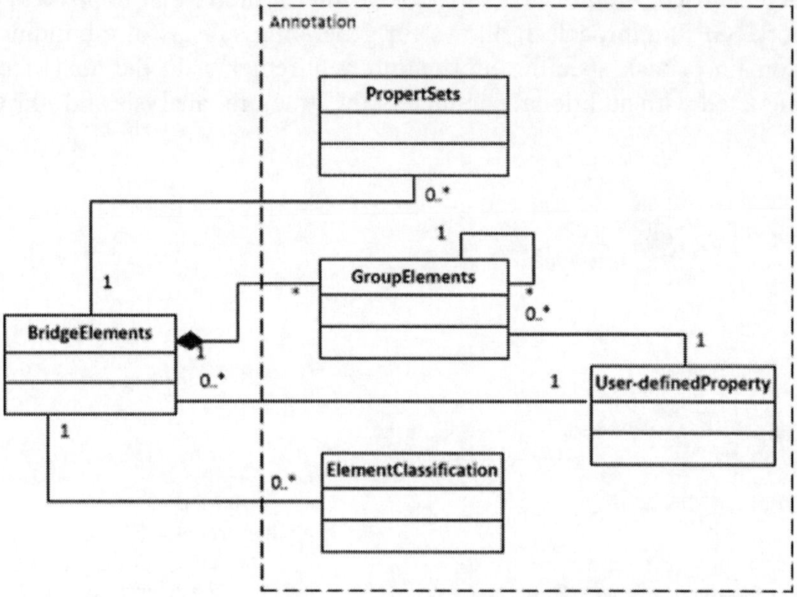

Figure 2: Annotation class model

The workflow of model annotation through BIM-Annotator (Fig.3):

a. Prepare the 3D model
   1. Convert an IFC/3D model into COLLADA format using IfcOpenShell geometry converter. Each object will have the same unique ID of the IFC model(GUID)
   2. Extract all property sets of elements using IFC2DB script based on the IFC server IFCWebServer.org and store them in a separate database.

b. Interactive model annotation through BIM-Annotator GUI
   1. Select one or more elements and set the class name (e.g. IfcBridgeSegmentPart)
   2. Edit the values of existing property sets and add new property sets using their templates. The changes on the original data will be tracked with a timestamp and the identity of the user.
   3. Create new groups/sub-groups of elements and assign them new class and property sets the same as for single elements

c. Data Exchange and filtering
   1. Export a Multimodal container which includes: the original IFC model, 3D COLLADA model, semantic model in XML format and a link model. The Multimodel export interface will export only the new entered or updated data.
   2. Apply hybrid filter criteria based on the original IFC data and the new semantic data to retrieve partial IFC and Multimodels. The user can for example retrieve an IFC model which includes only the load-bearing elements for structural analysis or only related elements for CFD analysis

The BIM-Annotator was applied successfully within the Eurostar project SE-LAB: Structural Engineering Lab: Cloud/Grid-Based Virtual Laboratory for Non-Linear Probabilistic Structural Analysis (www.selab.eu) in order to extend the IFC structural design models with additional parameters for probabilistic and non-linear analysis and special parameters for ATENA software in order to support the mapping of IFC models to ATENA models. A set of predefined filters on the original IFC models has been applied during the geometry conversion in order to exclude the elements which are not related or has a negligible effect on the structural analysis like doors, windows, non-bearing walls. For this purpose the BIMFit toolbox (BIMfit, 2012) has been used which is a JAVA-based filter toolbox that implements the Generic Filter Framework (GFF) approach. It allows for generating subsets of a building model that fulfill certain domain or task specific information requirements. In the next step the filtered models were annotated with additional parameters for structural analysis and FEM mesh generation.

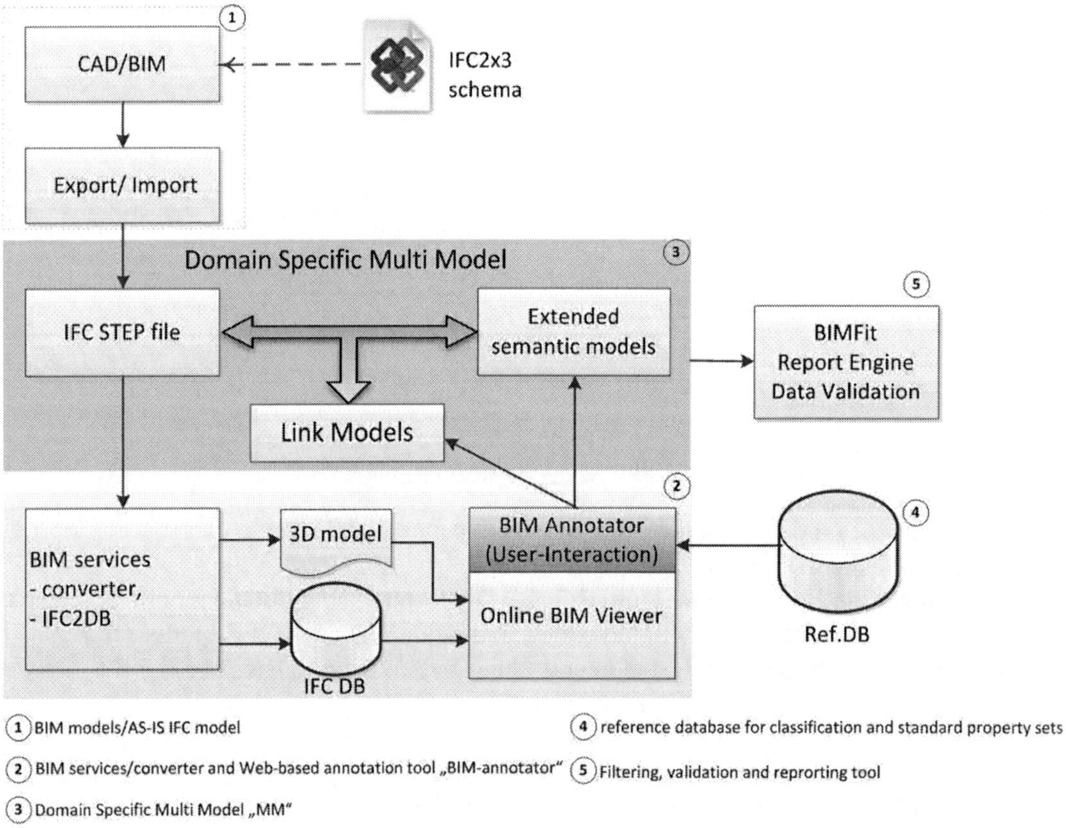

Figure 3: The data flow and system architecture

5. Data Exchange Scenarios and Test Cases for CFD Analysis of Bridges

For supporting the data exchange between BIM and CFD models within the BridgeCloud project the reference database has been extended with special classes and properties of bridge elements (Fig. 4). The following BIM services have been implemented:

- IFC to database converter based on the www.ifcwebserver.org
- IFC geometry converter based on the www.ifcopenshell.org
- 2D profile extractor for arbitrary and parameterized profiles
- IFC filter based on BIMFit toolbox

The first scenario of data exchange is carried out for simplified 2D aerodynamic simulation study of the bridge's parameterized cross section model. In this case the 2D geometry of bridge cross sections was extracted directly from IFC models. For this scenario a direct transformation of cross-section geometry parameters (shape and dimensions, vertices, polylines) into the equivalent entities of the CFD model input file in the target software can be done.

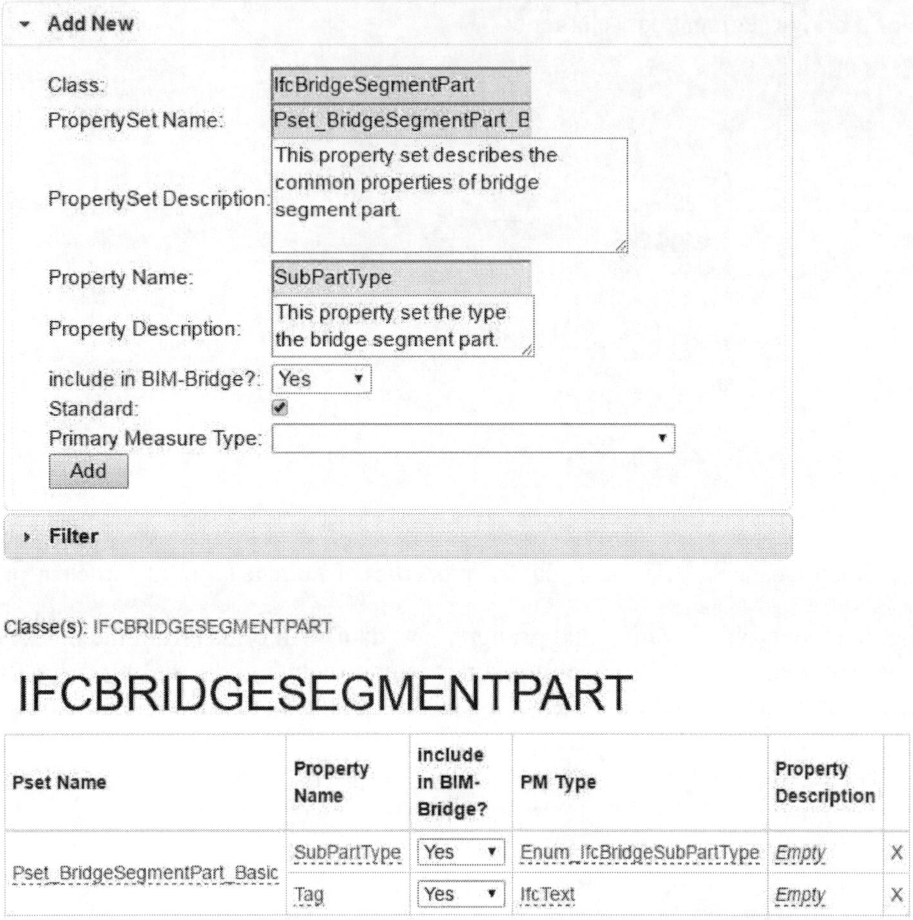

Figure 4: Extend the reference database with special bridge classes and properties

The second scenario of data exchange is carried out for a full 3D CFD analysis of the wind-bridge interaction analysis including the surrounding terrain topology. The bridge model, of this scenario was provided by the company “DENCO Development and Engineering Consultants S.A” (http://www.denco.gr). It concerns a real study that was carried out in the past.

The bridge model was provided as 3D DWG file (AutoCAD format) and not as BIM/IFC model. The BIM-Annotator was used in this scenario in order to demonstrate the possibility of annotating any 3D geometry model with poor semantic model (e.g. converted from CAD models or generated through laser scanning technology) and avoid recreating it again as a BIM model.

At first the bridge model was converted from DWG to WaveFront model file using the ABViewer (http://cadsofttools.com/products/abviewer), then it was imported to the open source modelling tool Blender (www.blender.org) for manual editing and geometry optimization (e.g. convert triangles to quads, assign colors, rename objects) and finally exported as COLLADA model to be ready for BIM-Annotator. After the annotation of the bridge model and adding special property sets for CFD analysis it was possible to extract partial models and support the mesh generation in the required level of details in the CFD model.

Figure 5 shows the process of assigning new class and use of the new added property set template of a bridge segment part element.

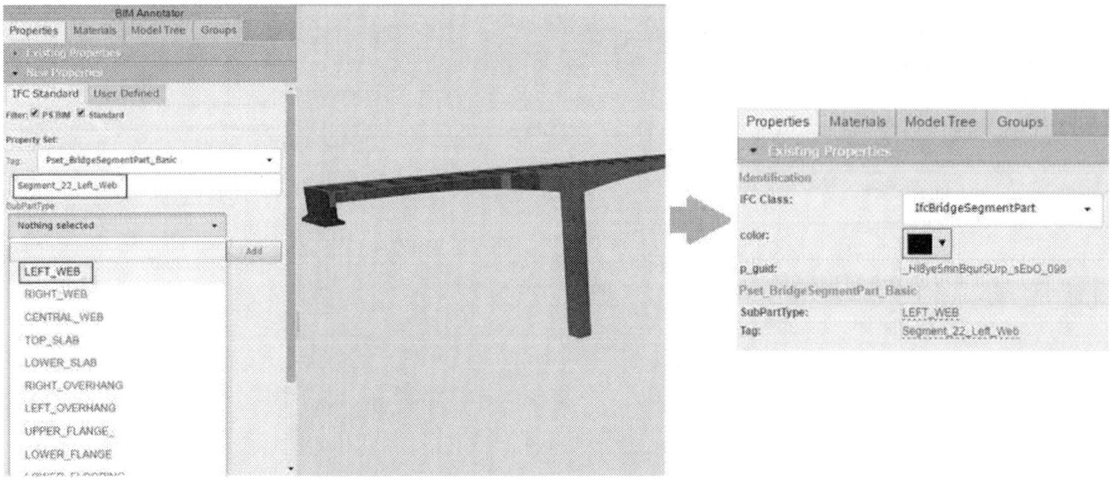

Figure 5: Change the class and add new properties of a bridge segment part element

The semantic model (classification and property sets data) will be saved in the model database and can be exported as a Multimodel container which includes the IFC model, COLLADA model, semantic model and a link model (Fig.6).

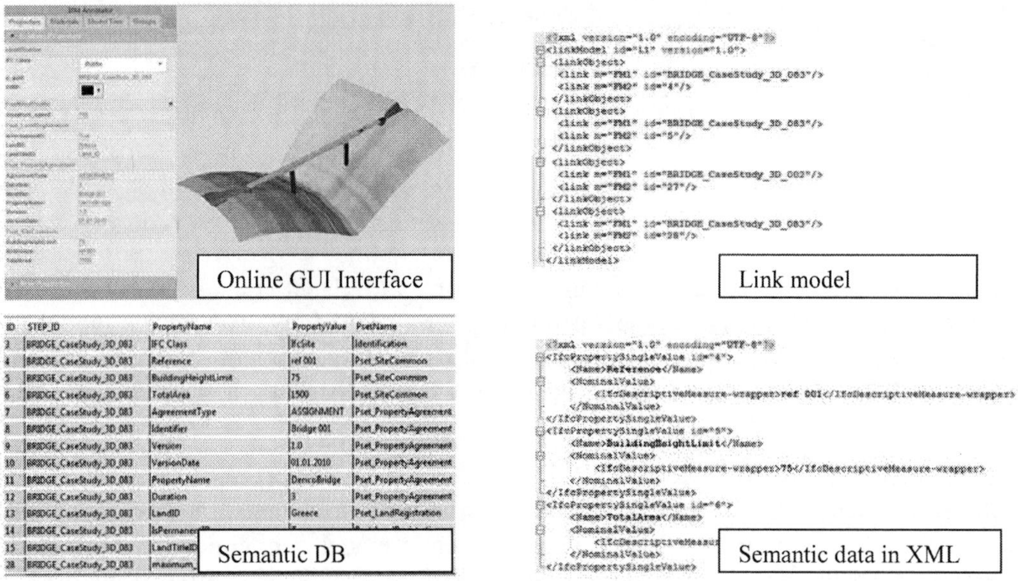

Figure 6: Export semantic and link models as a part of Multimodel Container

6. Conclusion and future work

This paper presented a concept and a prototype implementation tool for collaborative semantic enrichment and annotation of BIM models and the concept of linking data from different models through Multimodel approach for information exchanging in a standard way.

It presented also two data exchange scenarios between BIM and CFD models. The roadmap for further development of BIM-Annotator includes: adding basic geometry functions to allow the user to define and visualize the boundary conditions of the CFD model, quality control against specific data exchange requirement based on the mvdXML standard, improve the integration with BIMFit toolbox for advanced filtering and geometry filters on low level (e.g. faces of Brep), interactive filtering by selecting objects per mouse, re-export and convert the user-defined and updated properties back to the original IFC model, allow user to link non-BIM data like documents and photos to model elements.

Acknowledgements

The work presented in this paper was enabled by the financial support of the European Commission in the Eurostars research projects SE-LAB (E!7521) and BridgeCloud (E!7987). This support is gratefully acknowledged.

References

Yabuki, N. and Li, Z. (2006) "Development of new IFC-BRIDGE data model and a concrete bridge design system using multi-agents." in: CORCHADO, E., YIN, H., BOTTI, V. & FYFE, C. (eds.) Intelligent Data Engineering and Automated Learning - Ideal 2006, Springer-Verlag Berlin, pp. 1259-1266.

Lebegue, E., Fiês, B. and Gual, J., (2012). IFC-Bridge V3 Data Model – IFC 4, Edition R1
S.-H. Lee, B.-G. Kim, (2011) "IFC Extension for Road Structures and Digital Modeling", Procedia Engineering, Volume 14, Pages 1037-1042, ISSN 1877-7058

Amann, J.; Singer, D.; Borrmann, A. (2015) "Extension of the upcoming IFC alignment standard with cross sections for road design"In: Proc. of the ICCBEI 2015, Tokyo, Japan.

Bramann, H. and May, I (2015) "Graduated Scheme for Digital Design and Construction", Bundesministerium für Verkehr und digitale Infrastruktur, Berlin 2015, http://www.bmvi.de/SharedDocs/DE/Publikationen/DG/stufenplan-digitales-bauen.pdf?__blob=publicationFile

OpenBrIM, founded by FHWA, <http://openbrim.org/> (February 2016)

S.-H. Lee, B.-G. Kim, IFC Extension for Road Structures and Digital Modeling, Procedia Engineering, Volume 14, 2011, Pages 1037-1042, ISSN 1877-7058

Ji, Y., Borrmann, A., Beetz, J., and Obergrießer, M. (2013). "Exchange of Parametric Bridge Models Using a Neutral Data Format." J. Comput. Civ. Eng., 10.1061/(ASCE)CP.1943-5487.0000286, 593-606.

ASTM Standard E2103/E2103M - 13, (2013) "Standard Classification for Bridge Elements—UNIFORMAT II" ASTM International, DOI:10.1520/E2103_E2103M-13

BIMfit (2012) "BIMfit – BIM Filtering Toolbox" [online], Institute of Construction Informatics, TU Dresden, http://tu-dresden.de/die_tu_dresden/fakultaeten/fakultaet_bauingenieurwesen/cib/forschung/cib_software

Data driven method of pedestrian flow estimation for evacuation scenario using queuing model

Porzycki J.[1], Hrabák P.[3], Bukáček M.[2], Wąs J.[1], Lubaś R.[1]
[1] AGH University of Science and Technology, Poland, [2] Czech Technical University in Prague, Czech Republic,
[3] Brno University of Technology, Czech Republic
porzycki@agh.edu.pl

Abstract. In this paper the authors introduce an efficient tool for estimating pedestrian flow during an evacuation scenario. Estimations derived from this tool can be used to forestall possible threats like clogging in front of exits or congestion with a high density of pedestrians. A graph that represents the entire building is created – each room or group of rooms can be represented by a single node. Actual outflow from external nodes (leaves) is measured using depth map sensors. The flow then propagates through each node of the graph according to a queuing model. The proposed method is expandable, i.e. other flow sensors (e.g. CCTV underneath cameras or mobiles) can be used. The flow's propagation can also be estimated using other methods – e.g. crowd dynamics simulation. However, the authors believe that the described solution is the best choice for efficient estimation of pedestrian flow for indoor evacuation scenarios.

1. Introduction

The most popular application of crowd dynamics simulations is off-line testing of different scenarios in existing or developed buildings. However, in recent years an increasing interest in on-line, data-driven crowd simulations can be observed. In this approach, real data about passing pedestrians and their transport parameters (e.g. speed) are used in order to obtain short-term predictions of crowd movements. Such a solution can be used to increase pedestrian safety and comfort, in both buildings and outdoor areas. On the other hand, such an approach requires a compromise between reliability and efficiency.

In this article we introduce a reasonably simple estimation tool, based on the queuing model, which enables prediction of the outflow from a facility consisting of a network of rooms where the initial flow through the external nodes (leaves) is known. Initial flow can be measured by different sensors, however for indoor evacuation scenarios we suggest using depth map sensors. An original experiment shows that the tool is able to predict the outflow and evacuation time sufficiently.

The article is organized as follows: Section 2 reviews related works, whilst Section 3 refers to quantitative aspects of pedestrian flow. Sample experimental data are discussed in Section 4, along with the proposed methodology of cumulative flow estimation. The conducted experiments are described in Section 5, while Section 6 concludes the paper.

2. Related works

Crowd dynamics has been the subject of intensive research in recent years. Observations, experiments, and simulations are performed by scientists and practitioners. It should be stressed that various methodological approaches are used to simulate building evacuation, e.g., social-force models, Cellular Automata models, lattice-gas models, fluid-dynamic models, agent-based models, game theory models, approaches based on experiments with animals, and so-called hand calculation models (Zheng 2009). It is very popular to combine different approaches in a single model, for instance in the application of hybrid spatial discretization (Chooramun et al. 2012) or transition zones (Biedermann et al. 2014).

Regardless of the methodology applied, the key point is to obtain reliable outcomes from simulations. We believe that application of the data-driven paradigm (Johansson (2009), Brostow and Cipolla (2006) or Porzycki et al. (2015)), where real data serve as direct inputs into the simulation, makes it possible to create reliable patterns of pedestrian dynamics for specific geometries and situations.

On the other hand, a number of papers describe the application of graph representation to crowd dynamics simulation. Kneidl et al. (2012) introduce a navigation graph layer, which is used as a base for strategic level decisions – the selection of consecutive points of interest. Strug and Ślusarczyk (2014) propose a method for searching for accessible evacuation routes via analysis of the building graph representation.

Such results and patterns of crowd dynamics simulations, including different scenarios and populations, appear to be an important stage in the entire process of architectural design of buildings and other public facilities. An interesting example of a holistic approach to semantic building design was presented recently in (Schultz 2015).

3. Measuring pedestrian flow

In order to properly estimate pedestrian flow across an entire area, the technique proposed in this paper requires the inflow of pedestrians as input data. Since we model the area as a directed graph, we describe the pedestrian inflow stream as a flow from *leaves* (nodes without any predecessors).

Pedestrian detection and flow calculation is achieved by using depth maps sensors (e.g. Microsoft Kinect) mounted perpendicular to the ground. In this approach, pedestrians' heads are represented as local minima on a depth map. By detecting those local minima over time, one can calculate the in- or out- flow of pedestrians passing underneath the sensor.

Local minima on the depth map (Fig. 1C), can be easily detected with the usage of AND operation between the original depth image (Fig. 1A) and an eroded image (Fig. 1B). One should note that the size of structural element determines the size of the area in which local minima are detected (too small structural elements can lead to false detections – e.g. shoulders, too big can omit a short person next to a tall one). However, due to slight swinging from side to side during movement, as well as other factors, like hats, different hairstyles or just limited accuracy and noise from the sensor, the highest points on the head do not always correspond with the its center. In order to calculate the center of the head, we use *gradient fill* – starting from detected local minima in a depth map, consecutive pixels are denoted as head if the gradient between this pixel and its neighbors recognized as head pixels is smaller than a given threshold. Then, the mass center of the obtained figure is calculated (Fig. 1D). Detailed description of this method of pedestrian detection and tracing is described in Porzycki et al (2015).

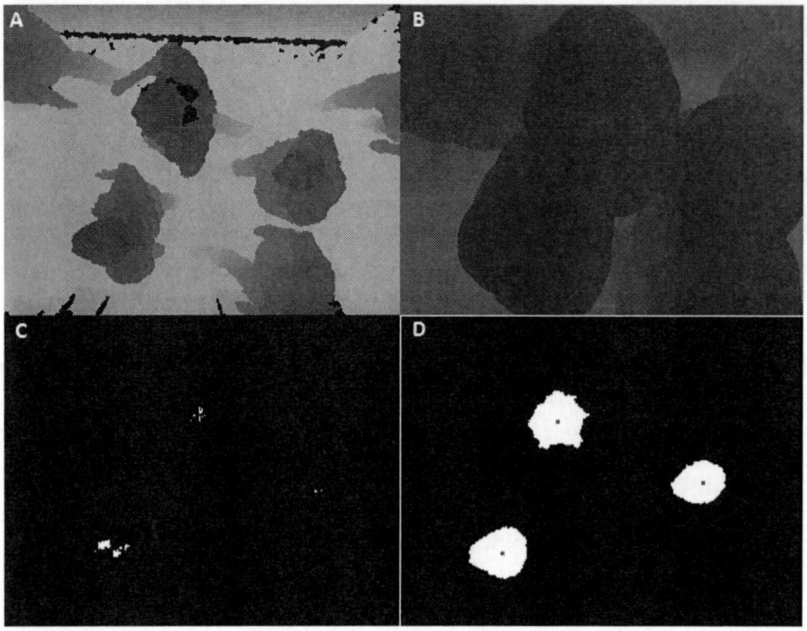

Figure 1: Consecutive steps of pedestrian detection. A – raw depth map from sensor mounted in the ceiling, B – map eroded with circular structural element with diameter roughly equal to half of average shoulder width, C – local depth map minima, D – mask of heads determined with gradient fill algorithm, with its mass center marked.

Of course, there are many different methods of detecting passing pedestrians. The most convenient way, in terms of usage of existing infrastructure, is the analysis of images from CCTV cameras. Johansson (2009) proposed a method based on head detection as circular objects by Hough transform, and then classification using Artificial Neural Network. Another method is clustering coherent motion vectors. This was described by Brostow and Cipolla (2006). There is also a group of methods that are based on the detection of tokens (typically mobile phones) carried by pedestrians. Schauer et al. (2014) propose a system that calculates flow based on numbers of devices with Wi-Fi and Bluetooth turned on. On the other hand, Nishimura et al. (2014) describes a method that estimates density on the basis of participatory sensing of movement speed and ambient sound by mobile phones. Smartphones are also used in a solution proposed by Li and Becerik-Gerber (2012), in which pedestrian location in a building is estimated using an ad-hoc established Wi-Fi network.

It is important to remember that each method has its own limitation and drawbacks. In the case of camera image analysis, obtained images can differ significantly according to camera quality and its setup. Moreover, in these kind of methods, one can usually observe a significant drop in accuracy while the density of crowd increases. Methods based on tokens provide only estimated information about flow, since the pedestrian has to carry a specific token (e.g. a mobile phone with Bluetooth turned on) in order to be detected. The main drawback of methods based on depth map analysis is its vulnerability to distortions from sunlight (for sensors that use structural infrared). Therefore, these methods can be applied only to indoor locations.

The method of pedestrian flow estimation proposed in the following sections can be used for different scenarios. However, this paper focuses on indoor, evacuation scenarios, and thus we decided that the most suitable pedestrian detection method is one based on depth sensors.

Here we note that the whole experiment has been recorded by cameras. These recordings serve to verification of the inflow/outflow estimation in the internal nodes, which are not covered by the depth maps sensors. The camera recordings have been processed manually in order to avoid automatic recognition errors.

4. Previous experiments

The queuing model for estimating pedestrian flow is based on experimental observations from Seyfried et al (2009) and Bukáček et al (2014). According to the study in Seyfried et al (2009), the capacity of a bottleneck (i.e. the maximal flow through it) depends linearly on the bottleneck width b as $J^{\text{out}}_{\text{max}} = 1.9 \cdot b$.

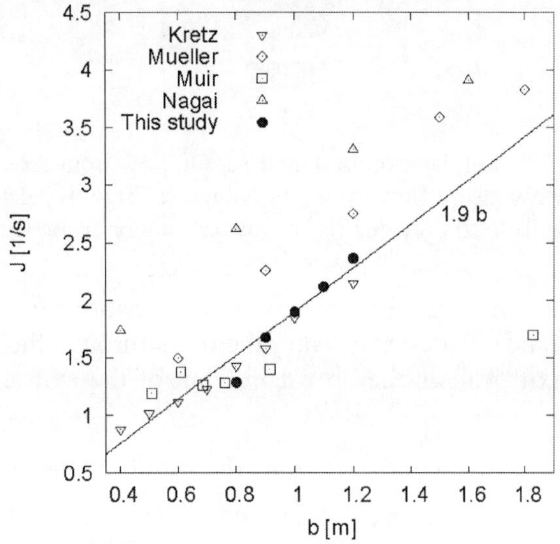

Figure 2: Plot of measurement from various experiments together with the estimated linear dependency. Source: Seyfried et al (2009).

This dependency is depicted in Fig. 2. This assumption is used in the estimation tool. However, it is important to mention that the dependency is valid for long time average flow under constant conditions. Other experiments, e.g. Bukáček et al (2014) or Bukáček et al (2015), show that the capacity of the exit changes according to other conditions. The outflow is mainly influenced by the number of pedestrians in front of the bottleneck, henceforth referred to as the occupancy and denoted by N. The flow through the bottleneck is then dependent on the occupancy as $J^{\text{out}} = J^{\text{out}}(N)$. Auxiliary influence of other conditions, like the dependence on the gradient of the occupancy, is neglected in this study.

5. Estimation of cumulative flow

The basic idea of the estimation is the application of the above mentioned stationary flow studies in order to predict nonstationary flow through a tree shaped, directed network of rooms (the choice between multiple exits is not considered). This is based on knowledge of the actual flow $J^{\text{out}}_j(t)$ in the *leaves* (external nodes) of the network. The flow is measured by a set of Kinects, as indicated in Fig. 3.

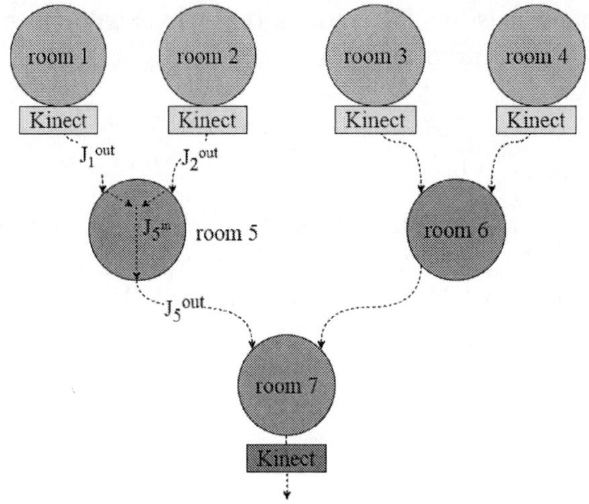

Figure 3: Schematic description of the proposed method. Outflow from external nodes – leaves (green) is measured using sensors, while outflow from internal nodes (blue) is calculated using the queueing model. Finally, one can easily verify the quality of flow estimation using Kinect mounted over the exit from whole area (red).

Each node of the tree is equipped with one exit and at least one entrance (except the *leaves*, which only emit pedestrians). Pedestrians enter the room through the entrances, walk through the room towards the exit, wait in the crowd in front of the exit, and then leave the room through the one exit.

In the following, let E_j stand for the exit from the room j and let $\mathrm{dist}(\cdot,\cdot)$ be the spatial distance between two points of the room using the optimal path. Each entrance to the room j is then characterized by the optimal walking distance $d_j = \mathrm{dist}(E_j, E_{\mathrm{parent(j)}})$ and optimal travel-time $TT_j = d_j / \overline{v}_j$ refers to the time between the entrance of the pedestrian and his/her approach to the cluster in front of $E_{\mathrm{parent(j)}}$. Here, $\overline{v}_j$ is the average velocity of pedestrians along the optimal path, i.e. $\overline{v} = 1.4$ m/s = 5 km/h if parent(*j*) is a room (interaction between pedestrians can be neglected) and $\overline{v} = J(\varrho)/\varrho$ if parent(*j*) is a corridor. Here ϱ [peds/m^2] is corridor density and $J(\varrho)$ [peds/s] refers to fundamental-diagram flow.

Let $J_j^{\mathrm{out}}(t)$ refer to the actual outflow through the exit E_j (number of pedestrians walking through E_j within 1 s) and $J_j^{\mathrm{in}}(t)$ to the cumulative inflow towards the cluster in front of the exit E_j (number of pedestrians joining the cluster within 1 s). The task is the following: *Based on knowledge of the measured outflow from the leaves, we aim to estimate the cumulative inflow to the next exit and further estimate the outflow from the exit. This is to be repeated until the outflow from the root is estimated.*

Let us focus on the estimation of the outflow $J_j^{\mathrm{out}}(t)$ given that the outflow from the previous attached rooms is known. Firstly, the inflow to the crowd in front of the exit is estimated as

$$\hat{J}_j^{\mathrm{in}}(t) = \sum_{\mathrm{children}(j)} J_{\mathrm{child}}^{\mathrm{out}}(t - TT_{\mathrm{child}}).$$

The number of the pedestrians in the crowd $N_j(t)$ is then estimated as

$$N_j(t) = N_j(t-1) + \left(\hat{J}_j^{\mathrm{in}}(t-1) - \hat{J}_j^{\mathrm{out}}(t-1)\right),$$

where $\hat{J}_j^{\text{out}}(t-1)$ is the estimated outflow from the previous step. The actual outflow is then given by

$$\hat{J}_j^{\text{out}}(t) = J^{\text{out}}\left(N_j(t)\right),$$

where J^{out} reflects the dependence of the outflow on the number of pedestrians in front of the exit. It is a monotonically increasing function

$$J^{\text{out}}(n) = n \text{ for } n \le J_{\max}^{\text{out}} \text{ and } J^{\text{out}}(n) = J_{\max}^{\text{out}} \text{ otherwise.}$$

6. Conducted experiment

The estimation tool was applied to data from an experiment organized at the Czech Technical University in Prague with the help of 54 volunteer students. The experiment layout corresponds to the presented concept of merging pedestrians flow in a network of consecutive rooms. Fig. 4 presents snapshots from the experiment.

Figure 4: Snapshots from the experiment conducted at the Czech Technical University in Prague. After a lecture 54 students were asked to leave the room as fast as possible. Two staircases lead to a gathering area in front of two exits leading to a common vestibule with one main exit. The experiment was recorded by multiple cameras. Each participant was equipped with a recognition hat to enable automatic extraction of data.

The volunteers were gathered on four staircases in the lecture hall. Two staircases (corresponding to rooms 1 and 2 from Fig. 3) lead to the gathering area in front of the left exit (room 5). Similarly, two other staircases (rooms 3 and 4) lead to the right gathering area (room 6). Both exits from the lecture hall open into a common vestibule. From the vestibule there is only one exit leading out.

The experiment was repeated three times with differently controlled inflow, i.e., outflow from rooms 1 to 4. The whole area was monitored by cameras in order to enable comparison of the experimental data with the estimation of marginal flows $J_j^{\text{out}}(t)$, $j \in \{5,6,7\}$ and the number of pedestrians in the room $N(t)$. Here we note that the Kinect measurement is related only to the leaves flow (1, 2, 3, 4) and the cumulative flow out of the premises ($j = 7$).

Pedestrian flow is then extracted from the records using the method of time headways. For two consecutive passes $t_1 < t_2$ of pedestrians through a given exit we define the actual flow function $J(s) = 1/(t_2 - t_1)$ for $s \in (t_1, t_2]$. The flow $J_j^{\text{out}}(t)$ measured in discretized time scale (elementary unit is 1 s) is then defined as

$$J_j^{\text{out}}(t) = \int_{t-1}^{t} J(s)\mathrm{d}s .$$

7. Implementation of the estimation tool

The appropriate values used for the estimation tool are given in Table 1. The layout is free of corridors, the travel-time TT_j is therefore considered as the walking time in a free room without any interactions. Here the reader can observe that the values of the maximal outflow are slightly higher than would be given by the relation $J = 1.9 \cdot b$. These values have been chosen to match the measured maximal flow, which was higher. There is an explanation for this: The width of the door is given as the narrowest place of the exit door, which is followed by a significant widening, which makes a difference to the motion within a corridor-like bottleneck..

Table 1: Values for the estimation tool

Room *j*	**1**	**2**	**3**	**4**	**5**	**6**	**7**
TT_j [s]	2	1	1	2	3	2	-
$J_{j,\max}^{\text{out}}$ [ped/s]	-	-	-	-	1.4	1.4	1.45
width [cm]	-	-	-	-	70	70	75
Parent	5	5	6	6	7	7	-
Children	-	-	-	-	{1, 2}	{3, 4}	{5, 6}

Comparison of the measured data and estimated data is given in Fig. 5. One can observe that the estimated flows are very close to the measured values. The most significant difference can be observed in exit 6.

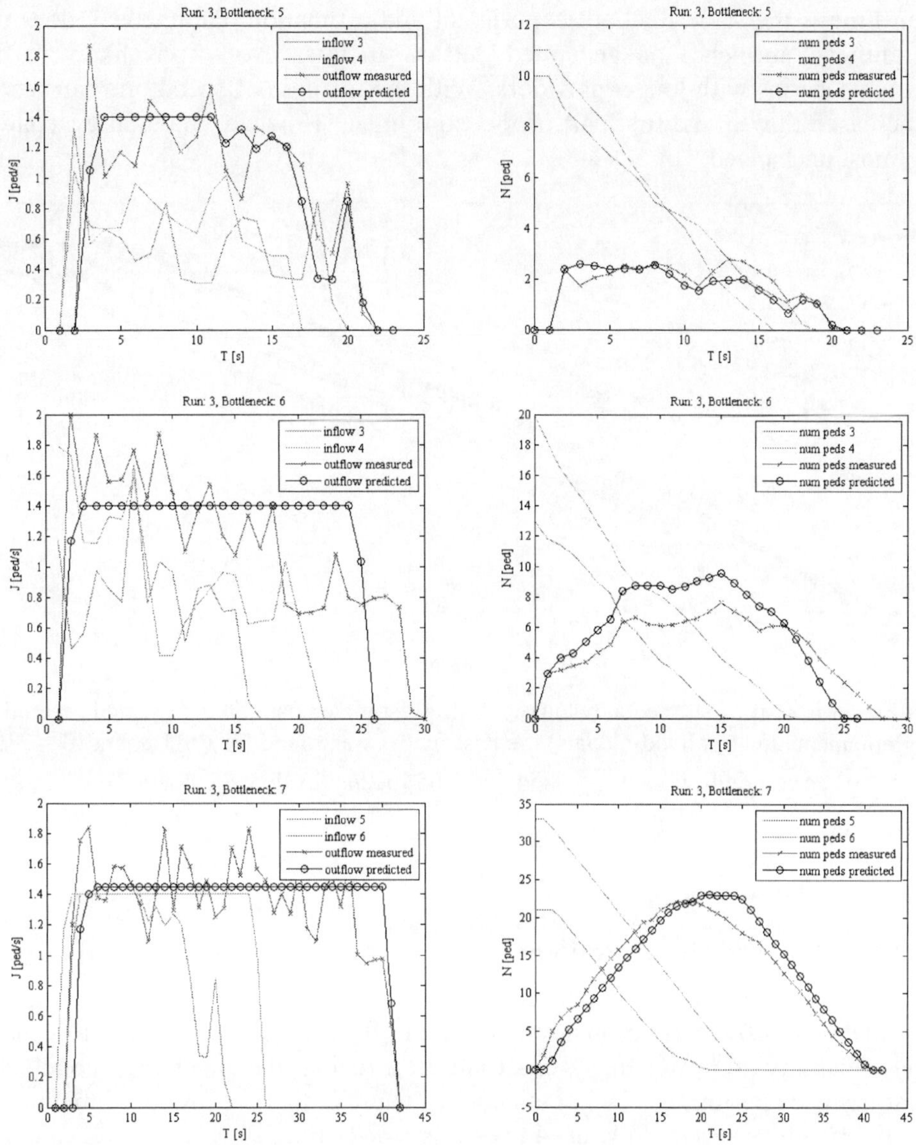

Figure 5: Comparison of measured and estimated outflow from rooms 5, 6, and 7. Left of the outflow plots are the corresponding plots of number of pedestrians in the whole room. Blue and green are the auxiliary values of children outflow and occupancy.

In the other implementation we consider the pedestrian as an individual – i.e. a given node releases another pedestrian when the sum of fractional parts of output exceeds 1. We discover that with such an approach and the time step that we use (1 s), it becomes important to allow immediate transfer to another room while a pedestrian approaches the doors. Without this condition, additional waiting time is added and whole evacuation process is delayed. It can be observed in Fig. 6 as the shift between the pink and dark blue plot.

We also analyze the influence of the slope C in the linear dependence $J_{\max}^{\text{out}} = C \cdot b$ of the maximal flow on the door width and the free-flow velocity v on cumulated outflow. We started from $v = 1.33$ and $C = 1.9$, that are standard values. Each estimation was compared with experimental data (thick, blue line). We observed that in this case C is the crucial parameter that is responsible for the *"slope"* of the plot. Flow generated with parameter C equal to 1.9, 2.0, 2.1, and 2.2 respectively is plotted in Fig.6. With the increase of C (in the presented range) the plot gets closer to experimental results. Finally for $C = 2.2$ total evacuation time is the same for both experiment and estimation. Parameter v does not have such a significant influence on generated outflow in this case – it is likely to be more important in scenarios with longer corridors. With the increase of speed one can recreate the slightly increased flow in the first part of the experiment. However the total evacuation time remains almost unchanged.

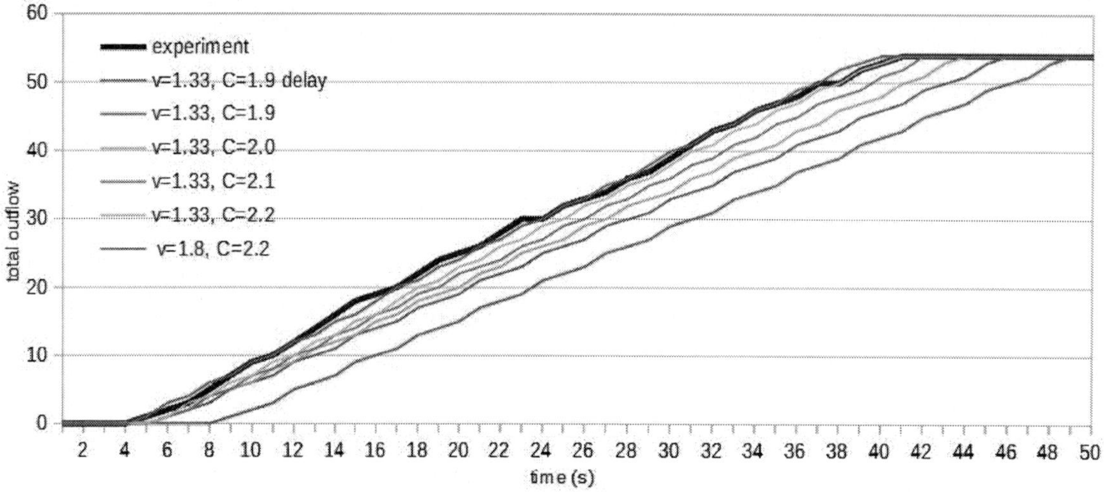

Figure 5: Comparison of experimental results with flow estimated using the presented method. In case of this implementation (with individuals) the best fitness was found for v = 1.8, and C = 2.2 (that corresponds with $J^{out}_{j,\max}$ 1.54 and 1.65 [ped/s] for doors 5, 6 and 7).

8. Conclusion and possible applications

In order to bypass the high computational complexity of pedestrian dynamics models we propose a method of efficiently estimating pedestrian flow in indoor evacuation scenarios. To assess the reliability of estimating pedestrian flow using the queueing model a simple experiment has been performed. The obtained results prove that the proposed method, despite of its simplicity, can be successfully used to estimate pedestrian flow.

The presented method of flow estimation, combined with reliable sensors, can be used to create valuable and useful tools. The application of a data-driven paradigm requires efficient and reliable tools in order to fully utilize the possibilities presented by this approach – the presented flow estimation method fulfills these requirements.

In this paper we focus on indoor evacuation scenarios. However, we believe that the presented approach can be easily extended to outdoor scenarios (by using different kinds of sensors), as well as to more complicated geometries and scenarios (by using a directed or undirected graph instead of a tree).

Acknowledgements

This work was supported by the Czech Science Foundation grant GA15-15049S and by the Czech Technical University grant SGS15/214/OHK4/3T/14.

This work was also supported by AGH University of Science and Technology, contract No. 11.11.120.859.

References

Seyfried A., Passon O., Steffen B., Boltes M., Rupprecht T., Klingsch W. (2009) New insights into pedestrian flow through bottlenecks. Transportation Science 43 (3) 2009, 395-406.

Bukáček, M., Hrabák, P., Krbálek, M., (2014) Experimental study of phase transition in pedestrian flow. In Pedestrian and Evacuation Dynamics 2014, Transportation Research Procedia, vol. 2, pp. 105-113. Elsevier Science B.V.

Bukáček M., Hrabák P. , Krbálek M. (2015) Experimental analysis of two-dimensional pedestrian flow in front of the bottleneck, in: M. Chraibi, M. Boltes, A. Schadschneider, A. Seyfried (Eds.), Traffc and Granular Flow '13, Springer International Publishing, pp. 93-101.

Johansson, A. (2009) Data-driven modeling of pedestrian crowds., Faculty of Traffic Sciences. Technische Universitäat Dresden, Dresden, Germany 2009.

Porzycki J., Lubaś R., Mycek M., Wąs J (2015) Dynamic data-driven simulation of pedestrian movement with automatic validation. In. Traffic and granular flow '13, pp. 129–136. Springer

Brostow, G. J., Cipolla, R. (2006) Unsupervised bayesian detection of independent motion in crowds. Computer Vision and Pattern Recognition, IEEE Computer Society Conference on. Vol. 1. IEEE, 2006.

Schauer L., Werner M. Marcus P., Estimating Crowd Densities and Pedestrian Flows Using Wi-fi and Bluetooth, Proceedings of the 11th International Conference on Mobile and Ubiquitous Systems: Computing, Networking and Services, 2014

Nishimura T., Higuchi T., Yamaguchi H., Higashino T. (2014) Detecting Smoothness of Pedestrian Flows by Participatory Sensing with Mobile Phones Proc. of ACM ISWC2015 (Proceedings of the ACM 18th International Symposium on Wearable Computing), pp. 15-18, 2014

Zheng X., Zhong T., Liu M. (2009) Modeling crowd evacuation of a building based on seven methodological approaches, Building and Environment, Volume 44, Issue 3, March 2009, Pages 437-445

Schultz C., Bhatt M., Borrmann A. (2015) Bridging qualitative spatial constraints and feature-based parametric modelling: Expressing visibility and movement constraints, Advanced Engineering Informatics, Available online 17 November 2015

Biedermann D., Kielar P., Handel O., Borrmann A. (2014), Towards TransiTUM. A Generic Framework for Multiscale Coupling of Pedestrian Simulation Models based on Transition Zones, Transportation Research Procedia, Volume 2, 2014, Pages 495-500

Chooramun N., Lawrence P., Galea E. (2012) An agent based evacuation model utilising hybrid space discretisation, Safety Science, Volume 50, Issue 8, October 2012, Pages 1685-1694

Strug, B., Ślusarczyk, G. (2014). Using graph representation of information extracted from IFC in building evacuation. In H. Li, Y. Rafiq, & P. de Wilde (Eds.), Proceedings of the 21st International Workshop : Intelligent Computing in Engineering (EG-ICE 2014), July 16-18, 2014 in Cardiff, The United Kingdom (pp. 1–10). Cardiff : Cardiff University School of Engineering.

Kneidl A., Borrmann A., Hartmann D., (2012) Generation and use of sparse navigation graphs for microscopic pedestrian simulation models, Advanced Engineering Informatics, Volume 26, Issue 4, October 2012, Pages 669-680, ISSN 1474-0346

Li N., Becerik-Gerber B., (2012) An Infrastructure-Free Indoor Localization Framework to Support Building Emergency Response Operation, Proceedings of the 19th International Workshop : Intelligent Computing in Engineering (EG-ICE 2012), Herrsching, Germany 2012

Rule Representation Using Linked Data Technologies

Chi Zhang, Jakob Beetz
Eindhoven University of Technology, The Netherlands
c.zhang@tue.nl

Abstract. In this paper, we report a prototype rule checking system based on Semantic Web and Linked Data technologies. This research aims to find a method to represent rules outside of specific systems, and can be used to integrate and share them among different organizations. In this system we propose to use SPARQL to represent rules. As the proof of concept, real use-cases from both BIM norms and domain regulations are used. A prototype implementation for the rule checking application is provided. Based on this application, additional issues are discussed including how to ease the process of writing rules and how to share and consume rules by developing a rule library based on Linked Data approach.

1. Introduction

Obtaining qualified building models and designs which fulfil requirements from stakeholders is essential for business success in the Architecture, Engineering and Construction (AEC) industry. These requirements can be constraints on explicit data captured in data instances e.g. required properties, as well as higher level norms and regulations for modeling and building designs. In order to automatically validate building models, these requirements need to be translated to computer processable languages to develop a rule-based checking system.

A general approach for developing a rule-based checking system has been summarized by Eastman et al 2009: *to provide a method for mapping the terms in written statements into the logic of testing conditions, then to define enriched data objects and methods capable of deriving properties and relations needed to respond to rule queries.* According to this approach, a rule-based checking application mainly consists of (a) building data objects, (b) domain ontologies according to terms in written statements, (c) a method to enrich data objects according to this ontology, and (d) a method to represent checking rules according to logics of written statements to query results. Conventional rule checking applications usually use proprietary systems and hard code the (b), (c) and (d) in specific systems, and process (a) captured by specific data models e.g. IFC. There are some limitations of such systems. First of all, this approach lacks transparency for public review and need many efforts if additional modifications are needed (Eastman et al 2009, Dimyadi et al 2015). Secondly, developed rules can hardly be reused by other applications. Another issue in this field which recently receives more and more attention is the collaboration of developing rules. There are many requirements and rules defined by different organizations with different vocabularies and classifications. Therefore, a method which is capable to integrate them is needed.

To address these issues, more and more researchers have proposed to use Semantic Web and Linked Data technologies to represent building data as well as rules to implement rule checking applications (Pauwels et al 2011, Zhang et al 2015). Unlike conventional rule checking approaches, Semantic Web technologies enable (b), (c) and (d) mentioned in the last paragraph outside of checking applications, hence they can be accessed and processed by different systems. Another advantage is that we can leverage many existing technologies of query and rule languages to facilitate the implementation of a rule checking environment instead of inventing domain specific languages from scratch. In order to make them applicable, however, there are still many issues to be further discussed. In this paper we address two of them. First of all, regarding implementations there are always some rules which cannot be easily formalized by any rule languages, hence an environment which supports them is needed. Secondly, to our knowledge, there is still no research talking about how to use Semantic Web technologies to represent rules in order to integrate and share them in the AEC industry.

In this paper, we describe a rule checking environment specially address these issues. All in all, the contents of this research are listed as follows:

- Development of a rule checking environment based on open standards and demonstrate use-case examples in different scenarios.
- Proposing a rule library for rule maintenance and sharing with a prototype implementation.

This paper is structured as follows: In section 2, the overall system is presented. Use case examples are demonstrated in section 3 according to their complexities. In section 4, the implementation of the system is briefly introduced. Two strategies are proposed in section 5 to ease the definition process for checking rules. In section 6, a rule library is proposed with a prototype implementation. Discussions and further work conclude this paper in the last section.

2. System design

The general architecture of this project is illustrated in Fig. 1. There are two applications in the entire system. One is to use rules to check models (section 4 and 5); the other is publication, sharing and consumption of rules (section 7). All the rules consist of domain concepts, underlying logics and operators. They are structured as formal vocabularies captured by OWL and SPARQL queries respectively. With the SPIN framework, all SPARQL queries are converted to the RDF representation. Therefore, all these resources are represented finally by RDF and identified by their Uniform Resource Identifiers (URIs). With a proper publication strategy, they are interlinked with each other and can be consumed by users and applied on building data, which is also represented in RDF. As all the operations are based on Linked Data standards of RDF and SPARQL, other types of data (e.g. product catalogue, city or sensor data) can be potentially integrated to facilitate rule checking across domains.

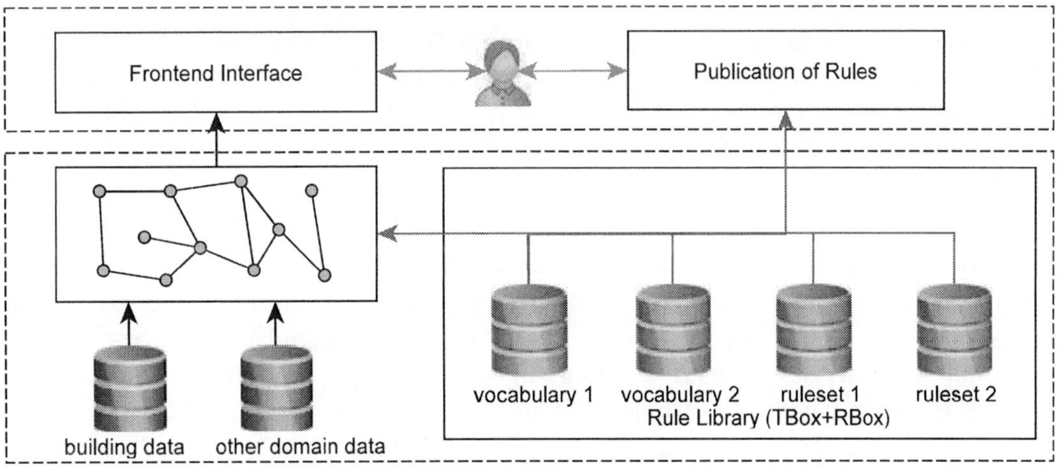

Figure 1. General architecture of the system

The core of this system is vocabularies and rules. Regarding their functionalities in the system, they are additionally grouped into four types (Fig. 2): (1) data ontologies, which are the Semantic Web version of conventional data schemas; (2) requirement ontologies, which consist of concepts used in requirements or regulations; (3) inference rules, which are used to transform from data captured by data ontologies to information represented by requirement ontologies; (4) checking rules, which are used to generate issues as the final output of the system. A hybrid reasoning strategy is used in this system, which means some of the inference rules are pre-processed before checking runtime, and the others are fired when they are called by checking rules.

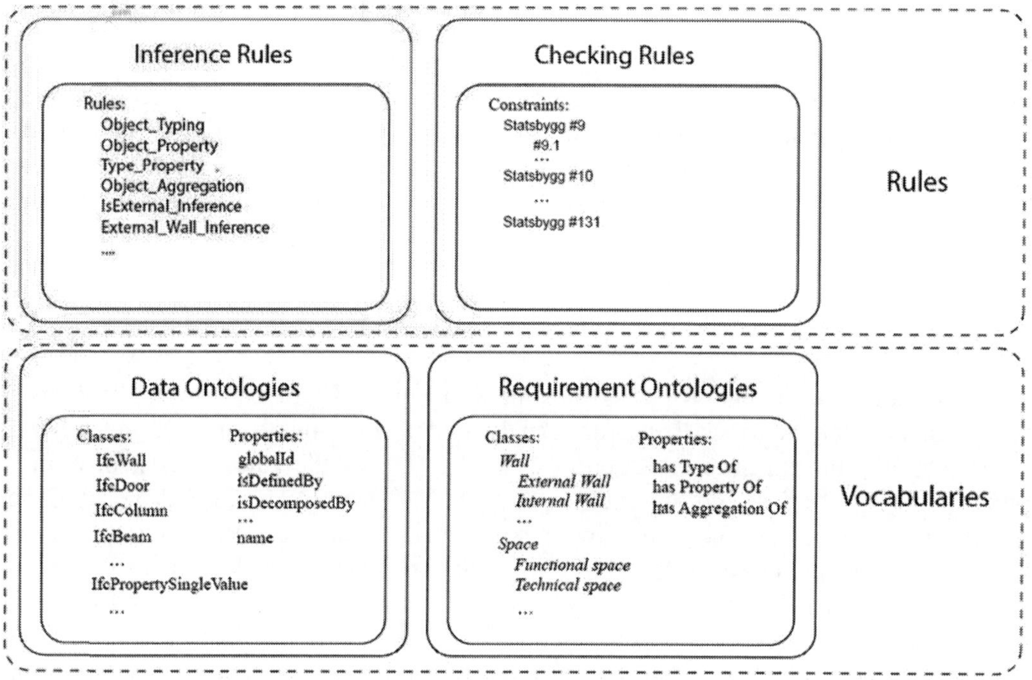

Figure 2. Vocabularies and Rules

3. Case study

We develop this application based on use cases from Statsbygg BIM manual and International Building Codes (Statsbygg 2011, IBC 2006). In this section, two examples are shown, namely rules to check explicit data and rules to check implicit data. In this section only checking rules are discussed, while inference rules which are more related to implementations are described in section 4.

In these two examples, besides concepts used in Statsbygg and IBC (identified by `statsbygg:` and `ibc:` namespaces), some other vocabularies are used. The vocabulary with namespace `spin:` is a meta-vocabulary published by TopBraid as a part of SPIN framework (SPIN, 2011). We use some concepts from this vocabulary to generate checking report and associate issues with building objects. Concepts identified by `qrw:` (query rewriting) is a locally defined vocabulary for deriving data from building models.

We only apply SPARQL `CONSTRUCT` queries to represent checking rules. `CONSTRUCT` queries use `WHERE-CONSTRUCT` to capture the IF-THEN logic. Since each query is applied to search data objects which violate requirements, all checking rules can be generally described as "where something violates the constraint, then construct an issue associated with it".

3.1 Example 1: checking explicit property

This example is to check an explicit name property of a site object to evaluate whether it follows the regular expression format of a cadastre number. It is from Statsbygg BIM manual. The rule is as follows:

- The site name shall contain the official ID of the Cadastre (Statsbygg).

The Fragment 1 shows a SPARQL equivalent of this rule. The `op:format` is a function to check the compliance with a pre-defined format. The `statsbygg:Site` and `statsbygg:siteName` are directly mapped to `IfcSite` and its `LandTitleNumber` property as how they are specified in Statsbygg.

```
CONSTRUCT {
    _:b0 a spin:ConstraintViolation .
    _:b0 spin:violationRoot ?site .
    _:b0 spin:violationPath statsbygg:name .
    _:b0 spin:violationLevel spin:Warning .
  }
WHERE {
  ?site a statsbygg:Site .
  ?site statsbygg:siteName ?name .
  FILTER (!op:format(?name,statsbygg:cadastraNumber))
}
```

Fragment 1. Example rule to checking site name and its SPARQL representation

3.2 Example 2: checking implicit property within building models

This example is from International Building Code to check implicit height property of stair flights with more complex logics. The rule is as follows:

- 1009.7 Vertical rise. A flight of stairs shall not have a vertical rise greater than 12 feet (3658 mm) between floor levels or landings (IBC).
  Exceptions:
  1. Aisle stairs complying with Section 1028.
  2. Alternating tread devices used as a means ofegress shall not have a rise greater than 20 feet (6096 mm) between floor levels or landings.

It has three sub rules on three types of stairs, but we only present the first one in the paper. A SPARQL query is made in Fragment 2. The keywords of `MINUS` and `UNION` filter out the exceptional situations when the stair is an aisle stair or an alternating tread device. In the `FILTER` expression, the function `qudspin:convertLiteral` uniforms different units to foot. This query provides a high level representation without concerning of how these concepts should be mapped to specific building data models. Therefore, it can be retargeted to different data models.

```
CONSTRUCT {
  _:b0 a spin:ConstraintViolation .
  _:b0 spin:violationRoot ?sf .
  _:b0 spin:violationPath geom:hasVerticalRise .
  _:b0 spin:violationLevel spin:Error .
}
WHERE {
  ?sf a ibc:StairFlight .
  ?sf ibc:hasVerticalRise ?vr .
  ?sf qrw:aggregates ?stair .
  MINUS {
  {?stair a ibc:AisleStair}
  UNION
  {?stair a ibc:AlternatingTreadDevice}
  }
  FILTER (qudspin:convertLiteral(?vr,unit:Foot)>12)
}
```

Fragment 2. Example rule to checking stair flight height and its SPARQL representation

4. Implementation

4.1 Mapping concepts in checking rules to specific data models

Regarding implementations referenced concepts in SPARQL queries need to be mapped to specific data models by "inference rules" described in section 2. These inference rules model knowledge from domains e.g. some mathematical equations as well as knowledge of specific data models. In this project, we use IFC as the targeted model and map these concepts to ifcOWL using SPARQL with functional extensions (Beetz et al 2009, Pauwels 2015).

The data captured by IFC model can be roughly classified as geometry data and domain semantic data. Depending on different situations, two mapping methods are implemented. For concepts only related to domain semantic data, standard SPARQL queries are usually sufficient to map them. In Example 2, the two classes of `ibc:AisleStair` and `ibc:AlternatingTreadDevice` are mapped to explicit classifications of `IfcStair`, and the `qrw:aggregates` is mapped to the semantic structure of `IfcRelAggregates` in IFC schema, which all can be enabled by SPARQL queries. All the mappings are transparent and no hard-coding is needed in this process. For properties related to geometry data, however, additional coding is usually needed as functional extensions for SPARQL. For example, the `ibc:hasVerticalRise` in Example 2 is coded as a SPARQL "Property Function" mapped to the geometric representations for `IfcStairFlight` objects. The SPARQL "Property Function" is a de facto mechanism which is supported by many platforms (W3C 2014). We develop SPARQL rules and extensions based on the open source Jena and SPIN APIs. Detailed information about implementation and rule reasoning is not discussed in this paper and will be reported in Zhang and Beetz 2016.

4.2 Checking results

The generated report is also in RDF triples, which consist of issue objects pointing to building objects and is maintained in a separated graph. As shown is Fragment 3, the generated report of Example 2 in section 3 is an issue object pointing to an `IfcStairFlight` instance.

```
_:b12 a                    spin:ConstraintViolation .
      spin:violationRoot   inst: IfcStairFlight_8915.
      spin:violationPath   ibc:hasVerticalRise .
      spin:violationLevel  spin:Error .
```

Fragment 3. Generated report of the Example 2 in section 4

5. Simplifying writing checking rules

An existing issue of using SPARQL is that it is not easy for users to write queries. Two possible solutions are described in this section.

5.1 Strategy 1: Templates

Templates are reusable generic rules with replaceable arguments, hence this strategy is especially applicable for rules with repeated logic patterns (Zhang and Beetz 2015). For example, rules of "a classroom should have at least two doors" and "a storey should have at least one floor slab" can share the same template which is used to check cardinality constraints. This has been implemented using the SPIN framework (SPIN 2011). Each of the templates is identified by its URI so is globally reusable.

```
#A {?subject_type} should {?predicate} at
least {?min} and at most {?max}
{?object_type}
CONSTRUCT {
  _:b0 a spin:ConstraintViolation .
  _:b0 spin:violationRoot ?s .
  _:b0 spin:violationPath ?predicate .
}
WHERE {
    ?s a ?subject_class .
  FILTER (
  (op:count(?s, ?predicate,
?object_type) > ?max) || (op:count(?s,
?predicate, ?object_type) < ?max)) .
}
```

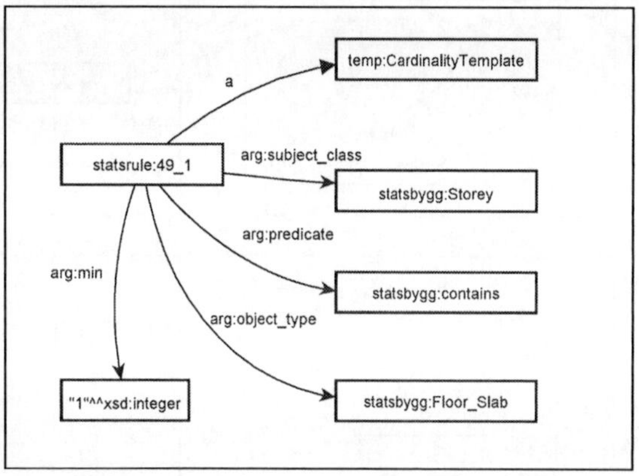

Figure 3. An example template instantiated by a concrete checking rule

Using this method, we have built a list of templates based on use cases from Statsbygg, which contain rules with repeated logic patterns.

5.2 Strategy 2: A high level interface for a subset of SPARQL expressions

A limitation of Strategy 1 is that a template can only capture static logic patterns, hence the expressivity of rules are limited by defined template sets. Another strategy is to develop a domain specific interface for describing rules and map it to a subset of SPARQL expressions. Although no systematic analysis can be provided, in our experiences only a small subset of SPARQL expressions have been used in writing checking rules. Therefore, to define a profile of SPARQL expressions for writing building rules might be a possible direction.

6. Maintenance and sharing of rules

6.1 A Rule library

An advantage of this checking system is that all rules and vocabularies are finally maintained in RDF and identified by their URIs. Therefore, rules, vocabularies and templates from distributed sources can be integrated together as a rule library. In order to manage them, we propose to use a simple meta-vocabulary to organize them. The top level is `Ruleset` which is an aggregation of `CheckingRules`. Each checking rule refers to vocabularies defined by different organizations, which additionally link to `InferenceRules` using SPIN property functions or other kinds of links e.g. `rdfs:seeAlso`. Inference rules also refer to lower level vocabularies (e.g. ifcOWL). For example, the rule defined in Section 6.1 can be maintained as Figure 4. The shaded node in this illustration is the resource of the checking rule, which is linked with related templates and concepts from different graphs.

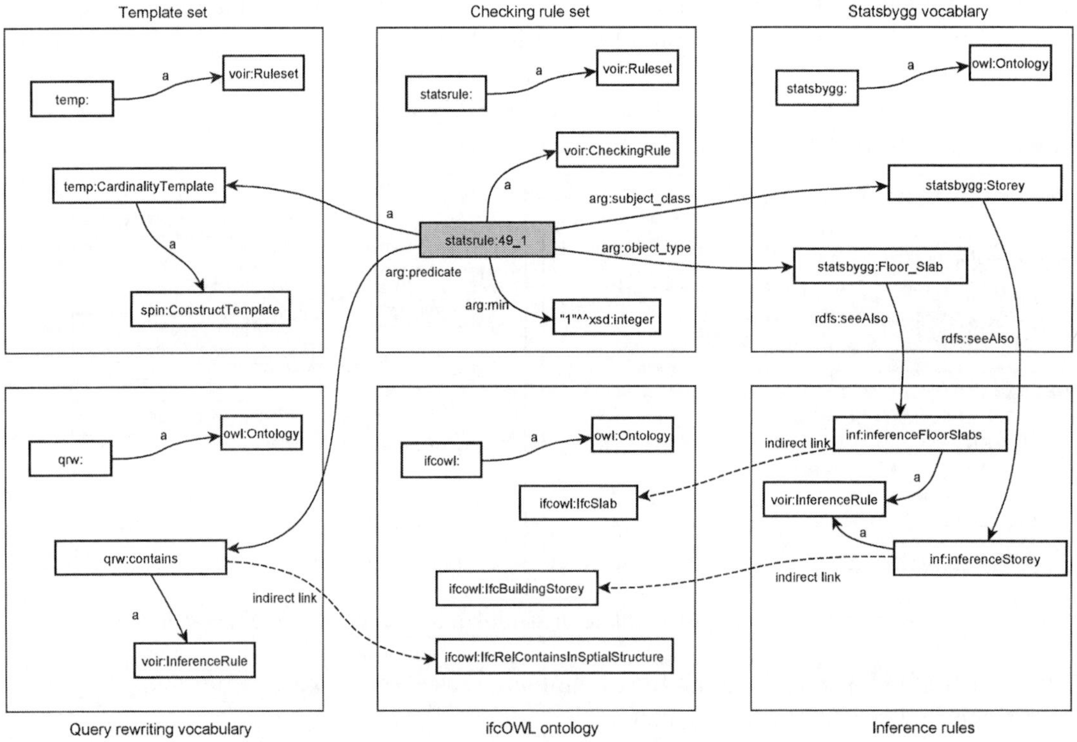

Figure 4. An example of how a checking rule can be linked with other resources

As an initiative work, we define a ruleset of more than 200 checking rules, 3 vocabularies (including ifcOWL) and 74 inference rules to load them into a triple store. They can be searched by users to find rules which are related to their topics. For example, a simple query can be written to find all the checking rules which are related to `statsbygg:Wall`.

```
SELECT ?x
WHERE {
  ?x a voir:CheckingRule .
  ?x ?arg1 statsbygg:Wall .
}
```

Fragment 4. An example of querying rules

6.2 Rule publication and consumption

As all the rules and vocabularies are represented in RDF graphs, in the long term, it is possible to publish them as Linked Data distributed on the Web based on the Linked Data principles (Berners-Lee 2006). Since rules are linked with all the related concepts, which are identified by their dereferencable URIs, additonal context information can be provided to help human and systems understand their semantics. For example, when we find checking rules which are related to `ibc:AisleStair` and `qrw:aggregates`, the publishers for these two concepts can provide or link to additional information about their semantics and how they are mapped to specific data models e.g. to declare that an `ibc: AisleStair` is a `ifcowl:Stair` associated with a classification resource. Therefore, the meanings of rules are transparent to the public to facilitate reusing of these resources.

To prove this concept, a prototype implementation is under development. We use Jena TDB and Fuseki as the SPARQL endpoint and Epimorphics Elda API as the Linked Data frontend.

7. Conclusion and further work

In this paper, we present a rule checking environment based on Linked Data technologies. Examples are demonstated by using this system. Two strategies are proposed to simplify writing rules using SPARQL. The advantage of this environment is that all the rules and vocabularies are finally maintained in RDF and independent from specific systems. Additional implementation and testing work is still needed.

In real practices, this approach requires maintenance of formal vocabularies. Therefore, to ensure the reliability of resources, a balance between centralized and federated systems need to be considered. A central vocabulary which can be reused by many requirements and regulations needs to be developed in the AEC domain. There are some existing candidates including some classification systems and libraries that can be considered as the basement e.g. buildingSMART Data Dictionary (bSDD). However, to make them applicable, additional reviewing, modeling and standardization work is needed.

References

Angles, R. and Gutierrez, C., 2008. The expressive power of SPARQL (pp. 114-129). Springer Berlin Heidelberg.

Beetz, J., van Leeuwen, J.P. and de Vries, B. 2009. "IfcOWL: A case of transforming EXPRESS schemas into ontologies." Artificial Intelligence for Engineering Design, Analysis and Manufacturing. vol. 23. no. Special Issue 01. 89-101.

Berners-Lee, T., 2006. Linked data. Available at: https://www.w3.org/DesignIssues/LinkedData.html.

Berners-Lee, T., Connolly, D., Kagal, L., Scharf, Y. and Hendler, J., 2008. N3logic: A logical framework for the world wide web. Theory and Practice of Logic Programming, 8(3), pp.249-269.

Bouzidi, K.R., Fies, B., Faron-Zucker, C., Zarli, A. & Le Thanh, N. (2012). Semantic Web Approach to Ease Regulation Compliance Checking in Construction Industry. Future Internet. 4 (3). pp. 830-851.

BuildingSMART. 2014. buildingSMART Data Dictionary. http://bsdd.buildingsmart.org/.

Dimyadi, J., Pauwels, P., Spearpoint, M., Clifton, C. & Amor, R. (2015). Querying a Regulatory Model for Compliant Building Design Audit. Proc. of the 31st CIB W78 International Conference.

Drummond, N. and Shearer, R., 2006, October. The open world assumption. In eSI Workshop: The Closed World of Databases meets the Open World of the Semantic Web (Vol. 15).

Eastman, C., Lee, J.M., Jeong, Y.S. and Lee, J.K., 2009. Automatic rule-based checking of building designs. Automation in Construction, 18(8), pp.1011-1033.

Fürber, C., & Hepp, M. (2010). Using sparql and spin for data quality management on the semantic web. In Business Information Systems(pp. 35-46). Springer Berlin Heidelberg.

Harris, S., Seaborne, A. and Prud'hommeaux, E., 2013. SPARQL 1.1 query language. W3C Recommendation, 21.

Heath, T. and Bizer, C., 2011. Linked data: Evolving the web into a global data space. Synthesis lectures on the semantic web: theory and technology,1(1), pp.1-136.

Horrocks, I., Patel-Schneider, P.F., Boley, H., Tabet, S., Grosof, B. and Dean, M., 2004. SWRL: A semantic web rule language combining OWL and RuleML. W3C Member submission, 21, p.79.

IBC, I., 2006. International building code. International Code Council, Inc.(formerly BOCA, ICBO and SBCCI), 4051, pp.60478-5795.

Knublauch, H. and Ryman, A. (2016). Shapes Constraint Language (SHACL). Available at: https://www.w3.org/TR/shacl/

Pauwels, P., Van Deursen, D., Verstraeten, R., De Roo, J., De Meyer, R, Van de Walle, R., & Van Campenhout, J. (2011). A semantic rule checking environment for building performance checking. Automation in Construction, 20(5), 506–518.

Pauwels, P. (2014). ifcOWL ontology file added for IFC4_ADD1. Available on https://www.w3.org/community/lbd/2014/12/12/ifcowl-ontology-file-added-for-ifc4_add1/.

Pauwels, P., and Zhang, S. 2015 "Semantic rule-checking for regulation compliance checking: an overview of strategies and approaches." 32rd international CIB W78 conference. 2015.

Solihin, W., and C. Eastman. "Classification of rules for automated BIM rule checking development." Automation in construction 53 (2015): 69-82.

SPIN (2011). SPIN SPARQL Inferencing Notation. http://spinrdf.org/ (Last visited on 12 June 2015).

Statsbygg, (2011). Statsbygg Building Information Modelling Manual Version1.2. Available at: http://www.statsbygg.no/bim, accessed January 2014.

W3C. (2014). SPARQL/Extensions/Computed Properties. Available at: https://www.w3.org/wiki/SPARQL/Extensions/Computed_Properties.

Zhang, C., Beetz, J., and Bauke de Vries. 2014 "An Ontological Approach for Semantic Validation of IFC Models." EG-ICE 2014. 2014.

Zhang, C., and Beetz, J. 2015 "Model checking on the Semantic Web: IFC validation using modularized and distributed rules". 32rd international CIB W78 conference. 2015.

Zhang, C. and Beetz, J. 2016. Querying linked building data using SPARQL with functional extensions". 11th ECPPM conference, submitted 2016.

Zhang, S., Boukamp, F. & Teizer, J. (2015). Ontology-based semantic modeling of construction safety knowledge: Towards automated safety planning for job hazard analysis (JHA). Automation in Construction. 52. pp. 29-41.

Super-Structure and Super-Structure Free Design Search Space Representations for a Building Spatial Design in Multi-Disciplinary Building Optimisation

S. Boonstra[†], K. van der Blom[‡], H. Hofmeyer[†], R. Amor[*], M.T.M. Emmerich[‡]
[†]Eindhoven University of Technology, The Netherlands
[‡]LIACS, Leiden University, The Netherlands
[*]University of Auckland, New Zealand
[†]h.hofmeyer@tue.nl

Abstract. In multi-disciplinary building optimisation, solutions depend on the representation of the design search space, the latter being a collection of all solutions. This paper presents two design search space representations and discusses their advantages and disadvantages: The first, a super-structure approach, requires all possible solutions to be prescribed in a so-called super-structure. The second approach, super-structure free, uses dynamic data structures that offer freedom in the range of possible solutions. It is concluded that both approaches may supplement each other, if applied in a combination of optimisation methods. A method for this combination of optimisation methods is proposed. The method includes the transformation of one representation into the other and vice versa. Finally, therefore in this paper these transformations are proposed, implemented, and verified as well.

1. Introduction

Many engineers in the built environment experience optimisation as a challenging task. This is because it is usually a time consuming trial-and-error procedure, in which knowledge and experience are first needed to create designs, which are then assessed and possibly modified. Many research projects involve the development of optimisation methods to create and analyse designs to aid engineers. These developments concern advanced optimisation methods, often specialised to small sub problems (for a single discipline) in the design process. Such a specialisation exists because design problems are too large for a single design tool, and engineers are invaluable to the design process since their experience can reduce a design problem drastically. However, it cannot be expected that an individual engineer oversees the complete design problem, and thus complex relationships between the disciplines might go unnoticed, leading to suboptimal designs. For this, multi-disciplinary building optimisation could be supportive, but it needs a method to handle the large design search spaces involved. This paper aims at developing such a method and focuses on the question of how to represent design search spaces such that optimisation methods find efficient solutions.

Prior to reading this paper it is important to understand the terminology concerning optimisation and data structures in optimisation. Optimisation aims to minimise or maximise an objective value by the variation of design variables, while at the same time satisfying certain constraints. What is important for optimisation is the representation of the design search space, which is the selection of design variables that are used to parametrise the solutions for the problem (design variables not part of the selection are constant or depend on the representation itself). The representation affects the possibilities and performance of the optimisation methods, e.g. a complex dynamic data structure might be too difficult to handle by most types of optimisation methods. In this paper, terminology will be used as found for optimal process synthesis in chemical engineering, where super-structure representations are distinguished from super-structure free representations (Voll et al. 2012). In a super-structure, the design search space has a fixed number of design variables, meaning all design alternatives are pre-encoded, which makes for a static data structure. This enables the search for an optimum in a systematic manner by using classical parameter-based optimisation methods. Super-structure free optimisation uses a design search space in which new design variables may originate or disappear, which can be seen as a dynamic data structure. Such a design search space allows for discovering unexpected new alternatives that were not pre-encoded. Typically, super-structures allow for formulating optimisation problems in the language of mathematical programming (using equations and inequalities). Free representations are formulated differently, for instance by describing initialisation procedures and variation operators that form the design search space. The difference between super-structure versus super-structure free approaches is a recurrent theme in specific fields of optimisation (Voll et al. 2012), whereas this topic has hardly been addressed for building design.

The design search space used in this paper entails the layout and dimensioning of building spaces, i.e. the building spatial design. For this design search space, a super-structure and a super-structure free approach have been developed and compared. Moreover, a method to carry out transformations between the two representations will be discussed, which is envisioned to enable both approaches to efficiently cooperate on a large design space.

2. Related Work

In literature, research on building optimisation can be found taking into account objectives like energy consumption, as is carried out by Wetter (2004) and Tuhus-Dubrow & Krarti (2010); structural stiffness by Liang, Xie & Steven (2000) and Baldock & Shea (2006); construction costs by Wang, Zmeureanu & Rivard (2005); and thermal comfort by Wright, Loosemore & Farmani (2002). Also, optimisation is thoughtfully combined with Building Information Modelling, Rafiq & Rustell (2014). Different energy performance criteria are combined in Emmerich et al. (2008) and Hopfe et al. (2012). A commonly used optimisation method is evolutionary optimisation, where design variables are stored in a so called genome that can be modified by means of mutation and recombination operators. Other optimisation methods are applied as well, like gradient-based optimisation for topology optimisation in Sigmund (2001), or the analytical derivation of an optimal truss layout by Chan (1960). The use of optimisation methods for building performance optimisation is however still not widespread and many issues need to be solved. One difficulty is to allow for more degrees of freedom in the optimisation. This is also addressed in this paper by defining design search space representations that allow for variations of the (global) building spatial design.

The super-structure terminology finds its origins in the process industry, where the optimal configurations of chemical engineering plants are sought. For example, Jackson (1968) described the structure of flow configurations of chemical reactors with a super-structure, although without explicit mentioning the term. Various recent works (Belegundu & Rajan 1988; Sekulski, 2009; Bandaru & Deb 2015) use the terminology for other engineering fields too. A super-structure prescribes the possible design alternatives to be considered in optimisation, which results in a selection of alternatives. This limited and fixed number of alternatives improves the chance of finding the global optimum. A super-structure enables an optimisation problem to be solved by mathematical programming, for which standard solvers exist (e.g. Floudas 1995).

Super-structure free optimisation has been suggested to overcome the limitations of super-structures for designing chemical process configurations. Emmerich, Grötzner & Schütz (2001) propose to use replacement, insertion, and deletion rules to modify (mutate, recombine) designs in evolutionary algorithms. However, the development of these local modification operators requires domain knowledge. Voll et al. (2012) suggest a more general framework that uses generic replacement rules in evolutionary algorithms. A similar strategy is followed by Droste & Wiesmann (2000), who exemplified it for the optimisation of decision diagrams. Other examples of super-structure free design spaces include the work of Koza et al. (1996) and Baldock and Shea (2006). There are only a few optimisation methods that can handle super-structure free representations, namely simulated annealing, evolutionary algorithms, and heuristic local search. Simulated annealing has been used in the design of processes, e.g. in Dolan, Cummings & Le Van (1990). In the field of structural design, Kicinger, Arciszewski & De Jong (2005) describe a super-structure free approach in the optimisation of structural topologies. Moreover, Hofmeyer & Davila Delgado (2015) use simulations of a co-evolutionary design process (these simulations can also be interpreted as asymmetric subspace optimisation, Martins & Lambe 2013) to find a building spatial design for which the structural grammar applied structural design shows minimal compliance.

3. Super-Structure Based Representation

3.1 Design Search Space

A so-called "super cube" (SC) is suggested to describe a building spatial design by means of a super-structure design search space representation. A super cube consisting of cells is described by four vectors: $B\{\overrightarrow{w_i}, \overrightarrow{d_j}, \overrightarrow{h_k}, \vec{b}^l_{i,j,k}\}$. Equation (1) shows the variables used. Here $b^l_{i,j,k}$ describes the existence of the cell with indices i, j and k in space l, where a value "1" means the cell is active and describes a part of space l while "0" means the cell is inactive. Following this, i is the x-, j is the y- and k is the z-index of a cell, while l is the space index. Finally, w_i, d_j, h_k describe the continuous dimensioning of the super cube's cells. The entire super cube is used to perform design modifications, therefore the complete design space is described by the vectors $\overrightarrow{w_i}, \overrightarrow{d_j}, \overrightarrow{h_k}$ and $\vec{b}^l_{i,j,k}$. Figure 1 shows the super cube notation for an example building spatial design. Building spaces are indicated by normal lines (and coarsely dashed hidden lines), whereas cells can be recognised by finely dotted lines. Each cell in the figure has a number in the left front corner that indicates the building space it belongs to.

$$
\begin{aligned}
&i \in \{1,2,\dots,N_w\} \qquad w_i \in \mathbb{R} \geq 0 \\
&j \in \{1,2,\dots,N_d\} \qquad d_j \in \mathbb{R} \geq 0 \\
&k \in \{1,2,\dots,N_h\} \qquad h_k \in \mathbb{R} \geq 0 \\
&l \in \{1,2,\dots,N_{spaces}\} \qquad b^l_{i,j,k} = \begin{cases} 1 & \text{if cell } (i,j,k) \text{ belongs to space } l \\ 0 & \text{otherwise} \end{cases}
\end{aligned} \tag{1}
$$

3.2 Constraints and Design Modification

Building spatial design modification is performed by re-assigning cells to building spaces through changes of the binary variables and by modifying distance values of the super cube's grid. Constraints are introduced to the design space so the search can focus on physically and technically feasible solutions. Constraints can be checked by algorithms or, when stated as equations, they can be part of the selection and generation of solutions. Stating constraints as equations has the advantage that their algebraic structure can be exploited by the optimisation algorithms employed. The super cube representation is suitable for such algebraic expression of constraints, and three constraints are presented here to demonstrate this suitability. The expressions enable the use of mathematical programming techniques like mixed integer non-linear programming (MINLP) which contribute to the efficiency of the optimisation. It should be noted that there may be differences between constraint representations and constraint implementations (not shown here). For example only "1"-values in binary variables are stored in memory to avoid inefficient constraint checking by large zero spaces in vector $\vec{b}^{l}_{i,j,k}$.

$\vec{w}\{w_1, w_2, w_3, w_4\}$,

$\vec{d}\{d_1, d_2\}$, $\vec{h}\{h_1\}$

$\overrightarrow{b^{l}_{i,j,k}}\{b^{1}_{i,j,k}, b^{2}_{i,j,k}, b^{3}_{i,j,k}, b^{4}_{i,j,k}\}$

$b^{1}_{i,j,k}\{1,0,0,0,0,0,0,0\}$

$b^{2}_{i,j,k}\{0,0,1,0,1,0,0,0\}$

$b^{3}_{i,j,k}\{0,1,0,0,0,0,0,0\}$

$b^{4}_{i,j,k}\{0,0,0,1,0,1,0,0\}$

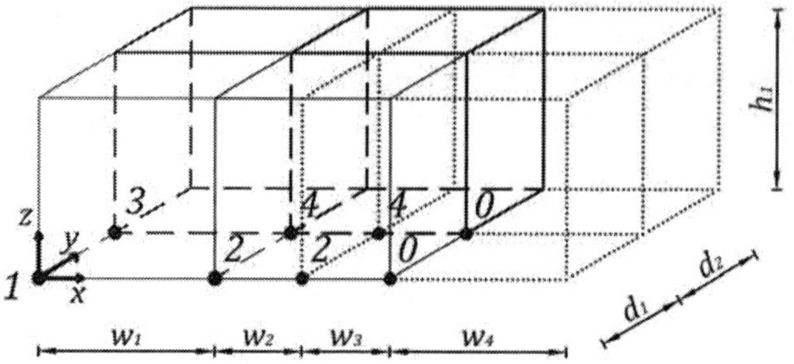

Figure 1 "Super cube" representation of a building spatial design, space 2 and 4 are described by two cells each, the two right cells are not used to describe a room

Condition 1: Non Overlap. Overlaps of building spaces are not allowed for they are not practical and might cause erroneous results in subsequent design analysis. And since every space is represented by a separate bit-mask (l) of all cells of the super cube, which does not automatically prevent non-overlap, this needs to be checked. Equation (2) achieves this by taking the sum of each cell over all masks. As a result of the binary representation, only if such a sum is smaller or equal to one, no overlap exists at that position.

$$\forall_l : \forall_{i,j,k} \sum_{l=1}^{N_{spaces}} b^{l}_{i,j,k} \leq 1 \tag{2}$$

Condition 2: Cuboid. Spaces are constrained to cuboid shapes for practicality and to delimit the design space to a manageable size. To check this condition by means of an equation, first the super cube will be extended with a single layer of cells all around, and these new cells will be set to be not related to a space ("0"), the latter described by equation (3):

$$\begin{gathered} \forall_l : \forall_{i,j,k} \in \{0, \ldots, N_w + 1\} \times \{0, \ldots, N_d + 1\} \times \{0, \ldots, N_h + 1\}: \\ i = 0 \vee j = 0 \vee k = 0 \vee i = N_w + 1 \vee j = N_d + 1 \vee k = N_h + 1 \Rightarrow b^{l}_{i,j,k} = 0 \end{gathered} \tag{3}$$

Then for each building space l, in each direction (x,y, and z) pairs of adjoining lines that run through the middles of the cells are imagined (e.g. for the z-direction a pair would be a line through all cells i_1=2, j_1=2 and a line through all cells i_2=2, j_2=3). Moving along a pair of lines, $b^{l}_{i,j,k}$ values are processed as shown in equation (4) for the z-direction (as an example, of course all directions should be studied). To obtain a cubic building space, if there is a change from zero to one in the binary string it should occur at the same position (k-value) for both lines. Otherwise in the equation the sums as shown will hold different values and the difference will be non-zero. The same should hold for changes from one to zero, as seen in the second part of the equation. Note that equation (4) allows for the occurrence of multiple changes from one to zero and from zero to one. In other words a space could be cuboid, however could still have internal voids, e.g. a courtyard. Therefore condition 3 is introduced next.

Condition 3: Ortho-Convexity. This condition enforces spaces to have a connected, ortho-convex shape. Note that, like condition 2, this also relies on the layer of "zero" cells as described by equation (3). With equation (5) the sum is taken of the number of times a change occurs from cell values zero to one in a building space for each direction. Any building space where there are multiple changes from zero to one is not fully connected and therefore invalidated. Note, that in conjunction with condition 2 this ensured that building spaces have a fully occupied cuboid shape.

$$\forall_l:$$

$$\forall_{i_1,j_1,i_2,j_2}: \left(\left(\sum_{k=1}^{N_h} k\left(1 - b^l_{i_1,j_1,k-1}\right) b^l_{i_1,j_1,k} \right) - \left(\sum_{k=1}^{N_h} k\left(1 - b^l_{i_2,j_2,k-1}\right) b^l_{i_2,j_2,k} \right) \right)$$
$$\left(\sum_{k=1}^{N_h} b^l_{i_1,j_1,k} \right) \left(\sum_{k=1}^{N_h} b^l_{i_2,j_2,k} \right) = 0$$
$$\forall_{i_1,j_1,i_2,j_2}: \left(\left(\sum_{k=1}^{N_h} k b^l_{i_1,j_1,k}\left(1 - b^l_{i_1,j_1,k+1}\right) \right) - \left(\sum_{k=1}^{N_h} k b^l_{i_2,j_2,k}\left(1 - b^l_{i_2,j_2,k+1}\right) \right) \right) \left(\sum_{k=1}^{N_h} b^l_{i_1,j_1,k} \right) \left(\sum_{k=1}^{N_h} b^l_{i_2,j_2,k} \right) = 0 \tag{4}$$

$$\forall_l :$$

$$\forall_{i,j}: \sum_{k=0}^{N_h} \left(1 - b^l_{i,j,k}\right) b^l_{i,j,k+1} \leq 1 \qquad \forall_{i,k}: \sum_{j=0}^{N_d} \left(1 - b^l_{i,j,k}\right) b^l_{i,j+1,k} \leq 1 \tag{5}$$
$$\forall_{j,k}: \sum_{i=0}^{N_w} \left(1 - b^l_{i,j,k}\right) b^l_{i+1,j,k} \leq 1$$

4. Super-Structure Free Based Representation

4.1 Design Search Space

A “movable and sizable” (MS) representation for spaces is suggested for the super-structure free design space representation. For this, a building is described with: $B\{\vec{S}\}$, in which a single $\vec{S}$ lists all the spaces. This vector is described by equation (6), in which S_i represents a space, C the coordinates of the space origin and D the geometry of the space with w, d and h the width in x-, depth in y-, and height in z-direction, respectively. Figure 2 shows the building spatial design of figure 1 in the "movable and sizable" representation.

$$\vec{S} = \left\{S_1, S_2, \dots, S_{N_{spaces}}\right\}$$
$$S_i = \{C, D\}; \quad C = \{x, y, z\}; \quad D = \{w, d, h\} \tag{6}$$

$$S_1\{\{x_1, y_1, z_1\}, \{w_1, d_1, h_1\}\}$$
$$S_2\{\{x_2, y_2, z_2\}, \{w_2, d_2, h_2\}\}$$
$$S_3\{\{x_3, y_3, z_3\}, \{w_3, d_3, h_3\}\}$$
$$S_4\{\{x_4, y_4, z_4\}, \{w_4, d_4, h_4\}\}$$

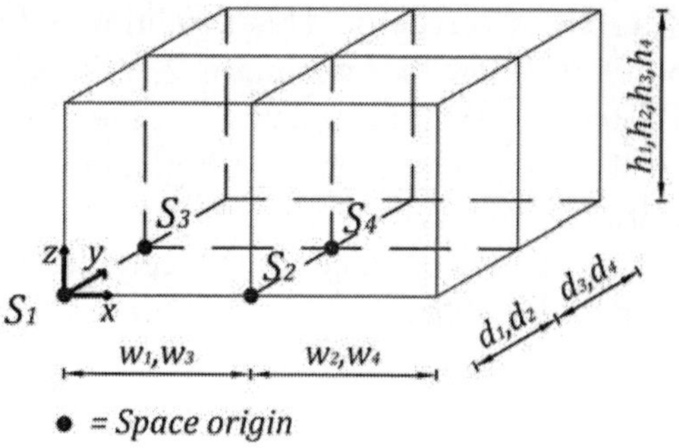

Figure 2 "Movable and sizable" representation of the building spatial design (first shown in figure 1)

4.2 Constraints and Design Modification

In the super-structure free approach, constraints are implicitly enforced by using design modification that naturally follow the constraints. The MS representation is intuitive for building engineers and allows for straight forward design modification. Here, this is carried out via removal, scaling and division of spaces. As an example, a modification of the spatial building design in figure 2 will be performed. Assume that after (e.g. structural or building physics performance) analyses, it is concluded that building space S_3 performs least well and thus could better be removed as shown in equation (7). Accordingly, the remaining spaces are scaled (equation (8)) to restore the initial volume (V_0) of the building design. To restore the number of spaces, hereafter a (e.g. randomly selected) space is divided (equation (9)) into two new spaces, resulting in a new spatial design (equation (10)). This process is further illustrated in figure 3 and has been used by Hofmeyer & Davila Delgado (2015) for real-world optimisation scenarios.

Deletion:
$$\vec{S}\{S_1, S_2, S_3, S_4\} \rightarrow \vec{S}\{S_1, S_2, S_4\} \tag{7}$$

Scaling:
$$\begin{pmatrix} S_1\{\{x, y\}, \{w, d\}\}, S_2\{\{x, y\}, \{w, d\}\}, \\ S_4\{\{x, y\}, \{w, d\}\} \end{pmatrix} \cdot \sqrt{\frac{V_0}{V}} \tag{8}$$

Division:
$$S_1\{\{x_1, y_1, z_1\}, \{w_1, d_1, h_1\}\} \rightarrow \begin{cases} S_5\left\{\{x_1, y_1, z_1\}, \left\{\frac{1}{2}w_1, d_1, h_1\right\}\right\}, \\ S_6\left\{\left\{x_1 + \frac{1}{2}w_1, 0, 0\right\}, \left\{\frac{1}{2}w_1, d_1, h_1\right\}\right\} \end{cases} \tag{9}$$

New design:
$$S\{S_2, S_4, S_5, S_6\} \tag{10}$$

5. Discussion

So far two design space representations have been defined for building spatial design optimisation: one suitable for the super-structure approach and another for the super-structure free approach. This section discusses the properties of the two approaches on a conceptual level with reference to the two presented representations.

From the super-structure based representation it becomes clear that its use requires expertise in the fields of mathematics, optimisation, and the built environment. This requirement should not however exclude building engineers from using this representation, because it can lead to the optimum design with a high confidence level. Additionally it can lead to new design insights when multiple solutions are assessed, e.g. relationships between design variables may be discovered. However, a design space representation draws a limit on what solutions can be considered by an optimisation algorithm. For the super-structure approach, this means all solutions are pre-defined by the engineer who developed the representation. This means that an optimum is only the best out of the pre-defined solutions, and better solutions outside the design space representation will never be found. A larger design space representation could solve this issue, but will almost always lead to a significant increase of computational time, and this without a prior guarantee of better optima.

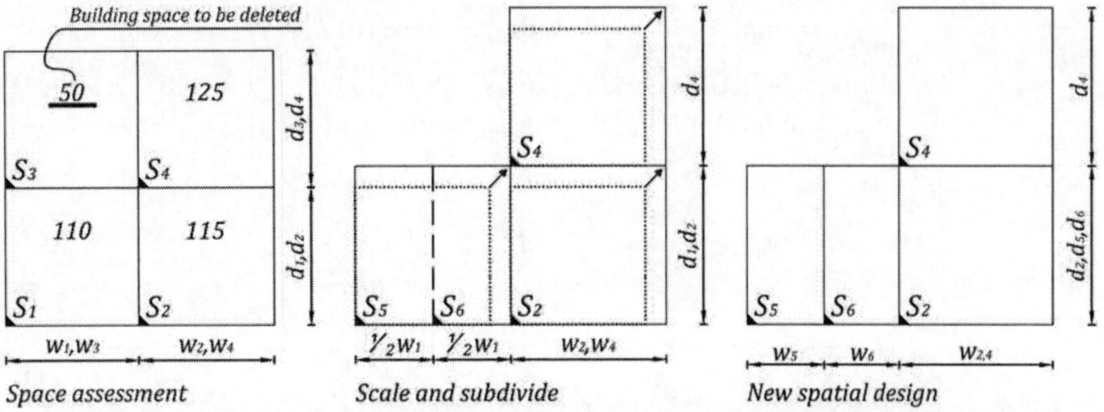

Figure 3 Super-structure free modification, numbers in spaces in the most left figure represent (structural or building physics) performance.

The super-structure free based approach to building optimisation can be developed even when only expertise in the built environment is available. Rules for modification of the considered design are then based on knowledge and experience in the field. This approach can combine design variables in (mathematically) unexpected ways and may therefore lead to new building designs that would otherwise not have been considered. It also provides a fast way to navigate a large design space, since the size of the design space does not influence the search for an improved design. However, this dynamic approach prevents the use of many classical search algorithms (global and parameter based search) and instead heuristic rules should be used to navigate the design space. Such heuristics are prone to the finding of local optima and cannot provide high levels of confidence concerning these optima (although comparisons between heuristics and global searches sometimes result in matching results). Compared to the super-structure approach, new design insights are more difficult to find when using heuristics, because less solutions are analysed and design evolution follows a path that is defined by the heuristics.

To consider large design spaces, it can be concluded that both approaches are eligible, although both have disadvantages as well: The super-structure approach is too costly in terms of computational effort and the super-structure free approach cannot provide the optimum with a high level of confidence. Therefore it is proposed to combine both approaches. Additionally, such a combination could enable the optimisation to discover both surprising designs and new design insights.

6. Combination of Super-Structure and Super-Structure Free Approaches

The combination of the approaches above is proposed by alternately employ each approach during the optimisation process for the same problem. This alternation requires mutual transformation between the two representations, this section will presents two suitable algorithms.

6.1 "Super Cube" (SC) to "Movable and Sizable" (MS)

To transform a building spatial design's "Super Cube" representation into the "Movable and Sizable" representation, it is suggested here to first find the smallest and largest indices i, j, k for the set of cells describing each space l as shown in equation (11). Space coordinates x, y, z can then be found as shown in equation (12), with the notion that if the smallest index equals 1, there is no term in the sum, and the degenerated sum is evaluated as 0 (which is appropriate here). The space dimensions are computed in a similar way using the minimum and maximum indices as shown in equation (13).

$$\begin{aligned} i^l_{min} &= \min(\{i \mid b^l_{i,j,k}\}) & i^l_{max} &= \max(\{i \mid b^l_{i,j,k}\}) \\ j^l_{min} &= \min(\{j \mid b^l_{i,j,k}\}) & j^l_{max} &= \max(\{j \mid b^l_{i,j,k}\}) \\ k^l_{min} &= \min(\{k \mid b^l_{i,j,k}\}) & k^l_{max} &= \max(\{k \mid b^l_{i,j,k}\}) \end{aligned} \quad (11)$$

$$x^l = \sum_{p=1}^{i^l_{min}-1} w_p, \qquad y^l = \sum_{q=1}^{j^l_{min}-1} d_q, \qquad z^l = \sum_{r=1}^{k^l_{min}-1} h_r \quad (12)$$

$$w^l = \sum_{i=i^l_{min}}^{i^l_{max}} w_i, \qquad d^l = \sum_{j=j^l_{min}}^{j^l_{max}} d_j, \qquad h^l = \sum_{k=k^l_{min}}^{k^l_{max}} h_k \quad (13)$$

6.2 "Movable and Sizable" (MS) to "Super Cube" (SC)

A transformation from "Movable and Sizable" to "Super Cube" first requires three steps to compute the super cube dimensions $\vec{w}$, $\vec{d}$, $\vec{h}$. First, for each space, the minimum and maximum coordinate values should be found, i.e. for each space $\{x, x+w\}, \{y, y+d\}, \{z, z+h\}$. Second, all these values are brought together, duplicate values are removed, and then values are grouped in three lists (each for either x, y or z values), and sorted in ascending order. Finally, vectors $\vec{w}$, $\vec{d}$, $\vec{h}$ are computed from these lists. For example, w is computed as $w_i = x_{i+1} - x_i$, for every $i \in [1, \ldots, n-1]$.

Regarding vector $\vec{b}^l_{i,j,k}$, for each space and for each cell the (derived) cell's coordinates are compared with the coordinates of the considered space. A cell is assigned to the considered space if the cell coordinates are completely within the coordinates of the space, e.g. for the x-direction $x_{space} \leq x_{cell} < x_{space} + w_{space}$.

6.3 Verification

The preceding transformation algorithms have been implemented and tested, including the modification of an existing visualisation tool to provide graphical support. The verification concerned: overlaps in spaces (figure 4), non-connected spaces, truncation errors, alterations in space identification, and fragmented spaces (figure 5). From the verifications it could be concluded that overlaps in spaces and non-connected spaces are preserved throughout transformations. Truncation errors can in special cases lead to small grid sizes in the "super cube" representation, which can be solved by deleting these grid size values ($\vec{w}$, $\vec{d}$, $\vec{h}$ and related $\vec{b}^l_{i,j,k}$). Further it could be concluded that building space identifications may get lost, however if desired this is easily solved by allocating a separate variable for space-identification. Finally, fragmented spaces in SC are not preserved. This is because in MS such a building space is naturally not possible, see figure 5. As a conclusion, it is expected that an alternation between search space representations is possible, provided that overlaps and fragmented spaces in SC are not allowed (i.e. the constraints in section 3.2 must be followed).

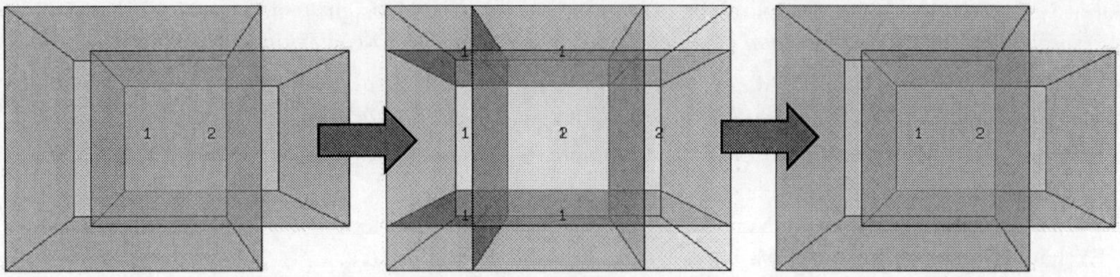

Figure 4 Building space overlaps subject to transformations are preserved. From left to right: Initial MS to SC, then SC to MS-representation.

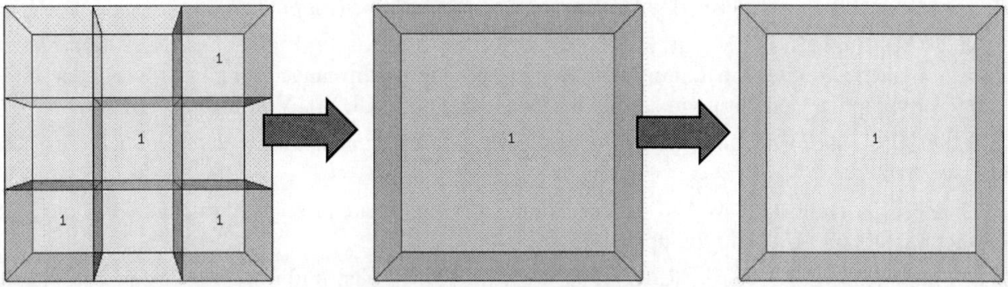

Figure 5 Fragmented space gets lost during transformation. From left to right: Initial SC to MS, then MS to SC representation.

7. Conclusions and Outlook

The difference between super-structure versus super-structure free approaches is a recurrent theme in specific fields of optimisation (Voll et al. 2012). In this paper, for the super-structure approach, a "super-cube" approach has been proposed, in which a fixed number of cells can be switched on and off to generate different building spatial designs, and constraints ensure practical designs, e.g. no overlap of spaces should occur. A super-structure free approach has been developed by a "movable and sizable" representation, listing the building spaces with their position and dimensions, and allowing these spaces to be deleted, split, and resized, as such automatically following the constraints.

Algorithms have been derived to transform the "super-cube" representation into the "movable and sizable" representation and vice versa, and these algorithms have been verified for successful operation for overlaps in spaces, non-connected spaces, truncation errors, alterations in space identification, and fragmented spaces.

In the near future, an optimisation approach will be developed where both representations are used alternately: The super-structure approach will allow a dedicated optimisation algorithm to find a global optimum (Van der Blom et al. 2016), whereas this solution in a super-structure free approach can be used to explore more freely another (possibly local) optimum. As such the design space is cyclically both explored in-depth (via the super-structure) and globally (via the super-structure free representation).

References

Baldock, R. & Shea, K., 2006. Structural Topology Optimization of Braced Steel Frameworks Using Genetic Programming. *13th EG-ICE Workshop*, pp.54–61.

Bandaru, S. & Deb, K., 2015. Temporal Innovization: Evolution of Design Principles Using Multi-objective Optimization. In *8th International Conference of Evolutionary Multi-Criterion Optimization*. pp. 79–93.

Belegundu, A.D. & Rajan, S.D., 1988. A shape optimization approach based on natural design variables and shape functions. *Computer Methods in Applied Mechanics and Engineering*, 66(1), pp.87–106.

Chan, A.S.L., 1960. The Design of Michell Optimum Structures. *The college of aeronautics* (Vol. 142), Cranfield.

Dolan, W.B., Cummings, P.T. & Le Van, M.D., 1990. Algorithmic Efficiency of Simulated Annealing for Heat Exchanger Network Design. *Computers Chem. Eng*, 14, pp.1039–1050.

Droste, S. & Wiesmann, D., 2000. Metric Based Evolutionary Algorithms, Proceedings of EuroGP'2000, Berlin: Springer-Verlag, pp. 29-43.

Emmerich, M., Grötzner, M. & Schütz, M., 2001. Design of Graph-Based Evolutionary Algorithms: A Case Study for Chemical Process Networks. *Evolutionary Computation*, 9(3), pp.329–354.

Emmerich, M. T. M., Hopfe, C. J., Marijt, R., Hensen, J. L. M., Struck, C., & Stoelinga, P. (2008). Evaluating optimization methodologies for future integration in building performance tools. In Proceedings of the 8th Int. Conf. on Adaptive Computing in Design and Manufacture (ACDM) (Vol. 29, p. 7).

Floudas, C.A., 1995. *Nonlinear and mixed-integer optimization: fundamentals and applications*, Oxford University Press.

Hofmeyer, H. & Davila Delgado, J.M., 2015. Co-evolutionary and Genetic Algorithm Based Building Spatial and Structural Design. *AIEDAM 29*, pp.351-370.

Hopfe, C. J., Emmerich, M. T., Marijt, R., & Hensen, J. (2012). Robust multi-criteria design optimisation in building design. Proceedings of Building Simulation and Optimization, Loughborough, UK, pp. 118-125.

Jackson, R., 1968. Optimization of chemical reactors with respect to flow configuration. *Journal of Optimization Theory and Applications*, 2(4), pp.240–259.

Kicinger, R., Arciszewski, T. & De Jong, K., 2005. Evolutionary computation and structural design: A survey of the state-of-the-art. *Computers and Structures*, 83(23-24), pp.1943–1978.

Koza, J.R., Andre, D., Bennett, F.H. & Keane, M.A., 1996. Use of Automatically Defined Functions and Architecture-Altering Operations in Automated Circuit Synthesis Using Genetic Programming. In *Genetic Programming 1996: Proceedings of the First Annual Conference*. pp. 132–149.

Liang, Q.Q.; Xie, Y.M.; Steven, G.P., 2000. Optimal topology design of bracing systems for multistory steel frames. *Structural engineering*, 126(7), pp.823–829.

Martins, J.R.R.A. & Lambe, A.B., 2013. Multidisciplinary Design Optimization: A Survey of Architectures. *AIAA Journal*, 51(9), pp.2049–2075.

Rafiq, M.Y. & Rustell, M.J., 2014. Building Information Modeling Steered by Evolutionary Computing. Journal of Computing in Civil Engineering, 28(4), pp.05014003-1-11.

Sekulski, Z., 2009. Least-weight topology and size optimization of high speed vehicle-passenger catamaran structure by genetic algorithm. *Marine Structures*, 22(4), pp.691–711.

Sigmund, O., 2001. A 99 line topology optimization code written in matlab. *Structural and Multidisciplinary Optimization*, 21, pp.120–127.

Tuhus-Dubrow, D. & Krarti, M., 2010. Genetic-algorithm based approach to optimize building envelope design for residential buildings. *Building and Environment*, 45(7), pp.1574–1581.

Van der Blom, K., Boonstra, S., Hofmeyer, H., Emmerich, M.T.M., 2016. A Super-structure Based Optimisation Approach for Building Spatial Topologies. Accepted for ECCOMAS 2016, Greece, June 5-10, 2016.

Voll, P., Lampe, M., Wrobel, G. & Bardow, A., 2012. Superstructure-free synthesis and optimization of distributed industrial energy supply systems. *Energy* 45(1), pp. 424-435.

Wetter, M. 2004. Simulation-Based Building Energy Optimization. *Ph.D. thesis*. University of California, Berkeley.

Wang, W., Zmeureanu, R. & Rivard, H., 2005. Applying multi-objective genetic algorithms in green building design optimization. *Building and Environment*, 40(11), pp.1512–1525.

Wright, J.A., Loosemore, H.A. & Farmani, R., 2002. Optimization of building thermal design and control by multi-criterion genetic algorithm. *Energy and Buildings*, 34(9), pp.959–972.

From Analysis of Information Needs towards an Information Model of Railway Infrastructure

Zaharah Allah Bukhsh[1], Timo Hartmann[2], and Irina Stipanovic[1]

[1]Department of Construction Management and Engineering, University of Twente, Enschede
[2]Chair of System Engineering, Institute of Civil Engineering, TU Berlin
z.allahbukhsh@utwente.nl, timo.hartmann@tu-berlin.de, i.stipanovic@utwente.nl

Abstract. Railway is a tightly coupled network, where the operations are directly effected by the condition of rail infrastructure. With the advancement of ICT, a railway network exploit various computerized systems for efficient railway monitoring, maintenance and operations. However, these systems suffer from number of limitations, mainly, the data related to each asset type (e.g. Track, Bridge, etc) are stored in separate database management system. Such scattered and isolated nature of data present the island of information, while making it impossible to perform the sound decision analysis. In this paper, we propose a nework wide information model of railway infrastructure that structure the railway object, specify their properties and identify their inter-relationships. The presented information model supports the railway monitoring, maintenance and operations by providing the layout of railway infrastructure. Structuring data in the form of railway assets, railway risk assessment, railway load management, railway maintenance, and railway failure will provide a solid base to railway stakeholders, e.g. infrastructure managers, to take informed decisions based on data properties.

1 Introduction

Railway network depends on information and communication technology (ICT) for day-to-day operations and infrastructure maintenance. Many computerized information solutions have been developed and deployed in the railway agencies to support the efficient railway operations, monitoring and maintenance. Immense amount of data is stored in the railway systems to keep track of assets' condition, network performance, maintenance records, etc . However, the data related to each network aspect are usually stored in separate database management systems (see Thaduri et al. (2015)), which expose the challenge of data integration (Galar et al., 2012). Such unavailability of data make it difficult to perform the sound decision analysis for cost-effective railway monitoring, maintenance and operations.

This research effort is a part of DESTination RAIL project, which seeks to develop a decision support tool based on network wide information management system. One of the main focus in the development of information management system is to understand the end-users data needs for the decision analysis. To deal with the challenges of data isolation and to comprehend the data needs, we choose to exploit the information modeling approach to design the information management system of railway infrastructure. Among other techniques, information modeling structures the problem domain and provide its semantic interpretation. An information model provides a neutral data model, with varying level of detail, which provides support in data exchange and data maintenance. Thus, the objective of this paper is to design the detailed information model of railway infrastructure, which cover monitoring, operation and maintenance aspects. An iterative design approach has been followed, where the draft version of an information

Submitted to:EG-ICE 2016

model is used in the process of requirements elicitation to stimulate the active discussion between project partners. Furthermore, semi-structured interviews, directed by a questionnaire, were conducted in order to examine and outline the specific data requirements of project partners. The main contribution of this work lies in presenting an information model, which not only represent the railway objects, but draft the monitoring, operations and maintenance aspects of the railway in the form of railway assets, railway risk assessment, railway load management, railway maintenance and railway failure. The final information model will be used as a blueprint for the development of a network wide information management system. Moreover, we believe that the presented information model is comprehensive and generic enough to be used for the development of railway infrastructure-related data applications.

The rest of the paper is structured as follows: the state of the art of information modeling in ACE domain is outlined in Section 2. Our development approach to design the information model of railway infrastructure is provided in Section 3. The detailed information model is discussed in Section 4. Finally, Section 5 and Section 6 provide the discussion and conclusions, respectively.

2 Related Work

To support the interoperability between softwares, development of information modeling and sharing protocols is trending in ACE domain. An information model can be defined as a simplified representation of a small, finite subset of the world. As such, each of the objects within a model corresponds to some real or abstract object that might exist in the world or within the state of mind of a group of persons or an individual (Turk, 2001; Kent and Hoberman, 2012). As explained by Zamanian and Pittman (1999), "information models formulate the concise description of the real-world artifact that can be communicated and processed effectively".

Few problem-specific information models have been suggested in the literature with respect to railway domain and in general for the ACE domain. Bosschaart et al. (2015) proposed an UML class representation of railway interlocking data in order to provide a common knowledge/data base of machine readable data formats. To reduce the cost and inefficiency of data exchange, UML classes are mapped to RailML. RailML is a XML based exchange format that ease the data exchange process among the railway applications (Kolmorgen and Huerlimann, 2005). Borrmann et al. (2014) followed the information modeling approach to design the track alignment and procedural geometric models. These data models are further used to facilitate the data sharing and synchronous modeling via collaboration platforms. To deal with challenges of railway data integrations from various data sources, Wang et al. (2012) proposed a neutral meta-data dictionary model. The proposed meta-data dictionary model is used for the development of XML-oriented three-dimensional data models where data objects are grouped into various types. Vossebeld and Hartmann (2014) proposed to use an information model to support part of safety assessment task for tunnels, instead of managing comprehensive dossiers with tunnel critical information. Lucas et al. (2013) developed a comprehensive object-oriented model and an ontology to help facility managers in managing the patient safety events and facility operations in an efficient manner.

There is increasing focus on the design of information and data models to facilitate efficient data exchange and to define data inter-relatedness. As noticed with aforementioned studies, information models are mainly contexts-specific and usually act as an initial step in the development of a computerized solution. Hence, it is important that information models are well developed, cover the problem domain sufficiently and are understood by their perspective end-users. In this paper, we also opted to consider the end-users' perspective for the development of information model for the domain of railway asset management, in order to understand information needs for decision analysis and to communicate the system design. Furthermore, the resulting information model will be a useful addition to the literature of railway engineering as no general railway infrastructure model was found during the literature search.

3 Information Modeling Approach

To design an Information Model (IM), we adopted a conceptual, specification-driven perspective. The presented IM is not aimed to exactly model and map the railway infrastructure network. Instead, it is targeted to specify and understand end-users' data needs by identifying the railway network objects and their relationships. Objects of the IM can be understood as physical entities of the railway infrastructure, such as tracks or bridges, or conceptual entities related to railway asset management tasks, such as risk types, failure reasons. In addition to identifying objects, the developed IM also represents important attributes of these objects and relationship between objects. To keep the IM simple, operational details, such as train schedules or railway stocks have been omitted. The Unified Modeling Language (UML) is used for supporting the model development process and for representing the model (Lee, 1999).

The design effort underwent three main iterations. During each iteration, we identified and refined objects and their properties related to the universe of discourse at hand. We started the design iterations by developing a first initial version of the IM capturing all the concepts and objects that were mentioned in the project proposal of DESTination RAIL. In a second iteration, this initial IM was then enriched by acquiring knowledge of railway infrastructure from various other sources. First and foremost, we consulted one of the state of the art railway engineering textbooks, Modern Railway Track (Esveld, 2001). Additionally, we consulted RailML an existing standard for describing railway infrastructure assets, railway timetables, and railway building stock. Identification of important domain related terms led to the specification of objects, their properties, their inter-relatedness and their overall operations. This led to the second version of IM.

To further improve the IM, semi-structured interviews were organized with twelve key project partners from nine different institutes. These participants belong to various railway agencies and research institutes and possess considerable experience working in the particular railway domain either as a researcher or engineer. These participants will also be the first end-users of the IM. The structuring of railway objects in IM is crucial, since all the innovations and methods developed in DESTination RAIL will depend on it. We used the draft IM developed out of the first two iterations to provide an example to the interviewees and to trigger thoughts and critical reviews. Moreover, we develop a questionnaire to guide the interview process. The questionnaire consists of questions related to railway infrastructure and asks questions about the data requirements of each participant. Interviews were conducted over Skype and telephone that lasted between 30 to 60 minutes. Overall, the interviews led to numerous comments on the conceptual IM from the second iteration. We used these comments to update the IM concept from the second iteration to arrive at the final IM described in the Section 4.

4 Information Model for Railway Asset Management

Railway infrastructure is comprised of physical objects, e.g. tracks, rolling stocks, etc. along with their functional capabilities and features. For the end-to-end railway management and smooth operations, three main aspects, i.e. monitoring, operation and maintenance of railway objects are required. By railway monitoring, current conditions of objects are assessed and required measures are taken. To store the data gathered from condition monitoring, properties of railway objects, their location and their geometrical details should be defined. We design an IM of railway infrastructure assets, which will store the data about the railway objects along with their current conditions, provided in Section 4.1. To assess the conditions and need of maintenance, an IM to support the risk assessment is introduced in Section 4.2. Operation of railway is core aspects in the railway network management, which consist of traffic control, timetable management, etc. Considering the defined scope of DESTination RAIL, we have modeled only railway load management aspect to capture the affect of rolling stocks on the network in Section 4.3. With respect to maintenance, we designed an IM to support railway maintenance in order to capture maintenance types, schedules, costs and affects on railway operations, presented in Section 4.4. Additionally, we model the IM of railway failures in order to keep a record of failure sources in the network, provided in Section 4.5.

Figure 1 shows the objects of the IM representing the main components of rail infrastructure. The *RailInfrastructure* is composed of *Track*, *Platform*, *Signaling* and *ElectrificationSystem*. Among others, *Track* is the most integral component of the rail infrastructure. The objects related to rail infrastructure are mainly associated with the physical objects (i.e. track, platform, etc) of the railway network. For example, any object of infrastructure can be regarded as *Hotspot*, as it is defined as a part/component/place of the network that is vulnerable to fail. To understand the needs of maintenance, one or more types of *RiskAssessmentMethod* can be associated with each component as well. Moreover, to allow the representation of different failure reasons of each object, the IM allows to track possible problems with a class named *FailureSource*. Similarly, IM can store the data about the spots that are undergoing with certain maintenance operations through *SpotMaintenance*. A *RailInfrastructure* component has one or more associated *ConstructionTechniques* that can be used to store different maintenance and replacement methods for each of the components in the network. Be noted that all of these information models are related to each other in terms of exchange of data. For the sake of discussion and to keep the models readable, we have discussed each model separately in the following sections.

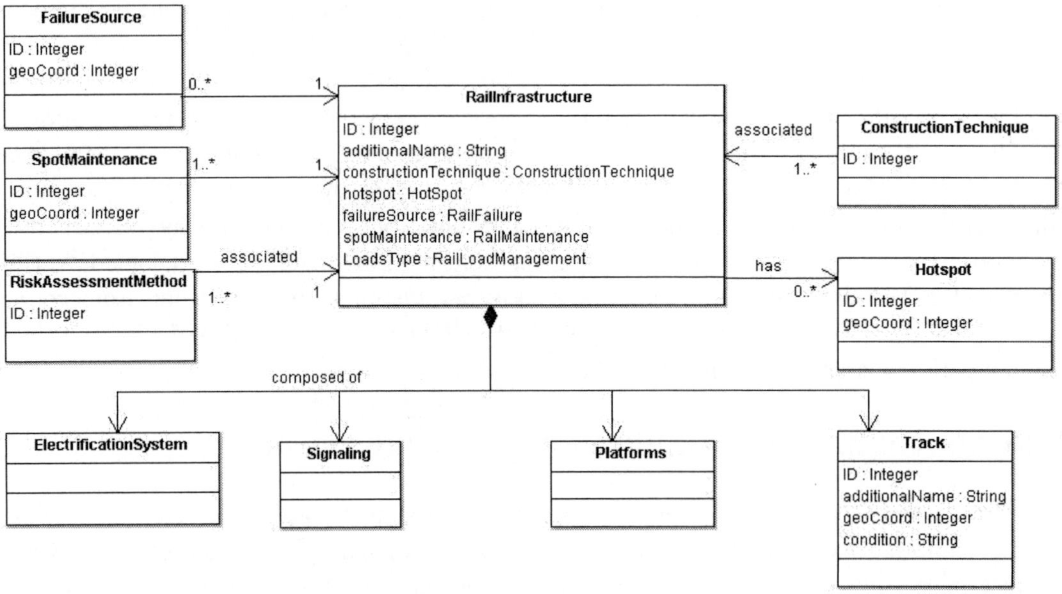

Figure 1: Information Model of Rail Infrastructure

4.1 Model of Railway Infrastructure Assets

A track consists of a number of sub-components as illustrated in Figure 2. Components of tracks are divided into *superstructure* and *substructure*. *Superstructure* includes all those components that are above the foundation. While, *substructure* provides the details of underlying support components.

Every railway track has a specific *layout*. We have defined *layout* using objects for track *curves* and *gradients*. The *substructure* of the track is composed of cutting, embankment, drainage and subgrade. The IM represent the related properties of all these components. A substructure can have zero or more *cutting* and underlying *embankment*. It is necessary to keep the information regarding the *drainage* system updated because most track failures occur due to malfunctioning of the drainage system. The *subgrade* is further based on *subsoil*. It is important to be able to specify subgrade and subsoil behaviour under various load cases.

The *superstructure* of the track consists of all those components that are built over the substructure. The key component of the superstructure is the *rail* itself. A *rail* object is further decomposed into sleepers, ballast, and fastening system. Definition of objects along with their properties will be helpful to store the data about these physical components. As shown in Figure 2, a track can have zero or more *SwitchesAndCrossings*. Each switch or crossing can include additional information regarding its type, crossing point, length and exchange radius. Additional structures can be represented, such as, track tunnel or bridge. Each track element can have zero or more of these structures.

Along with geometrical and location properties, each object has a condition property which will be used to store the current conditions of asset. This condition property will be updated frequently as a result of monitoring.

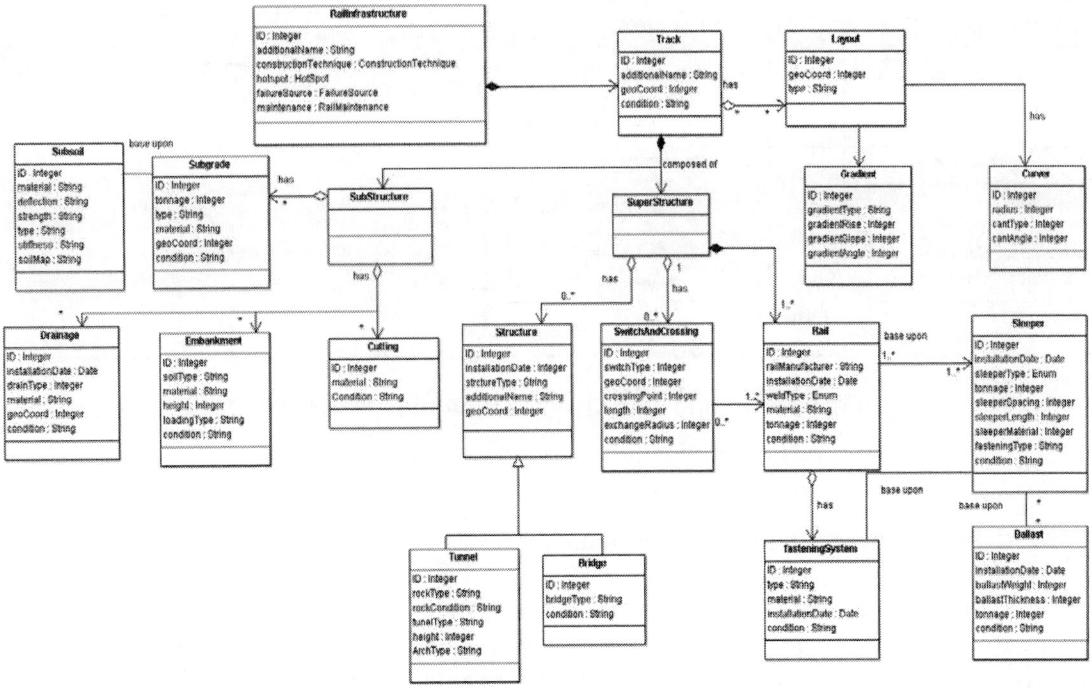

Figure 2: Information Model (Railway Infrastructure Assets)

4.2 Model of Risk Assessment Method

Figure 3 shows how the IM can represent the important concepts of the general *Risk Assessment Method* adopted from ISO (2009). The risk assessment method consists of classes of *RiskIdentification*, *Risk-Analysis*, *RiskEvaluation* and *RiskTreatment*, each of which can be modeled in IM. The *RiskIdentification* capture the possible risks, their effects, and their analysis techniques based on a particular *RiskSource*. In the *RiskAnalysis* process, the identified risks are further analysed by considering further information of risk factors, risk likelihood, risk consequences, risk levels, or risk causes, among others. Based on the *RiskAnalysis* methods, a risk evaluation method prioritise the risk and suggest treatment requirements. Finally, *RiskTreatment* captures the treatment assessment, treatment selection and treatment priority for the sake of risk mitigation. For a single risk, it is possible to assign a number of risk treatments. IM presented in Figure 3 is able to capture the whole process of risk assessment in a form of defined data entities.

The risk assessment method presented here are of generic nature and can be applied to any infrastructure, system, and organization. The development of risk assessment method specific to railway infrastructure is part of our future work.

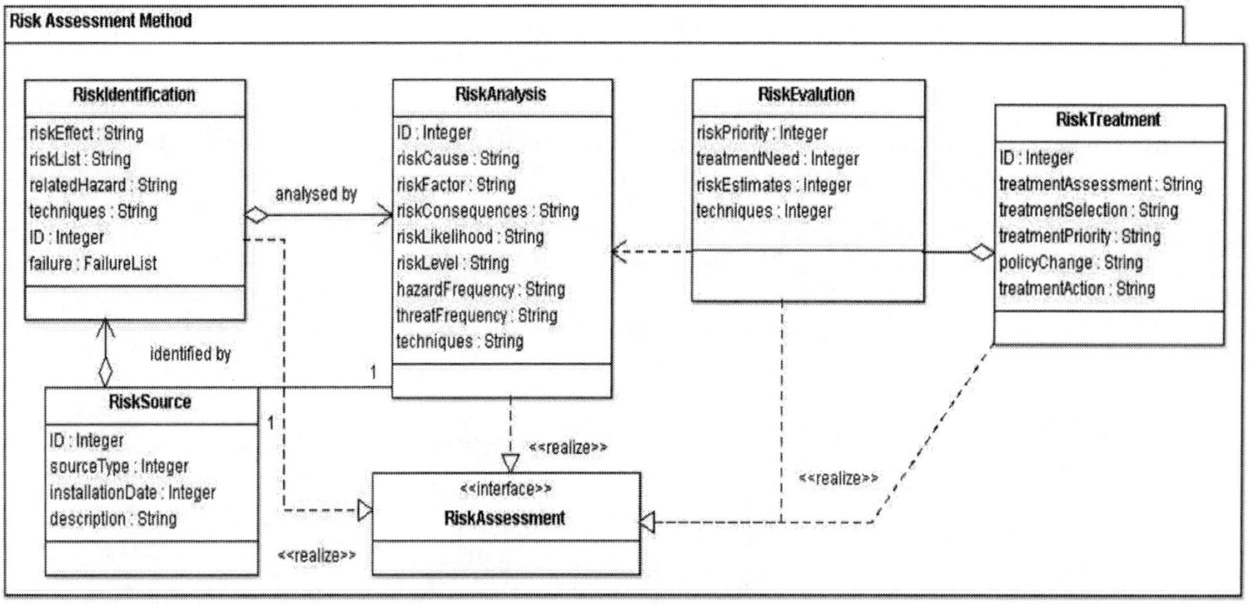

Figure 3: Information Model (Risk Assessment Method)

4.3 Model of Railway Load Management

As discussed earlier, railway load management belongs to the area of railway operations. Data about loads and rolling stock is important to store as it can be used to simulate the behavior of substructures under various loadings. Moreover, information regarding various vehicle types, weight of load, axle load, load speed, load length, caused deflection, force and load type are important properties to be stored. The information model of *RailLoadManagement* is provided in Figure 4. Several other properties of load can also be stored in the system, if needed.

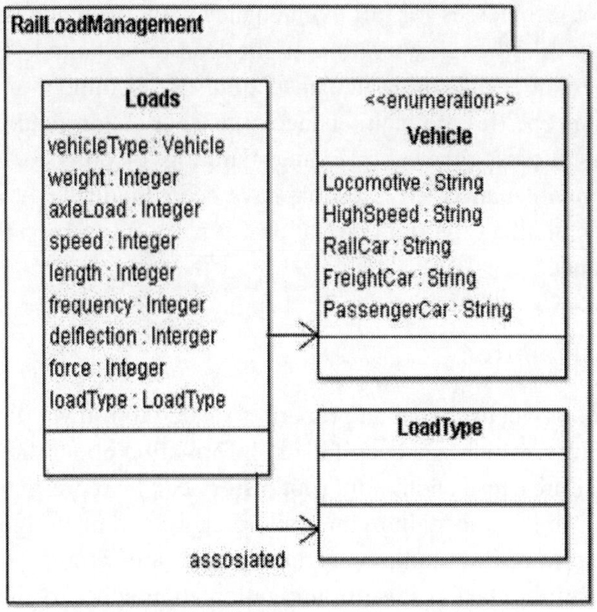

Figure 4: Information Model (Railway Load)

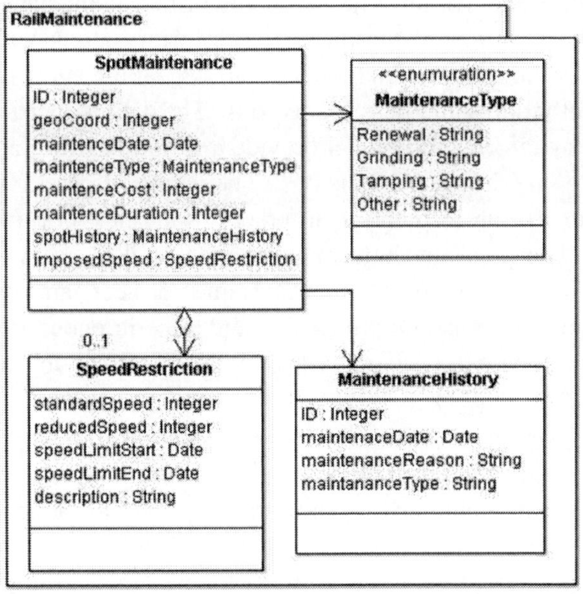

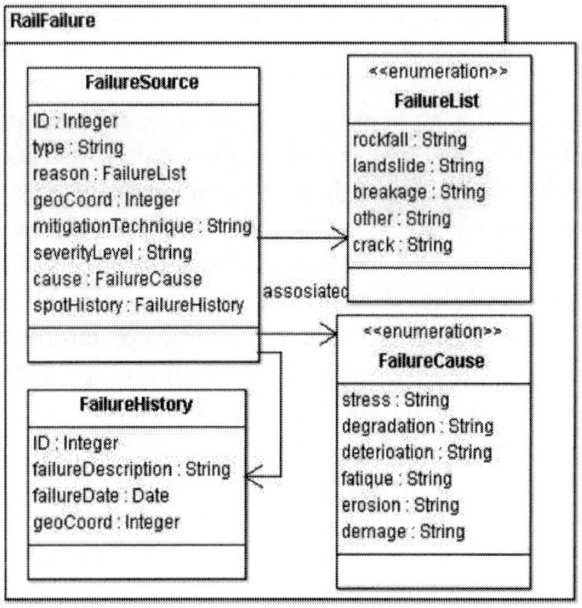

Figure 5: Information Model(Railway Maintenance)

Figure 6: Information Model (Railway Failure)

4.4 Model of Railway Maintenance

Figure 5 shows the main object classes for rail maintenance management accounted for in the IM. As a result of rail maintenance work, the rail operation might need to be halted or speed restrictions need to be applied. Regarding the maintenance of particular section/spot, a number of important information can be stored. Most important properties are maintenance type, spot history and imposed speed. The maintenance type can be represented as renewal, grinding, tamping, or others. Additionally, the IM allows to store data about all the maintenance activities that have been conducted at a particular section/spot in the past. As maintenance can affect the train operations, it is useful to keep the data about the imposed speed during the maintenance.

4.5 Model of Railway Failure

Figure 6 shows the main components and data properties related to railway failure. Failure source is the main object of railway failure, which has been failed. Information about the location of failure, failure reasons, failure severity, failure cause and failure spot history can be represented using the IM. Additionally, information regarding the type of failure and failure cause can be assigned to each railway failure element to for example determine how common certain failures are. Similarly, information regarding the history of failure will be useful to take the useful mitigation approaches to avoid failures in future.

5 Discussion

The presented information model not only provides a layout of railway infrastructure, but it provides the data support to monitoring, maintenance and operational domain of railway. Data structured by information model of railway assets represents the geometrical specification and inter-relations of core assets, which is further useful in the process of monitoring. An information model of rail maintenance specifies the planned schedule of maintenance as well as record the maintenance history along with maintenance reasons and maintenance type. Moreover, an information model of railway failure supports the identification of failure sources, types of different failures and possible reasons. The data properties of all the physical and conceptual entities specified by information model provide a strong base of data for stakeholders, such as infrastructure managers, to take informed decisions. The nature of decisions could vary from identification of failure sources, to risk assessment of an object in the network and management of load assessment of rolling stock. The presented information model will be used to provide a digitalized framework of data in a form of information management system to project partners. Moreover, we believe that the presented information model is comprehensive and generic enough to support the development of those railway applications where the data/record about the identified objects is required to be stored.

The key concept in the design of information model is to define the optimum level of granularity. High level of granularity provides in-depth and detailed knowledge of objects and their inter-relationship. However, it could result in an information model which is complex to understand and too difficult to modify. While, with the low level of granularity, the chances of leaving out the important objects is high. We mitigated this problem by taking two steps: first, we represent the rail infrastructure into different domains as shown in previous sections. Within each domain, we focused only on main components. Secondly, during our interview sessions, we asked the interviewees to suggest about the inclusion and exclusion of considered objects as well as any modification in the objects inter-relationship. The main focus of the developed information model is to communicate the system design instead of outlining the implementation details. Thus, we mainly focused at the level of granularity that kept our model easy to communicate and understandable.

As with any information model, many concerns can be raised based on the selection of objects, their considered properties, and their interrelationship among them. Thus, it is important for an information model to act as a dynamically updated model, during design and development phase, instead of a static model which reflect the system design. To support the need of continuous modification, the design and implementation techniques for the system development should be flexible enough. It can be noted in the information models, provided above (for instance see Figure 1), that few class attributes e.g. geo-Cord, condition is repeatedly defined for each class, while the concept of inheritance could have been employed for this purpose. Many standardized data models (e.g. CityGML, IFC) use the inheritance to achieve the reusability. We avoid the use of inheritance intentionally as even though inheritance improve the reusability of code but it induces the unnecessary coupling in the system design and implementation (Burn, 2014). With the compelling need to support the dynamic system design and implementation, a prominent shift has been noticed, in database management techniques, from the static database schema definition (relational databases) to dynamic schema definition (NoSQL databases) (Moniruzzaman and Hossain, 2013).

6 Conclusion

The information model of railway infrastructure developed in the paper is the part of an on-going effort of DESTination RAIL project, which require the development of network wide information management system to mitigate the challenges of data isolation. We followed an iterative development approach to design information model, where the data item from the project proposal is identified, standard data sharing format (RailML) of railway along with seminal railway engineering literature is considered, finally semi-structured interviews with twelve participants from nine different institutes were conducted. Instead of focusing only on railway assets and railway operations, the information model presented here can store data about the all the important aspects of railway maintenance, railway assets, railway failures, railway loads and railway risk assessment. Finally, the resulted information model provides a strong base of data that can be used by infrastructure managers to take well grounded operations and/or maintenance decisions.

The developed information model has served two main purposes: first, it structures the railway infrastructure based on its data properties, which will be further used for the development of information management system. Secondly, it is used as a communication tool to understand the end-users' perspective with respect to data needs and domain knowledge. We believe, the provided information model is generic enough to be used by other railway application where the data about considered objects is required to be stored.

References

Bernardi, S., Flammini, F., Marrone, S., Merseguer, J., Papa, C., and Vittorini, V. (2011). Model-driven availability evaluation of railway control systems. In *Computer Safety, Reliability, and Security*, pages 15–28. Springer.

Borrmann, A., Flurl, M., Jubierre, J. R., Mundani, R.-P., and Rank, E. (2014). Synchronous collaborative tunnel design based on consistency-preserving multi-scale models. *Advanced Engineering Informatics*, 28(4):499 – 517.

Bosschaart, M., Quaglietta, E., Janssen, B., and Goverde, R. M. (2015). Efficient formalization of railway interlocking data in railml. *Information Systems*, 49:126 – 141.

Burn, S. (2014). Inheritance is Bad: Code Reuse. Available at: http://blogs.perl.org/users/sid$_b$*urn*/2014/03/*inheritance* – *is* – *bad* – *code* – *reuse* – *part* – 1.*html*.

Esveld, C. (2001). Modern railway track. MRT-productions Zaltbommel, Germany.

Galar, D., Gustafson, A., Tormos, B., and Berges, L. (2012). Maintenance Decision Making Based on Different Types of Data Fusion. *Eksploatacja I Niezawodnosc-Maintenance and Reliability*, 14(2):135–144.

Jeff Leighton, BIM Manager, V. (2015). Evolution of Building Information Modeling. Available at: http://www.sbcmag.info/news/2015/nov/contractor-bim-process-not-software.

Kent, W. and Hoberman, S. (2012). *Data and reality: a timeless perspective on perceiving and managing information in our imprecise world*. Technics publications.

Kolmorgen, V. and Huerlimann, D. (2005). Railml-a standard interface for railway data. *EUROPEAN RAILWAY REVIEW*, (4).

Lee, Y. T. (1999). Information modeling: From design to implementation. In *Proceedings of the second world manufacturing congress*, pages 315–321. Citeseer.

Lucas, J., Bulbul, T., and Thabet, W. (2013). An object-oriented model to support healthcare facility information management. *Automation in Construction*, 31:281–291.

Moniruzzaman, A. and Hossain, S. A. (2013). Nosql database: New era of databases for big data analytics-classification, characteristics and comparison. *arXiv preprint arXiv:1307.0191*.

Thaduri, A., Galar, D., and Kumar, U. (2015). Railway assets: A potential domain for big data analytics. *Procedia Computer Science*, 53(1):457–467.

Turk, Z. (2001). Phenomenologial foundations of conceptual product modelling in architecture, engineering and construction. *Artificial Intelligence in Engineering*, 15(2):83 – 92.

Turkaslan-Bulbul, M. T. and Akin, O. (2006). Computational support for building evaluation: Embedded commissioning model. *Automation in construction*, 15(4):438–447.

Vossebeld, N. and Hartmann, T. (2014). Supporting tunnel safety assessment with an information model. In *2014 International Conference on Computing in Civil and Building Engineering*.

Wang, H., Xu, W., and Jia, C. (2012). Metadata-oriented data model supporting railway distributed system integration. *Journal of Software*, 7(4):814–822.

Young, R. R. (2002). Recommended requirements gathering practices. *CrossTalk*, 15(4):9–12.

Zamanian, M. K. and Pittman, J. H. (1999). A software industry perspective on aec information models for distributed collaboration. *Automation in Construction*, 8(3):237–248.

Towards Knowledge-Based Building Navigation with the Use of a Hierarchical Graph Model

Wojciech Palacz, Grażyna Ślusarczyk, Andrzej Łachwa, Barbara Strug, Anna Paszyńska, Ewa Grabska
Jagiellonian University, Kraków, Poland
wojciech.palacz@uj.edu.pl

Abstract. This paper is an attempt to develop an effective method of indoor navigation with a dynamic target selection. Knowledge needed to locate a desired place and the shortest path leading to it is represented in the form of a graph with many hierarchies. This representation allows us to express different types of hierarchical dependencies between building parts, like geometrical and functional ones, in one structure. Moreover, such a structure is useful to extract subgraphs containing information necessary for a given computational task, for instance route searching. The paper presents an example of searching for a target, illustrating the approach that can be used for various applications.

1. Introduction

Although many new buildings are built on university campuses there are no effective facilities to find departments, lecture halls, canteens, etc. The visitors and also students and staff often face the problem how to reach easily and timely a desired place from the current location. There exists a need for navigation tools to locate a target place and the shortest path leading to it.

Navigation systems are, in general, concerned with determining the current location of their user, finding the optimal path to a target point, and then guiding the user along this path. Outdoor devices usually use satellite-based location services, but these services are unreliable inside buildings. Indoor systems use alternative approaches based on Wi-Fi (Köbben et al., 2006), UWB, RFID (Khoury & Kamat, 2009), etc. Approaches based on matching images from smartphone cameras to the database of unique landmarks were also proposed (Basiri et al., 2016). In the last resort, the user can simply be asked to mark their current location on a map.

The optimal path is usually defined as the shortest one, and calculated by an appropriate graph algorithm. This implies that the system must have an alternative map in the form of a graph. This graph will usually have nodes representing doors and other important points in the building, and edges representing possible movements of a person walking from one point to another one (Büchel & Gilliéron, 2004). The most common graph algorithm for route calculation is the Dijkstra's algorithm. Other graph algorithms like A*, Floyd-Warshall or Bellman-Ford (Cormen et al., 2001) are also used to determine the shortest path from a source to a destination. In (Kneidl et al., 2011) a reduced visibility graph is used to reflect possible route choices and the Fastest-Path Algorithm finds the fastest path for travelers (Höcker et al., 2010). In (Whiting et al., 2007) metrical-topological models constructed from labelled floor plan geometry are used to describe the shape and connectivity of space, and constitute useful underlying tools for wayfinding. However, for almost all current navigation applications complex building interiors with large open spaces and vertical communication means present challenges.

The guidance part can be limited to showing a map with a drawn path, or can be provided as a list of commands ("go straight 100 meters, then turn right and walk another 50 meters"). Humans do not have an innate understanding of numeric distances and angles, therefore instructions using landmarks ("walk up the stairs, then turn towards the coffee machine") are easier to follow (Basiri et al., 2016). In the extreme case, when the navigation device does not use any location service and cannot update its own position in real-time, the guidance instructions may simply be a sequence of photos showing landmarks the user should walk by on their way from the starting to the target point (Faure et al., 2006).

The approach proposed in this paper deals with indoor navigation dedicated to pedestrians. Navigation strategy is based on knowledge about the building layout stored in the hierarchical graph structure. Its multiple hierarchies allow for building models which represent not only the spatial hierarchy of rooms and floors, but also other functional and administrative dependencies. This additional knowledge stored in the graph can be used in the target selection phase.

Currently available navigation tools require users to specify a single point as a target, either by directly marking it on a map, or by providing a description which can be translated by the device to point coordinates ("the room with the number 303", "the coffee machine closest to my current position"). The system based on the graph model proposed in this paper will be able to find targets described in a parametric way or specified by selected attributes (e.g., office rooms with printers). The hierarchy grouping graph nodes into larger entities makes it possible to accept requests for "the closest laboratory belonging to the Department of Organic Chemistry". What's even more important, specifying targets which resolve to a set of points will also be possible: "all office rooms belonging to the Department of Games" will make the navigation device guide the user from one room to the other.

The hierarchical nature of the graph model can be also useful for path searching algorithms. It provides the possibility of filtering the graph by hierarchy type and level, eliminating knowledge not related to the task of finding a path between two points in the chosen fragment of the building. The number of data to be analyzed is greatly reduced, thus speeding up the search.

2. Related Works

Graph structures are commonly used to model relations in many systems (Strug et al., 2013; Minas, 2002). They can be used in design systems to model topological relations between components, in databases to model logical relations between objects as well as to model data and control flow or specification and analysis of software systems. In many real applications, modelling systems by plain graphs (graphs where edges and nodes are sets without additional structure) is insufficient. The complex systems are very often hierarchical, thus graphs with hierarchy should be used as the models (Grabska et al., 2007, 2013; Strug et al., 2014). Graphs of this kind allow not only for modelling hierarchical relations between components of the system but also for hiding some details of "encapsulated" subgraphs.

During the last years several models based on graphs with hierarchy have been defined (Milner, 2008; Ferrari & Montanari, 2000; Bruni et al., 2012; Barendregt et al., 1987; Drewes et al., 2002; Poulovassilis & Levene, 1994; Sowa, 2008, 1976, 1984; Harel, 1988; Chen & Zhong, 2011, 2012). They were used for modelling global computing systems, syntactical structure of agents, mobile systems, design systems, granular computing, etc. It turns out that existing hierarchical graphs are not sufficient to efficiently model objects considered in architectural design and engineering problems. The good representation should allow for expressing multi-argument relations between parts of different components, hierarchical dependencies between different parts of design, as well as many hierarchies of different types, where not all components must belong to the hierarchy. None of the mentioned models allows for modelling of all required features.

Therefore in this paper hierarchical hypergraphs with multiple hierarchies of various types are proposed as representation of building models. The considered graphs are composed of nodes, which represent object components, and edges representing relations between them. In given graph nodes other nodes and edges can be nested. Graph nodes with nested atoms are called hierarchical. Hierarchical nodes may be used to hide certain details of a designed object that are not needed in a given moment or to group objects having common features (geometrical or functional). Graph hierarchies enable us to group elements according to different objectives, and consider the project at a chosen level of detail. Hierarchical graphs encode the knowledge about created designs and therefore enable to efficiently reason about the conformity of designs with specified design criteria (Grabska & Ślusarczyk, 2011).

In this paper a multi-hierarchical graph model is used to search for possible routes in a given building. Searching for routes in buildings is a problem related to autonomous navigation of robots in indoor environments (Shen et al., 2011; Latombe, 1991) and establishing the best escape routes from buildings in case of emergency (Stringfield, 1996; Gilliéron & Merminod, 2003; Cepolina, 2005; Shen & Chien, 2005; Chiu et al., 2007; AlShboul & Al-Tahat, 2007; Papinigis et al., 2010; Ronchi & Nilsson, 2013).

3. The Graph-Based Representation of Building-Related Knowledge

In this section the extended graph-based data structures, which better reflect the intrinsic nature of design objects, are described. They enable to express geometrical properties of objects together with their attributes and different types of relations between object components.

The proposed multi-hierarchical graphs can represent a complex object at different levels of detail and at different stages of the building lifecycle. They allow for hiding unnecessary at the moment low-level data and presenting only an outline of the object or showing a detailed view of the whole object (or of its part). The considered multi-hierarchical graphs are an extension of labelled and attributed graphs. They are composed of nodes, which represent object components, and edges representing relations between them. Nodes and edges are labelled by names of components and relations, respectively. Semantic aspects of components and relations are encoded in sets of attributes assigned to nodes and edges.

Use of multiple graph hierarchies, instead of a single hierarchy, allows for additional knowledge to be encoded in the graph structure. Each hierarchy can correspond to different element grouping criteria. Reasoning about designs (Grabska & Ślusarczyk, 2011) can be more efficient thanks to the possibility of selecting both the hierarchy type, level, and the appropriate components of the object.

Let us introduce a formal description of the proposed multi-hierarchical graph model.

Let Σ_V and Σ_E be two disjoint alphabets of node and edge labels, respectively. Let A be a nonempty, finite set of node and edge attributes. Let D_a denote a fixed, nonempty set of admissible values for attribute $a \in A$, called the domain of a.

Let the set of nodes and edges of a graph G, known together as graph atoms, be denoted by U, i.e., $U = V \cup E$. It can be assumed without loss of generality that Σ_V, Σ_E, A, V and E are pairwise disjoint.

The graphs considered are hierarchical, i.e., nodes and edges can be nested inside other nodes. Graph nodes with nested atoms are called hierarchical. Hierarchical graphs allow for expressing relationships between components located on different hierarchy levels, i.e., edges can connect nodes nested in different parents.

Some graph atoms may be completely outside the hierarchy, in the sense that concepts like "set of children" and "parent" are not applicable to them at all. Let $\perp$ be a fixed value, different from all graph atoms, which will be used to denote this case in the following.

Definition 1 *A mapping* $ch : V \to 2^U \cup \{\perp\}$ *is a* ***child nesting function*** *if and only if:*

- $\forall v, w \in V : w \in ch(v) \Rightarrow ch(w) \neq \perp$, *i.e. if a node is a child of some other node, then it is a part of the hierarchy and thus must have its own set of children (which may be empty),*
- $\forall x \in U\ \forall v, u \in V : x \in ch(v) \wedge x \in ch(u) \Rightarrow v = u$, *i.e., an element cannot have two distinct parents,*
- $\forall v \in V : v \notin ch^{+}(v)$, *i.e., no element can be its own descendant.*

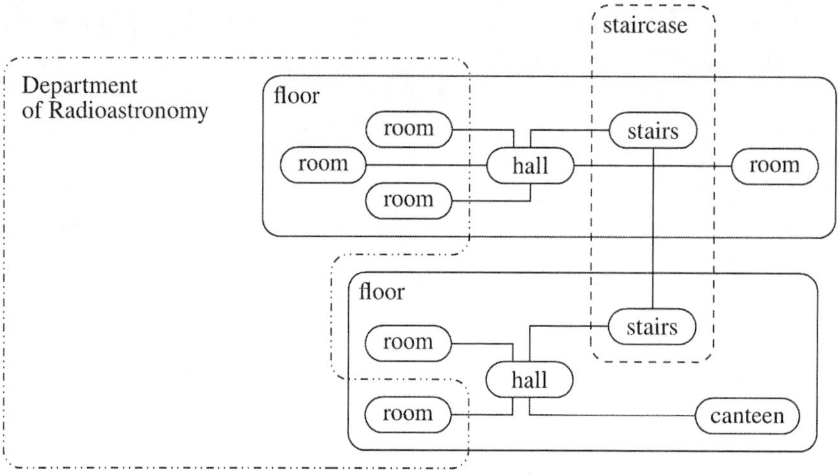

Figure 1: An example graph model with three hierarchies.

For node $v \in V$, $ch(v)$ is known as a set of its children, $ch^{+}(v)$ as a set of its descendants, and $ch^{*}(v)$ denotes a set containing both node v and its descendants.

The proposed graphs are multi-hierarchical, i.e., there is a possibility to define hierarchies of different types in one graph. Many hierarchies defined in one graph allow us to specify different types of hierarchical dependencies between graph elements. Such a representation makes it possible to filter the knowledge stored in the graph by selecting specific hierarchies. Moreover, there is a choice of different views of the project consisting of selected hierarchies including only relevant subsets of graph atoms.

Definition 2 *A **multi-hierarchical graph** over Σ_V, Σ_E and A with n hierarchies (where n is a fixed natural number) is a system $G = (V, E, s, t, ch_1, \dots, ch_n, vlb, elb, atr, val)$, where:*

- *V and E are disjoint finite sets, with V being non-empty, whose elements are called nodes and edges, respectively,*
- *$s : E \to V$ and $t : E \to V$ are mappings assigning to edges their source and target nodes, respectively,*
- *$ch_i : V \to 2^U \cup \{\perp\}$, where $i = 1, \dots, n$ are child nesting functions,*
- *$vlb : V \to \Sigma_V$ and $elb : E \to \Sigma_E$ are node and edge labelling functions, respectively,*
- *$atr : U \to 2^A$ is a node and edge attributing function,*
- *$val : U \times A \to D$, with $D = \bigcup_{a \in A} D_a$, is a partial function such that for all $x \in U$ and $a \in A$ if $a \in atr(x)$, then $val(x, a) \in D_a$.*

In Fig. 1 an example of a graph with three different hierarchies is presented. In the first hierarchy, nodes representing rooms and other spaces are nested in hierarchical nodes representing floors. Edges which connect nodes represent accessibility. All graph elements belonging to this hierarchy are drawn as solid ovals and lines.

The second hierarchy is used to group stair segments into staircases. While stair runs and their landings are contained in their specific floors, staircases considered as a whole do not belong to any floor. Therefore, the node in Fig. 1 which represents a staircase is not a part of the first hierarchy, and is drawn with a dashed line to underline this fact.

The third hierarchy stores knowledge about administrative room assignments. In this example there are four rooms assigned to the Department of Radioastronomy. Nodes representing these rooms are nested in the node representing the department.

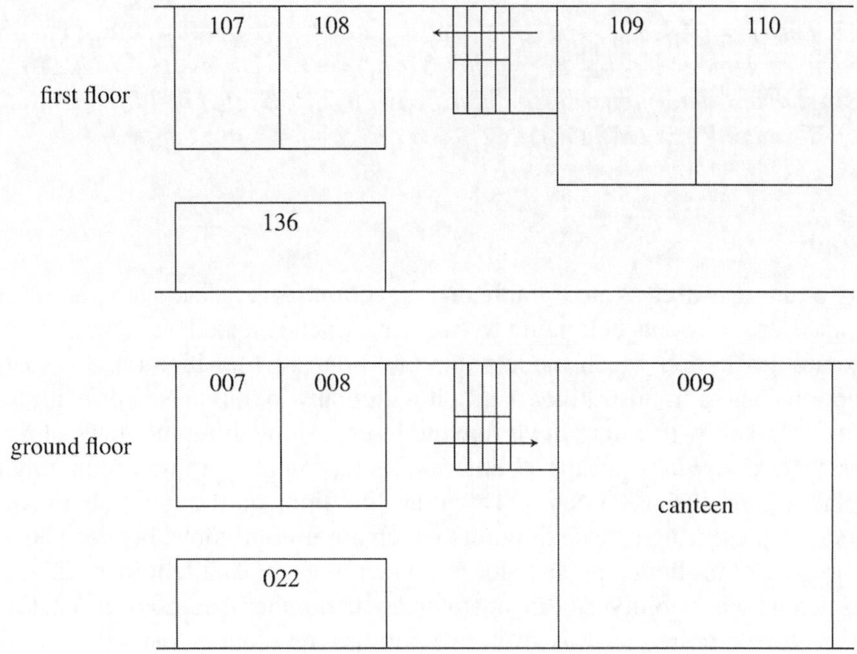

Figure 2: A fragment of a university building floor plan.

It should be noted that a graph atom can belong to several hierarchies at the same time. For example, nodes representing stair segments are a part of the spatial and of the vertical spatial hierarchy; they are not a part of the administrative one.

Notions of a subgraph of a multi-hierarchical graph, an induced subgraph and a single view are useful tools for filtering the knowledge stored in a graph model.

Parts of an object represented by a multi-hierarchical graph correspond to its subgraphs.

Definition 3 *A graph* $G = (V_G, E_G, s_G, t_G, ch_{1\,G}, \dots, ch_{n\,G}, vlb_G, elb_G, atr_G, val_G)$ *is a* ***subgraph*** *of a graph* $H = (V_H, E_H, s_H, t_H, ch_{1\,H}, \dots, ch_{n\,H}, vlb_H, elb_H, atr_H, val_H)$ *if:*

- $V_G \subseteq V_H$;
- $E_G \subseteq E_H$ *and* $\forall e \in E_G : s_H(e) \in V_G \wedge t_H(e) \in V_G$;
- $s_G = s_H|_{E_G}, t_G = t_H|_{E_G}$;
- $\forall x \in V_G : ch_{i\,G}(x) = ch_{i\,H}(x) \cap (U_G \cup \{\perp\})$ *where* $i = 1, \dots, n$,
- $vlb_G = vlb_H|_{V_G}, elb_G = elb_H|_{E_G}$;
- $\forall x \in U_G : atr_G(x) \subseteq atr_H(x)$,
- $\forall x \in U_G, a \in A : val_G(x, a) = val_H(x, a)$.

A subgraph in which all edges connecting selected nodes of a given graph are present is called an induced subgraph.

Definition 4 *A graph* $\boldsymbol{Ind(V_I)} = (V_I, E_I, s_I, t_I, ch_{1\,I}, \dots, ch_{n\,I}, vlb_I, elb_I, atr_I, val_I)$ *is an* ***induced subgraph*** *of an graph* $H = (V_H, E_H, s_H, t_H, ch_{1\,H}, \dots, ch_{n\,H}, atr_H, val_H)$ *if* $Ind(V_I)$ *is a subgraph of* H*, where* $E_I = \{e \in E_H : s_H(e) \in V_I \wedge t_H(e) \in V_I\}$.

Searching for specific information about the design, the designer often needs to take into consideration only one graph hierarchy. A subgraph which contains all nodes of the selected hierarchy and edges representing relations between them is called a single view.

Definition 5 *Let* $H = (V_H, E_H, s_H, t_H, ch_{1\,H}, \ldots, ch_{n\,H}, vlb_H, elb_H, atr_H, val_H)$ *be a graph and let i be a fixed number* $1 \leq i \leq n$. *A graph* $\mathbf{S(ch_i)} = (V_S, E_S, s_S, t_S, ch_{i\,S}, vlb_S, elb_S, atr_S, val_S)$ *is a* ***single view*** *determined by the hierarchy* $ch_{i\,H}$ *if* $S(ch_i)$ *is a fragment of an induced subgraph of H where* $V_S = ch^*_{i\,H}(V_H) \cap V_H$ *and* ch_j *for* $j \neq i$ *are omitted.*

4. Case Study

A university building is used as an example in this section. Fig. 2 displays a part of its floor plan, which includes several rooms belonging to two departments, a student canteen and a staircase. A multi-hierarchical graph which models this building has four hierarchies: spatial, vertical spatial, functional and administrative. A graph with many hierarchies is difficult to arrange on a diagram in a clear way, therefore the following figures show different views of this graph.

The first hierarchy, which groups together nodes representing rooms belonging to the same floor and places them inside a node representing this floor, is the most obvious one. It also provides nodes representing entry/exit points which are used to move between adjacent spaces in the building. Most of them represent doors, some represent stair landings. Edges connecting these points denote accessibility, and are attributed with numbers representing costs of traversing the edges (i.e., time required to walk from one point to the other). A single view showing this spatial hierarchy is displayed in Fig. 3.

The second hierarchy is also based on physical containment, but it groups spaces in the vertical direction. It is named "vertical spatial" and provides hierarchical nodes representing staircases and lifts – that is, objects which cross floor boundaries.

The third hierarchy (see Fig. 4) divides the building into functional areas. All corridors and stairs are assigned as children of the "communication" node, personal rooms of university employees as children of the "staff offices" node, canteens and other places where food can be bought are assigned to the "gastronomy" node, and so on.

The fourth hierarchy (see Fig. 5) provides nodes corresponding to the administrative structure of the university (chairs, departments, etc.) and places rooms inside these nodes. This allows the system to answer questions like "how can I get to the Department of Design"?

Let us consider finding a place to print a large-format poster as an example of a complex navigational problem which requires knowledge from several hierarchies. Rooms with necessary equipment are marked by the presence of a specific attribute. It should be noted that there are rules determining which printers can be used by any given employee. The prescribed order of searching for an available large-format printer is: in office rooms belonging to that person's

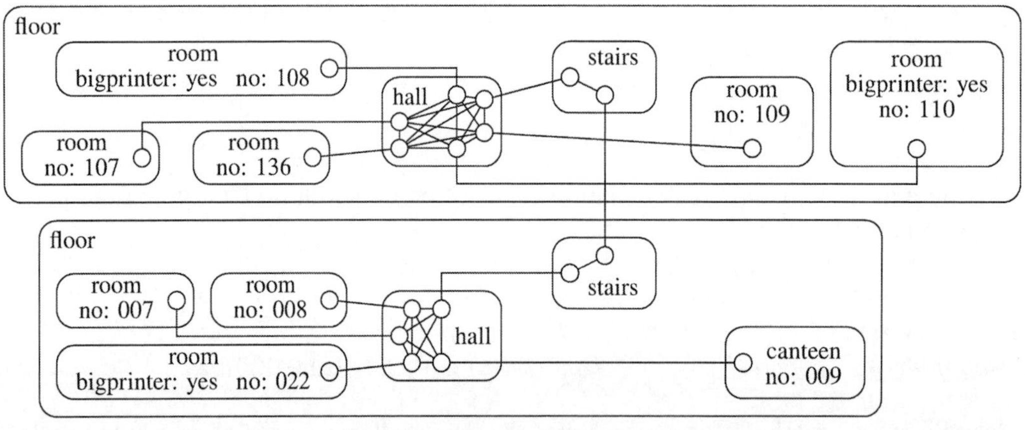

Figure 3: A view showing the spatial hierarchy of the building model (edge costs omitted).

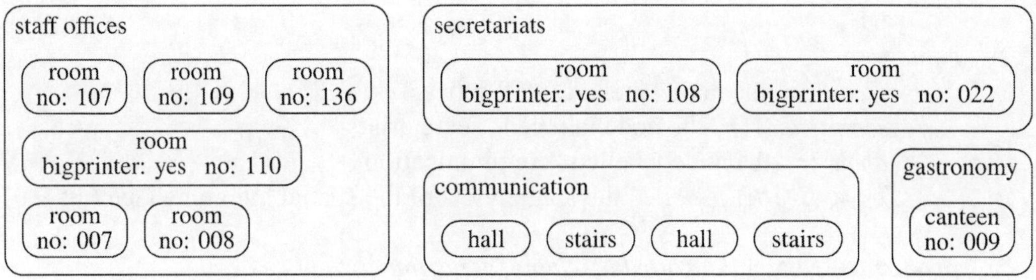

Figure 4: A view showing the functional hierarchy of the building model.

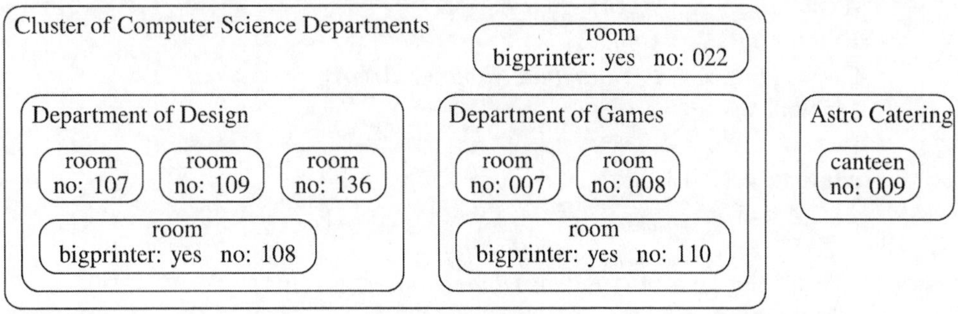

Figure 5: A view showing the administrative hierarchy of the building model.

department; in the secretariat of that department; in secretariats of higher-order administrative units.

A navigation tool implementing these rules must know which department is the considered one. Pseudocode in Fig. 6 assumes that this information is externally provided as the invocation argument of the *SearchFor* procedure, along with the name of an attribute signalling the presence of a large-format printer. It can then take the set of all nodes which are contained in the node representing this department (administrative hierarchy), intersect it with the set of nodes nested in the "staff offices" node (functional hierarchy), and discard nodes without the required attribute. This determines the set of rooms to check in the first search phase.

Then, the tool needs to direct the employee to the nearest room from this set. This is implemented in the *TryNodes* procedure. The code finds the shortest path from the node representing the room the employee is currently in to any of the nodes representing rooms to check; or rather, from a node representing an entry/exit point in the current room to any node representing a point in the destination rooms. To speed up the search the Dijkstra's algorithm is applied not to the complete graph model, but to its subgraph, specifically to a spatial hierarchy subgraph induced by start and destination nodes as well as by nodes which in the functional hierarchy are nested in the "communication" node.

If, upon arriving to the destination point, the employee finds the room closed or the printer busy, then they command the navigation tool to direct them to the next room with a printer. The tool removes the node representing the failed room from the set of destination nodes, and repeats the procedure described in the previous paragraph. If all rooms in the department turn out to be failures, the tool proceeds to phase two, i.e., to secretariats.

Secretariats belonging to a given unit can be found by intersecting the set of nodes which represent rooms and are directly contained in a node representing that unit, and the set of nodes contained in the "secretariats" node. Not all secretariats have large-format printers, therefore filtering based on attribute presence is still required. The resulting set of printer-equipped secretariats will usually have either one or zero elements.

```
constants
    offices := the node labelled "staff offices"
    secretariats := the node labelled "secretariats"
    comm := the node labelled "communication"
    D := S(ch_spatial), i.e., the single view of the spatial hierarchy (see Fig. 3)

procedure SearchFor (attributeName, departmentName)
    n := the node labelled departmentName

    A := ch_administrative(n)
    B := ch_functional(offices)
    C := {v ∈ A ∩ B : attributeName ∈ atr(v)}
    TryNodes (C)

    while n ≠ NULL do
        A := ch_administrative(n)
        B := ch_functional(secretariats)
        C := {v ∈ A ∩ B : attributeName ∈ atr(v)}
        TryNodes (C)

        n := par_administrative(n)
    endwhile

    report failure and end program, all possibilities exhausted
endproc

procedure TryNodes (setOfRoomNodes)
    while setOfRoomNodes ≠ ∅ do
        curr := node representing the point user is currently in
        A := subgraph of D induced by
                    ch*_spatial (ch_functional(comm) ∪ {curr} ∪ setOfRoomNodes)
        use Dijkstra's algorithm on A with curr as the source node
                    and entry points of setOfRoomNodes as the target nodes
        let target be the closest target point
        targetRoom := par_spatial(target)

        display map with the route from curr to target
        direct user to target
        wait for user's decision

        if user wants to check another room then
            setOfRoomNodes := setOfRoomNodes − {targetRoom}
        else
            report success and end program
        endif
    endwhile
endproc
```

Figure 6: Outline of an algorithm used by the navigation tool.

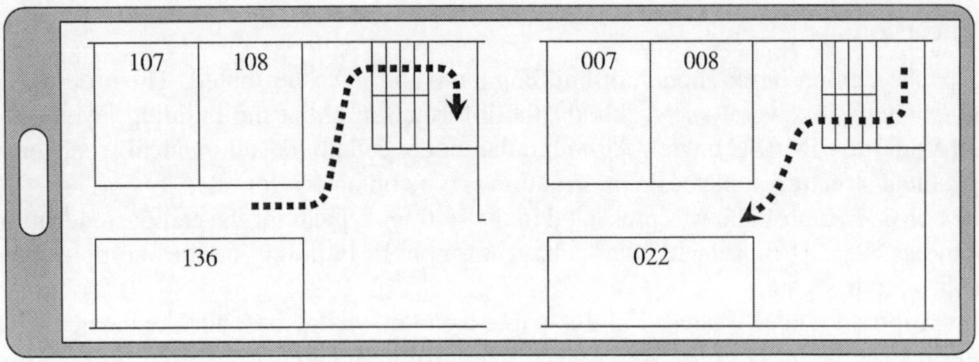

Figure 7: A smartphone with the navigation tool.

The navigation tool takes as destination nodes the ones which represent secretariats belonging to the department and directs the employee to successive rooms from this set using the procedure outlined above. If visiting departmental secretariats does not succeed, then the tool checks the administrative hierarchy to find the parent unit of the department, and considers secretariats serving that unit. If necessary it then proceeds to the grandparent unit, the great-grandparent unit, etc.

Fig. 7 illustrates the result of this process – the Department of Design secretariat is closed, and the navigation tool displays directions to the secretariat belonging to the Cluster of CS Departments. This path was calculated by the Dijkstra's algorithm invoked on a graph displayed in Fig. 8.

It should be noted that while *SearchFor* implements a particular set of rules governing access to large-format printers and is higly specific to this case, *TryNodes* is a general navigational procedure, able to direct people to successive rooms from the set given as its invocation argument. It should be possible to reuse *TryNodes* without modification in many other algorithms solving different navigation problems faced by university visitors, students and staff.

As demonstrated by this case study, the use of multiple hierarchies in a graph model allows that model to represent several different hierarchical relations in a natural way. Knowledge stored in these relations can be combined and used to extract subgraphs which contain information necessary for a given computational task. This reduction of data size speeds up processing.

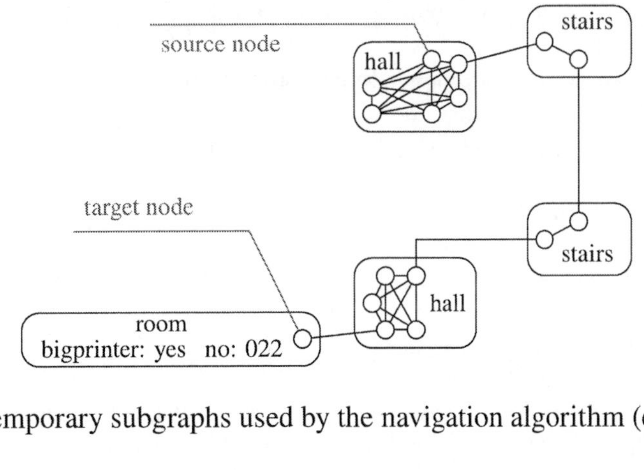

Figure 8: One of temporary subgraphs used by the navigation algorithm (edge costs omitted).

5. Conclusion

In this paper a graph-based model for building navigation was presented. The proposed model can be extended in several ways. Firstly the information about the building layout could be derived from the BIM/IFC model. Although the model can not be automatically converted into a hierarchical structure some basic information can be obtained from it.

The considered problem was presented in the settings typical for the campus/educational establishments but can be used with minor changes for public buildings or other complex buildings people have to navigate.

The proposed model was used in this paper as a knowledge base for the navigation within the building on the basis of the shortest path algorithm. It can also be used for creating tools which would support persons with disabilities helping the to find the easiest/most accessible route (not always the shortest).

References

AlShboul, A. A. & Al-Tahat, M. D. (2007). Modelling of public building evacuation processes. *Architectural Science Review*, 50(1), 37–43.

Barendregt, H., van Eekelrn, M. C. J. D., Glauert, J. R. W., Kennaway, J., Plasmeijer, M. J., & Sleep, M. R. (1987). Term graph rewriting. *Lecture Notes in Computer Science*, 259, 141–158.

Basiri, A., Amirian, P., Winstanley, A., Marsh, S., Moore, T., & Gales, G. (2016). Seamless pedestrian positioning and navigation using landmarks. *The Journal of Navigation*, 69(1), 24–40.

Bruni, R., Montanari, U., Plotkin, G., & Terreni, D. (2012). On hierarchical graphs: reconciling bigraphs, gs-monoidal theories and gs-graphs. In *13th Italian Conference on Theoretical Computer Science*.

Büchel, D. & Gilliéron, P.-Y. (2004). Pedestrian navigation inside buildings. *Géomatique Suisse*, 11/2004, 664–668. (in French).

Cepolina, E. M. (2005). A methodology for defining building evacuation routes. *Civil Engineering and Environmental Systems*, 22(1), 29–47.

Chen, G. & Zhong, N. (2011). Granular structures in graphs. *Lecture Notes in Computer Science*, 6954, 649–658.

Chen, G. & Zhong, N. (2012). Three granular structure models in graphs. *Lecture Notes in Computer Science*, 7414, 351–358.

Chiu, Y.-C., Zheng, H., Villalobos, J., & Gautam, B. (2007). Modeling no-notice mass evacuation using a dynamic traffic flow optimization model. *IIE Transactions*, 39(1), 83–94.

Cormen, T. H., Leiserson, C. E., Rivest, R. L., & Stein, C. (2001). *Introduction to Algorithms (2nd ed.)*. MIT Press.

Drewes, F., Hoffmann, B., & Plump, D. (2002). Hierarchical graph transformation. *Journal of Computer and System Sciences*, 64, 249–283.

Faure, C., Benci, P., Danzart, A., & Lecolinet, E. (2006). Design of mobile services for students. In *Proceedings of the UbiMob'06 Conference*. (in French).

Ferrari, G. & Montanari, U. (2000). Tile formats for located and mobile systems. *Information and Computation*, 156(1-2), 173–235.

Gilliéron, P.-Y. & Merminod, B. (2003). Personal navigation system for indoor applications. In *Proceedings of the 11th IAIN World Congress*.

Grabska, E., Łachwa, A., Ślusarczyk, G., Grzesiak-Kopeć, K., & Lembas, J. (2007). Hierarchical layout hypergraph operations and diagrammatic reasoning. *Machine GRAPHICS & VISION*, 16(1/2), 23–38.

Grabska, E. & Ślusarczyk, G. (2011). Knowledge and reasoning in design systems. *Automation in Construction*, 20(7), 927–934.

Grabska, E., Ślusarczyk, G., & Gajek, Sz. (2013). Knowledge representation for human-computer interaction in a system supporting conceptual design. *Fundamenta Informaticae*, 124, 91–110.

Harel, D. (1988). On visual formalisms. *Communications of the ACM*, 31, 514–530.

Höcker, M., Berkhahn, V., Kneidl, A., Borrmann, A., & Klein, W. (2010). Graph-based approaches for simulating pedestrian dynamics in building models. In *8th European Conference on Product & Process Modelling (ECPPM)* Cork, Ireland: University College Cork.

Khoury, H. M. & Kamat, V. R. (2009). Evaluation of position tracking technologies for user localization in indoor construction environments. *Automation in Construction*, 18(4), 444–457.

Kneidl, A., Borrmann, A., & Hartmann, D. (2011). Generating sparse navigation graphs for microscopic pedestrian simulation models. In *18th EG-ICE International Workshop* Twente, Netherlands.

Köbben, B., van Bunningen, A. H., & Muthukrishnan, K. (2006). Wireless campus LBS: Building campus-wide location based services based on WiFi technology. In E. Stefanakis, M. P. Peterson, C. Armenakis, & V. Delis (Eds.), *Geographic Hypermedia: Concepts and Systems* (pp. 399–408). Springer.

Latombe, J.-C. (1991). *Robot Motion Planning*. Kluwer Academic Publishers.

Milner, R. (2008). Bigraphs and their algebra. *Electronic Notes in Theoretical Computer Science*, 209, 5–19.

Minas, M. (2002). Concepts and realization of a diagram editor generator based on hypergraph transformation. *Science of Computer Programming*, 44(2), 157–180.

Papinigis, V., Geda, E., & Lukošius, K. (2010). Design of people evacuation from rooms and buildings. *Journal of Civil Engineering and Management*, 16(1), 131–139.

Poulovassilis, A. & Levene, M. (1994). A nested-graph model for the representation and manipulation of complex objects. *ACM Transactions on Information Systems*, 12, 35–68.

Ronchi, E. & Nilsson, D. (2013). Fire evacuation in high-rise buildings: a review of human behaviour and modelling research. *Fire Science Reviews*, 2(1), 1–21.

Shen, S., Michael, N., & Kumar, V. (2011). Autonomous multi-floor indoor navigation with a computationally constrained MAV. In *2011 IEEE International Conference on Robotics and Automation (ICRA)* (pp. 20–25).

Shen, T.-S. & Chien, S.-W. (2005). An evacuation simulation model (ESM) for building evaluation. *International Journal on Architectural Science*, 6(1), 15–30.

Sowa, J. F. (1976). Conceptual graphs for a database interface. *IBM Journal of Research and Development*, 20(4), 336–357.

Sowa, J. F. (1984). *Conceptual Structures: Information Processing in Mind and Machine*. Addison-Wesley.

Sowa, J. F. (2008). Conceptual graphs. In F. van Harmelen, V. Lifschitz, & B. Porter (Eds.), *Handbook of Knowledge Representation* (pp. 213–237). Elsevier.

Stringfield, W. H. (1996). *Emergency planning and management*. Rockville, MD, USA: Government Institutes.

Strug, B., Grabska, E., & Ślusarczyk, G. (2014). Supporting the design process with hypergraph genetic operators. *Advanced Engineering Informatics*, 28, 11–27.

Strug, B., Paszyńska, A., Paszyński, M., & Grabska, E. (2013). Using a graph grammar system in the finite element method. *International Journal of Applied Mathematics and Computer Science*, 23(4), 839–853.

Whiting, E., Battat, J., & Teller, S. (2007). Topology of urban environments: Graph construction from multi-building floor plan data. In *Computer-Aided Architectural Design Futures 2007: Proceedings of the 12th International CAAD Futures Conference* (pp. 115–128). Dordrecht, Netherlands: Springer.

AUTHOR INDEX